W9-BZK-433

DEAR BUNNY,

DEAR VOLODYA

Dear Bunny,

Dear Volodya

The Nabokov-Wilson Letters,

1940–1971

Revised and Expanded Edition

EDITED, ANNOTATED,

AND WITH AN

INTRODUCTORY ESSAY BY

Simon Karlinsky

UNIVERSITY OF CALIFORNIA PRESS   *Berkeley Los Angeles London*

University of California Press   Berkeley and Los Angeles, California

University of California Press, Ltd.   London, England

Originally published in English as *The Nabokov-Wilson Letters*, © 1979 by Harper & Row, Publishers, New York

Library of Congress Cataloging-in-Publication Data
Nabokov, Vladimir Vladimirovich, 1899–1977.
    Dear Bunny, Dear Volodya : the Nabokov-Wilson letters, 1940–1971 / edited, annotated, and with an introductory essay by Simon Karlinsky.—Rev. and expanded ed.
        p.   cm.
    Original ed. published in 1979 under title: Nabokov-Wilson letters.
    Includes bibliographical references and index.
    ISBN 0-520-22080-3 (pbk. : alk. paper)
    1. Nabokov, Vladimir Vladimirovich, 1899–1977—Correspondence.   2. Wilson, Edmund, 1895–1972—Correspondence.   3. Authors, Russian—20th century—Correspondence.   4. Authors, American—20th century—Correspondence.   5. Critics—United States—Correspondence.   I. Wilson, Edmund, 1895–1972.   II. Karlinsky, Simon.   III. Nabokov, Vladimir Vladimirovich, 1899–1977. Nabokov-Wilson letters.   IV. Title.
    PG3476.N3 Z548 2001
    813'.54—dc21
    [B]   00-061995

Printed in the United States of America

08   07   06   05   04   03   02   01

10   9   8   7   6   5   4   3   2   1

The paper used in this publication is both acid-free and totally chlorine-free (TCF). It meets the minimum requirements of ANSI/NISO Z39.48-1992 (R 1997) *(Permanence of Paper)*.

Contents

EDITORIAL NOTE   vii

*Introduction: Dear Bunny, Dear Volodya;
or, Affinities and Disagreements*   1

The Letters   31

INDEX   375

Editorial Note

When Elena Wilson wrote to me in February 1975, inviting me on her own behalf and that of Vladimir Nabokov to edit and annotate the correspondence between the two writers, I accepted with delight. Because of prior commitments, I could not begin the actual work until after the death of Nabokov on July 30, 1977. By that time, I had received two batches of letters, one by Nabokov from the Wilson holdings in the Beinecke Library at Yale University and the other by Wilson from the Nabokov archive in Montreux.

What I was sent, it was assumed by everyone involved, constituted the entire corpus of the correspondence. In the Editorial Note to the first edition (1979), I wrote: "The present volume includes the extant correspondence between Vladimir Nabokov and Edmund Wilson." This rash statement must have unleashed the jinx that inexplicably attached itself to this project.

The hardback version of the first edition went on sale while both Elena Wilson and I were still reading the galleys. It was, consequently, full of errors and misprints. The paperback version, carefully checked by Véra Nabokov, Elena Wilson and myself, appeared in 1980. But shortly after the appearance of the hardback, Brian Boyd (already working on his definitive two-volume biography of Nabokov) informed me that he had located a number of Nabokov letters not included in my collection, letters that had been misfiled at the Beinecke Library. At the time the paperback was going to press, I had obtained copies of these new letters. But in the meantime, new Wilson letters began turning up in Montreux, including some dating from the summer and fall of 1945, which had been placed in a small suitcase and stored in the attic. Rather than delay the already announced paperback, the publisher chose to bring it out as it was, not waiting for the end of the continuing new discoveries.

(The jinx mentioned above continued when the French edition of

The Nabokov-Wilson Letters [Rivages, 1988], splendidly translated by Christine Raguet-Bouvard, was made from the uncorrected hardback edition. In a development reminiscent of Nabokov's novel *Pnin*, a self-styled "Russian-language expert" reviewed the Russian quotations and translations from the Russian and changed them, introducing numerous absurdities and howlers.)

The present volume incorporates the fifty-nine letters that came to light between 1980 and 1993. No rash claims are made this time that this is the exhaustive corpus of *all* the letters the two writers addressed to each other, only that this is all I was able to find. The commentary for the second edition has been greatly facilitated by the publication, in the intervening years, of such fundamental sources as the five volumes of Edmund Wilson's diaries, broken down by decades, from the 1920s to the 1960s; Vladimir Nabokov's *Selected Letters 1940–1977*, Dmitri Nabokov and Matthew J. Bruccoli, eds. (1989); his *Perepiska s sestroi* (Correspondence with his sister, Elena Sikorskaya, 1985); and, of course, Brian Boyd's indispensable two-volume biography, *Vladimir Nabokov: The Russian Years* (1990) and *Vladimir Nabokov: The American Years* (1991).

Brian Boyd's help has also been essential in the preparation of the present edition, especially with the problem of the correct dating of the letters (he showed me how unreliable the two writers were in this respect). I would also like to thank Gennady Barabtarlo, who shared with me four letters he discovered in the Wilson archive and provided valuable information on other matters. Dieter E. Zimmer was my co-editor in the German version of this volume (Rowohlt, 1995); some of the additional footnotes he suggested have been retained in this edition. Francis M. Nevins, Jr., kindly wrote to correct the mistakes of Vladimir Nabokov and myself in the area of crime fiction. This edition incorporates the information and/or corrections provided earlier by Sergei Davydov, Alfred Appel, Jr., Hugh McLean and Francis J. Whitfield. The research assistants who helped with the present volume were Anna Primrose, Glen C. Worthey and Robin Ladouceur.

Very sadly, this time I did not have the help of the late Véra Nabokov and Elena Wilson, who shared their knowledge and recollections with me with unfailing patience and graciousness during the work on the first edition.

●

The correspondence has been edited in accordance with the following guidelines:

1. Corrections. Obvious slips of the pen and chance misspellings have been corrected and occasional missing letters (of the alphabet) reinstated. In the very few cases where an inadvertently omitted word has been added, it appears, as do other editorial additions, in brackets. For the sake of historical authenticity (and because of their charm), some of the gallicisms ("semestre," "Octobre") that were typical of Nabokov's English during his first few years in America have been left intact, as have the grammatical and orthographic idiosyncrasies of Wilson's Russian, which are usually pointed out and explained in the footnotes.

2. Dating. Edmund Wilson's dates followed the standard American practice, while Nabokov's had for the most part the continental format of 1.IX.44 for September 1, 1944. For the convenience of the readers, all the dates have been standardized. When the internal evidence indicates that a letter has been misdated, the correct date has been supplied whenever possible.

3. Capitalization. Each of the two correspondents adhered to the capitalization practices of his native language in both English and Russian. Wilson capitalized all the words, except for prepositions and conjunctions, in the titles of Russian (and French) literary works in accordance with English usage, while Nabokov would capitalize in English only the first word of a title, as is customary in Russian. This idiosyncrasy has been retained. Nabokov's frequent failure to capitalize proper adjectives, another Franco-Russian habit, has been corrected throughout.

4. Russian orthography. There is a definite interplay in the correspondence between the old (pre-revolutionary) and the new (post-revolutionary) Russian orthographies. In the beginning, Nabokov systematically used the old orthography and Wilson the new one, but later on Wilson learned to use the old orthography, while Nabokov occasionally switched to the new. The two orthographies (and, occasionally, a mixture of both) have been retained as they appear in the original manuscripts.

5. Transliteration. Transcriptions of Russian words into the Latin alphabet by the two correspondents for the most part followed no particular system. Transliteration has been normalized, except for instances

where it is deliberately humorous or whimsical, or where Nabokov is demonstrating a new transliteration system of his own devising, as in Letter 147.

6. Deletions. In a few cases, statements that might have offended surviving friends or associates of one or the other of the two writers have been deleted. A few names left out in the first edition have been restored here. The remaining cuts have been retained in accordance with the wishes of Véra Nabokov. All such deletions are indicated by [...].

In my annotations, I have striven to be as impartial as possible about the points of contention and disagreement between the two writers, supplying the readers with the necessary factual background to enable them to reach their own judgments and conclusions. The same kind of objectivity was my goal when I started writing the introductory essay, which aims at sketching the background of the correspondence and elucidating the topics on which the two correspondents agree or disagree. This goal may have proven illusory in certain portions of my essay. It would have been dishonest and hypocritical to pretend that I go along with Nabokov's contention that the Russian and English versification systems are by and large interchangeable or with his denial of the literary worth of a number of writers and works, ranging from the plays of Molière to Pasternak's *Doctor Zhivago*, which I admire.

Similarly, thirty years of close study of Russia's literary and political history of the first two decades of the twentieth century make it impossible for me to ignore that Edmund Wilson's views on the Russian literary scene after 1905 and on the nature of the October Revolution (as expressed in *The Triple Thinkers* and *To the Finland Station*) were based on some highly misleading sources. While I fully realize that the reader of this volume is interested not in my views but in those of the two major literary figures whose correspondence it has been my privilege to edit, I saw no way of explaining the issues and viewpoints involved if I were to block out my own knowledge and outlook. The introduction has dwelled on Nabokov's background at greater length than on Wilson's because the formative experiences of Russians of his generation are less well known or understood than the corresponding experiences of Americans of Wilson's generation.

DEAR BUNNY,

DEAR VOLODYA

Introduction

Dear Bunny, Dear Volodya;
or, Affinities and Disagreements

A memorable literary sensation of 1965 was created by Edmund Wilson's highly critical review of Vladimir Nabokov's four-volume annotated edition of Pushkin's *Eugene Onegin*. Wilson's article appeared in *The New York Review of Books* in July. Nabokov's reply in August was followed by his additional detailed rebuttal in the February 1966 issue of *Encounter*. The exchange generated the kind of excitement that an evenly matched, no-holds-barred fight usually does and a number of literary and scholarly figures jumped into the fray, taking sides, egging on the two opponents and administering a few indiscriminate kicks of their own in this or that direction. In the excitement of the scuffle few people noticed that in the very first lines of his review Wilson qualified himself as "a personal friend of Mr. Nabokov's, for whom he feels a warm affection sometimes chilled by exasperation," or that Nabokov's reply to the review began with a confirmation of the two writers' old friendship and an assurance of reciprocated affection. "In the 1940s, during my first decade in America, he was most kind to me in various matters, not necessarily pertaining to his profession," Nabokov wrote in the opening paragraph of his reply. "We have had many exhilarating talks, have exchanged many frank letters."

As the frank letters in the present collection will testify, the embittered debate over the *Onegin* translation and commentary was preceded by a quarter of a century of close personal and intellectual contact. The restless and stimulating relationship between the two writers, their continuous lively exchange of ideas, were reflected in significant ways in their respective literary biographies. It was during his period of closeness with Nabokov that Wilson's thoroughgoing involvement with Russian literature and culture hit its full stride. The beginnings of Nabokov's second literary career (as an American author writing in English) can hardly be imagined without Wilson's help, advice and literary contacts. Writing to Elena Wilson after Wilson's death about their joint plans to publish the present correspondence, Nabokov concluded his letter with the words: "I need not tell you what agony it was rereading the exchanges belonging to the early radiant era of our correspondence" (unpublished letter of May 17, 1974).

There were many factors that contributed to their affinity and mutual sympathy. They came from cultivated upper-class homes within their respective cultures. Each had an interest and an involvement in the other's literature and native traditions. Both were at home in French literature and language. Both had a skeptical, albeit divergent, view of religion and mysticism. Both were sons of jurists who were involved in politics. Wilson believed that his father might have been appointed to the U.S. Supreme Court had a vacancy opened up during Woodrow Wilson's presidency. Nabokov's father, a major participant in the opposition movement of pre-revolutionary Russia, may well have ended up with a cabinet post in a democratic post-revolutionary government, had Lenin and Trotsky not established their repressive dictatorship after the October Revolution. Wilson is remembered by most people as a literary critic and Nabokov as a novelist; yet both men wrote and published fiction, literary criticism and plays as well as verse, and for both of them literature was the central passion of their lives. Wilson was also one of the very few literary associates of Nabokov who was able to take at least a minimal interest in the latter's other major sphere of interest, lepidopterology.

In Russian as well as American culture, literary works have often been valued for their message and held in suspicion if they displayed technical brilliance. Nabokov and Wilson, however, both knew that there is no substitute for literary quality—though they often differed about what constitutes quality in literature. There was also a curious parallelism between the impact of certain of their respective books, which they themselves may not have realized at the time. Wilson's *To the Finland Station* is one of the best guides to the Western sources of Marxism-

Leninism, just as Nabokov's novel *The Gift* is an imaginative examination of its native Russian roots, so that, read together, the two works almost form two sides of an equation. The prosecution and banning of Wilson's novel *Memoirs of Hecate County* contributed to the collapse of the Victorian moralistic censorship that had persisted in Western countries till the end of the 1950s; the publication of Nabokov's *Lolita* in America and England signaled the completion of that collapse.

With all their affinities and wide areas of shared mutual interests, it was fortunate that Nabokov and Wilson met when they did, in 1940. Only five years earlier, the vicissitudes of our century's history and the intellectual currents of the 1930s might have kept them apart, with nothing to say to each other. Their two decades of closeness as well as their eventual painful cooling off had their sources in views and attitudes formed long before their first meeting. The relationship might perhaps be understood with greater clarity if we examine briefly the intellectual trajectories that each traveled before encountering the other.

Edmund Wilson had on several occasions described his childhood in New Jersey and upper New York State. A formative, indeed traumatic, experience occurred when Wilson was taken to play with a rich boy and was shocked by this boy's highhanded treatment of family servants and by his matter-of-fact acceptance of his superior status. The episode was later described in Wilson's memoir "At Laurelwood" (included in his *Night Thoughts*) and also in his novel *I Thought of Daisy*. His biographer Sherman Paul sees in this experience—rightly, to my mind—the source of Wilson's lifelong dislike of the "world of wealth which annihilates every impulse toward excellence" and of any kind of entrenched privilege. It also accounts for his early sympathy with writers such as G. B. Shaw and H. L. Mencken whom he saw as disturbers of the status quo and of bourgeois complacency.

During the glittering Jazz Age of the American 1920s in which Wilson participated as the friend and associate of almost every important literary figure (many of whom he had known since his college days) and which he helped define, he was not especially interested in Russian literature or the Russian Revolution. He was too busy discovering the exciting new changes in literary sensibility which he examined in his epoch-making book *Axel's Castle*. *Axel's Castle* crowned the decade of the twenties, consolidated Wilson's reputation as the foremost critic of his time and asserted, once and for all, the importance of the Symbolist mode for the development of literature in the twentieth century. With the publication of this book it was no longer possible in America to dismiss Marcel Proust as an unreadable bore, to regard Joyce as a pornographer or to mock Gertrude Stein as absurd—as sometimes had been done. It was Wilson who more than any other critic brought them their recognition as modern masters and pointed out their common roots in French Symbolism.

With the coming of the depression, Wilson, like the majority of American writers of the time, was swept by a wave of doubts about the validity of his society's traditional structure and institutions. The Sacco and Vanzetti case, the Harlan County miners, the unemployment and the breadlines convinced many that a newer and better social model was needed. Daniel Aaron's book *Writers on the Left* documents the groundswell of enthusiasm for Soviet Russia among America's intellectuals which came just as Stalin was consolidating his power and plunging the country into the worst nightmare in its history. What amazes a person even minimally acquainted with Soviet realities about the intellectual climate of America in the thirties is the almost inconceivable gullibility of the intellectual community, its lack of any meaningful criteria for comparing the situations in the two countries. The judicial railroading of two Italian anarchists which aroused so much passionate protest— what was it against the frameups and executions of hundreds of Russian anarchists, Socialist Revolutionaries and non-Leninist Marxists in the first few years of Lenin's rule? Nor could the breadlines of the American unemployed be meaningfully compared to the death by starvation of millions of Ukrainian peasants due to forced collectivization during the same years.

It was in that decade of famine, repressions and proliferating GULAG camps in the Soviet Union that the prestige of the October Revolution as humanity's best hope for a free and just society reached its highest point in the West. Edmund Wilson studied the theory of Marxism-Leninism, made common cause with American Communists during the various protest actions of the period, but, unlike many of his colleagues and associates, reserved the right to think and judge for himself even at the height of his involvement with Marxism. In the spring of 1935 he traveled to the Soviet Union on a Guggenheim Fellowship, hoping to do research on the Russian Revolution at the Marx-Engels Institute in Moscow, a pilgrimage very much in the style and spirit of the time.

Wilson did not possess the visceral poetic sensitivity of E. E. Cummings who had made a similar trip three years earlier and who, knowing as little of Russian language and history as Wilson did when *he* set off, managed to capture the very essence of the Soviet reality of the 1930s ("an altruistic game of human prisoners, uncircus of noncreatures calling itself 'Russia' ") and to embody it in his unappreciated masterpiece *Eimi*, a book that dovetails uncannily with Boris Pasternak's letters of the same year to his wife and with the memoirs of Nadezhda Mandelstam.[1] Wilson's account of his Soviet impressions (published in a self-censored form in *Travels in Two Democracies*, 1936, and in a more explicit version in *Red, Black, Blond and Olive*, 1956) is an affecting mixture of his own naive expectations and the harsh realities he does his best to explain away. The three Soviet engineers he meets on the boat from London to Leningrad are polite and courteous, and this is instantly credited to the advanced new post-revolutionary culture. But the crowds in Leningrad look shabby and glum—as well they might, considering the purges, arrests and starvation with which they were living. Their appearance and behavior are attributed to the "old subhuman life of serfdom" which they supposedly still remembered from the pre-revolutionary days (not too many people in 1935 could have remembered serfdom, which was abolished in 1861).

Unlike such Western travelers as G. B. Shaw, who visited the U.S.S.R. at the height of the post-collectivization famine and declared after his return that Soviet citizens were the best-fed people in Europe, Wilson perceived enough of Soviet realities to make him see that this was not the free and idealistic utopia, run by workers and peasants, which he had

1. Cummings minimized his book's impact and severely limited the circle of its potential readers by couching it in a dense verbal idiom reminiscent of both Joyce and Gertrude Stein and also by disguising the Soviet celebrities he describes, e.g., Meyerhold, Pasternak and Lili Brik, under whimsical nicknames such as Somebody, Something and Madame Potiphar. Readers unfamiliar with the Soviet scene had no way of knowing who some of the book's principal characters were.

hoped to find. During his visit an encounter with the literary historian D. S. Mirsky[2] stimulated Wilson's interest in Pushkin, an interest which lasted for the rest of his life and which was so important in bringing him together with Nabokov. It was in order to read Pushkin in the original that Wilson undertook to learn Russian at the end of his trip. Disillusioned with Stalin (but still keeping his illusions about Lenin and the liberating character of the October Revolution), Wilson embarked on researching and writing *To the Finland Station*, a study of the origins of Marxism that has become a classic. Shortly after its publication he met Nabokov.

If the environment in which Edmund Wilson spent his childhood and youth can be imagined and understood by any literate person with almost no effort, the world into which Vladimir Nabokov was born and in which he lived out the first two decades of his life—the Russia of the period between the liberation of the serfs, the introduction of trials by jury and the other reforms of the 1860s and the October Revolution—has been so enveloped in myth in the Western imagination, so distorted by propaganda, so reduced to simplistic clichés, that most people in the West have a less clear idea of it than they do of the Egypt of the pharaohs. The reality of turn-of-the-century Russia that is reflected in, say, the personal letters of Tolstoy, Chekhov and Gorky or found in the Russian press of the period is so at variance with our popular notions that a simple statement of historical facts (such as we find in some of Nabokov's letters to Wilson) is likely to be dismissed as either perverse revisionism or nostalgic idealization.

The usual image is that of an inflexible autocracy, not changed a jot since Ivan the Terrible, a country populated by a handful of high-living, whip-wielding aristocrats and by masses of cringing, starving peasants, with an occasional great writer or starry-eyed revolutionary in the background. This was the country Oscar Wilde depicted in his 1883 melo-

2. D. S. Mirsky (Prince Dmitri Svyatopolk-Mirsky, 1890–1939) lived in England from 1922 to 1932 and there published, in English, two books on Russian literary history which remain to this day the best surveys on Russian literature available in any language, and also a book on Pushkin. He returned to the Soviet Union in 1932 and later perished in the purges.

drama *Vera; or, The Nihilists;* and this was the image that influenced Edmund Wilson to write in his section on Russia in *A Piece of My Mind* (1956) about "the swinish back-country of Gogol, full of overeaten landowners and overgrown orchards, wretched slaveys and maniacal masters; the old nests of gentlefolks of Turgenev, with their messiness of family relations and their herds of ill-treated serfs [. . .] Lenin, of course, declared war on all this and the Communists have made efforts to clear it away."

What the West has so systematically overlooked in all this is the six decades of momentous social change that preceded the Revolution and that had made the world of Gogol's *Dead Souls* and Turgenev's *Sportsman's Sketches* and *A Nest of Gentlefolk*, alluded to by Wilson, a thing of the past by the time Vladimir Nabokov was born. One of the most prominent features of those decades was the widespread and enormously influential *obshchestvennoe dvizhenie,* the civic protest movement which Nabokov invokes again and again in his letters to Wilson. It was rapidly spreading in the pre-revolutionary decades, it embraced a broad political spectrum, from moderate to ultra-radical, and it was gradually bringing about a very real and tangible liberalization of the social and political life of the country despite the obstinate and at times violent efforts of the last two tsars to curb or reverse it. With the abolition of censorship of books and periodicals, the legalization of all political parties and the establishment of a parliamentary system after the 1905 revolution, the civic protest movement acquired the right of open advocacy. The illegal leaflets and terrorists' bombs of the end of the nineteenth century were largely replaced after 1905 by other means of social protest, such as the burgeoning labor and feminist movements, a vocal and highly critical opposition press (the Bolshevik organ *Pravda* went legally on sale in 1912) and a multitude of contending political parties, ranging from extreme right, pro-monarchy and anti-Semitic through moderate and liberal groups, such as the Constitutional Democratic party (of which Nabokov's father was one of the founders), to socialist and Marxist organizations, the most prominent of which, the Socialist Revolutionary party, had a million active members on the eve of the Revolution. It was only a matter of time before a broadly based coalition of reformist and socialist parties brought down the monarchy in February 1917, only to see all the laboriously won rights and freedoms wiped out when Lenin took over less than a year later.

Nabokov's father was an important political figure during the parliamentary period of Russian history (1905–1917). A man who represented the finest traditions of pre-revolutionary democratic anti-government dissent, he was the Head of the Chancellery and a member of several of the key councils in the Provisional Government between the February and October Revolutions. His memoirs about that period, praised for their objectivity by both Trotsky and Kerensky, show that the Provisional Government was doomed by its devotion to fair play, its concern with securing the consent of the governed and its determination to guarantee civil rights and freedom of expression to everyone, including those who were determined to destroy it. The Socialist Revolutionaries and the Constitutional Democrats, schooled in the pre-revolutionary principle of cooperation between the anti-tsarist parties (as described by Nabokov in Letter 6) were simply not prepared for Lenin's fanaticism, cruelty and lack of all scruple.

And yet they should have been. There was a definite dogmatic, authoritarian component within the Russian pre-revolutionary civic protest movement. It is very much there in the radical-utilitarian literary criticism of the Belinsky-Chernyshevsky school which dominated the Russian literary scene during much of the nineteenth century. Chekhov was aware of it when he showed how despotic radicals such as Dr. Lvov in *Ivanov*, Lida in "The House with a Mansard," and Pavel Ivanovich in "Gusev" could regard themselves and be regarded by others as partisans of freedom and civil rights. Tolstoy went right to the heart of the matter in his portrayal of the "famous Marxist" Novodvorov (in his novel *Resurrection*), respected and supported by appealingly depicted, idealistic revolutionaries whom he intends to discredit and destroy once he seizes power. Andrei Bely's *Petersburg*, a novel without which Nabokov's literary origins would be hard to imagine, deals with the interchangeable nature of revolutionary discipline and reactionary repression and with their ultimate convergence.

Vladimir Nabokov encountered the phenomenon of ideological compulsion and conformity masquerading as liberation during his school years. Enrolled by his liberal father at the advanced Tenishev School in St. Petersburg, the eleven-year-old Nabokov was put under tremendous pressure by the teachers and the other students to join various extra-curricular clubs and, later on, political discussion groups. He resisted the pressure, but the taunts and remonstrations he endured must have stayed with him. He described the situation in both the English and the Russian versions of his autobiography and also based on it the episode in *Bend Sinister* (Chapter Five) in which the headmaster threatens to flunk the young Adam Krug unless he joins a student discussion group. "The headmaster, while stressing the purely voluntary nature of attendance, warned Krug (who was at the top of his class) that his individualistic be-havior constituted a dreadful example [. . .] Indeed, so broadminded was he that he positively *wanted* the richer boys to form strongly capitalistic clusters, or the sons of reactionary nobles to keep in tune with their caste and unite in *Rutterheds*. All he asked for was that they follow their social and economic instincts, while the only thing he condemned was the complete absence of such instincts in an individual."

The reflection of this experience in both autobiographies and in the novel suggests that it might have been as formative for Nabokov as the encounter with the privileged rich boy described in "At Laurelwood" was for Wilson. It may well have been the source of Nabokov's later vehe-ment rejection of Freudian or Marxist or any other kind of analysis that pigeonholes people into convenient, mostly imaginary slots and classi-fies them in accordance with arbitrary principles whose validity the classified person may not even recognize. This rejection forms one more link that connects Nabokov to Chekhov ("my predecessor," as he called him in one of his letters to Wilson), whose lifelong objections to "labels" and "tags" that subdivide people into illusory groups, categories and classes Nabokov found highly congenial. Nabokov's later distaste for or-ganized politics in any form and his distrust of mass movements must have been enhanced by the spectacle of the defeat of the major socialist and democratic parties, with their membership in the millions, by the small band of Bolsheviks led by Lenin. The aversion to politics must have been further reinforced by the assassination of Nabokov's father by right-wing, pro-monarchist fanatics in Berlin a few years after the fam-ily's emigration.

The world of Russian emigration in which Nabokov was to spend the next two decades of his life was as complex and diversified as pre-revolutionary Russia had been. There were the exiled major and minor royalty and aristocracy who, because of the senseless murder of the last tsar and his family by the Bolsheviks, acquired considerable sympathy and popularity in the West. There were the nationalistic rightist émigrés, with their samovars and gypsy choruses, their anti-Semitism and militarist mentality, who in the 1930s tended toward supporting Hitler's Germany and in the forties were occasionally moved to pro-Soviet positions by their admiration for Soviet military might and Stalin's ultra-nationalistic policies. Nabokov described this variety of émigrés with undisguised distaste in his stories of the forties, "Conversation Piece, 1945" and "The Assistant Producer," the latter based on a real case of a rightist émigré leader who turned out to be both a Soviet and a Nazi agent. There was also among the émigrés a large percentage of peasants and working-class people, including Jews and other minorities, who had left the country because they found living under Lenin's Communism far more harsh and oppressive than anything they had known before the Revolution.

The people responsible for the densely rich intellectual and literary life of the Russian emigration between the two world wars were the thousands of exiled liberals, socialists and democratic Marxists. It was this segment that operated the leading émigré publishing houses, brought out excellent literary journals (the two leading ones, the Prague *Freedom of Russia* and the Paris *Contemporary Annals*, were both published by the Socialist Revolutionaries) and provided the readership for the more serious literary productions of émigré writers. Nabokov's letters to Wilson mention a number of leading pre-revolutionary dissidents, friends of his, who belonged to this group: Ilya Fondaminsky, Iosif Hessen, Boris Nikolaevsky, Irakly Tseretelli. These were and still remain invisible men and women as far as Western popular thought and media are concerned. While some in the West could mourn for Nicholas and Alexandra and romanticize all Russian émigrés as genteel aristocrats who had lost their fortunes, and others could acclaim Stalin's U.S.S.R. as the "first truly human culture" and a triumph of true Marxist socialism, there was simply no place in the Western view of Russia and Russians for a liberal faction that was opposed both to the tsarist regime before the Revolution (and had, in fact, brought about its downfall) *and* to the theocratic police state founded by Lenin. Yet, without understanding this aspect of Russian political and intellectual history, there is no way of understanding Vladimir Nabokov.

He began his first literary career as a Russian writer writing for Russians in exile—those invisible people who lived, as he put it, in "material indigence and intellectual luxury"—shortly after completing his studies at Cambridge. Publishing his work under the pen name V. Sirin (*sirin* was a fabled bird of paradise of Russian folklore), he was one of a number of young literary hopefuls who made their debuts in the same period and under similar circumstances. The older generation of émigré writers numbered in its ranks such luminaries of twentieth-century Russian literature as Bunin, Remizov, Khodasevich and Marina Tsvetaeva. After the publication of his first few novels, it was generally recognized that Sirin was the most interesting and gifted of the younger émigré prose writers. At the same time there was a certain perplexity and even hostility on the part of émigré critics, primarily because of their inability to fit his novels into either the realist or the Symbolist mold and also because of his steadfast refusal to join any groupings or coteries.

The two crowning achievements of his European period are, interestingly enough, his two Russian novels on political themes. *Invitation to a Beheading* (1935–36) is a surrealistic anti-utopia that takes the twentieth-century police state to its ultimate future conclusion: a provincialized backwoods with a decaying, obsolete technology, where all privacy and individuality have been abolished and a person can be sentenced to be beheaded for possessing a modicum of intellectual independence. *The Gift* (1937–38), surely among the three or four greatest novels written in Russian in this century, is about a young man who discovers and develops his literary gift and finds love while researching a literary biography of Nikolai Chernyshevsky, the radical nineteenth-century critic and novelist and the man from whom Lenin and the Bolsheviks derived their political style and their aesthetics. In *The Gift* Nabokov initiated his method of hybridizing his fictional narratives with scholarly literary genres, such as biography, annotation and literary history, a method that was later developed and expanded in *Pale Fire, Ada, Look at the Harlequins* as well as in the *Onegin* commentary.

When Nabokov sailed for America with his wife and son in May 1940, he was a recognized major writer in all the cultural centers of the Russian diaspora, from the Baltic countries to China. A few of his novels had been published in translation in England, France and Germany (Jean-Paul Sartre's adverse review of the French translation of *Despair*, mentioned in Letter 173 and in note 3 to that letter, is a typical reflection of the prevalent Western attitude toward émigré writing in the thirties and forties). In America, however, there could not have been more than a hundred people who were aware of his literary achievement at the time of his arrival. It is to Edmund Wilson's credit that he was able to ignore the widespread anti-émigré prejudice of those days (which had, for example, led to an attempted boycott of the Book-of-the-Month selection of a novel by Nabokov's friend Mark Aldanov in 1943 on the grounds that an anti-Stalinist émigré had to be an enemy of freedom and democracy) and extend a helping hand to a man who was a virtual unknown in the United States.

Within months after Nabokov's arrival, we see Wilson arranging for him to do book reviews for *The New Republic* (of which Wilson was then the literary editor). In subsequent months and years Wilson became something of an unpaid literary agent and adviser for Nabokov. He was behind every important literary outlet that Nabokov was to find in his early years in America. It was Wilson who put him in touch with James Laughlin of New Directions, Edward Weeks of *The Atlantic Monthly* and Klaus Mann of *Decision*. This began before Wilson could have had any real inkling of Nabokov's full literary stature and it continued for a number of years regardless of whether Wilson appreciated Nabokov's latest book (as he did *The Real Life of Sebastian Knight*) or not (as was the case with *Bend Sinister*). What drew Wilson to Nabokov was not a realization of Nabokov's literary achievement—which he seemed to have taken for granted—but personal friendship and a community of literary interests.

As we study the first few letters of their correspondence, the two opposite magnetic poles of their intellectual relationship emerge: the positive, which is Pushkin, and the negative, which is Lenin. Shortly after returning from the U.S.S.R., Wilson published his essay on *Eugene Onegin* and two years later his essay on "The Bronze Horseman" accompanied by his prose translation of this narrative poem. The inclusion of these two essays in Wilson's book *The Triple Thinkers* (1938) was a pioneering event in American criticism, since for most American critics and readers of that time Russian literature started with Turgenev (and probably ended with Gorky). The beginning of his contact with Nabokov coincided with a renewed interest in Pushkin on Wilson's part. Their letters reflect his study of the entire corpus of Pushkin's work, in part under Nabokov's guidance. Nabokov's translation of Pushkin's verse play *Mozart and Salieri*, first published in *The New Republic* in April 1941, with a prefatory piece by Wilson, was actually done in collaboration with him—a rare instance in Nabokov's literary career where he collaborated on anything with another writer.

Wilson's Pushkin articles of 1943, initially published in *The Atlantic Monthly* and later included in his book *A Window on Russia*, were the direct results of his discussions and exchanges on the subject with Nabokov. With the passage of years, we can see the very intensity of each writer's involvement with Pushkin's writings and biography giving rise to something like a proprietary attitude on each side. The initially amicable disagreements about Pushkin's metrical variety or lack of it and the extent of his proficiency in Latin or English gradually acquire an impatient edge, pointing toward the later explosive disagreement over the *Onegin* translation and commentary.

When Nabokov received and read Wilson's *To the Finland Station* in December 1940 (apparently the first book by Wilson that he ever read), he was far better equipped to evaluate and appreciate it than Wilson could have realized. Only a few years earlier, Nabokov had written the biography of Chernyshevsky which is ascribed to the hero of *The Gift*, forms a considerable portion of that novel and is, by Nabokov's own admission, a far more thoroughly researched piece of biographical writing than his later study of Gogol. If we accept the one-time Russian Marxist Peter Struve's definition of Bolshevism as a "mixture of imported foreign potions with native Russian rotgut," the first two sections of *To the Finland Station* document the "foreign potions" while Nabokov's biography of Chernyshevsky (who is not mentioned in *To the Finland Station*) addresses itself to an important aspect of the "rotgut" component. In the course of his work on Chernyshevsky, Nabokov had occasion to study in depth several of the protagonists of Wilson's book: Hegel, Feuerbach, Fourier, Saint-Simon and Marx. It is therefore understandable that Nabokov was charmed and captivated by Wilson's broadly researched, carefully objective and highly entertaining account of Marx and Engels, of their utopian socialist predecessors and of the origins and results of Marxism.

It was equally predictable that Nabokov, who through his family connections had a ringside seat for observing the Russian Revolution and who in the course of his work on *The Gift* had acquired a thorough knowledge of that revolution's origins, could not go along with the third section of Wilson's book, with its view of Russian history based almost entirely on Leninist and Trotskyite sources, its acceptance of Lenin as the only true spokesman for Russian socialism and Marxism, and its unfair dismissal of Lenin's socialist and liberal opponents as "representatives of the bourgeoisie" who were supposedly interested only in preserving private property. What Nabokov took exception to most strongly was Wilson's portrayal of Lenin himself (both in *To the Finland Station* and in *The Triple Thinkers*) as a warm-hearted humanitarian, a freedom-loving democrat and a sensitive critic of literature and the arts.

The American propensity for sentimental idealization of the founder of the Soviet Union became manifest shortly after the October Revolution. In his account of his interview with Lenin in 1919, Lincoln Steffens (*Autobiography*, 1931) reported that Lenin spoke to him primarily of the necessity for dictatorship and renewed terror; Steffens then added on his own that Lenin was "a liberal by instinct" who "defended liberty of speech, assembly and Russian press" and was in all probability personally opposed to terror. This is the recognizable pattern of replacing the real Lenin, the one who can be found in his personal correspondence or in the memoirs published abroad by his one-time political associates, such as Nikolai Valentinov and Peter Struve—the irascible fanatic, a man in love with the idea of violence, a politician whose prime motivations were a lust for boundless personal power and a murderous hatred of anyone who presumed to interpret Marxism or socialism in ways different from his own—with a saintly icon that bears little resemblance to the actual man.

For a person as closely familiar with the historical record as Nabokov, it was inconceivable that Lenin, who began his political career at the age of twenty-one by trying to sabotage the efforts of relief organizations to feed starving peasants during the 1891 famine (he believed that the more peasant families starved, the greater the likelihood was of the survivors starting a revolution) and who maintained his grip on power by unleashing a wave of indiscriminate terror unprecedented in modern times, could be regarded by anyone as a kindly humanitarian. Nor did it make sense that Wilson repeatedly represented Lenin as a defender of literary freedom, the very same Lenin who reinstated the censorship of books in a far more sweeping form than had ever existed under the tsars, who in 1920 issued an index of prohibited books and in 1923 allowed his wife Krupskaya to ban from public libraries a long list of "anti-artistic and counterrevolutionary literature," including the writings of Plato, Kant, Schopenhauer, Nietzsche and Tolstoy (the ban was lifted after protests from abroad and threats by Maxim Gorky to give up his Soviet citizenship if it were allowed to stand).

Wilson's assertion in his reply to Nabokov's critique of his portrait of Lenin that he had steered clear of official biographies and had based his view on "family memoirs, Trotsky's writings, Lenin's own works, and the memoirs of people like Gorky and Clara Zetkin," who were all "trying to tell the truth" (Letter 7), makes one think of a historian of Christianity who is sure that his account is factual because all his information comes straight from the Vatican. Wilson did not have at his disposal the more complete Soviet editions of Lenin's writings (which began appearing in the 1960s) when he was working on *To the Finland Station*. They contain such basic texts as "On the Tasks of the People's Commissariat of Justice Under the Conditions of the New Economic Policy" of February 20, 1922, where Lenin makes plans for staging a series of "exemplary" trials at which non-Leninist Marxists and Socialist Revolutionaries were to be convicted in advance, sets up quotas of people to be found guilty of subversive activities, and promises to expel from the Communist Party those judges and prosecutors who fail to fulfill their quotas of guilty verdicts. The study of such documents gives full support to Nabokov's recurrent assertion that Stalinism was not a betrayal of Lenin's policies but their direct continuation.

Wilson eventually came to realize that the sources on Lenin which he had used in *To the Finland Station* were examples of "deliberate myth-making."[3] In the "Introduction, 1971" which was added to the 1972 edition of the book, Wilson cited a wide array of sources of which he had not been aware in the 1930s, including the testimony of Peter Struve and Nikolai Valentinov, which documented the ruthless, brutal aspects of Lenin's personality and political style, as well as Bertram D. Wolfe's demonstration of the historical falsifications in Gorky's memoirs. While one admires Wilson for having had the courage to admit his earlier misconceptions, it is regrettable that this came too late to have made any difference in his relationship with Nabokov.

If the disagreement on the personality of Lenin was due to two divergent interpretations of the same set of historical facts, the even more vehement disagreement on the nature of Russian versification is an instance of an argument in which the participants either talk past one another or talk about two different things. The argument, initiated in personal discussion, was then reflected in Wilson's comparison of Pushkin's verse to Shakespeare's and finding Pushkin pedantically regular (Letter 47). What Wilson had clearly done was to apply *English* versification principles to Pushkin. Nabokov's reply (Letter 48) was a long, detailed and copiously illustrated treatise—not on the Russian system of stress or the standard Russian meters, for it never occurred to Nabokov that Wilson might not know them—but on the interplay between meter and rhythm in the Russian iamb as used by Pushkin. An earlier version of "Notes on Prosody" which Nabokov was to append to his commentary on *Eugene Onegin* and also publish as a separate booklet, this treatise outlines the discovery by Andrei Bely that a "variable rhythmic current" ran "through the constant structure of the Russian iamb." In trying to teach Wilson this "counterpoint of Russian verse," Nabokov did not realize that he was addressing his contrapuntal lesson to a person who had not been told about the pitch and length of various notes, or, to draw on

3. Letter to Arthur Mizener of April 4, 1950, *Letters on Literature and Politics, 1912–1972*, p. 479.

a different field for comparison, that he was giving a lesson in algebra to a pupil who did not know the four rules of arithmetic or the Arabic system of numerals.

Not until seven years later did Wilson learn from Gleb Struve (Letter 200) how Russian words are accented and that Russian has only one stress per word and no secondary stresses—a crucial piece of information, without which one cannot hope to understand Letter 48. Nor was Wilson aware that Russian meters and versification had been studied by generations of poets and theoreticians far more thoroughly than had ever been done with English verse. Nabokov was not communicating a versification theory of his own devising or something that he was taught at school, as Wilson believed, but a highly sophisticated analysis, advanced and developed during the Symbolist period, mostly by Annensky and Bely (and superseded in recent decades by computerized and semiotic studies of metrics developed in the Soviet Union). The Greek terminology, with its paeons, amphibrachs and pyrrhics, which in modern Russian stand for something quite different from what they stood for in classical Greek, made Wilson suspect Nabokov of pedantry and led him to point out in his reply (Letter 49) that English had gotten away from trying to fit its prosody and grammar into the mold of the classical languages.

Nabokov may well have confused the issue further and hampered Wilson's understanding by his attempts to invent for Wilson's benefit examples of English verse based on Russian-style prosody. These examples disregard the English secondary stresses, something that most Russians who learn English—no matter how well—instinctively do, while native speakers of English, just as instinctively, make these stresses a part of the metrical scheme. Wilson ostensibly went along with this confusion of the two versification systems when he wrote in his reply that Russian verse "seems to me basically, from the point of view of metrics, just like English verse." Thus, the misunderstanding was consolidated and in their subsequent arguments on metrics it is all too clear that Wilson has English prosody in mind when he writes of either English or Russian verse, while Nabokov for the most part seems to do just the opposite. As the entry of May 25–28, 1957 in his journal published in *Upstate* (p. 157) indicates, Edmund Wilson never did learn how the Russian stress system, metrics or prosody work. Nabokov's unwitting withholding of essential information, based on his apparent failure to perceive some fundamental gaps in Wilson's command of Russian, was the obstacle to communication in this case, just as it was later in the case of Nabokov's less than comprehensive elucidation of the grammatical problems that Wilson encountered while reading Chekhov in the original and for which he sought Nabokov's help.

Despite their disagreements on Lenin and on Russian iambics, the letters for the early 1940s document the ever growing closeness of the two writers and their steady involvement in each other's literary and academic interests and pursuits. Both of them held temporary teaching jobs at various colleges during that time. Their correspondence for 1942 shows them sharing available job information and recommending each other for academic positions. In March 1945 Wilson wrote to Nabokov that their "conversations have been among the few consolations" of his life during the past years (Letter 118), and a year later, in a letter to his teacher Christian Gauss (cited in note 1 to Letter 139), Wilson stated that Nabokov had become one of his closest friends, adding "I have a tremendously high opinion of his abilities." Another aspect of their intimacy was Nabokov's sharing with Wilson his observations of America and the Americans, collected on his travels around the country as a lecturer. The portrait gallery of academic and non-academic types in the remarkable Letter 55 shows Nabokov as a social observer, amassing and storing away the supply of impressions that he was later to put to such good use in *Lolita* and *Pnin* (in fact that letter can be read as a preliminary sketch to certain passages in these two novels).

In November 1943 Wilson proposed and Nabokov accepted a plan for the two of them to collaborate on a book on Russian literature. The initial idea was for a book of Wilson's essays, accompanied by Nabokov's translations. The project was energetically discussed and elaborated in their correspondence of 1944, and it is mentioned again and again in letters of subsequent years. There were several changes in the proposed format of the book. Doubleday eventually agreed to publish it and paid advances on it to the two prospective co-authors. The book was still being discussed in 1948, albeit with diminishing enthusiasm. Needless to say, it never materialized.

Introduction

Irving Howe has perceptively pointed out that one of Wilson's most salient and attractive qualities was his open-minded approach to all literatures and his eagerness to share every pleasure of literary discovery with his friends. Nabokov, who like the hero of *The Gift* recognized "only two kinds of books: bedside and wastebasket," was to prove a constant disappointment to Wilson, the bearer of literary gifts. Not since Tolstoy had there been a writer with as little reverence for established literary reputations as Nabokov. Against Wilson's broad catholicity of tastes, there was Nabokov's attitude, best expressed by Fyodor in *The Gift*, of "Either I love a writer fervently, or throw him out entirely." Because of the unpredictable pattern of his rejections, it is widely but erroneously assumed that by best writers Nabokov always means the best stylists, that is, that he chooses his favorite authors solely for their style, regardless of the content of their work. But this supposition is belied by his deep attachment to Tolstoy and Chekhov, neither of whom is an exemplary stylist in Russian, and by his rejection of Racine and Stendhal. Nabokov invariably finds uncongenial those writers who subjugate themselves to the prevalent normative poetics of their age (hence his contempt for neo-classicism *in toto* and especially for eighteenth-century literature, with the exception of Pope and Sterne in England and of Fonvizin and Derzhavin in Russia); writers who rely too much on readymade conventions and formulae (as Stendhal and Conrad did, to his way of thinking); or those who strive for effects which are emotional rather than artistic (such as Dostoevsky and Faulkner).

Because Nabokov felt more at home in the Russian literary tradition than in any other, he was apt to transpose the Western writers Wilson held up for his admiration into their Russian equivalents. Thus, Henry James, that "pale porpoise," as Nabokov described him, was for him a watered-down version of Turgenev (of whom Nabokov was not especially fond), Faulkner the equivalent of the socially conscious minor Russian novelists of the 1860s, and André Malraux a poor relative of Soviet writers of the 1920s who imitated Dostoevsky and Leonid Andreyev and who resembled Malraux in their themes and locales. Nabokov took a more accepting view of F. Scott Fitzgerald and John Peale Bishop, but this was due, one suspects, to his personal fondness for Wilson, whose classmates and close personal friends these two writers had been. For the greater duration of the correspondence, the literary pedagogue in Wilson was again and again stymied by Nabokov's stubborn refusal to appreciate his literary offerings.

Then, in the spring of 1950, the correspondence having intensified because the two writers were bedridden with various ailments, Wilson scored, one after another, three direct bull's eyes when he succeeded in getting Nabokov to appreciate the unlikely literary trio of Charles Dickens, Jane Austen and Jean Genet. Dickens happened to have been a particular favorite of Nabokov's father. As a child, Nabokov had been exposed to a great deal of Dickens when his father read his books out loud in English to the family. He later lost his interest in Dickens as he did in his father's two other favorite novelists, Balzac and Zola. Persuaded by Wilson of the particular value of Dickens' later novels, Nabokov made *Bleak House* one of the mainstays of his course in comparative literature at Cornell.

With Jane Austen, who for Wilson shared with James Joyce "the almost unique distinction in English novels of having a sense of form,"[4] it was his particular triumph to overcome Nabokov's typically Russian prejudice against women novelists. It so happens that while there have been major Russian women poets, some of whom were also able playwrights, there have been until very recently no novels in Russian written by women that rise above the level of the kind of women's pulp fiction that Nabokov satirized in his story "The Admiralty Spire." There was also the fact of Jane Austen's total lack of reputation in Russian culture. Other English women novelists had done quite well in Russia. Ann Radcliffe and the Brontë sisters enjoyed considerable renown throughout the nineteenth century. Mary Elizabeth Braddon's potboiler *Lady Aurora Floyd* was not only unaccountably liked by Tolstoy, but even served as a model for certain episodes in *War and Peace*. Austen, however, was and remains an unknown. The first Russian translation of *Pride and Prejudice* did not come out until the 1960s and it was received without much enthusiasm.

Once persuaded by Wilson to read *Mansfield Park*, Nabokov not only included it in his Cornell course, but proceeded to draw on Austen's work

4. Letter to Gilbert Troxell, *ibid.*, p. 74.

Introduction

for a number of parallels in his *Onegin* commentary (indeed, Austen comes closer to the quality of Pushkin's prose than any other foreign writer; his prose fragment "Roslavlev" reads like a chapter from a lost Jane Austen novel set in Russia). Much later, Nabokov was to incorporate references to *Mansfield Park* in *Ada*. In the case of Jean Genet, Nabokov's third literary discovery of that spring which he owed to Wilson, his evident distaste for certain aspects of Genet's subject matter was overcome by the originality of that writer's artistic vision and by Nabokov's appreciation of its roots in the art of Flaubert and Baudelaire.

Nabokov and Wilson's correspondence and friendship were founded in no small measure on their mutual esteem as writers. Nabokov had greatly admired the literary qualities of *To the Finland Station* and from then on he invariably praised all of Wilson's essay collections, individual articles, novels and plays. The cause of Nabokov's specific disagreements and strictures was always either Wilson's tendency to idealize the October Revolution and its makers or what Nabokov saw as Wilson's arbitrary introduction of social commentary, brought in in response to current intellectual fashion rather than the inner logic of the piece of writing. Puzzled by Nabokov's recurrent advice to disregard the sociological angle and tone down the ideological content of his writing, Wilson ventured (Letter 186) that Nabokov must have taken over in his youth *fin de siècle* art for art's sake slogans and had been applying them mechanically ever since.

There can hardly be a better illustration of the chronological disjunction between Russian and Western intellectual trends than this assumption of Wilson's. The debates over art for art's sake as opposed to socially engaged art took place in Russia not at the turn of the century, as in the West, but back in the 1860s. Freedom of the arts was defended primarily by Turgenev and his and Tolstoy's friend, the poet Afanasy Fet; their opponents were the radical utilitarians led by Chernyshevsky, who decreed that all writers address themselves to current social and political issues and who had the power to drum out of literature anyone who did not comply with their demands, as they did in Fet's case. For more than three decades, between the sixties and the mid-nineties, Russian literature and the other arts had to contend with the virtual dictatorship of radical utilitarian criticism. Their hegemony was quietly challenged by Chekhov; in retaliation, influential utilitarian critics did their best to discredit him and wreck his reputation. The overt challenge to their power was flung, defiantly and with deliberate insolence, by Sergei Diaghilev's journal *The World of Art* at the very end of the nineteenth century and this challenge was taken up by the entire Symbolist generation.

The issue for Nabokov, as it had been for Chekhov and the Russian Symbolists, was not ignoring or suppressing the economic or social factors, but, as he makes clear in his praise for Wilson's portrayal of the working-class girl Anna in *Memoirs of Hecate County* (Letter 185), of incorporating them organically into a literary work in ways that do not reduce the work to a sociological sermon or lesson and do not pander to quotidian topical preoccupations. Readers of Nabokov's numerous interviews in which he was wont to proclaim his "supreme indifference" to social purpose or moral message or general ideas are usually not aware that he was reacting to a powerful Russian tradition which twice within a century had enslaved literature and the other arts in the name of the same social purpose, moral message and general ideas. The first time was in the nineteenth century, when Tolstoy and Chekhov were systematically attacked and some good lesser writers expelled from literature for not having the right kind of social awareness. The second time came in the Soviet period, when a number of writers whom Nabokov in various ways admired, such as Zoshchenko, Olesha, Zabolotsky and Mandelstam, were persecuted and in some cases destroyed by a government that began enforcing the Belinskian-Chernyshevskian demand for social relevance with labor camps and death sentences. The very vehemence of Nabokov's disclaimers stems from the fact that he was the only major Russian writer in history who had an effective forum for such a denunciation.

More often than not, this aspect of Nabokov is not properly understood in the West, and this was one of the things that handicapped Edmund Wilson's full grasp of some of Nabokov's novels. Another handicap was Wilson's persistent ignoring of the Russian literary scene of the first two decades of the twentieth century, that is, of the very period in which Nabokov's personality and artistic outlook were formed. Edmund Wilson delved into Russian literature deeper than any American critic who was not a full-time Russian literature specialist. More than anyone else, he made literate American readers aware of the importance of Pushkin and Gogol. His essays on Turgenev and Tolstoy were based on study of sources available only in the original Russian. In his essay on Tyutchev—which is not entirely fair to the poet, in my view—Wilson ranged into areas of Russian literature most American critics do not even know exist. The same can be said about his interest in the two outstanding playwrights, Griboyedov, whose *Misfortune of Being Clever* Wilson aptly described as "something halfway between Beaumarchais and *Hamlet*," and Alexander Sukhovo-Kobylin, to whom he devoted a remarkable essay.

Yet, for all this wide scope, Wilson took almost no notice of the remarkable Silver Age of the early twentieth century—just as he had avoided when he wrote *To the Finland Station* looking too closely at the socialist and Marxist groups that opposed Lenin. Wilson was acquainted with D. S. Mirsky's books on the history of Russian literature, which do that period full justice; but his view of the post-1905 situation had been formed earlier by Leon Trotsky's *Literature and Revolution*, a book that cleverly discredits and slanders some of the finest Russian writers of the early twentieth century in the name of the proletarian writers who were to supersede them, in Trotsky's scheme of things, but who never materialized (or perished in the purges if they did). Anyone familiar with the spectacular explosion of Russian literary creativity after 1905, when the official censorship was abolished and the radical-utilitarian countercensorship weakened, is amazed to read Wilson's Trotsky-influenced statements in "Marxism and Literature" (originally published in 1937, but allowed to stand in all subsequent editions of *The Triple Thinkers*, where this essay was included) that there was a decline of Russian literature after 1905 or that the only important literature that the Russian Revolution produced was the writings of Lenin and Trotsky and Blok's poem "The Twelve" (which is like saying that English romanticism produced no literature of note except the writings of Thomas Paine, William Godwin and Shelley's poem "The Mask of Anarchy").

It was precisely in the brilliant literary flowering of that age, which Trotsky had concealed from Wilson, that Nabokov's art originated— from the experimental prose of Remizov and Bely, from the more traditionalist, but stylistically exquisite prose of Bunin and, even more importantly, from the great and innovative poetry that was then being written by Annensky, Blok, Bely and, later, Mandelstam and Pasternak, among so many others. (Wilson began taking an interest in some of the figures of that age, such as Pasternak, Mandelstam and Akhmatova, at the end of his life, when it was too late for this to have any effect on his understanding of Nabokov.)[5]

When he warned Nabokov, in the first letter to him we have (Letter 3), to avoid playing with words and making puns, something for which he took Nabokov to task also in his responses to the two of his books that he most admired, *The Real Life of Sebastian Knight* and *Nikolai Gogol*, Wilson could not have been aware that this was less a personal idiosyncrasy of Nabokov's than an aspect of a widespread trend in the literature of Russian modernism. Interest in paronomasia, in discovering the hitherto unperceived relationships between the semantic and phonetic aspects of speech, pursued not for the purpose of playing with words but for discovering and revealing hidden new meanings, was basic to the prose of Remizov, Bely and other Russian Symbolists. It was even more basic to the poetry of Mayakovsky, Pasternak and Tsvetaeva, the three poets whose work had some of the same roots as Nabokov's prose and with whom he shared the bent for verbal experimentation that at first puzzled and then delighted readers of his novels written in English.[6]

It is all the more remarkable, then, that with this lack of awareness of Nabokov's literary origins, Wilson was able nevertheless to capture their very essence when he wrote in his evaluation of *The Real Life of Sebastian Knight* that "it is all on a high *poetic* level, and you have succeeded in being a first-rate poet in English" (Letter 23). Indeed, just as Boris Eichenbaum in his splendid study of the sources of Tolstoy's *Anna Kare-*

---

5. Russian Symbolism is not mentioned in *Axel's Castle*, Wilson's great study of the impact of the Symbolist movement on twentieth-century literature. When Wilson wrote in the beginning of his chapter on Proust that "Marcel Proust is the first important novelist to apply the principles of Symbolism to fiction," he was not aware—as no one in the West was at the time—that Sologub, Remizov and Bely had been publishing major Symbolist novels at least a decade before the first volume of *A la recherche du temps perdu* appeared.

6. What Nabokov's Western reviewers and interviewers have tended to attribute to the influence of James Joyce is actually Nabokov's own continuation and development of the features of Russian modernism to which he had been exposed long before he had ever heard of Joyce.

nina has shown the importance of the lyric poetry of Tyutchev and Fet for the genesis of that novel, Nabokov's English prose, for all his tremendous originality and undoubted individuality, frequently draws on some of the significant procedures of Russian Symbolist and post-Symbolist poetry.

Wilson liked *The Real Life of Sebastian Knight*, which Nabokov had written in English prior to his departure for America, better than he was ever to like any of Nabokov's later books. In 1942 he read the two earlier Nabokov novels that had been published in English translation, but he liked *Laughter in the Dark* less than *The Real Life of Sebastian Knight*, and *Despair* even less. He seemed enthusiastic about the drafts and separate sections of *Bend Sinister* which Nabokov had shown him while the novel was being written, but he totally rejected it when he read it in its finished form.

Together with *Invitation to a Beheading* and *The Gift*, *Bend Sinister* forms something like a trilogy of Nabokov's novels about totalitarian revolutions. Where *The Gift* dealt with the roots of totalitarianism in the ostensibly libertarian but actually dogmatic and fanatical ideologies of an earlier generation, and *Invitation to a Beheading* was concerned with the bleak remote results of such a system, *Bend Sinister* was a fantasy about the coming to power of a despotic dictator. Drawing on his own experiences during Lenin's takeover in Russia and Hitler's in Germany, Nabokov interlarded the book, as he was to admit in an introduction to a later edition, "with bits of Lenin's speeches, and a chunk of the Soviet constitution, and gobs of Nazist pseudo-efficiency." Because it was fresher in Nabokov's memory due to its greater proximity in time, the Nazi experience was given a greater prominence in the novel, but the Bolshevik experience is also an essential component. The relationship between the dictator Paduk and his ideological predecessor Skotoma is a distorted, parodistic version of the connection between Chernyshevsky and Lenin that was dealt with in *The Gift*.

Despite Nabokov's earlier urging, Wilson had not read *The Gift* or *Invitation to a Beheading* when he was confronted with *Bend Sinister*, feeling rightly that his command of Russian was not sufficient for tackling these two complex novels (not yet translated into English at that time). Therefore, Wilson was not aware of the important political strain in

Nabokov's earlier work, of which *Bend Sinister* was a continuation. His statement in Letter 160 "You aren't good at this kind of subject, which involves questions of politics and social change, because you are totally uninterested in these matters and have never taken the trouble to understand them" is truly astounding, considering that it is addressed to the author of *The Gift*. Equally astounding is that this was to remain Wilson's view to the end of his life. In the 1971 postscript to his critique of the *Onegin* commentary (in *A Window on Russia*), we read that Nabokov "despises the Communist regime and, it seems to me, does not even understand how it works or how it ever came to be. His knowledge of Russia, in fact, is very special, extremely limited."

Yet it was Wilson, as Nabokov tells us in his introduction to the 1964 edition of the novel, who helped arrange the publication of *Bend Sinister*. With the same impartial generosity, Wilson refrained from reviewing this novel, which he disliked, trying to arrange good reviews for it by other critics; still later, he offered Nabokov his help in finding a producer for a dramatized version of *Bend Sinister* (Letter 265). He went on championing Nabokov's cause with editors, publishers and universities throughout the forties and the early fifties. But the only book by Nabokov which Wilson actually reviewed in print was *Nikolai Gogol*. The review, which appeared in *The New Yorker* and was later included in Wilson's collection of essays *Classics and Commercials,* was laudatory, but it also contained a number of strictures that reflected the standing disagreements between the two writers on topics which have already been covered in this essay.

The crack in the relationship caused by Wilson's dislike of *Bend Sinister* must have widened into a fissure with his reaction to *Lolita*. As had been the case with *Bend Sinister,* Nabokov's letters kept Wilson informed of his progress on the new novel. Once again Nabokov was extremely anxious to have him read the finished book, all the more so because he considered *Lolita* his best work in English. In November 1954 Wilson read it and informed Nabokov that he had "liked it less than anything you wrote." It is hard to account for Wilson's aversion. There were no political dimensions in *Lolita* of the kind that caused him to reject *Bend Sinister*. The criticism he offers sounds almost puritanical, but this is hard to credit, coming from the author of *Memoirs of Hecate County,* who was furthermore an enthusiastic admirer of Jean Genet. Be that as it may, Wilson displayed his characteristic fairness by enclosing with his negative evaluation of *Lolita* two other opinions: an equally negative one by his former wife Mary McCarthy and an admirably perceptive, even prescient dissenting opinion by Elena Wilson, who was the only one of the three to see the beauty and the value of the book.

Things went downhill in 1955–56. The arguments about versification and the October Revolution had by now been repeated so often that they had become predictable. Nabokov was dismayed and hurt by the section on Russia in *A Piece of My Mind. Reflections at Sixty* (1956), with its quotations from Melchior de Vogüé intended to demonstrate that, except for Lenin's democratic reign, Russia had remained unchanged from the Middle Ages to Stalin. It showed how little Wilson had learned from all their letters and conversations about that particular topic. Equally depressing for Nabokov was Wilson's 1956 edition of Chekhov's stories, with its numerous errors of translation and its almost exclusively sociological introduction in which Wilson expressed the curious view that Chekhov's characters were the very people in charge of things in Stalinist times.

But the correspondence and occasional family visits continued for two more years. The publication and international acclaim in 1958 of *Doctor Zhivago* by Boris Pasternak (in whose poetry Nabokov had tried to interest Wilson back in January 1941) put a further strain on the relationship. Wilson devoted to Pasternak's novel an ecstatic review in *The New Yorker*, one of his finest pieces of writing in the field of Russian literature, in which he qualified the book as "one of the great events in man's literary and moral history." For Nabokov, *Doctor Zhivago* was a piece of pulp fiction, regrettably written by a poet he admired, a book, as he put it in the afterword to the Russian version of *Lolita*, about a "lyrical doctor with penny-dreadful mystical urges and philistine turns of speech and an enchantress straight out of Charskaya" (Lydia Charskaya wrote widely popular treacly novels for and about teen-aged girls in pre-revolutionary Russia). After a disagreement as profound as this, it was but a short step to the 1965 clash over *Onegin*.

In the 1960s, there was estrangement. With the international recognition of Nabokov's stature that came with *Lolita* and *Pnin*, there appeared, partly in response to his growing influence, new writers and literary trends to which Nabokov could respond in ways that he could not to the literary figures of his and Wilson's generation in whom the latter had tried to interest him during the two decades of their correspondence. In America, there were John Cheever, John Updike, John Barth. In France, there was Alain Robbe-Grillet. There was Raymond Queneau (whom Nabokov admired far more than Wilson did). There were the prose fictions of Samuel Beckett, which Nabokov greatly valued while rejecting his plays as imitations of the forgotten chamber dramas of Maurice Maeterlinck. All these writers, highly rated by Nabokov, meant very little to Wilson, who during the sixties took less notice of new literary developments than he had done in preceding decades. Nor would Wilson have been likely to share Nabokov's great enthusiasm for Edmund White's elegantly stylized novel about the semiology of snobbery, *Forgetting Elena*, had he lived to read it. Their last meeting of the minds on literary matters was a negative one, when they agreed on what is surely an underevaluation of the talent of Alexander Solzhenitsyn, whom Nabokov dismissed with greater severity than did Wilson.

Both sides were hurt by their 1965 clash over *Onegin*. In later years, there were several efforts to patch things up. The last two letters of the present collection betray a nostalgia for their one-time closeness and mutual confidence. But, as better-informed readers know, there was more acrimony to come: Wilson's less than generous portrayal of Nabokov's person in *Upstate*, Nabokov's angry rebuttal in his letter to *The New York Times Book Review*, as well as Wilson's near-sighted summary of Nabokov's themes and literary significance in *A Window on Russia*. Yet it is fitting that Wilson's last written communication with Nabokov, which closes their extant correspondence, deals with a scholarly point that involves Nabokov's family and a great Russian writer, Anton Chekhov, whom both correspondents loved, even if they did see him in widely divergent ways.

For all of Edmund Wilson's awesome scope as a literary critic, the one major writer whose reputation he did not help to establish or assert was, paradoxically, his close friend and correspondent Vladimir Nabokov. Wilson had enjoyed *Speak, Memory*, which had preceded *Lolita*, and he very much liked *Pnin*, which followed it, but he said so in his letters to

Nabokov, not in critical reviews. He had nothing to say about *Pale Fire*, the novel for which his one-time wife Mary McCarthy had led the chorus of critical acclaim. *Ada*, with its rich contrapuntal variations on themes from Russian literature which never fail to delight Slavic scholars, was pronounced unreadable by Wilson. And he seems never to have read *The Gift*, the one Nabokov book which, had he properly understood it, could have supplied him with the missing key both to the art of Vladimir Nabokov and to an understanding of much of modern Russian history.

But if he had left it to others to reveal the full dimensions of Nabokov's genius, Wilson has the historical priority of having discovered, encouraged and shared with others the unique originality of Nabokov the man, thus enabling him to pursue and develop his second literary career, as an American writer. This was also no mean critical achievement and it constitutes Edmund Wilson's additional, hitherto unrecognized contribution to the enrichment of the American literature of our century.

SIMON KARLINSKY
Kensington, California

The Letters

1940

1

c/o Prof. Karpovich[1]
West Wardsboro
Vermont

August 30, 1940

My dear Mr. Wilson,

My cousin Nicholas[2] has suggested my writing to you. I would be very happy to meet you. I am staying with friends in Vermont (goldenrod and wind, mostly), but shall be back in New York in the second week of September. My address there will be: 1326, Madison Ave. Tel. At. 97186.

Съ искреннимъ привѣтомъ[3]

V. Nabokoff

1. Michael Karpovich (1888–1959), professor of history at Harvard and editor of the New York–based Russian émigré literary journal *Novyi Zhurnal (The New Review)*.

2. Nabokov's cousin, the composer and memoirist Nicolas Nabokov (1903–1978); he is mentioned in this correspondence as Nicholas, Nikolai and Nika.

3. "With sincere regards."

2

October 7, 1940
35 W. 87

Dear Mr. Wilson,

I shall be delighted to come and see you. I could come on Tuesday at 2 or 6. Let me know, please, which suits you best. My telephone is Sc 49270 and I shall be at home to-morrow till 10 a.m. I would have telephoned myself, but cannot find your number.

Yours sincerely

V. Nabokoff

3

THE NEW REPUBLIC
40 East 49th Street
New York, N.Y.

November 12, 1940

Dear Nabokov:

This review of Rust'hveli[1] is admirable—and very entertaining.

In doing future reviews, please follow exactly *The New Republic* usage in giving the title, author, etc., at the top. You will note that the number of pages and the price are included. I am enclosing an example. Another thing: do please refrain from puns, to which I see you have a slight propensity. They are pretty much excluded from serious journalism here. Also, the expression *I for one* is not precisely in the tone of reviewing. You ought simply to say *I*, or if you want to emphasize it, *for myself* or *for my part*.

Won't you call me up soon and come in and have lunch again? I hope I didn't offend you in going to the Greenbergs'[2] house when you had invited us first. We have as a rule only Wednesday night in New York, and I thought it would be a good opportunity to combine seeing the Greenbergs with having you and the Eastmans[3] meet. I feel under special obligations to the Greenbergs, as his mother and sister were extremely kind to me in Moscow.

Yours sincerely,
Edmund Wilson

Mr. V. Nabokov
35 W 87
New York City

EW:MB

1. Nabokov's review of the English translation of *The Knight in Tiger's Skin* by the twelfth-century Georgian poet Shot'ha Rust'hveli ("Crystal and Ruby," *The New Republic,* November 25, 1940).

2. Roman and Sophie (Sonya) Grynberg. Roman Grynberg published literary and political commentary in the émigré press under the pen name "Erge." In the 1950s, he co-edited the literary journal *Opyty (Experiments)* and during the 1960s he brought out the important periodic literary miscellany *Vozdushnye puti (Aerial Ways).* Unless otherwise noted, the "Roman" mentioned in this correspondence is always Grynberg.

3. Max and Elena Eastman.

4

Dear Wilson,

Your suggestion regarding *Mozart and Salieri*[1] has worked havoc with me. I thought I would try with the idea—and then suddenly found myself in the very deep waters of English verse. After a week of hard work I have finished the first scene. Will you please tell me whether it is worth while going on?

I have also brought you my novel *Invitation to a Beheading*.

The review of the Dukhobor book[2] will be ready in two or three days.

Yours truly

V. Nabokov

1. Wilson had suggested that Nabokov translate *Mozart and Salieri*, one of the series of brief verse plays by Pushkin which are known collectively as Pushkin's "little tragedies." The translation was completed in collaboration with Wilson and published in *The New Republic* (April 21, 1941) and in Nabokov's volume of translations *Three Russian Poets* (1944), in both cases with a prefatory note by Wilson.

2. See Letter 6, note 2 below.

5

THE NEW REPUBLIC
40 East 49th Street
New York, N.Y.

December 12, 1940

Dear Nabokov: How are you getting along with *Mozart and Salieri?* Here is a check, which is in the nature of an advance on the work. Your Приглашение на казнь[1] has stumped me, and I think I had better go back to Tolstoy till my Russian is stronger. I suppose it is like being confronted with Virginia Woolf after having read no English fiction since Thackeray.

Best regards,

Edmund Wilson

1. *Invitation to a Beheading*.

6

V. Nabokov
35 W. 87th St.
New York

December 15, 1940

Dear Wilson,

This is going to be a very long letter. First, let me thank you for the cheque. It is really wonderful to be living at last in a country where there is a market for such things. I am sending you the second scene, though I am still struggling with the murderer of the Vatican whose hindquarters protrude whenever I manage to get his head squeezed in—and vice versa.[1]

I am sending you also the Dukhobor review.[2] If you find the last sentence (about "beggar" and "bugger") superfluous, just leave it out.[3]

I want to speak to you about your book.[4] I enjoyed it immensely, it is beautifully composed, and you are extraordinarily unbiased although here and there I did notice two or three little thistles of conventional radicalism sticking to your freely flowing gown. You would be branded (as I have been) by the judges in Moscow as a "*bezotvetstvennyi*[5] eclectic" while your "clearing up" of Marxism's difficulties (page 187 and elsewhere) would have maddened Marx. Personally I find that you have simplified his idea a little too drastically. Without its obscurities and abracadabra, without its pernicious reticences, shamanic incantations and magnetic trash, Marxism is not Marxism. The paradox which explodes Marxism and other dreams of the Ideal State is that the first author is potentially the first tyrant of that state. You have hinted at this in a gnoseological excursion but here, I think, is the crux of the problem. The individual whims of a ruler tell deeper truths about a corresponding period than the vulgar generalisation of class war etc.; and the peculiar mathematical and historical howlers, in the *Capital* and capitaloids, are transfigured by the synthesis of Revolution into the beastly cruel stupidities it commits. You've got all that, but I think you ought to have stressed that point. Your criticism of Marxism is so ferocious that you kick out the Marxism stool from under the feet of Lenin, who is left dangling in midair. Incidentally, you are quite wrong about Hegel's triad being based upon the triangle (with a phallic implication which reminds me of a solemn Freudian contention that children like playing ball because balls remind boys of their mother's breasts and girls of their father's balls). The triad (for what it is worth) is really the idea of a circle; to give a rough example: you come back (synthesis) to your starting point (thesis) after visiting the antipodes (antithesis) with the accumulated impressions of the globe enlarging your initial conception of your home town.

Such is the artistic deceptiveness of nature's methods that the thing that eventually brings the most evil or the most benefit to most people is an unpredictable casual freak of a thing which could never have been suspected of developing into a general boon or blight. How glum Engels would have looked were he shown some modern factories. And electric plants. There are also earthquakes, and banana skins, and indigestion.

I wonder where you got your statistics when you say that Thiers executed more people than did the Terreur? I object to this kind of excuse for two reasons. Although from a Christian's or a mathematician's point of view a thousand people killed in battle a hundred years ago equal a thousand people killed in a battle of to-day, historically the first definition is "slaughter" and the second "some casualties." Secondly: one cannot compare the slapdash suppression, however abominable, of a revolt with the thorough application of a system of murder. By the way, speaking of the Terreur, do you know that, long before the Russian revolution, radical thought was so powerful in the Russian publishing business that the works of Lenôtre[6] could not appear in Russian: we had really *two* censorships!

I have noted some little mistakes you have made: жестокость *is* cruelty, *not* severity. It is жёсткость (lacking the howling O in the middle) that may mean "severity" or rather "harshness." You might have mentioned that Gapon was an agent provocateur and died a traitor's death (hanged by the social revolutionists). The legend of the Tsar and Tsaritsa "trying to make peace with Germany" is an absolute fabrication of Bolshevik propaganda just as the legend of Lenin promising the Germans to ruin Russia was invented by his adversaries.

And now we come to Ilyitch[7]—and here I itch (sorry). I am afraid the portrait of his father is a little too much in the celestial colors of his Soviet biographers. Ulianoff senior was according to people who knew him a very ordinary pleasantly liberal minded gentleman. Thousands of his likes founded thousands of the same kind of schools—it was quite a competition. The atmosphere of the Ulianoff family (free tuition, etc.) was practically the same in all liberal teachers' or doctors' families and goes back to the fifties. Nothing quite similar to the moral purity and *beskorystie*[8] of Russian *intelligenty*[9] is to be found abroad. Whatever group they belonged to, Bolshevik or Cadet,[10] Narodovoltsy[11] or Anarchist, their *byt*[12] during half a century of *obshchestvennoe dvizhenie*[13] was marked by a sense of duty, self-sacrifice, kindness, heroism; nor were these traits sectarian. I know of a case when a famous Cadet taking part in a secret meeting of different groups for a conference that had to be hastily dissolved because it was learnt that the Cheka had got wind of it, risked his life staying behind in order to warn an obscure Menshevik (whom he hardly knew and of whose party he disapproved) who, it was apprehended, might come later and be trapped.[14]

Your Ulianoff-père is not an individual but merely a type. (Whereas your other people are splendidly alive). If, in addition to the blues and pinks, you had put in a dash of sepia (as you did with your other portraits) the man would have been less "iconic."

As to his son . . . No, not even the magic of your style has made me like him, and I have read years ago the official biographies you have faithfully and fatally followed (what a pity you have not dipped into Aldanov's *Lenin*).[15]

Family reminiscences are apt to be sickly sweet, and poor Krupskaya lacked both humor and taste. An ironic reader confronted with Lenin's remark about the fox he did not shoot because he was "beautiful" might retort: pity that Russia was homely.

That bluff geniality, that screwing up of eyes *(s prishchurinkoy),*[16] that boyish laugh, etc., on which his biographers dwell so lovingly, form something particularly distasteful to me. It is this atmosphere of joviality, this pail of milk of human kindness with a dead rat at the bottom, that I have used in my *Invitation to a Beheading* (which I still hope you will read). The "invitation" is so kindly meant, all will be so nice and pleasant, if only you don't MAKE A FUSS (says the executioner to his "patient"). A German friend of mine, whose hobby was capital punishment, and who saw it done with an axe in Regensburg, told me that the headsman was positively paternal.

Another horrible paradox about Leninism is that these materialists found it possible to squander the lives of millions of real people for the sake of the hypothetical millions that would be happy some day.

But I loved your Marx. The way you examine those letters of his which hurt Engels who had lost his mistress, is beautifully shrewd; and they are really very pathetic, the clumsy attempts of a boorish person trying to atone for a "gaffe" and making it still worse. The book is so entertaining that I could not stop it, let alone stop myself. You will not be irritated by my criticising certain passages? I felt it would be somehow unfair to your very important book, if I did not express the whirl of thought that its shimmering propeller produced.

Yours very cordially
V. Nabokov

1. At the end of *Mozart and Salieri,* Antonio Salieri, who has just poisoned Mozart out of envy, reflects on whether a man of genius can be capable of murder. He evokes the legend that Michelangelo ("the creator of the Vatican") murdered a model so that he could use his body to depict the dead Christ. Because of the extreme compression of Pushkin's text,

Nabokov's English version uses five lines to convey this passage, where Pushkin had only three.

2. "Home for Dukhobors," Nabokov's review of *Slava Bohu. The Story of the Dukhobors* by J. F. C. Wright (*The New Republic*, January 13, 1941).

3. The last paragraph of "Home for Dukhobors" reads:

> An irritating feature of the book is Mr. Wright's dismal trick of sticking in Russian words, all of which are misspelled, or misplaced, or ridiculously wrong. It is always rather perilous for a writer to try to toy with a foreign idiom. I like to recall the case of the famous Russian writer Herzen who, living in Putney and knowing very little English, illustrated a brilliant essay on the Britisher's innate contempt for poverty by the unfortunate remark that the worst invective commonly heard in London was the word "beggar."

Nabokov's final point was apparently laundered for magazine publication; a more explicit version is to be found in Chapter Three of *The Gift*, where the hero notices that Herzen "had confused the sounds of two English words 'beggar' and 'bugger' and from this had made a brilliant deduction concerning the English respect for wealth."

4. *To the Finland Station.*

5. "Irresponsible."

6. Louis Gosselin ("Georges") Lenôtre, 1857–1935, the conservative historian of the French Revolution.

7. Lenin.

8. "Selflessness."

9. "Intellectuals."

10. Members of the Constitutional Democratic party.

11. Members of the People's Freedom party.

12. "Daily life."

13. "Civic [protest] movement."

14. Véra Nabokov had pointed out that it was Nabokov's father who did this.

15. *Lenin* by M. A. Landau-Aldanov (New York, 1922). The book is a debunking of the cult of the wise and benevolent Lenin, written from the position of Russian prerevolutionary liberal socialism. Member of one of the lesser Socialist parties before the Revolution, Mark Aldanov (1889–1957; his real name was Landau) developed during his emigration into a popular and prolific historical novelist. Edmund Wilson met Aldanov in the 1940s; he discusses Aldanov's novel *The Fifth Seal* in his essay on Leonid Leonov which is included in *Classics and Commercials*.

16. Nabokov's rendition of this phenomenon into English is found in Chapter Six of *The Real Life of Sebastian Knight:* "Puckering about the eyes which stands for wisdom and humor." Wilson's essay "A Little Museum of Russian Language" (in *A Window on Russia*) comments on the numerous Russian terms for voluntary and involuntary ways of narrowing one's eyes, terms which are ubiquitous in Russian literature and a constant source of difficulty for translators.

7

THE NEW REPUBLIC
40 East 49th Street
New York, N.Y.

December 19, 1940

Dear Nabokov:

Thank you very much for your letter. I was glad to get your detailed criticism. I was aware of the weakness of my Russian background. I do feel, though,
that you are mistaken in your conception of Lenin and the whole type of revolutionary personality which he represents—because you conceive a monster
and don't explain him in human terms. In writing about him, I tried as much as
possible to steer clear of the official lives and depended on the family memoirs,
Trotsky's writings, Lenin's own works, and the memoirs of people like Gorky
and Clara Zetkin. It seems to me that all these people are trying to tell the
truth, and a pretty consistent picture emerges. I don't believe that Gorky,
differing as he did so seriously in matters of opinion from Lenin, could ever
have been on such close terms with a man such as you imagine.

I am glad you like the book, which has weaknesses on the German side, too.

Thank you for the *Mozart and Salieri*. Let us have a discussion of it some
time before the first of the year. I want to go through the whole thing very carefully, and I have to write an article this weekend, so that I can't do anything
about it until after that. And thank you for the Dukhobor review.

Yours sincerely,
Edmund Wilson
(over)

Mr. Vladimir Nabokov
35 W. 87
New York City

[On reverse]

You are mistaken in thinking that I confused жёсткость with жестокость.
In the speech which I quote on page 400, Lenin says, «Мы страдаем от этого
зла жестоко.»[1] This appears in the official English translation as "severely."

I am also relieved to find that I had not done so badly as I said with «В
Европу прорубить окно».[2] I translated it, "We shall break a window through
to Europe"—I suppose *hack out* would, as you suggest, have been better. I was
very much interested in your letter. I know from reading French books on

American subjects how peculiarly uncomfortable it is to read books about one's own country by people who have got the subject up but don't really know much about it at first hand.

1. "We suffer cruelly from this evil."

2. This line from the prologue to Pushkin's "The Bronze Horseman" appears in Wilson's translation of the poem (in *The Triple Thinkers*) as "break a window through to Europe." "To hack out" or "to chop out" would have indeed been closer to the Russian original.

8

Dear Wilson,

I am afraid my imitation English has rather let me down. No, there was nothing wrong about your Russian background; in fact I wrote to you as I would have done to a compatriot. What I objected to was merely your sources being a little too much *ad usum Delphini;*[1] and if I suggested others, it was because anything remotely hinting at the ghost of the ghost of a critical attitude towards Lenin could not have been printed in Russia; but insofar as you adopted a certain point of view, your rendering of the atmosphere is perfect. I am sure that had I attempted to portray any of our dismal rulers, from Vladimir the Lovely Sun[2] to Lenin the Lenient, I would have gone to the other extreme and made them look more inhuman and ridiculous than they were. *Du choc des opinions jaillit la vérité*[3] like a football which provokes a wild scramble all over again.

Yours съ дружескимъ привѣтомъ[4]

V. Nabokov

P.S.

I am returning a cheque that was sent me to-day by mistake.

1. "Suitable for children."

2. The formulaic appellation in Russian folklore for the Grand Prince Vladimir (956–1015), also known as St. Vladimir, the Kievan ruler who brought Christianity to Russia.

3. "The truth springs forth from the clash of opinions."

4. "With friendly regards."

9

THE NEW REPUBLIC

40 East 49th Street

New York, N.Y.

December 27, 1940

Dear Nabokov:

Thank you for your letter. I am leaving *The New Republic* at the end of this week, but I have arranged with Bruce Bliven to have you do a periodical article (if you would care to) about contemporary Russian literature. I suppose each one ought to be limited to perhaps 1,500 words, unless there is a good deal that is very important, which I imagine is not the case at present.

Sometime during January when I come to town, perhaps we could have a conference on *Mozart and Salieri*.

All the good wishes of the season from us both to you and Mrs. Nabokov.

Yours sincerely,

Edmund Wilson

Mr. Vladimir Nabokov

35 W. 87

New York City

EW:MB

I am writing a little note to your review of Maximoff,[1] which I hope you won't mind. I'll have a copy enclosed with this letter. Correct it if you don't approve.

1. Nabokov's review of *The Guillotine at Work* by G. P. Maximoff. It was said to have been published in *The New York Sun* in 1941, but Michael Juliar in his *Vladimir Nabokov: A Descriptive Bibliography* (1986) was not able to locate it.

10

[Véra Nabokov to Mary McCarthy and
Vladimir Nabokov to Edmund Wilson]

December 28, 1940

Dear Mrs. Wilson,

My husband and I would be very happy if you and Mr. Wilson could come on Sunday the 5th at 9.

Our lodging being very small and uncomfortable, we are going to entertain a few friends in the apartment of our very old friends Bertrand and Lisbet Thompson,[1] Hotel Bolivar, Central Park West at the 83rd St. (Incidentally B. C. Thompson had written an article about France for *The New Republic*). We are also asking the Kerenskys.

Please let me know as soon as you can whether the 5th suits you and your husband.

I wish you both a very happy New Year.

Yours sincerely,
Vera Nabokoff

Dear Wilson,

I think your footnote[2] is splendid; and I feel very grateful.

Отъ души благодарю васъ[3] for arranging the periodical articles. I certainly shall be delighted to do them.

Thanks for the cheque.

Yours truly
V. Nabokov

Съ новымъ, новенькимъ, новёхонькимъ, новѣйшимъ Годом![4] Please come!

1. The Nabokovs' friendship with the Thompsons dated from 1926. On C. Bertrand and Lisbet Thompson, see Brian Boyd, *Vladimir Nabokov: The Russian Years*, pp. 393–394.

2. To the Maximoff review. See the postscript to Wilson's letter of December 27, 1940.

3. "I heartily thank you."

4. "Wishing you a Happy New, [Nice little] New, [Sweet little] New, Newest Year!" (A crescendo of Russian diminutives.)

1941

11

[Postcard, postmarked January 5, 1941]

Dear Wilson,

We were extremely sorry to have to postpone our party (the Thompsons had the flu').

Could you come next Saturday evening instead, to the same address? As we all are particularly eager to see you both, we shall wait for your consent before calling the others.

Yours cordially,

12

January 11, 1941
Trees,[1] RFD 1
Stamford, Conn.

Dear Nabokov: The situation about the *New Republic* is this. I arranged with Bruce Bliven[2] to have you do a periodical article about contemporary Russian literature (all kinds: you can find out from Yarmolinsky[3] what is being published). He asked me to tell you not to let it run too long, so I'd try to keep it between 1000 and 1500 words. Just go ahead and write one and send it to Nigel Dennis, who is now in charge of the literary department, reminding him that I had arranged for the article with Bliven. I have told Dennis about it. Inquire at the same time when they would like another. I am going to write Laughlin about bringing out your books.

It was nice to see you last night. I wish we had had more chance to talk. We will get together presently over *Mozart and Salieri*. I hope you got the second check for this that was supposed to be sent you. If you didn't, let me know.

As ever,
Edmund Wilson

1. "Trees" was the name of the house Wilson rented.
2. Bliven was the president of the editorial board of *The New Republic*.
3. Historian and translator of Russian literature, Avrahm Yarmolinsky was Chief of the Slavonic Division of the New York Public Library.

13

35 W. 87
February 9, 1941

Dear Wilson

a big *spaseebo*[1] for "contacting" me with *Decision*[2] and "New Direction[s]." I had a very pleasant talk with Klaus Mann who suggested my writing for them

The Letters, 1941

an article of 2000 words. I got a letter from James Laughlin[3] and am sending him my English novel *The Real Life of Sebastian Knight* which I retrieved from my agent. (I should have loved your reading it if I had a spare copy and you time.) Laughlin has also written me about a collection of modern Russian poems—particularly Pasternak (a first class poet—do you know his stuff?).

I have been reading at the library all the monthlies for the Soviet year 1940,—a ghastly and very amusing task. This week my article for the *New Republic* (for which I have no more that warm feeling since you have gone,—that stimulating warmth) will be ready. I am working hard at my lectures. In March I have got a fortnight of them at Wellesley Coll[ege] and yesterday I came back from Wells Coll[ege] where, to put it modestly, I had some success. Nicholas was charming.[4]

When shall I see you?

My best regards to your wife and a good Russian hand shake for you.

Yours truly

V. Nabokov

Жена шлетъ сердечный привѣтъ вамъ обоимъ[5]

1. "Thank you."

2. *Decision*, "a review of free culture," was published in New York from 1941 to 1942 and edited by Klaus Mann.

3. Founder, editor and president of the New Directions publishing house.

4. Nicolas Nabokov was teaching at Wells College at the time.

5. "My wife sends both of you her cordial regards."

14

35 W. 87

March 5, 1941

Dear Wilson,

I want your advice. What kind of magazine or review might accept the story which I am enclosing? Will you please read it—perhaps you could suggest something? I thought of showing it to Klaus Mann for *Decision*, but I am afraid it might strike him as anti-German,—not merely anti-Nazi,—although really it could have happened in other countries too.[1]

I liked Kim but I did not like the Russian spy. There is also a line in one of his poems about tropical "blazoned butterflies flapping their wings" that pleased the entomologist in me. Vermont, a cross little gentleman on a bike,— very good.[2]

I got into rather a fix with my article on Sov[iet] Literature 1940. I reviewed the latest issues of *Krasnaya Nov'* and *Novyi Mir*³ for *Decision* thinking I would write about the poetry and the novel for the *New Republic;* but what I have found and read made me so sick that I can't force myself to proceed . . . I have got ready an examination of "the characters in Soviet drama,"—would that do?⁴

I would *very* much like to see you before I go to Wellesley Coll[ege] for a fortnight course of lectures. I am going on the 15th of March.

My and my wife's greetings to Mrs. Wilson.

Крепко жму вашу руку; кажется, скоро разучусь писать по-русски, такъ много пишу на своемъ «пиджин»'е.⁵

Yours very truly

V. Nabokov

1. Probably "Cloud, Castle, Lake," which appeared in English translation in *The Atlantic Monthly* for June 1941.

2. This paragraph refers to Wilson's essay "The Kipling That Nobody Read," included in his book *The Wound and the Bow.*

3. *Red Virgin Soil* and *The New World,* two leading Soviet literary journals.

4. This essay apparently remained unpublished.

5. "I firmly clasp your hand; it seems that I will soon forget how to write Russian, since I write so much in my 'pidgin'."

15

March 7, 1941

Trees, RFD 1

Stamford, Conn.

Dear Nabokov: I tried to get you on the phone when I was in town yesterday, but you weren't home. Perhaps we could arrange something towards the end of next week. I'm going away tomorrow, but shall be back by Thursday. I want to go over *Mozart and Salieri* with you. I've been finishing up a book and haven't had a chance to do anything about it.

I like your story very much. I'm going to see the editor of the *Atlantic Monthly* while I am in Boston and will try to get him to take it. About the *New Republic* article: I think you ought to write to Nigel Dennis and tell him that you are concentrating on Soviet Drama—or send him the article, if you have written it. Tell him that I approve and talk as if you more or less assumed that it would be all right. I am sorry that they are not going to run your review of the anarchist book, which they seem to be scared of for political reasons.¹ I have told them that they ought to send it back to you, because it is a good piece (though I disagree with you about Lenin), and ought to be published. Why don't you give it to Klaus Mann? It is a good thing at this time for your name to appear in print, and you oughtn't to waste this article.

Nikolai came out to see us when he was over, and we had an awfully good time with him. He has pretty well persuaded me that I ought to do something about trying to provide him with a scenario for his opera on *Арап Петра Вели-кого*[2]—though I think it really ought to be done by a Russian.

As ever,
Edmund Wilson

1. Nabokov's review of *The Guillotine at Work* by G. P. Maximoff. The book is an examination of political terror in the Soviet Union.
2. *The Blackamoor of Peter the Great* (by Pushkin).

16

Wellesley College
Wellesley, Massachusetts

March 27, 1941

Dear Wilson,

You *are* a magician. I have had a delightful lunch with Weeks[1] who received my story and me with very touching warmth. I have already corrected the proofs and have been asked for some more little masterpieces.

I had been looking forward to seeing you under the oaks of New England. Where are you? The general atmosphere here reminds me, in patches and whiffs, of my Dear Old College in England (and Weeks is also a Trinity man) where I had been so unhappy,—in the gaps between the remembered patches.

My lectures are a purring success. Incidentally I have slaughtered Maxim Gorky, Mr. Hemingway—and a few others—corpses impossible to identify. The professors (♀ ♀) are very charming. My predecessor Prince Sergei Volkonsky who lectured here in 1894 is very lyrical in his memoirs about the "delightful girlish laughter ringing, etc."[2]

I shall leave for Chekhov's Stadion in Ridgefield, Conn.,[3] on the 29th and shall be back in N.Y. on the 4th.

Hoping to see you soon somewhere
Yours дружески[4] V. Nabokov

1. Editor of *The Atlantic Monthly*. His brief memoir about his association with Nabokov, combined with his review of *Speak, Memory*, is to be found in his column, "The Peripatetic Reviewer," *The Atlantic Monthly*, January 1967.

2. "What a charming sight it is to see these young girls surrounded by nature and science. And everywhere—in the woods, on the lake, in the lofty corridors, you hear the Wellesley cheer in young ringing voices." *My Reminiscences* by Prince Serge Wolkonsky (Sergei Volkonsky), translated by A. E. Chamot, London, 1924, Vol. 1, p. 242. Volkonsky (1860–1939), theoretician of theater and the dance, one-time director of the Imperial Theaters, memoirist and, at the end of his life, a close friend and associate of the poet Marina Tsvetaeva (who dedicated to him her cycle of poems "The Disciple" and wrote an essay about his memoirs), made two lecture tours of the United States during the 1890s. His memoirs offer a fascinating outsider's-eye view of the American universities at that time.

3. Mikhail Chekhov (1891–1955), the famed Russian actor and the nephew of Anton Chekhov, had invited Nabokov to visit his drama school for the purpose of discussing a collaboration on a dramatization of *Don Quixote*. During his emigration, Mikhail Chekhov tended to regard literary works from a mystical anthroposophic angle. Unsurmountable differences in artistic outlook soon led him and Nabokov to give up the envisioned project.

4. "Amicably."

17

April 9, 1941

Dear Bunny,

it is quite perfect now—you have played your Mozart to my Salieri. But one thing troubles me: why does not your name appear with mine at the end? The important part in such translations is the finish, the last touch—and that touch is yours. Will you agree to add your signature?

In preparing my Russian course, I have been forced to translate a dozen Pushkin poems and numerous passages. I do not know what my versions are worth but they satisfy my sense of his poetry more than the existing translations. I am sending you one poem and 3 others. I tried to render in the last line of "The Poet" the «широкошумные дубравы»[1] phonetically.

Yes, I felt very cross not to have said goodbye to your wife, but your energy overwhelmed me. I went to see Nigel Dennis the other day; we had a very nice talk, he gave me a book to review *(Mr. Shakespeare of the Globe)* and we arranged about the article (Art of Translation).[2]

I did not find anything*) to correct in the proofs—except the absence of your signature, but I don't know how to do it.

Yours truly
Vladimir

The Letters, 1941

*) one little thing: I put "compose" instead of "create" ("Haydn may *compose*") because there was "creation" on the next floor, just overhead and stamping.[3]

I wrote this before our telephone talk.

1. "The broadly-soughing leafy groves" (from Pushkin's poem "The Poet"). Nabokov's translation of this poem has apparently not been published.

2. Nabokov's review of *Mr. Shakespeare of the Globe* by Frayne Williams appeared in *The New Republic,* May 19, 1941; his article, "The Art of Translation," in the same journal on August 4, 1941.

3. In the published version of Nabokov's translation of *Mozart and Salieri,* the line in question appears as: "Perchance another Haydn may achieve/Some great new thing . . ."

18

April 27, 1941
Wellfleet, Mass.

Dear Vladimir: This translation of "Anchar"[1] is the best Pushkin translation and one of the best translations of poetry of any kind I ever saw. (The only thing I'd criticize is *His neighbors* in the last line. Would *The dwellers* be better?) "The Poet" is also excellent.

I think you really ought to publish these two. I'll send them to the *Partisan Review,* if you like or I should think Klaus Mann would be glad to have them. I imagine he'd pay you more than the *P. R.* There's also *The Kenyon Review,* to which I'd be glad to send them. You've got the compression and energy of the language which is what the translators usually don't get.

We've acquired a house up here, but it will be sometime before it will be in shape for us to live in it. We hope you'll come up to see us sometime. Our best to your wife and good luck with California. I have a fear, though, that you may become bewitched out there and never come back—one of the worst things that can happen in America to gifted Europeans. Consider the fates of Huxley and Isherwood (not that I ever thought much of Huxley). You know, it is like getting into Yeats's fairyland or under the Venusberg. The weather is fine every day, and the rest of the world seems very unreal. So remember the East from time to time. As ever,

Edmund W.

P.S. I forgot to say that if I were you I shouldn't hesitate to ask Weeks to pay you for your story right away—I always do. Just explain that you're leaving in May and would like to have the money before you go. I don't want to mention it to him, because I do a good deal of recommending as to what he ought to print in *The Atlantic,* and he might resent it if I tried to tell him when he ought to pay his contributors as well.

E. W.

1. "The Upas Tree." Nabokov's translation was included in his collection *Three Russian Poets.*

19

35 W. 87
April 29, 1941

Dear Bunny,

I am so glad that you liked them. In a couple of years I shall be doing that sort of thing much better.

Yes, I think Klaus Mann's review is a good idea. I shall ask him whether he wants them.

I did write to Weeks and he sent me 150. I was very touched that you remembered my query.

Two more stories (longer ones, too) are now being translated for the *Monthly* and seem to be shaping out rather well. You will appreciate this: Rakhmaninov has asked me to translate the words of his "Bells" into English.[1] These words are Balmont's reckless translation of Edgar Poe's "Bells." But as the Edgar Poem does not fit the music I am supposed to re-shuffle the thing according to Balmont's drivel. The result will be rather uncanny. I have also translated some Lermontov poems for my lectures and will soon have to tackle Tute-chev.[2] I have sent a novel I wrote straight in English to New Directions, but I am afraid it may not click.[3] I have described some new species of butterflies in the Museum and have had 8 teeth extracted—howlessly, but the pain *after* the drug stops acting is horrible. So you see I am fairly busy—and if I keep talking about my affairs in such detail it is because I feel it is you who have given me the great Push.

I think you are quite right about the West. I am practically certain of coming back here in Octobre or even earlier. Even without a regular job (which I have never had in my life) I have managed to keep afloat this winter. The only thing that really bothers me is that apart from a few sneaking visits I have had no regular intercourse with my Russian muse and I am too old to change Conradically (this is a *good* one) and have left Europe in the middle of a vast Russian novel[4] which will soon start to ooze from some part of my body if I go on keeping it inside.

Shall I see you before my trip? I am starting with wife, child and three butterfly nets on the 26th of May.

Дружески жму Вашу руку.

Вашъ В. Набоковъ[5]

1. Sergei Rachmaninov's cantata *The Bells* (1913) is a setting of Poe's poem in a Russian adaptation by the Symbolist poet Konstantin Balmont.

2. Fyodor Tyutchev (1803–1873), one of Russia's truly great nineteenth-century poets. The spelling of his last name, which occurs in this correspondence in a bewildering number of variants, has been normalized, except when the spelling is deliberately humorous, as in the present instance. Nabokov's translations of Tyutchev's poetry were included in *Three Russian Poets*. Wilson's essay on Tyutchev appeared in *The Atlantic Monthly* in January 1944; a revised version of it was included in *A Window on Russia*.

3. *The Real Life of Sebastian Knight*.

4. Portions of this novel were published in Russian under the Latin titles of *Solus Rex* and *Ultima Thule*. The novel was never completed in Russian, but the two published sections eventually evolved into another novel written in English: *Pale Fire*.

5. "I amicably clasp your hand. Yours V. Nabokov."

20

Stanford University
Slavic Department
Palo Alto, Calif.

May 25, 1941

Dear Bunny,

I am driving off to California to-morrow with butterfly-nets, manuscripts and a new set of teeth. I shall be back by Septembre. Is there any chance of your dashing to Palo Alto in summer?

I am afraid I am sending you another translation. *The Scoopoy Ritzer*'s[1] monologue. This time I have tried to follow Pushkin's rhythm as closely as possible. Even mimicking some of the sounds. And the so-called alliteratio puschkiniana. It would be too long for Mann,—and I do not quite know where to send it. Could you god-father it—if you find the translation all right? And I would be immensely grateful to you for any corrections. Are you bringing out another Supplement?

We are reaching the climax in the drama of packing; the anti-climax will come when we find that—after the trunks have been crammed and locked—the child's bricks or my Dahls[2] are still sulking in a corner. Our best regards to your wife and a good shake-hand for you.

Yours

V. Nabokov

1. *I.e.,* the second scene of another of Pushkin's "little tragedies," *The Covetous Knight* (the title is transcribed in whimsical phonetics). The translation appears in *Three Russian Poets.*

2. *The Reasoned Dictionary of the Great-Russian Language* by Vladimir Dahl, in four volumes.

21

230 Sequoia Ave.

Palo Alto

July 18, 1941

Dear Bunny,

My English novel has been accepted by New Directions and Laughlin came to see me here from Los Angeles. The terms are 10% straight and an advance of 150 dollars. It will appear in Octobre. This is another tip of one of your rays. On the other hand Weeks rejected a second (and much better story) I had sent him, and then *two* weeks later asked me to send it back for re-examination. I also sent him the story which somebody told me had been stolen by an extinct magazine, but this proved false—the magazine died before I wrote the story.

Thanks for your delightful book.[1] I had read most of the articles when they appeared in the *N. R.* and liked them very much—re-liked them. The poem bounces beautifully.[2]

Did you get a Pushkin translation *(The Covetous Knight)* which I sent you before leaving N.Y.? I have now translated the little *Feast during the Plague.*[3]

Yes the climate here is just what you say of it. Though I have only seven lectures per week I feel that I require all the energy I can summon to leave my deck chair and talk about Russian versification or the way Gogol used the word «даже»[4] in «Шинель.»[5] During our motor-car trip across several states (all of them beauties) I frantically collected butterflies. There is, in that connection, a certain little bit of desert in Arizona which I shall never forget. I have a good time with the lepidoptera here, too. We have a nice little house. In September I shall go to Wellesley where I have a very comfortable engagement for a year,—a dozen lectures and lots of time to write. For more than a year I have had no relation with my Russian muse; there is also something I would like to write in English.

For almost 25 years Russians in exile have craved for something—any-thing—to happen that would destroy the Bolsheviks,—for instance a good bloody war. Now comes this tragic farce. My ardent desire that Russia, in spite of everything, may defeat or rather utterly abolish Germany—so that not a German be left in the world, is putting the cart before the horse, but the horse is so disgusting that I prefer doing so. First of all I want England to win the war. *Then* I want Hitl[er] and Stal[in] dispatched to Christmas Island and kept there together in close and constant proximity to each other. And then—I quite realize that everything will happen in some ridiculously different way—just as an automobile advertisement juicily interrupts the account of hideously dramatic events.

Напишите мнѣ два слова[6]

Yours
В. Набоковъ[7]

1. *The Boys in the Back Room: Notes on California Novelists* (a collection of Wilson's arti-cles, all of which had previously appeared in *The New Republic*).

2. "The Playwright in Paradise: A Legend of the Beverly Hills," included in *The Boys in the Back Room*.

3. Another one of Pushkin's "little tragedies." Nabokov's translation of it is in *Three Rus-sian Poets*.

4. "Even."

5. "The Overcoat." Nabokov preferred his own, more precise translation of this title, "The Carrick."

6. "Write me two words."

7. "V. Nabokov."

22

19 Appleby Rd.
Wellesley, Mass.
Tel: Wellesley 3257R

September 18, 1941

Dear Bunny,

We have just rolled back to the East. I shall be teaching Comparative Litera-ture here for a year. I want to see you very much.

I am afraid that the Russians who told you that *сволочь* comes from *cheval* are donkeys. *Сво́лочь* (which comes from *своло́чь* = to dump, to drag down; same root as *волоки́та* = philanderer) is, thank God, as old as the Russian language. But there is *another* Russian word *шваль* (meaning "old rubbish" or "a rotter") which is *said* to be derived from *cheval* (with the explanation you quote) but is really a corrupted form of *шушваль* (or *шушера*) which in its turn is derived from the ancient *шваль* = *швецъ* = a tailor.[1] This reminds me of: «поваръ вашъ Илья на боку» = "pauvres vaches, il y en a beaucoup" or the one I invented myself: я люблю васъ = yellow-blue väse.[2]

I happen to be working on the question of the exact relationship between Wilson's "City of the Plague" and Pushkin's version.[3] Apparently Mirsky did not see the original.[4] I shall send you my notes later on.

Did I tell you that I liked your collection of critical studies very much?[5]

Have you noticed when reading *War and Peace* the difficulties Tolstoy experienced in forcing mortally wounded Bolkonsky to come into geographical and chronological contact with Natasha? It is very painful to watch the way the poor fellow is dragged and pushed and shoved in order to achieve this happy reunion.

I have sold another story to Weeks, "The Aurelian," it will appear in the Christmas number of the A. M.[6]

We are very comfortable and happy here. My first lecture will be on October 1. There will be three in Octobre, three in February and half-a-dozen public ones,—that is all; but I am expected to participate in "social life" (College lunches, etc.). I have been working a good deal lately in my special branch of entomology, two papers of mine have appeared in a scientific journal,[7] I am describing a new butterfly from the Grand Canyon and am writing a rather ambitious work on mimetic phenomena.

Крепко жму вашу руку, кланяюсь вашей женѣ, вашъ В Набоковъ[8]

My wife greets you both.

---

1. There exists a widespread misconception that the Russian word *shval'* (meaning "scum" or, as Nabokov has it, "a rotter" when applied to one person and "old rubbish" or "riff-raff" when applied collectively to objects or groups of people) comes from the French word for horse, *cheval*, and that it originated during Napoleon's retreat in 1812, when many rotting horse carcasses were left in Russia by the French army. As Nabokov points out, the word *shval'* has an old Russian etymology and existed long before the Napoleonic invasion.

Wilson's Russian informants compounded the error by confusing *shval'* with another word, similar in meaning, but coarser in tone: *svoloch'*. This word, a noun stressed on the first syllable, is a derivation of the identically spelled infinitive of the verb *svoloch'* (to drag off or drag down), which is stressed on the last syllable.

2. The confusion between Russian *shval'* and French *cheval* suggests to Nabokov a word game in which a phrase in one language is matched with a phrase in another language, identical in sound but having an unexpected, usually nonsensical, new meaning. This is the game on which an entire book was based, *Mots d'Heures: Gousses, Rames* [i.e., *Mother Goose Rhymes*] by Luis d'Antin van Rooten (New York, 1967), where the familiar English nursery rhymes were represented by nonsensical French phrases of similar sound.

Nabokov's Russo-French example matches the Russian for "your cook Ilya is on his side" with the French for "poor cows, there are many of them." The Russian for "I love you" (*ya lyublyu vas*) yields the English "yellow-blue väse." This last pun was later used in *Ada* ("Three young ladies in yellow-blue Vass frocks," p. 187).

3. Pushkin's "little tragedy" *The Feast during the Plague* is a free adaptation of *City of the Plague* by the English poet John Wilson (1785–1854).

4. D. S. Mirsky's *A History of Russian Literature* states that *"The Feast during the Plague* is a fairly accurate translation of a scene of John Wilson's *City of the Plague."*

5. *The Wound and the Bow.*

6. Nabokov's "The Aurelian" (originally titled "Pilgram") appeared in the November (1941) issue of *The Atlantic Monthly.*

7. "On Some Asiatic Species of Carterocephalus" and *"Lysandra cormion*, a New European Butterfly," both in Volume 49 of the *Journal of the New York Entomological Society,* New York, 1941.

8. "I firmly clasp your hand [and] send my regards to your wife, yours V. Nabokov."

23

October 20, 1941
Wellfleet,
Mass.

Dear Vladimir: I've just read *Sebastian Knight,* of which Laughlin has sent me proofs, and it's absolutely enchanting. It's amazing that you should write such fine English prose and not sound like any other English writer, but be able to do your own kind of thing so subtly and completely. You and Conrad must be the only examples of foreigners succeeding in English in this field. The whole book is brilliant and beautifully done, but I liked particularly the part where he is looking up the various Russian women, the description of the book about death and the final dreamlike train-ride (as well as the narrator's long dream). It makes me eager to read your Russian books, and I am going to tackle them when my русский язык[1] is a little stronger.

I hope you will get somebody at Wellesley to read your proofs—because there are a few, though not many, mistakes in English. You tend to bend over backwards using *as* instead of *like* and sometimes use it incorrectly. The critic's remark about Sebastian's first being a dull man writing broken English, etc. is not a pun, but rather a bon mot.[2] If the conjuror with the accent is supposed to be American, he would never say *I fancy*, but probably *I guess*.[3] I am sure that your phonetic method of transliterating Russian words is one of those things that you are particularly stubborn about; but I really think it's a mistake. It looks outlandish to people who don't know Russian and is confusing to people who do. I boggled for some time over your version of А у нея по шейку паук.[4] Combinations like *neigh* and *sheik* (and do these really represent the Russian vowels?)—into which I fear you have been led by your lamentable weakness for punning—are not the logical phonetic way of representing these sounds, they introduce irrelevant ideas. You were right in thinking I should object to *smuggled smugness*,[5] though in other cases your sensitivity to words provides you with some admirable observations and effects. I agree about the word *sex*—it is an awful word.[6] But what about *Geschlecht—das Geschlecht!*[7]

Now can't you and your family come up here and spend Thanksgiving (the 3rd Thursday in November) with us, staying on afterwards? We'd love to have you and have plenty of room for you all. If you're tied up for the holiday at Wellesley or otherwise, perhaps you could come up some week-end—almost any after the first of November? In the meantime, we may be in Boston some week-end before then, and we might have lunch or something.

We saw Nikolai at Aurora last summer. I suppose you know about his facial paralysis. I hope he is getting over it. I haven't heard from him since he has been at St. John's.

I haven't really told you why I like your book so much. It is all on a high *poetic* level, and you have succeeded in being a first-rate poet in English. It has delighted and stimulated me more than any new book I have read since I don't know what.

Our best regards to you both. As ever,

Edmund Wilson

1. "Russian language" (the original has the Latin *u* instead of the Russian *y*).

2. In Chapter One, "a celebrated old critic" remarks: "Poor Knight! he really had two periods, the first—a dull man writing broken English, the second—a broken man writing dull English." In the rest of the paragraph, this remark is mentioned as "a nasty dig" and as a "jest," indicating that the word "pun" in the original version was removed in response to Wilson's comment.

3. Similarly, the conjuror in the published novel says: "They don't kinda like my accent [...] but I guess I'm going to get that turn all the same" (Chapter Ten).

4. In Chapter Seventeen, the narrator traps Nina Lecerf into revealing her true national-

The Letters, 1941

ity by saying in Russian "Why, there is a spider on her neck" and thereby eliciting a violent reaction from Nina, who claims to know no Russian. Nabokov transcribed the Russian phrase *(A u nei na sheike pauk)* into punning English phonetics *(Ah-oo-neigh na-sheiky pah-ook)*. Wilson's reconstruction of the phrase in its Russian form has the wrong preposition *(po* instead of *na)* and puts the word for "neck" into the contextually inappropriate accusative case due to a repeated confusion between the Russian *y* and the Latin *u*.

5. "Well did he know that to flaunt one's contempt for a moral code was but smuggled smugness and prejudice turned inside out" (Chapter Nine).

6. ". . . secondly because the very sound of the word 'sex' with its hissing vulgarity and the 'ks, ks' catcall at the end, seems so inane to me that I cannot help doubting whether there *is* any real idea behind the word" (Chapter Eleven).

7. The German word for sex (in the sense of gender, however, rather than the one Nabokov had in mind).

24

19 Appleby Rd.
Wellesley, Mass.

October 21, 1941

Dear Bunny,

Sebastian's ghost makes you a *земной поклонъ*.[1] I am very happy that you liked that little book. As I think I told you, I wrote it five years ago,[2] in Paris, on the implement called *bidet* as a writing desk—because we lived in one room and I had to use our small bathroom as a study. There is another fishy "as" in that sentence. You are quite, quite right about the slips. There are many clumsy expressions and foreignish mannerisms that I noticed myself when reading the book again after five years had passed; but if I started correcting them I would rewrite the whole thing. My suggestion (which I know is not quite fair) is that the assumed author of the *Life* writes English with difficulty. I am itching to improve it after your letter, but I have already returned the proofs—am writing to Erskine[3] asking him to send them back if it is not too late. What tortures me when I try to write "imaginative" prose in English is that I may be unconsciously copying the style of some second-rate English writer although I know, theoretically, that "form" and "content" are one.

I am a little ashamed to confess that the other day I wrote my first English poem and sent it to Weeks who called it "a darling" and will print it in the Christmas issue of the *A.M.*[4] I who hate so intensely the way "sincerity" is considered by some critics to be the main *quality* of a writer, must now rely upon "sincerity" in judging that poem!

We would love to come on Thanksgiving day, but do not quite know whether we shall be free to do so, though we hope we will. Anyway, I shall write you again as soon as we are fixed.

Áwe-chin ya dove-áll-in váh-shim peace-máugham![5]

Yours
V. Nabokov

You just rang up: no—except for the sketchy chess-game alluded to in one chapter there is *no "chess-idea" in the development of the whole book*. Sounds attractive, but it is not there.

1. "Bow to the ground."

2. Véra Nabokov thought that this was a memory lapse because the apartment where the novel was written was rented only in 1938.

3. Albert Russell Erskine, Jr. was associate editor at New Directions in 1940–1941.

4. "The Softest of Tongues," which appeared in the December 1941 issue of *The Atlantic Monthly*.

5. A whimsically phonetic transcription of the Russian for "I am very pleased by your letter."

25

October 24, 1941
Wellfleet, Mass.

Da-rogue-oy Val-odd-ya:[1] If you haven't corrected the page proofs yet, just get him to send them to you when they are ready and you will be able to make the corrections then.

We'll probably be going to Boston the week-end of November 8, and perhaps we can arrange something then. Do try to come up for Thanksgiving.

I don't believe a word you say about your book and am furious at having been hoaxed by it (though my opinion of it has rather gone up than otherwise).

Yah j'm('en f)ou rook-oo,[2]
E. W.

[Added at the top]
How about—

> Nous avons eu beaucoup de jolies dames.
> Ну, завозы боку де(р)жали дам?[3]
> ↑
> eliminated by grasseyement[4]

1. "Dear Volodya," transcribed in a manner that parodies Nabokov's transcription of the phrase about the spider on the neck.

2. An amalgam of Russian for "I clasp your hand" and of French for "I don't give a damn."

3. Wilson tries his hand at the word game in Nabokov's letter of September 18 by constructing a Russian sentence meant to be similar in sound to the Swiss hotel manager's French words from Chapter Thirteen of *The Real Life of Sebastian Knight* ("We have had many pretty ladies"). The Russian word sequence translates approximately as "Well, deliveries [from out of town] [on or to] side held ladies," which does not form a coherent sentence.

4. French pronunciation of *r.*

26

[November 28, 1941]
Thursday

Dear Bunny,

I do hope you did not take my "Refrigerator"[1] as implying that I spent a bad night at your house. I did not. I really cannot tell you, at least in English, how much I enjoyed my stay.

Yesterday I read the *Aspern Papers.*[2] No. He writes with a very sharp nib and the ink is very pale and there is very little of it in his inkpot. Incidentally he ought to have proved somehow that Aspern was a fine poet. The style is artistic but it is not the style of an artist. For instance: the man is smoking a cigar in the dark and another person sees the *red tip* from the window. *Red tip* makes one think of a red pencil or a dog licking itself, it is quite wrong when applied to the glow of a cigar in pitch-darkness because there is no "tip"; in fact the glow is blunt. But he thought of a cigar having a tip and then painted the tip red—rather like those false cigarettes—menthol sticks with the end made to look "embery"—that people who try to give up smoking are said to use. Henry James is definitely for non-smokers. He has charm (as the weak blond prose of Turgenev has), but that's about all.

I am enclosing a passage from my agent's letter on which I would like your advice. I wonder if the "old timer" might not be asked to pay a little more. I also got "we-are-interested" letters from a publisher or two. And an article on a Hil[aire] Belloc book which I sent exactly *a year ago* to the N.Y. Times—and which I understood was too snappy for them—has appeared last Sunday.[3] I am wondering whether this pleasant little flurry is not due to your fine blurb which perhaps Laughlin has been sending around.

My very best regards to your wife and the same to you both from Véra.

Дружески вашъ
В. Набоковъ[4]

[In margin]
I'm sorry—these spots are due to a hair lotion I tried.

[In the envelope of this letter, an unsigned typewritten note, apparently from Wilson, was found.]

An old time agent who worked a lot with central Europe called me saying he had a client who wished to dramatize your *Laughter*.[5] The person being quite unknown, I am going to say that you want two hundred dollars down against future royalties. Also that the play must be done and placed in one year after which all rights will revert back to you in case of non-success; play should also be submitted to you for approval.

1. Nabokov's visit with the Wilsons resulted in his poem "The Refrigerator Awakes" (*Poems and Problems*, pp. 153–154).

2. By Henry James.

3. "Belloc Essays—Mild But Pleasant," *The New York Times Book Review*, November 23, 1941.

4. "Amicably yours, V. Nabokov."

5. *Laughter in the Dark*, the English title of Nabokov's novel first published in Russian as *Kamera obskura* in 1932 and in England as *Camera Obscura* in 1936. For the American edition of 1938, Nabokov revised the novel and gave it a new title, which has been retained in the numerous subsequent editions in English.

27

December 3, 1941
Wellfleet, Mass.

Dear Vladimir:

① It might be a good thing to have your agent tell the theatrical agent that in as much as you understand that the customary payment in such cases is $100 a month, you think you ought to have at least $500 for an option of a year. Of course you risk losing the $200 in this way—it is something of a gamble.

② I don't think my blurb has anything to do with the attention you seem to be attracting. I have written blurbs and recommendations for lots of people who have never gotten anywhere. I think that your rapid progress has been due to the merits of your writing. One of the strangest cases on record—especially in view of the fact that your vein does not fall into any of the current fashions.

③ It is hard to explain to people about Henry James. I didn't like him when I first read him at college and his work has serious deficiencies, but he is really, I am now convinced, a great writer. I am impressed by the number of young people nowadays who read him completely through. On the other hand, it is very difficult to persuade people who have been put off by their first acquaintance to read any more of him at all. I am curious to see whether he will make any impression on you. I wish you would try something from his early phase— *The American* or *Washington Square*—and then something from his latest, *The Golden Bowl*. There is always an element of slackness in his prose—except perhaps in something from his middle period like *What Maisie Knew*. Those others I suggested your reading are all from the middle period.

As ever,
Edmund W.

[In margin]
I do like very much his Proustian autobiography, *A Small Boy and Others, Notes of a Son and Brother.*

1942

28

V. Nabokov
19 Appleby Rd.
Wellesley, Mass.

January 5th, 1942

Прошу прощение за нелѣпое
збсентъ маиндлесъ ! [1]

Dear Bunny,

I should like to have your advice, as I felt you were interested in my blunderings anent publishers.

Here are the facts. I am writing a new novel in English; but moreover there are at least three Russian novels of mine which I would like to have translated and published. I wrote to Laughlin telling him that several publishers have approached me and that if he did not want those three Russian novels I might try and offer them elsewhere keeping for him the English novel I am writing now.

I also told him that I could not find the right kind of translator (the first chapters of *Invitation to a Beheading* which one of my translators has just sent me are one long shudder).

> Now, here is Laughlin's answer: "I daresay you will receive many inquiries from publishers, but please believe I am most anxious to keep you on with New Directions as I feel the standard of your writing fits perfectly with our aims and ideals.
>
> The titles that you mention sound fine for us. I would like to do one of your books each year. Can they be translated at that rate? Will you make the translations yourself or have them done? Do you need financial assistance with the translations? Let me know so that we can make our plans.
>
> I hope you are pleased with the appearance of the book. I am confident that we will soon have to order another edition. After the Christmas scramble the reviews will begin to appear and then it should start to build."

As I hope to produce an English book in the course of this year and another in the course of the next one, the translations of the three Russian volumes will always lag behind. What would you advise me to do about them?

Do you think I could ask him to have at least one of them (independently from the publishing of my English book) translated *vprok?*[2] I like New Directions immensely and am by no means on the lookout for another publisher, but don't you think that perhaps my keeping all my Russian translatable material clogging my bowels for years ought to entitle me to some kind of more definite agreement and profit?

Incidentally the translation of my Russian works is in itself a nightmare. If I were to do it myself it would obviously prevent me from writing anything new. Correcting the efforts of my present translators would take almost as much time. If, however, a translator writing perfectly dependable English could be found (which would limit my cooperation to the gnoseological side) do you think Laughlin would pay for it, even if this translation would have to wait for a year or two while he publishes my English stuff? Do you happen to know what is the customary fee of a first-class translator?

Thanks for the delightful butterfly. It buzzed out of the card like a real lepidopteron.[3] We wish you both a very happy new year and hope to see you soon.

Yours very cordially
Vladimir Nabokov

1. "I beg forgiveness for [my] absurd absent-mind[ed]ness" (the last two words are in English transcribed into the Cyrillic alphabet). The original, through a slip of the pen, has *proshenie* (petition) instead of *proshchenie* (forgiveness).

2. "For future use."

3. On several occasions Wilson sent Nabokov cutout paper butterflies, propelled by a wound-up rubber band.

29

January 7, 1942
Wellfleet,
Mass.

Dear Vladimir: You sent me only the second page of your letter so that it's difficult to advise you—do send me the rest. I've just come back from New York, where I saw the Greenbergs. They seem to be flourishing: Roman has gotten fat and Mrs. G. has some kind of job. They are living in very strange quarters, which are enormous but do not resemble an apartment but rather the reception room of an institution.

The Holliday bookshop in New York (which has, to be sure, rather a special clientele) told me that they had sold thirty copies of your book—which isn't bad.

As ever,
Edmund W

30

January 12, 1942

Dear Bunny,

I am returning the *Accent*. The style of Delmore's article is vile, but I like the subject.[1]

I am also sending you "Spring in Fialta" which *Harper's Mag[azine]* finds "subtle, evocative, beautifully written but too long and not the sort of piece they could use right now" i.e. after Pearl Harbour. I want you and Mary to read it. Perhaps you could suggest some harbour for it.

We enjoyed so much your short visit and Dmitri has made me repeat all your фокусы[2]—it was an indifferent performance.

Вашъ
В. Набоковъ[3]

1. "The Writing of Edmund Wilson" by Delmore Schwartz (*Accent*, Spring 1942) was a detailed examination of Wilson's writings from *I Thought of Daisy* to *The Wound and the Bow*.

2. "Conjuring tricks." Like Wilbur Flick in his *Memoirs of Hecate County*, Wilson was an amateur magician. He loved performing for his friends and, especially, for children.

3. "Yours, V. Nabokov."

31

January 18, 1942

THE PRINCETON CLUB
OF NEW YORK

Dear Vladimir: I can't advise you very well about your books without seeing your contract with Laughlin. You probably ought to have another publisher besides New Directions. If I were you I'd call up Bob Linscott of Houghton Mifflin in Boston, arrange to see him and discuss the matter with him. Be sure to take your contract when you see him. I saw him when I was going through Boston last week, and he told me that he had written you some time ago and had never heard from you. He is anxious to see you, and he will give you sound advice. He says that the *Atlantic Monthly* people are also complaining that they can't get in touch with you.

I'm enclosing a not very interesting review of your book. P. M. Jack was extremely stupid in the *Times*.[1]

1. P. M. Jack's review of *The Real Life of Sebastian Knight* ("Novelist's Life," *The New York Times Book Review*, January 11, 1942) compared the book adversely to *Cakes and Ale* by Somerset Maugham and *The Quest for Corvo* by A. J. S. Symons and complained that Nabokov had "neither the style of Maugham nor the research of Symons." Nabokov's English style is, according to Jack, "interesting in a Walt Disney sort of way," which "might sound interesting in another language." The review concludes: "I am afraid that altogether this is a rather silly story."

32

February 3, 1942
Wellfleet, Mass.

Dear Vladimir: Would you mind addressing this letter to Aldanov?[1] He has sent me some of his writings, and I have lost his address, if you know it. Did you see the relatively intelligent review of your book by Kay Boyle in *The New Repub-*

lic?[2] I have just read *Laughter in the Dark*. I liked it, but I liked it better before it got rather implausible toward the end. I thought that the unfortunate hero was going to develop color audition and detect the whereabouts of the girl by hearing her red dress, or something. Did you do the translation yourself?—because it is very good. I noticed, by the way, that at one point the *tip* of somebody's cigar is referred to. I'll bet that the *soulful conversation* that the landlady has with the girl in the early part of the book is a mistranslation for душевная беседа.[3]

As ever,
Edmund Wilson

Is Nikolai coming
to Wellesley in March?
We were terribly sorry
to have missed him.

We don't have any telephone now, and expected him to wire or write.

1. On Mark Aldanov, see Letter 6, note 15.
2. Kay Boyle's perceptive appreciation of Nabokov's qualities as stylist and storyteller in her review of *The Real Life of Sebastian Knight* ("The New Novels," *The New Republic*, January 26, 1942) might well be the earliest such instance in American criticism.
3. Wilson must have meant задушевная беседа ("a heart-to-heart talk").

33

[Postcard, postmarked April 30, 1942]

Dear Bunny,

I just want to tell you that I shall be coming alone Saturday. To my wife's and my own great regret we cannot bring the child. He is going to have his tonsils removed next week.

I am bringing Pushkin and my butterfly net.

Yours, дружески,[1]
V. Nabokov

1. "Amicably."

34

Dear Bunny,

I'm afraid I shall not be able to catch the 8:20 milk train. I shall come with the 2 one—though I hate coming so late, as I shall have to dash back on Sunday: I am speaking on the Wellesley Coll[ege] radio on Monday, afternoon.

Вашъ В. Набоковъ[1]

1. "Yours, V. Nabokov."

35

May 6, 1942
Wellfleet, Mass.

Dear Vladimir: I was very much impressed by the mimicry article—want to talk to you about it when I see you again. I don't know where to tell you to send it. You might try *The Yale Review*, a dreary quarterly, which won't pay you much. You ought to write to Miss Helen MacAfee: *Yale Review*, Drawer 1729, New Haven, Conn. Quote me if you like as being very much interested in the article and having suggested your sending it there. I see that Karpovich has done some reviewing for them, and his recommendation might help. *The Virginia Quarterly* is also a possibility. The editor is a man named Archibald B. Shepperson—address University of Virginia, Charlottesville, Va. You could mention me to him, too. (*The Atlantic* would be better than either of these.)

I've read the poem carefully and like it, but parts of it I don't understand. Should like to go through it with you.[1]

Now the circus is coming to Boston next week and couldn't we all go together? Will your boy be over his tonsil operation by then? On this account, it might be better to go the end of the week—though there are two performances every day through Sunday, and we could go, I think, any day. If you would get tickets in advance (not too expensive), I'll pay you later. I think we ought to hear Stravinsky's music for elephants, don't you?[2]

I made a few suggestions and corrections in pencil on the mimicry article. It was great fun to have you, and we were sorry you had to go so soon. As ever,

Edmund W

1. Possibly "Slava," written in March 1942. The English translation, "Fame," is in *Problems and Poems*, pp. 102–103.

2. *Circus Polka (For a Young Elephant)* by Igor Stravinsky was performed in the spring of 1942 by the Ringling Brothers and Barnum & Bailey Circus, with choreography by George Balanchine and a cast of "fifty elephants and fifty beautiful girls."

36

May 6, 1942

Dear Mary and Edmund,

Those 24 hours were lovely. We shall be very disappointed, my wife and I if we do not see you on Sunday.

Now about Mary's book.[1] I have read it. It has been a habit of mine to be absolutely outspoken in such cases, i.e. especially when it concerns friends. So I hope you will take what I have to say in the right spirit. When I see you I shall discuss the book exhaustively but until then I want to tell you that it is a splendid thing, clever, poetic and new. In fact I am quite flabbergasted—if that's the right word.

> Yours
> V. Nabokov

Just got your letter, Bunny. Thanks for the advice. We'd love to go to the circus, but Dmitri will be at the hospital next week and somehow we would not like to go without him: family ethics!

1. *The Company She Keeps* by Mary McCarthy.

37

May 10, 1942
Wellfleet, Mass.

Dear Vladimir: I have just been let down with a crash by Cornell, where I thought I had a job for next fall. The president won't appoint me, due to the war and low finances. I'm not clear whether that job you've had at Wellesley was something specially created for you or whether it is a regular thing for which they get a different person every year—but if the latter is the case, I'd be grateful if you would mention me to them (unless of course there's any chance of your continuing yourself). I've taught classes at the University of

The Letters, 1942

Chicago and lectured at Columbia, and am just the thing for young girls of tender age.

Mary was delighted that you liked her book. I hope we will get to Boston next weekend and I'll let you know if we are coming.

As ever,
Edmund W

38

Dear Bunny,

I was sorry to learn that Cornell let you down. My position at Wellesley is, unfortunately, an ontogenetic, not phylogenetic, phenomenon. It was created especially for me. I had about a dozen lectures in all for an annual fee of 3000 dollars. Recently a gallant attempt was made by several professors to have me stay for another year, or at least to arrange a course of Russian Literature, but it all fizzled out, the obstacle being the same lack of funds. I came here with the understanding that my job had no evolutionary future, but being human I developed a sneaking hope that it might breed. It did not—and the rocks are beginning to feel slimy.

Dmitri's operation proved to be more serious than we thought. He came home yesterday and will have to stay in bed for some time. Did you see in a recent *Life* a remarkably obscene photograph of the prettiest Russian ballerina (Tumanova, I think) reclining upon the head of an elephant with the elephant's trunk thrust between her bare thighs from beneath and curving up most phallically?[1]

Надѣюсь васъ скоро повидать, дорогой другъ

Вашъ В. Набоковъ[2]

I have just been informed by the Professor of French who is also an astrologist that Hitler will die on the 23rd of May, i.e. ten days to wait.

1. Page 29 of the April 20, 1942 edition of *Life* featured the described photograph, not of Tamara Toumanova, however, but of Vera Zorina (née Eva Brigitta Hartwig) who was at the time married to George Balanchine. She was appearing in the Ringling Brothers and Barnum & Bailey production of Stravinsky's *Circus Polka,* mentioned earlier.

2. "I hope to see you soon, dear friend. Yours, V. Nabokov."

39

I have indicated
one or two corrections.
↓

Dear Vladimir: The thing to do with "Spring in Fialta" is first to send it to *The New Yorker*. Write to Wm Maxwell and tell him I suggested your doing so. I am afraid it is too long for them, but they may offer to run it if you will cut it. If they won't take it, try *Harper's Bazaar* (572 Madison Ave., N.Y.) Write to Mary Louise Aswell and mention Mary and me. Mary and I both liked it, but felt that from the magazine point of view—and perhaps from our point of view, too—it hasn't quite enough story. You expect more of an episode at Fialta.

Under separate cover, I'm also returning *Despair* and *Новый Журнал*.[1] I enjoyed the former, but, in the same vein, I don't think it's quite as good as *Laughter in the Dark*. The best part, I think, is after he commits the murder. I read *Русалка* and your ending.[2] Knowing your tendencies as I do, I was rather surprised that you handled it so soberly. I thought at first that the prince was going to refuse to believe the child, dismiss the whole story as preposterous and send the little nymph about her business—thus frustrating the русалка's fell purpose.

I enjoyed my visit very much. Please remember me to your wife and Dmitri. I hope he is all right now. If you should ever care to come up here before you leave for the summer, you have a standing invitation, you know. Just write us or send us a wire.

As ever,
Edmund W

1. *The New Review.*
2. Nabokov's "Concluding Scene" for Pushkin's unfinished verse play *The River Nymph (Rusalka)* appeared in *The New Review*, No. 2, 1942.

40

Dear Bunny,

I have sent "S. in F." to Harp[er's] B[azaar]—thanks for the suggestion.[1] I am sorry you did not care for it. I wrote it ten years ago, but still think the crescendo of the circus theme throughout the story and the intertwining of the retrospective romance rather neat.

I am immersed in my Gogol book. It begins with a scientific description of the Russian subspecies of the Devil in his immature stage—the little "pod-lenky, gadky"[2] Russian "chort."[3]

I have talked to Miss Perkins,[4] of the English Department here, about you, and also to Dean De Vane,[5] at Yale. Wellesley is going to concentrate on Chinese and Yale on Japanese so that English is not popular. I was glad to see a huge photograph of Mary in the centre of the Yale bookshop. The two days I spent there were very pleasant—though nothing came of it. They had offered me the position of assistant teacher of Russian in the summer course, but as I would have to teach the main professor Russian too, I refused. He is a little man called Trager[6] with a system of phonetics which I should have to follow obediently—a system of which I totally disapprove

djenj, vjesj,[7]

and the list of examples of sentences is a scream. He was born in America, but his parents came from Odessa; and he has been engaged for 5 years. Odessa speaks the worst lingo in Little Mother Russia—and learning it from one's parents in Brooklyn does not improve it. He is a nice energetic little chap, but as the method of teaching will consist in—sorry, of—inspiring the students with the mere sound of Russian for the first two or three weeks, with him and me taking on the same students alternately, a variety of odd situations would ensue. Со Ай римэйнъ джоблесъ.[8]

Thanks for the little corrections in the article and in the tale. I handed the former to DeVane for the *Yale Review*. Are you thinking of coming to Boston soon?

Yours very djrjužjesjkjjj[9]

V. Nabokov

1. The English translation of Nabokov's story "Spring in Fialta" was finally published in *Harper's Bazaar* in May 1947.

2. "Base little, nasty."

3. "Devil."

4. Agnes Perkins, professor of English at Wellesley and author of *Vocations for the Trained Woman*, who helped Nabokov edit the manuscript of *The Real Life of Sebastian Knight*.

5. William Clyde DeVane, the noted specialist in the poetry of Robert Browning.

6. George L. Trager was an assistant professor of Russian at Yale from 1942 to 1944. The present annotator's friend and Berkeley colleague Hugh McLean took beginning Russian with Trager during that time; he confirms the use of the incredible "methodology" which Nabokov here describes.

After his departure from Yale, Trager specialized in anthropology and linguistics, teaching these subjects at various universities in the subsequent decades. On Nabokov's later encounters with the incompetent instruction of foreign languages (often disguised by supposedly advanced methodologies), which was widespread at American universities in the 1940s and 1950s, see his letters to Professor Jean-Jacques Demorest and to the *Cornell Daily Sun* in his *Selected Letters, 1940–1977*, pp. 262–264 and 266–267. The same topic is also treated in sections 2 and 3 of Chapter Six in *Pnin*, where the protagonist is denied a job teaching French at a college because he can actually speak and read the language.

7. Transcriptions of Russian words for "day" and "entire" which indicate palatalization of consonants by having such consonants followed by *j*'s.

8. "So I remain jobless" (English words transliterated into old orthography Russian alphabet).

9. "Amicably" (a parody of the Yale professor's transliteration system).

41

June 12, 1942
Wellfleet, Mass.

Dear Vladimir: When I went up to Bennington to see my daughter the other day, I found that they had been looking both for somebody to teach Russian and for somebody in Comparative Literature. They had appointed for the former a Mme Hasenclever, who, though German, had been brought up in Russia; and for the latter a great-great grandson of Benjamin Constant or something of the kind. The president, a man named Lewis Jones, told me that if either of them didn't work out, you might be just the thing for them, and suggested that you write him explaining your qualifications and experience. It is a very pleasant place up there, and I think pays rather well.

We hope to get down to Boston the week-end of the 20th. Couldn't we arrange something for Saturday or Sunday, if you are there?

By the way, don't you think that Pushkin in the *Русалка*[1] intended to have the Prince come back insane after an interview with the mother русалка herself? Isn't that what his speech about insanity at the end of the scene with the miller-raven portends? He would come back and be unable to make connections with the human family at home. The wife is developed on a scale which makes one think that she must be meant to figure later in an even more pathetic way.

I was very much surprised when Hitler did not die on the 23rd of May, and I think you ought to consider very seriously whether your astrological authorities are sound.

As ever,
Edmund W

Mary was cheered by what I told her you said about her book, as she has been getting pretty dreadful reviews. Almost nobody has said that the book was well written. I don't think people notice the difference nowadays.

1. *The River Nymph.*

42

Dear Bunny,

Thanks so much, Bennington sounds awfully attractive. I am writing to Lewis Jones to-day. Funny—to know Russian better than any living person— in America at least,—and more English than any Russian in America,—and to experience such difficulty in getting a university job. I am getting rather jittery about next year. The only thing I have managed to obtain is the position of re-search fellow, for one year (1200 dollars) beginning Sept. 1, at the Mus[eum of] Comp[arative] Zool[ogy]—three hours a day and all the butterflies at my dis-posal. If I could combine this with college lectures it would be perfect. And of course I would chuck it if I got a better paid position elsewhere.

There is a racy review of Mary's book in the *Mercury.* I have made all my students promise to read the "C° she K." (what would it be in Russian? «Общес-тво, въ которомъ она вращается»? No. «Съ кѣмъ она водится»).[1]

We had several splendid days in Vermont, but I was dreadfully sorry that they clashed with your arrival at Boston.

I have just had a visit from the secretary of the man—whatever his name— who wrote something called *Tobacco Road* and who is now writing a novel of Soviet Life.[2] *Vous voyez ça d'ici.*[3] He wanted to know the English spelling of "nemetzky," "collkhoz"[4] (which he writes "kholholtz") and such things. The hero is called Vladimir. All very simple. I was half impelled by my private devil to palm him a set of obscene words which he would use for "good-morning" and "good night." (e.g. "Razyebi tvoyu dushu,"[5] said V. gravely).

The thoroughly americanized Karpovich children were awfully tickled by Prof. Fedotov[6] shaking hands with them before retiring for the night.

I got a letter from Pearce[7] asking me very nicely for some more *virshi*[8] and I sent him a poem which I composed at your instigation and which I append. *Harper's Baz[aar]* sent back "S. in F." which apparently belongs to the boomer-ang variety of MS.[9]

We are going to Vermont in the beginning of next week, and will stay there (in a ram-chakal[10] farmhouse haunted by great sulky porcupines, song-of-

Bernadette-smelling skunks, fireflies and a number of good moths) until well into August.

No, Bunny, you are utterly wrong. Economic Pushkin would have *never* had *two* characters develop madness,—the old miller *and* the prince. The end I tagged on is in perfect keeping with the general ending of all legends connected with mermaids and fairies in Russia—see for instance Lermontov's "Rusalka" or Al[eksei] Konst[antinovich] Tolstoy's "Rusalka" poem etc. Pushkin never broke the skeleton of tradition,—he merely rearranged its inner organs,—with less showy but more vital results. I grant you it would have been more amusing to have the prince [go] howling home in a rich fit of dementia praecox—or better still to have him sneak in quietly and mumble nightmare innuendoes to his wife—but that was never Pushkin's intention.

I want to see you soon. Will you ring me up Saturday? My son has composed what he calls an "anecdote" about a mother who was so kind that when she had to spank her child she gave him some laughing-gas first.

Yours very дружески

В. Набоковъ[11]

1. Two idiomatic Russian ways of saying "The company she keeps."

2. Erskine Caldwell published in 1942 a novel called *All Night Long* set in the Soviet Union and describing guerrilla warfare.

3. "You get the picture."

4. Russian words for "German" and "collective farm" *(kolkhoz)*.

5. A violent but untranslatable Russian obscenity.

6. The theologian and literary critic George Fedotov (1886–1951), author of *The Russian Religious Mind*.

7. Charles ("Cap") Pearce, the poetry editor of *The New Yorker*.

8. Archaic and slightly contemptuous term for "verses."

9. *Harper's Bazaar* was to change its mind five years later (see Letter 34, note 1).

10. Combination of the English "ram" and the Russian word for "jackal."

11. "Amicably, V. Nabokov."

43

June 30, 1942

West Wardsboro

c/o Prof. Karpovich

Vermont

Dear Edmund and Mary,

it's heartbreaking to have to refuse your invitation, but circumstances here have tapered to our leaving Friday morning for Vermont.[1] Shall we see you there by any chance?

The Io moth and its elegant companion are in the museum labelled "Coll. Edm. Wilson, Cape Cod". We shall be back here in the last days of August.

Wishing you both a summer as fair as possible (under the circumstances). We remain

Yours very drujesky[2]
Vladimir and Véra Nabokov

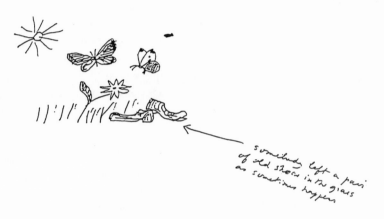

something left a pair
of old shoes in the grass
as sometimes happens

1. At the invitation of Michael Karpovich, the Nabokovs went to Vermont to give their son Dmitri, who had been ill most of the winter, a chance to recuperate in the country (see Brian Boyd, *Vladimir Nabokov: The American Years*, p. 45).

2. "Amicably," in a whimsical quasi-French transcription.

44

August 8, 1942
Wellfleet, Mass.

Dear Vladimir: How are you? I've been reading more Pushkin, with great enthusiasm, and wish you were around to talk to—Nina Chavchavadze[1] is rather inadequate on such subjects. I was disappointed in *Каменный Гость*,[2] and don't quite see why Mirsky thinks it a masterpiece. *Цыганы*[3] *is* a masterpiece, though; and the humorous ones, *Граф Нулин*[4] and *Домик в Коломне*[5] seem to me absolutely wonderful, though they don't seem to be so much read. (I found at Cambridge, however, that the beginners in Russian at the summer school, were being made to memorize *Граф Нулин*. What are the theories about *Домик в Коломне* of which Mirsky speaks? There *is* something a little queer about it?

The Letters, 1942

Do you know what the theory is about the countess whom he sees at church and who has no obvious connection with the story? Also, do you think he had any intention beyond what is obvious in the *Гавриилиада*?[6] Did he mean to imply that we can't be sure whether Christ was the son of Gabriel, the Devil or God? The part about the Garden of Eden is quite beautiful—I prefer it to Milton on the same subject.

We are still pursuing our activities up here regardless of Clifton Fadiman and Pearl Harbor. I hope that Vera is better in the country. Do let us know when you are back.

As ever,
Edmund W

1. Nina (née Romanov, the daughter of the Grand Duke George of Russia) and Paul Chavchavadze (of noble Georgian extraction and Russian culture) were Edmund Wilson's neighbors and friends. Paul Chavchavadze (1899–1971) was a writer and literary translator.
2. *The Stone Guest*.
3. "The Gypsies."
4. "Count Nulin."
5. "The Little House in Kolomna."
6. "The Gabrieliad," also known in English as "Gavriliada."

45

Vermont
August 9, 1942

Dear Bunny,

I have not heard from you for quite a while. *Scoo-cha-you pa vass.*[1] Thanks for sending me the *Accent* review.[2]

I am following Gogol through the dismal maze of his life and have selected as basic rhythm of my book the *en passant* move of the Pawn. (Please note this). I wonder if it would be physically possible to trace a certain (anonymous) "citizen of the American states" with whom Gogol sat at the table d'hôte of an (anonymous) boarding house at Lübeck in August 1829.[3] Or the wise Englishman who gave lessons of atheism to Pushkin.[4] The book is progressing slowly, mainly because I get more and more dissatisfied with my English. When I have finished it, I shall take a three months' vacation with my ruddy robust Russian muse.

I am begging Laughlin to find me a translator for my *Gift*. Sex ♂, nationality American, knowledge of Russian good, vocabulary *richissime*, style his own.

Laughlin asked Knopf, and Knopf suggested Yarmolinsky whose English is no better than mine and whose translations of Pushkin (with Babette D.)[5] are worse than mine. So I am still looking for somebody who might make a translation of that 500 page book, with myself only controlling the meaning and nuance. I know of one man who could do it if I helped him with his Russian. This is a roundabout way of putting it but I am afraid you have other dogs to beat whereas I have no illusions about the sums Laughlin can pay,—at least such sums as have come to me; they might come in bulkier form to others.

I am going to Cambridge on the 31st of August as my duties at the Mus[eum of] Comp[arative] Zool[ogy] begin on the 1st of Sept. We have taken a flat there—8 Craigie Circle. It is amusing to think that I managed to get into Harvard with a butterfly as my sole backer. I am capturing a good deal of them here, chiefly moths. It is one of the most perfect pleasures I know of—to open the window wide on a muggy night and watch them come. Each has its own lamp-side manner: one will settle quietly on the wall to be boxed in comfort, another will dash and bang against the lampshade before falling with quivering wings and burning eyes upon the table, a third will wander all over the ceiling. The system is to have several tumblers with a piece of "carbona" soaked cotton-wool stuck to the bottom, and you overturn the tumbler upon the bug. When stunned it is transferred to another jar to be pinned later. Tonight I shall sugar for them: you mix: a bottle of stale beer, two pounds of brown sugar (or treacle) and a little rum (added just before applying); then just before dusk you smear (with a clean paint brush) a score of tree trunks (preferably old lichened ones) with the concoction and wait. They will come from nowhere, settling on the glistening bark and showing their crimson underwings (especially brilliant in the flashlight) and you cover them with a tumbler beginning with the lower ones. Try, Bunny, it is the noblest sport in the world.

My very best greetings to Mary. Véra присоединяется.[6] Do write me a few (slanting) lines.[7]

Yours
V. Nabokov

1. "I miss you" (in whimsical phonetics).

2. James Laughlin's review of Mary McCarthy's *The Company She Keeps*, which appeared in the Summer 1942 issue of *Accent*.

3. In a letter to his mother of August 25, 1829, Nikolai Gogol briefly mentioned an American he had met at the inn in Travemünde where they were both staying. In *Nikolai Gogol*, Nabokov has a little fantasy about this American: "One may thus imagine a retired businessman in the Boston of 1875, casually telling his wife of having dreamt the other

night that together with a young Russian or Pole whom he had once met in Germany when he was young himself he was buying a clock and a cloak in a shop of antiques."

4. In a fragment of a letter dating from 1824 and possibly addressed to his school friend, the poet Wilhelm Küchelbecker, Pushkin wrote of an elderly Englishman he had met in Odessa, who was writing a thousand-page treatise intended to disprove the existence of an intelligent Creator. As Nabokov was later to point out in his commentary to *Eugene Onegin*, this Englishman is now thought to have been one Dr. William Hutchinson (who, incidentally, became a zealous minister of the Church of England upon his return from Russia).

5. Yarmolinsky's wife, the poet Babette Deutsch, who collaborated with him on translations of Pushkin.

6. "Joins me."

7. Most of Wilson's handwritten additions and marginal notes in his letters were written at a slant.

46

Dear Bunny,

that was indeed funny—our writing to each other on the same day and both referring to Pushkin's atheism. I think you are right about the "Gavriliada" implication. And of course the "heads covered with their azure wings" or better "with heads enveloped in their bright blue wings" (закрывъ главу лазурными крылами)[1] is a bit of paradisical ornithology unsurpassed. Have you noted in the «Домикъ въ Коломнѣ»[2] the wonderful discourse on metres and rhymes (with examples subtly inserted) and the hair breadth escape from the rhyme *Жена*[3] (there are very few rhymes in *ona* in Russian and that is the most popular one) in the stanza about smoked tongue and the restaurateur Kopp?[4] But there is one curious blunder: Pushkin says he is selecting the alexandrine, a 6 feet line whereas he uses a 5 feet one. I have never quite understood what happened.[5] The countess, whom I remember but vaguely, seems to be there mainly in order to provide a romantic contrast to the simple Parasha, (or perhaps the latter was not so simple?).

The "Guest of Stone" is the most perfect of the four dramas. I shall make you see its beauties when we meet. Чего стоитъ напримеръ строчка «скажи ... нѣтъ, после переговоримъ»—строчка въ которой передается скороговорка и одышка страсти. Или «далеко на сѣверѣ въ Парижѣ»[6] which physically was south to Pushkin, but north in regard to Madrid. And loads of other things.

Yours очень дружески[7]
V. Nabokov

1. Nabokov slightly misquotes this passage from Pushkin's description of Heaven in "The Gabrieliad." His first variant in English is actually closer to the Russian original which goes: Архангелы в безмолвии сидят, / Главы закрыв лазурными крылами. (Archangels are seated in silence,/ Heads covered with their azure wings.)

2. "The Little House in Kolomna."

3. "Arse."

4. This occurs not in the text of "The Little House in Kolomna," but in a discarded earlier draft of the poem, usually printed as an appendix in academic editions of Pushkin. Because it so obviously rhymes with the still unprintable Russian word for "backside" or "arse," Kopp's restaurant in St. Petersburg is remembered in Russian scatological folklore to this day.

5. Another reference to the discarded earlier draft. Pushkin does not actually say that he is writing the poem in the alexandrine meter, but only that he had considered the possibility.

6. "How priceless, for example, is the line 'tell me . . . no, we'll talk later'—a line in which the rapid speech and breathlessness of passion are conveyed. Or, 'far away in the north in Paris'." Both quotations are from Scene II of *The Stone Guest*, Pushkin's play about Don Juan.

7. "Very amicably."

47

Edmund Wilson
Wellfleet, Massachusetts

April [mistake for August] 20, 1942[1]

Dear Vladimir: If I had the leisure, I'd be glad to translate your book. I'd like to see you translated, and I'd probably learn a lot of Russian. But I've got so many things to do that I couldn't possibly. I'm working on a couple of books, and I think I'll have to take on a part-time job that has been offered me at Smith. The truth is, besides, that my Russian is so uncertain that going over my work would probably be nearly as much trouble for you as translating the book yourself. How about Alexander Werth, who translated Ognyov's *Communist Schoolboy?* You don't have to have an American, do you?

I acquired in New York a volume of your poems called Горній Путь.[2] I didn't know it existed. It looks like an *oeuvre de jeunesse.*

I'm glad you'll soon be back in this vicinity—will look you up when I get to Boston.

By the way, I find that Henry Sweet in the article on Phonetics in the Encyclopaedia Britannica confirms my opinion that in Russian all the vowels tend to be long. What we do with longs and shorts you do with softs and hards. Since reading more Pushkin, I think I understand better the misunderstandings behind our argument at Stamford. Mirsky speaks of the versification of one of Pushkin's dramas—I forget which—as showing the flexibility of Shakespeare's later plays. When I read the play, I found that this was ridiculous. Beside the verse of Shakespeare's later plays, Pushkin seems pedantically regular. He almost never varies the iamb, whereas with Shakespeare any substitution is possible. I don't remember in Pushkin even any such verse as "Never, never, never, never, never" in *King Lear*. It may be that neither you nor Mirsky, trained on classic Russian verse, quite realizes what English verse is like. I read French poetry for years without really understanding what they were up to—and probably don't fully understand yet.

There is a wonderful example of the handling of soft and long l's in the *Skazka o Tsare Saltane:*

Ты, волна моя, волна!
Ты гульлива и вольна—[3]

This kind of thing, of course, we have in English; but my theory is that it is more important in Russian. Don't you think that Pushkin is particularly good when he is describing the way things *move?*—as he gives the movement of the wave with the alternating l's. Don't the l's *look* like waves, too? Also the ballet girl in *Evgeni Onegin* and the wonderful picture of the cat creeping after a mouse in *Graf Nulin*.[4]

Best regards from us both to Vera—I hope she is better for her vacation. It will be nice to see you again.

As ever,

Edmund W

1. This letter was dated April 20 by Wilson and so printed in the first edition of this book. As Nabokov's biographer Brian Boyd has pointed out (in a private communication), the first paragraph of this letter is clearly a reply to Nabokov's veiled request in his letter of August 9 that Wilson undertake a translation of his novel *The Gift*. Nabokov's detailed treatise on Pushkin's meters in his letter of August 24 is a response to Wilson's complaint about the supposed regularity of Pushkin's meters ("He almost never varies the iamb, whereas with Shakespeare any substitution is possible") in the present letter. All this indicates that the "April" Wilson wrote must have been a slip of the pen for August.

2. *The Empyrean Path* (Berlin, 1923).

3. For Wilson's and Nabokov's respective translations of and commentary to these two lines from Pushkin's "Tale of the Tsar Saltan," see Letter 72 of this collection.

4. Pushkin's verse tale "Count Nulin."

48

Dear Bunny,

I am going to steal an hour from Gogol and thrash out this matter of Russian versification, because you are as wrong as can be.[1] Phonetics have nothing to do with Russian versification. The fact that Russian vowels tend to be long, or soft, or hard, bears no relation whatever to the structure of Pushkin's verse. I do not recall what Mirsky says about Pushkin's Shakespearean flexibility; but I do know that there is absolutely nothing regular or pedantic about Pushkin's iamb. Except perhaps in *Boris Godunov* (which is a failure) Pushkin does nothing but vary and almost dislocate the iamb. What you call "substitution" is another kind of variation, that's all, and just as in Shakespeare (or in English classic verse generally) you will find only here and there a few of the numerous Russian rhythmical variations (which I am going to discuss), so, in Russian verse, the kind of substitution you refer to (a false pyrrhic) is found only in a rudimentary form. You say that you don't remember in Pushkin e v e n any such verse as the five never's in *Lear;* do you mean that you remember a similar kind of line anywhere *else* in Shakespeare (come, come, Bunny)? Incidentally we are not trained, Mirsky and I, on classic Russian verse; we are trained on the verse of Blok, Annensky, Bely and others who revolutionized the old ideas about Russian versification and introduced into Russian verse breaks and substitutions and mongrel meters that are far more syncopic than anything even Tyutchev had dreamed of. My knowledge of English versification is merely a "shapochnoye znakomstvo",[2] but I am quite, quite sure that Russian versification can be explained better to an English poet by the vague similarities between it and English versification than by the blatant differences between the two languages. I have tried once or twice to tell you of the counterpoint in Russian verses, of the variable rhythmic current running through the constant structure of the Russian iamb, for here lies or stands the crux of the matter. In order to understand the various melodies of the iambic line of five feet it is necessary to study these rhythms in the simpler form they assume in the octosyllabic line.

We shall agree to designate the iambic foot as $\cup^{\prime}$ and the octosyllabic line consisting of these feet as R^0 which implies that a given line contains no Rhythmical Variation (Ritmicheskiye Khody), i.e., that all the four accents of the metrical line coincide with the normal accentuation of the words, for instance: «Да вой волковъ. Но то-то счастье»[3] which may be rendered as: "And howling wolves. But oh! the rapture" (here and elsewhere I have been mainly concerned with preserving the stress—not the exact shade of sense).

Now owing to some words being *themselves* (i.e., apart from their rhythmic form in an iambic line) anapests, dactyls, paeons, or such combinations as for instance "neosmotritelneishyi muzh"[4] where the first word is ∪∪∪$\acute{}$ (so-called "fourth paeon") plus ∪∪∪, and also owing to other, mainly monosyllabic words (such as «и», «по», «на», «надъ»,[5] etc.) being unstressed in speech, but happening to coincide with the metrical accent of the verse, an octosyllabic line consisting of such words while nominally retaining its iambic scheme will fail to receive in one or two places the corresponding stress-accent of the word, for instance «Воображенье очень живо»[6] which I render as "Im<u>a</u>gination's brush is vivid" where the metrical accent on the first foot falls on an unstressed syllable (which I have underlined); this weak spot is termed a "half-accented" foot and designated as ∪– (instead of ∪$\acute{}$), meaning that the wave of the meter rises where there is no cork to bob (the "cork" being the regular accent in the word). Further it is clear that such a half-accent may coincide with any of the feet (except the last one—although even this has been tried, by Max Voloshin, 1918, in the line «и неосуществимая» which is made to rhyme with моя (or «твоя»)[7]— and something of that sort is found in English versification too when some long word ending in "ity" is made to rhyme with "sea" or "me"), so that three rhythmic varieties of the octosyllabic line may be produced according to whether the half-accent occurs in the first, second or third foot, and these varieties I designate as R^1, R^2 and R^3 respectively. As, moreover, owing to the presence of some long adjective «неугомо́нная забота» or «таинственныя времена»[8] the line may consist of two "fourth" paeons ∪∪∪$\acute{}$ ∪∪∪$\acute{}$ or a "second" paeon plus a "fourth" one ∪$\acute{}$∪∪ ∪∪∪$\acute{}$ (a third possible combination ∪∪∪∪∪$\acute{}$∪$\acute{}$ being extremely rare and almost unpronounceable) there occur two more varieties R^{1+3} and R^{2+3} (incidentally the former can be scanned also as an amphibrachic line of three feet with a half-accent on the middle one) i.e. lines in which there are two half-accents. In all these five cases of course the line may be designated either from the "paeonic" point of view (that is with only the absolute verbal value of the accents taken into account) or from the "half-accent" one (that is bringing in the shadow of the metrical scheme) so that the line «неугомонная забота» can be designated either as ∪∪∪$\acute{}$∪∪∪$\acute{}$[∪] or ∪–∪$\acute{}$∪–∪$\acute{}$[∪], but the second designation is the clearer one as it shows the rhythmic relation of a concrete line to its abstract basic meter.

Now will you please study the following six examples of R^0, R^1, R^2, R^3, R^{1+3} and R^{2+3}, all of them taken from "Count Nulin," with translation attempting to render the rhythm in English. Let me repeat that this is not an attempt to force alien rhythms upon English versification but an effort to show that similar rhythmical variations may be—artificially perhaps—illustrated by En-

	and	how	ling	wolves.	But	●!	the	rap	ture
R^0 (4 iambi)	∪	⌣	∪	⌣	∪	⌣	∪	⌣	
R^1	i	ma	gi	na	tion's	brush	is	vi	vid
	∪	—	∪	—	∪	—	∪	—	
R^2	our	he	ro	ine	t'is	sad	to	men	tion
	∪	—	∪	—	∪	—	∪	—	
R^3	with	pleas	ing	dig	ni	ty	is	beam	ing
	∪	—	∪	—	∪	—	∪	—	
R^{1+3}	an	in	sur	mount	a	ble	tempt	a	tion
	∪	—	∪	—	∪	—	∪	—	
R^{2+3}	a	for	mid	a	ble	en	nouf	let	to
	∪	—	∪	—	∪	—	∪	—	

glish lines, bad as they are, or, in other words, that there is no need whatever to resort to phonetics in order to understand Russian versification. [see page 82]

Pushkin's octosyllabic iambic verse shows a very peculiar combination of such lines, extraordinary richness and variety of rhythm being produced by torrents of such lines, remaining unbroken by the dam of plain R^0 for a length of several verses, thus forming rhythmic series (one of Pushkin's peculiarities is the wonderfully musical combination of adjacent lines R^2 and $R^{1(+3)}$). If we designate the half-accent feet by black circles and the full accent ones by white circles (so that for instance the R^{1+3} line $\cup-\cup\overset{\prime}{-}\cup-\cup\overset{\prime}{-}[\cup]$ «неугомонная забота» will look like this ●○●○) and then join the half-accent feet, in adjacent verses only, by means of lines from verse to verse, then we get the following rhythmic pattern or profile (quite distinctive, in the repetition of certain combinations, in the case of every Russian poet) [see page 84]

I shall only just allude to the vexed question of English versification in relation to the Russian rhythms. I have no books here to illustrate my remarks, my memory is untrustworthy and anyway I have not studied the subject thoroughly enough. First of all it is clear that half-accents produced by long words are of seldom occurrence in English verse because English words are so much shorter. If the English word for "man" or "tree" was as long as its Russian counterpart (growing moreover the tails of declensions) the face of English poetry would be changed as Pascal said in reference to Cleopatra's nose. But if we take in account such particles as "on," "in," "with," "as," which correspond to the similar unaccented particles in Russian then certain rudimentary rhythms of the half-accent type can be found in English too; and if you concede that the difference (mind you, the difference, not the lines themselves) between, say, "the flush of morn, the sunset calm" and "while westerly, along the hills" corresponds to the difference between «разсвѣта блескъ, заката тишь» and «на западѣ по склонамъ горъ»[10] i.e. to the difference between R^0 and R^2,—if you concede only this, then all I say here is mathematically correct.

Here is a little horror (which took me considerable pains to compose) containing four kinds of rhythmic variations in both languages:

R^{1-3}	Вдоль *по* аллеѣ *и* въ тени
R^0	(Амуръ скамью поставилъ тамъ)
R^2	слоняюсь, *и* меня Нини́
R^0	французскимъ учитъ тамъ словамъ.
R^3	Учебникъ съѣхалъ *на* траву,
R^0	ромашка смотритъ, словно ждетъ,
R^1	и *на* жилетъ ко мнѣ главу,
R^0	зардѣвшись вся, Нини́ кладетъ.

The Letters, 1942

slap

slap stile echoes

pause on tiptoes

hurried retreat

troubled night

Она, торжественно саркастна ......

Затем почему — да, да —

почему, да вздохнула!

Спорь/ной мой Нунуя собака, — ...

обижу прочить такую.

Не знаю, зач...за показать оне ......

досадой страшною полад — ..

но тихие косматы, вздул залал,.....

прервал парами приляжи сонь....

услыщавъ зарь ея походку.....

и проклиналъ свои ночёвъ ...

и своенравную красоту .....

въ гостиномъ обратился въз...

Какъ оне хозяйка и Параша"..

провод...съ остальную ноге .....

(поправившіе, воля ваша, ...

и не...тре въ ване номоге .....

9

R^{1-3}	Down <u>in</u> the garden, <u>in</u> the shade
R^0	where Cupid placed an artful bench
R^2	I linger <u>with</u> the little maid
R^0	who daily tries to teach me French.
R^3	The grammar flutters <u>to</u> the grass,
R^0	a daisy nods a knowing head,
R^1	and <u>on</u> my breast a little lass
R^0	outflushes all the rose's red.

Inversely, though the quantity and possibility of what I call "seesaw" words (e.g. "whether t'is nobler") far surpass anything of that kind occurring in Russian (and thus, together with slurred syllables, verbal dimples and other special varieties of English intonation make the fullest amends for the lack of rich series of Russian rhythms) there do exist a few Russian words capable of accomplishing the seesaw trick. Such words as for instance «между», «передъ» (not «перёдъ»,[11] of course), «полу-» (half-), «какъ-бы»[12] and some others which are normally accentuated on the first syllable as "never," "under" or "whether" are (by the way, I often have wondered why participles, adverbs and double syllable words ending in "er" make the best seesaws) alter the stress balance by coinciding with the ∪∪ of the paeon or rather with the ∪– of the meter. Thus «передъ окномъ возникшей дракой»[13] may be rendered rhythmically as "under the window started fighting" and «полу-влюбленный, полу-сонный»[14] as "rather enamored, rather sleepy". And I still fiercely maintain that such seesaw words do not introduce a trochee into the iambic line (just as the feminine ending of the line cannot be said to turn the last foot into an amphibrach, or just as such a line as R^3 cannot be said to be formed of an iamb, an amphibrach and an anapest, as Russian old-fashioned teachers taught us at school), but merely form an iambically influenced pyrrhic or more correctly a half-accent foot, that is are slightly dipped in the first syllable and slightly tilted in the second by the impulse of the iambic meter. The Russian iamb of five feet is more complicated than the octosyllable as more rhythmic variations are possible (R^0, R^1, R^2, R^3, R^{1-3}, R^{2-3}, R^{1-4}, R^{2-4}, R^{3-4}, R^{2-3-4}, R^{1-3-4}) and also because the shuttling of the cesura affords many possibilities. Pushkin's last drama (to which he put the finishing touches on the day of his fatal duel) with its acrobatic *enjambements*, exploded cesura, extraordinary rhythmic angulations etc., is as different in its much richer rhythmical structure from *Boris Godunov*, as *King Lear* is from *Romeo and Juliet* although of course rich Russian versification and rich English versification are not governed by the same rules.

Here, however, are some instances from this *Guest of Stone* which seem to me to have certain counterparts in English.

Что́ за бѣда́, *хо́ть и узна́ютъ!* Только
Whát of it, pray? lét them expóse me! Only

Ведь я не госуда́рственный престу́пникъ
for am I a polítical offénder?

Разве вы́ вино́вны
Are you réally guílty?

пе́редо мной?
Vérily so?

What we call a regular iamb of five feet (R^0) is «~~уби́лъ~~ его родного брата. Право, жаль»,[15] and I bet you do not find many such lines in the *Guest of Stone*. Something of the rhythmical richness of that masterpiece can be gathered from the pattern produced by the following lines—beginning of Scene 3 from «Все къ лучшему . . .» to «. . . любовной пѣсни».[16]

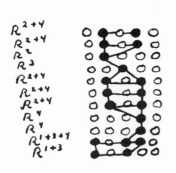

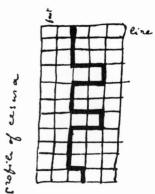

I do hope that I have explained the variations of the Russian iamb and for the time being will not complicate matters by discussing in detail the half-accent varieties of the *piatistopnyi* (there is also the *shestistopnyi*[17] one), but if you will insist on obscuring the issue by referring to phonetics and telling me that "dignity" or "insurmountable" is shorter than "vazhnostiu" or "(ne)ugomonnaya"[18] (which is quite true but irrelevant), or that such English varieties as say "The unforgettable, unforgotten" breaking in among iambic octosyllables have no counterpart in Russian, or that a trochaic line may appear among them, or that my rhythmic renderings do not scan properly to an English ear, then in despair I shall have to suggest your perusing the treatise *Poetica* by Andrei Bely which is probably the greatest work on verse in any language.[19] What I want you to do is to forget the softs and hards and check the "half-accents"

affair by the vague similarities that English verse offers insofar as neither Russian nor English versification is syllabic. I simply cannot believe that phonetics must be brought in to explain a matter which is quite satisfactorily, and I might add elegantly, expressed in terms of relationship between metrical scheme and rhythmical pattern. And for an English-speaking person to better understand Russian versification (which has been actually borrowed from Germany and England and not from France, as Kantemir[20] tried to do) it is necessary to assume a basic similarity of stress between the languages regardless of the special features that make English and Russian so different to the ear.

I am glad you bought the *Gorny Put*[21] though it is a rather miserable little thing. The poems it contains were written when I was still in my teens and are strongly influenced by the Georgian poets, Rupert Brooke, De la Mare, etc., by whom I was much fascinated at the time. It also contains, if I remember right, a very poor translation of "La belle dame sans merci." Funny to think all this was almost a quarter of a century ago. Stalin in his wildest dreams never imagined he might be emitting pleasant noises in the company of Meester Churchill—just as I could not have guessed that one day I would be discovering new butterflies in the wilds of Arizona, or that you would buy my *Gorny Put*. I quite agree with you concerning the *alliteratio puschkiniana* and rendering of motion. One of the best things of that kind occurs in the end of his "Imitation of Dante" which begins «Въ началѣ жизни школу помню я».[22] The Smith lectures sound good. Werth (whose last book on Russia is extremely good) must be too busy, I am afraid.

Hearty *privety*[23] from Véra and me to both of you.

V. Nabokov

I append some quotations from my translation of *Hamlet*,[24] *pour la bonne bouche.*[25]

[Added in longhand at the top of the first page]
After the 1st of Sept. our address will be: 8, Craigie Circle, Cambridge, Apt. 35

1. This letter is Nabokov's detailed response to Wilson's misguided application of the English versification system to Pushkin's meters. See the Introduction, pp. 16–17. See the discussion of this letter in G. S. Smith, "Notes on Prosody," in *The Garland Companion to Vladimir Nabokov*, Vladimir E. Alexandrov, editor (New York and London, 1995).

2. "Nodding acquaintance."

3. Almost all the Russian examples cited to demonstrate metrical patterns come from Pushkin's verse tale "Count Nulin." The few examples from the same poet's *The Stone Guest* are identified as such in the text.

4. "A most imprudent husband."

5. "And," "on/along/over/by," "on," "over/above."

6. In "Count Nulin" Pushkin had Воображает очень живо, "He imagines very vividly."

7. "In 1918, during the Civil War, I remember Maksimilian Voloshin, an excellent and erudite poet (1877–1932), reading to me at a Yalta café, one cold and gloomy night with the sea booming and splashing over the parapet onto the pavement, a fine patriotic poem in which the pronoun *moya* or *tvoya* rhymed with *i nepreodolimaya*" (*Eugene Onegin*, translated from the Russian, with a commentary by Vladimir Nabokov, Vol. 3, p. 534). *Moya* and *tvoya* mean "mine" and "thine" (feminine singular); *i neosushchestvimaya* (in the letter) means "and unrealizable" and *i nepreodolimaya* (in the *Onegin* commentary) is "and insurmountable." These two adjectives are also in the feminine singular form.

8. "Irrepressible concern" or "mysterious times."

9. "She gives Tarquin a swinging slap—Yes, yes!—And what a slap! Count Nulin burned with shame to swallow such an insult. I don't know what he might have done, consumed with dire chagrin, if the woolly Spitz had not begun to bark and waked Parasha from her heavy slumber.* The count, hearing her steps and cursing his night lodgings and the capricious beauty, beat a shameful retreat. It is up to you to imagine how he, the hostess and Parasha spent the rest of the night—I do not intend to help you." Up to the point marked by the asterisk, the translation is by Edmund Wilson, who cited this passage in the section on Pushkin in "Notes on Russian Literature," later included as "Pushkin" in *A Window on Russia*. Wilson's commentary on this episode reflects Nabokov's marginal notes on the right side of this example.

10. "The glitter of dawn, the stillness of sunset" and "In the west over the slopes of hills."

11. "Between," "in front of" (not "the front").

12. "As though."

13. "A fight that arose before the window."

14. "Half-enamoured, half-sleepy."

15. In the original, the line Nabokov quotes is a highly unusual six-foot line imbedded in iambic pentameter: Убил его родного брата? Правда: жаль/[Что не его]. ("He killed his brother? It's true; I'm sorry / [He didn't kill him].") After citing the line, Nabokov crossed out the first word to make it a five-foot line for the purpose of illustration.

16. "All's for the best . . ." to ". . . lovesong."

17. "Five-foot" [. . .] "six-foot."

18. "Of importance" or "(ir)repressible."

19. There is actually no treatise by Bely bearing this name. Nabokov must have had in mind Bely's series of epoch-making essays on the relationship between meter and rhythm that were collected in his book *Symbolism* (1910).

20. Prince Antioch Kantemir (1708–1744), who wrote Russian satires in syllabic verse, patterned on the French verse of Boileau.

21. *The Empyrean Path.*

22. "At the beginning of my life I remember a school."

23. "Regards."

24. Several fragments from *Hamlet* in Nabokov's translation appeared at the end of the 1920s in émigré periodicals.

25. "For dessert."

49

Edmund Wilson
Wellfleet, Massachusetts

September 1, 1942

Dear Vladimir: Your letter about versification is partly based on a false assumption about what I was trying to say in mine. I did not mean that the long Russian vowels produced metrical differences from English. This is quite a separate matter from the metrical question.

Now about the metrics: the terminology you use—of amphibrachs, pyrrhics, etc.—is obsolete in English. We now speak of these feet only in analyzing choruses from Greek plays—because Greek verse is quantitative and you have feet made up of combinations of long and short syllables that require special names to designate them. Thus in this line from the *Agamemnon*—

$$\text{πĕρĭβᾰλōν / γᾰρ οῐ / πτĕρŏφŏρŏν / δĕμᾱσ / Θεοί}^{1}$$

περίβαλον and πτερόφόρον[2] are paeons; but when an English-speaking reader reads them, he accents the first syllable of each word, imposing on the line his own metrical system (nobody seems to know what the Greeks did, because nobody seems to know precisely what the written Greek accent indicated); and since we have got away in English in prosody as well as in grammar from trying to fit English into the molds of the classical languages, we have simplified our metrics to five kinds of feet. We couldn't have any such thing as a line beginning uuu– in English, so we don't need to talk about fourth paeons. (If they taught you those other feet in school, the analysis of Russian verse—which seems to me basically, from the point of view of metrics, just like English verse, as you say—then the Russian discussion of prosody was still in a backward state.)

Our five English feet are these: trochee, iambus, anapest, dactyl, spondee. We do not need any more. The notation is the same we use for Greek and Latin, but here the little curves mean unaccented syllables instead of short syllables, and the dashes mean accented syllables instead of long syllables. (Sometimes they write a / instead of a dash; but I have got into the habit of writing it the other way.) These five feet suffice for analyzing any English verse. In our metrics,

or ‿‿

$$\text{Ĭmāg / ĭnā / tiŏn's brūsh / ĭs vīv / ĭd}$$

is scanned like this; and

Dōwn ĭn / thĕ gār / dĕn ĭn / thĕ shāde /

like this. Your system has the advantage of distinguishing the primary from the secondary accent in a word like imagination; but it can't seem to show the inversion of accent produced by the trochee in the first line of *Down in the garden.*

Now before proceeding further, I must confess that your examples have convinced me that I did underestimate the flexibility of the verse in *Kamenny Gost,*[3] due to the fact that I don't know where the accent falls in a great many Russian words and so tend to read it all as regular iambics. However, here is a famous passage from Shakespeare's *Winter's Tale:* [opposite page]
—I have had several interruptions in writing this letter and am now finishing it in the Belleview Hotel, after vainly trying to reach you by phone. I was going on to cite more complex passages from Shakespeare, but will have to wait for this till I see you. Observe, however, in the above the two beats dropped out in the line that begins *From Dis's wagon.* It gives the effect, I think, of the flowers dropping out of the wagon; and the pulling the rhythm up with the first syllable of *daffodils* is like beginning to pick them up.

> Madame Sostrosis famous clairvoyante
> Hās ă / bād cōld ̆ / nōne / thĕlēss
> Is the wisest woman in London with a wicked pack of cards,[5]—

where the beat left out makes a pause for a snuffle or blowing of the nose. It all seems perfectly natural: you don't notice at first that the line is short two syllables. Did Pushkin ever reach the point where he was capable of anything like this?

Your metrical system seems to me a combination of conventional and antiquated Russian teaching with original discoveries about how Pushkin gets effects by locating the main accent of the line according to certain patterns. What you show about this is very interesting. Your diagram of the slapping passage in *Nulin* makes me appreciate it better. I hope you will give this whole question your earnest consideration, as the establishment of a durable peace, after Hitler has been beaten, may depend on it.

I am going to be in Boston till Saturday morning. Do call me up, if you are here—though I imagine you will be staying in the country till after Labor Day.

As ever,
Edmund W

I haven't yet had a chance to compare the *Hamlet* passages carefully. I see that Pasternak has published a translation.[6]

- Now, my fair'st friend,

I would I had some flowers o'the spring that might

Become your time of day; and yours, and yours,

That wear upon your virgin branches yet

Your maidenheads growing: - O Proserpina!

For the flowers now, that frighted thou lett'st fall

From Dis's waggon! daffodils, ~~daffodils~~ *daffodils*

That come before the swallow dares, and take

The winds of March with beauty; violets dim,

But sweeter than the lids of Juno's eyes

Or Cytherea's breath; pale primroses,

That die unmarried ere they can behold

Bright Phoebus in his strength, a malady

Most incident to maids: bold oxlips and

The crown-imperial; lilies of all kinds,

The flower-de-luce being one. O, these I lack,

To make you garlands of, and my sweet friend,

To strew him o'er and o'er / [4]

my correction

V.N.

1. "Her the gods cloaked in a feathered shape." Aeschylus, *Agamemnon*, 1147–1148 (Cassandra's words about the nightingale).

2. "Cloaked" and "feathered."

3. *The Stone Guest.*

4. *The Winter's Tale,* Perdita's speech in Act Four, scene iv.

5. A somewhat garbled quotation of lines 43–46 from T. S. Eliot's "The Waste Land." In terms of Russian versification, the meter used by Eliot is not iamb, but accentual verse. The Russian accentual verse *(dol'niki)* was known to and used by Pushkin's contemporaries, especially Zhukovsky; but it really came into its own in the work of Russian Symbolists of the early twentieth century.

6. Boris Pasternak's translation of *Hamlet* was first published in Moscow in 1941.

50

September 13, 1942

Dear Bunny,

It took me exactly ten minutes to compose the following little masterpiece consisting exclusively of 4th paeons, a sequence that is seldom found even in Russian prosody.

> The complicated variation
> of Lepidoptera affords
> a fascinating occupation
> for proletarians and lords.

And here is the same thing in Russian:

> Разнообразное сложенье
> чешуекрылыхъ мотыльковъ
> уготовляетъ услажденье
> для королей и бѣдняковъ.

The composing of the amphibrachic poem proved more difficult.[1] I had to struggle against slipping into anapest, just as there are horses that sbivaiutsia s ryssi na galop.[2] I have tried to relieve the jogging monotony of the meter by using various enjambements and shortening every third line. You will find it appended.

We were really tremendously glad to see a bit of you here and hope it happens again soon.

My lecturing tour through Virginia, Georgia and Florida begins apparently on the 1st of October and will last a couple of months.

My son is still worrying about the genesis of your mouse.[3]

Yours

B.[4]

P.S. I have suddenly remembered two cases in Pushkin similar to the Shakespearean lapse in the "daffodil" line. In the poem which begins, I think, (it is omitted in the bloody edition I have here) Нѣтъ, я не дорожу мятежнымъ наслажденьемъ all the lines are of six feet except one which is of five: торопитъ мигъ послѣднихъ содроганій[5] ("Precipitates the moment of seminal ejaculation"). Erotic haste shortens this line quite naturally, but only expert attention discloses this.

1. Nabokov's poem "Amphibrachs." It was later re-named "Exile" (see Letter 52) and published in *The New Yorker* on October 24, 1942. Russian amphibrachs are a three-syllable metrical unit in which the second syllable is stressed and the first and third are not. This meter is similar to that of Anglo-American limericks: "There WAS a / young MAN from / Nan-TUCK-et."

2. "Break from a trot into a gallop."

3. Dmitri Nabokov remembers that Wilson used to delight him with a trick where he turned a handkerchief into a mouse.

4. B is a V in the Cyrillic alphabet.

5. See note 2 to Letter 51.

51

September 19, 1942

Wellfleet, Mass.

Dear Vladimir: I think that this supposedly amphibrachic poem is probably your best yet of verses in English, and I imagine that the *New Yorker* would take it. I don't quite like the way *some* is used in the last line. You really mean *others.*[1] *Some* is always the first member of the formula: *some ... others. Eavesdropping* is spelt like this.

From my point of view, this is simply an anapestic poem, with an iamb in the first foot. Even according to your own metrical system, there is an extra non-amphibrachic syllable at the end of each line, which gives the whole line an anapestic movement. The other poem, according to my system, is just iambic tetrameter. You have placed the two main emphases in each line so that they fall on every fourth syllable; but in a true fourth paeon the first three syllables are all of equal value, which is not the case here and only possible in qualitative verse like the Greek.

I have to go to Cambridge Wednesday. Could I come to see you in the evening? I'll call you up when I get in—about noon.

As ever,
Edmund W

In my edition, that line of the Pushkin poem is metrically the same as the others:

Она торопит миг последних содраганий.[2]

Your idea about it is a happy one, though. The Shakespeare translations seem to me awfully good. I'll talk to you about them when I see you.

1. The last line of "Exile" in its published form reads: "while others were grouped in a glade."

2. "She hastens the moment of ultimate quivers." This rendition would be closer to Pushkin's wording than Nabokov's overly literal "seminal ejaculations" in the preceding letter. The line is from Pushkin's untitled lyric that begins "No, I do not treasure the stormy rapture." Nabokov misremembered that the line he cited begins with the pronoun "she." Wilson quotes the correct version of the line.

52

[Postcard from Véra Nabokov to Edmund Wilson]

October 13, 1942

Dear Edmund,

Thank you very much for your letter with the introduction letter. I can at last forward latter to V. to-day: until now his whereabouts were too uncertain. Owing to some change in schedule he spent an unexpected week at a "black Wellesley"[1] in Georgia, for room and board, but seems to have enjoyed it.

It might amuse you to learn that "Amphibrachs" (re-baptized "Exile") were enthusiastically hailed by *New Yorker* and will appear in an early issue.

I am looking forward to seeing you both as soon as V. returns.

Yours sincerely,
Véra Nabokov

1. See next letter. Nabokov referred thus to Spelman College, an all-black women's college in Atlanta, where he gave a lecture on Pushkin (stressing the poet's African ancestry) on October 8, 1942.

The Letters, 1942

53

8 Craigie Circle, Suite 35

Cambridge, Massachusetts

November 3, 1942

I found a few sheets of this
aristocratic paper in this "suite"

Dear Bunny,

I came back from my Chichikov Travels[1] for a couple of days to Cambridge and am going away again, this time to places in Illinois, to-morrow. Colleges visited: Cokes near Florence, Spelman in Atlanta, Georgian State Col[lege] for ♀ ♀ at Valdosta and Univ[ersity] of the South, Sewanee. My admiration for American education has increased still more—perhaps owing to the quite remarkable appreciation which my iridescent lectures obtained. I have met most charming and brilliant people (especially the President of Spelman, Miss Read and the president of G.S.C.W. Frank Reade);[2] I have roamed over palmetto wilds and pine barrens and swamps in pursuit of most brilliant and charming butterflies; I have played tennis, canoed, danced; and I have made very little money. I did not pass through, or stay at, Louisville so that I did not see your friend. Thanks all the same. The amphibrachic poem won great praise from Pierce,[3]—the magic of your approbation always works. You have probably received a certain letter from the Guggenheim Society to which I have applied for a grant (my financial position is becoming disastrous). I made a (rather silly, I'm afraid) synopsis or description of the novel I am working at ("The Person from Porlock").[4] I gave you as reference.

I have been working hard in my Museum these few days I have stolen from my tour; and I have been ill. I am not very eager to renew my jogging. There will not be any lepidoptera in Illinois and Minnesota. A child in Georgia called a butterfly a "flutter-by"—which almost solves the puzzling origin of that word (a good try was a "better fly" i.e. larger, brighter than other flies).

I have been talking a lot about Mary's book.

Love from both of us to both of you.

V.

---

1. Reference to Gogol's *Dead Souls*.

2. Florence Matilda Read had been the President of Spelman College since 1927. President Frank Reade of the Georgia State College for Women is also mentioned in Chapter Six of *Pnin*.

3. Apparently, Charles Pearce (see Letter 42, note 7).

4. "Person from Porlock" was the working title of the novel that eventually became *Bend Sinister*. The "person from Porlock" was the man who interrupted Coleridge as he was writing down "Kubla Khan," causing him to forget the rest of the poem.

54

November 7, 1942
Wellfleet, Mass.

Dear Vera:

I have just had a letter from Vladimir, who says that he is setting out on the road again. We had hoped you could all come up here for over the weekend of Thanksgiving. Wouldn't there be any chance of this?

If I knew precisely where he is going in the West, I could perhaps send him some letters to people. Of course, I'll be delighted to recommend him for a Guggenheim.

We do hope you can come up here Thanksgiving.

As ever,
Edmund Wilson

EW/S

55

8 Craigie Circle, Suite 35
Cambridge, Massachusetts

November 24, 1942

Dear Bunny,

instead of going to Virginia last Wednesday I went to bed with a bad attack of flu. Dmitri has done the same. In Russia this illness was dubbed "ispanka" (the Spanish lady).

Here are some aberrations of Homo sap and Homo sapiens that I have collected during my tour:

1) Woman teaching Drama. Hobby: resemblance to the Duchess of Windsor. The resemblance *is* rather striking. When the Duchess (according to press-photos) changes her coiffure, she changes it too (*keeping up with her model*, as some mimetic butterflies are known to do). Classifies the people she meets into a) those who mention the likeness at once; b) those who take some time to realize it; c) those who speak of it only to a third party; d) (the best) those who,

in her presence, automatically refer to Wally without consciously defining the association of thoughts; and e) those who ignore it—or do not see it. She is a spinster with a few Windsors in the past, and this hobby of hers is what makes life worth living.

2) A little man, with mild watery eyes; of somewhat clerical appearance. Very quiet, untalkative, small false teeth. Blurts out some obvious question ("how long have you been in this country?") in a ventriloquist's voice and then is dismally silent again. Profession: secretary of several clubs. Bachelor. Sexual life either limited to a poor little solo once in a while, or non-existent. Led me to the Lincoln Monument. And then suddenly the miracle happened: stopped abruptly, staring at a flagpole. Eyes ablaze, nostrils a-quiver, awfully excited. Challenged one of the watchmen: "Is that a *new* flagpole you've got there?" Wanted to know (voice trembling) its exact height. "70 feet, I guess." Sighed with relief. You see[,] his passion was flagpoles and the new one he had just acquired for his back yard was 75 feet tall (he would get a 100 f[oot] one next year, he said). Embraced the silver-painted rotundity and looked up. Yes, about 70. "But don't you notice," I said, "that it deviates a little up there." Quite happy now because it *was not* quite straight, while *his* displayed a most perfect erection. The little man was bright and alive for at least half an hour. And next day I noticed him tingle for a moment when I happened to mention Poland and Poles. Good case for the Viennese Wizard (who might also observe that "pol" means "sex" in Russian).

3) Celebrated Negro scholar and organizer. 70 years old, but looks 50. Dusky face, grizzled goatee, nice wrinkles, big ears,—prodigiously like a White Russian General in mufti played sympathetically by Emil Jannings. Piebald hands. Brilliant talker, with an old-world touch. *Très gentilhomme.*[1] Smokes special Turkish cigarettes. Charming and distinguished in other, more important, ways. Told me that when he went to England he was listed as a "Colonel" on the Channel boat, because his name bore the addition "Col." on his passport.

4) Man in shirtsleeves at my hotel. Stuck out his pink head as I was walking along the passage to my room at about 10 P.M. and suggested a night-cap. I did not want to offend him, so we sat on his bed and had some whiskey. He had been evidently bored to death and was now making much out of my skimpy company. Began telling me, with copious details, all about his sugar business in Florida, his reasons of coming to Valdosta (to hire colored labor) and lots of extravagant particularities about his factory. My whole body felt like one big yawn. I kept peeping at my watch—thought I'd give him another 10 minutes and then turn in. As I was fumbling in my pocket for matches, a little pill-box I used for collecting moths on lighted porches fell out and rolled on the floor.

He picked it up and remarked: "might be mine: I use these for collecting moths." He turned out to be an entomologist who had at one time been in touch with the Amer[ican] Mus[eum of] Nat[ural] Hist[ory] where I had worked. I did not look at my watch any more. It is the second time I have been fooled that way (first time was with Prof. Forbes in a Boston subway).

5) Big heavy man, College President. First thing he did was to discuss with most amazing subtility Browning's "Last Duchess" and "Eagle's Feather." Has the students call him by his Christian name—and called me McNab[2] because could not pronounce it properly. Shocked the community by bringing Mrs. Roosevelt from the station in a hideous little rickety car which he uses on weekdays instead of his luxurious Packard. Talked very entertainingly about his grandfather, a Confederate hero—but then gave me to read what he was writing on the subject—family memoirs you know—and it was very poor. Otherwise a most tremendous gentleman as egocentrical as I.

6) Old man in the "lounge" (really, lavatory) of the Pullman. Talking volubly to two nice self-controlled unsmiling privates. The main words he used were "Christ," "hell" and "fucking" coming all in a bunch towards the end of every sentence. Horrible eyes, black fingernails. Somehow reminded me of the militant type of Russian "chernosotenetz."[3] And as if in answer to my passing thought he started on a wild attack against Jews. "They and their pissing children," he said. Then he spat into the wash basin and missed by several inches.

I have more in my collection but this is enough. I like writing in bed. Thanks so much for inviting us for Thanksgiving day, but I am exhausted—and my finances are exhausted too. My tour (which I will resume 3–12 December) was a very great success in the way of appreciation etc., but proved financially a failure as my Institute does not pay the traveling expenses.

I want to see you very much. I saw Weeks the other day [...] and he will bring out a story and a poem of mine in the January number.

Yours,

V.

1. "Very much a gentleman." This was W. E. B. DuBois.

2. "McNab" is to be found in Nabokov's last completed novel, *Look at the Harlequins,* as the nickname of the narrator-hero.

3. Member of the Black Hundreds, a reactionary, anti-Semitic organization in pre-revolutionary Russia.

The Letters, 1942

56

November 25, 1942
Wellfleet, Mass.

Dear Vladimir: We are very disappointed at your not being able to come up here for tomorrow. I am not surprised at your collapsing as a result of that lecture tour. Can't you get Laughlin to come through with some more money, so that you can write your books? Would you like me to try to sell *Partisan Review* the idea of bringing out part of your Gogol? What ever happened to the butterfly piece? I approved of the new end of the French professor poem—though it was a pity to sacrifice *askew*.[1]

I was fascinated by your description of your adventures, and it made me rather envious, as I used to do a certain amount of this kind of traveling around myself, and usually enjoyed it.

Nina Chavchavadze and I read Pushkin together two or three times a week. She hoped you would be here Thanksgiving. I have just discovered how truly awful the Russian numerals are, and it has about killed any faint hopes I may have had of ever learning to speak the language. The article in the *Encyclopaedia Britannica* is quite funny about the numerals, as the writer gets positively bitter.

I was sorry not to see you in Cambridge, but I was only stopping overnight and had already arranged to have dinner with the Levins.[2]

As ever,
Edmund W.

1. "Exile" (see Letter 51, notes 1 and 2).
2. Harry and Elena Levin.

57

8 Craigie Circle, Suite 35
Cambridge, Massachusetts

December 13, 1942

Dear Bunny,

I have two answers to your dedicatory[1] quiz: one (of which you may be unconscious—but it is absolutely right) refers to the opening lines

After writing,
reading late

which in tone, rhythm and atmosphere are most beautifully like Pushkin's mumble:

мнѣ не спится,
нѣтъ огня[2]

("Verse composed during a sleepless night").

The other answer is, of course, "Lesbia in Hell" which mimics in rather a startling way the macabre bonhomie and tippling brackets of some of Pushkin's rhymed tales.

I liked both your verse and your prose enormously—and this is not a case of «кукушка хвалитъ пѣтуха.»[3] I loved the bit about languages—though personally I would not have compared the «ж» to a butterfly[4]—good as the resemblance is—for you see «ж» is most essentially the symbol of *beetle*, жукъ, жужжаніе, жудъ,[5] etc.,—and so when I look at that letter I see a coleopteron on its back with legs outspread—not having made up its mind whether to sham dead or perform the six-limbed passes that might help it to turn over. One of my favourites is "Dawns, dawns."

I have just returned from my last series of lectures and have found Véra ill with pneumonia at the hospital. She will have to stay there a fortnight, the doctor says.

The one about MacLeish is just splendid.[6] "Paul-Montgomery-Vincent Green was the very best boy that ever was seen"—a line from some nursery-book which I have kept in my head 37 years. I envy so bitterly your intimacy with English words, tumbling them as you do, that it seems rather silly to send you the poem you will find on a separate page. I have been pining away ever since the chairman of a Women's Club where I had been reading my verse said to me with a lyrical leer: "What I loved best was the broken English." I wrote it on my way to Washington where I went for the only purpose of sorting out some butterflies I had described (not the one referred to here, which is in New York and which I visited too—and also had a drink with Pierce[7]). Wars pass, bugs stay. Do please give it an expert look soon, because I want to send it [to] the *N[ew] Y[orke]r*, and need money badly.

When will you be here?

"Privet"[8] to you and Mary

Yours

V.

1. Apparently on a copy of Edmund Wilson's *Note-Books of Night*, a collection of verse and prose, which was published by The Colt Press, San Francisco, in 1942 and later reissued

The Letters, 1942

with additional material as *Night Thoughts*. "After writing," "Lesbia in Hell," and "Dawns, dawns," cited in this letter, are Wilson's poems included in *Note-Books of Night*.

2. "I can't sleep, there is no light." Nabokov breaks up the first line of Pushkin's poem into two separate lines.

3. "The cuckoo praises the rooster." This line from Ivan Krylov's fable "The Cuckoo and the Rooster" (1834) has become, like so many of Krylov's lines, a popular proverb. The last three lines of the fable read: "Why then, without fear of blame / Does the cuckoo praise the rooster? / Because he praises the cuckoo."

4. Wilson's short essay "Word-Fetishism" (in *Note-Books of Night*) mentions the Russian "*zhe's* that vibrate like butterflies."

5. "Beetle, buzzing, (low-pitched) buzzing"—words that begin with ж *(zhe)* and pertain to beetles while imitating their sounds.

6. "The Omelet of A. MacLeish."

7. Pearce.

8. "Regards."

1943

58

230 East 15th St.
New York

January 11, 1943

Dear Vladimir:

I am sorry that I did not have a chance to stop off in Cambridge but had to come straight to New York. The above is my address, and our telephone number is Gramercy 7-4579.

I think I have perhaps found a solution to the problem of getting a translator for your books. I met while I was lecturing at Smith an extremely intelligent Russian woman who speaks and writes English absolutely perfectly. She has been over here ever since she was about eleven but has kept up her Russian and studied Russian literature with Mirsky in London. I have read her doctor's thesis on the influence of Dostoevsky in English, and it is interesting and well written. She has some very good stuff on bad English translations and has printed the various English translations of a passage from *The House of the Dead* in parallel columns and compared them with the Russian, demonstrating that they are all extremely bad. She spent Christmas with us and we liked her very much. I gave her your *Podvig*[1] to read and she was very much impressed by it. I will warn you that she is devoted to Dostoevsky, thought not in any mystical or obnoxious way. She is Helen Muchnic, 69 Belmont Avenue, Northampton, Mass. It might be worth your while to see her in Boston some time.

You know that you played on me unintentionally a more successful hoax than any that you premeditated. I was sure that you had invented the Pushkin poem about lying awake at night which sounded so much like mine. I told Mary and other people so and cited it as an example of the lengths to which you would go in the concoction of literary frauds, and swore that I would not for anything in the world give you the satisfaction of looking it up and of not being able to find it. Then I did look it up one night and found that it did actually exist. I was furious.

I hope that Vera is back at home and all right. If you ever get on to New York, do let us know.

By the way, are you an American citizen now? I believe that this may make some difference to the Guggenheim people.

I like the *Atlantic* piece very much.[2] It is beautifully written.

Best regards from us both—
Edmund W

I have discovered a formula in Russian poetry:

И божество, и вдохновенье,
И жизнь, и слезы, и любов[ь].[3]

Ночь, ледяная рябь канала,
Аптека, улица, фонарь.[4]

Both these repeated in a different order from preceding stanzas.[5] Isn't there something similar in your «Расстрел»?[6]

1. *Glory*, cited under its original Russian title *The Exploit*.
2. "Mademoiselle O," which later formed Chapter Five of *Speak, Memory*, was published in the January 1943 issue of *The Atlantic Monthly*.
3. "And deity, and inspiration, / And life, and tears, and love." The last two lines of Pushkin's poem "I recollect a wondrous moment . . ."
4. "Night, icy ripples of the canal, / Pharmacy, street, lantern." The last two lines of Alexander Blok's poem "Night, street, lantern, pharmacy . . ." which is the second poem of his cycle "Dances of Death" (1912–1914).
5. The formula Wilson discovered is that Russian poets like ending a poem with a two-line list composed of items that were mentioned in the course of the poem.

The Letters, 1943

6. Nabokov's poem "The Execution" (1927), the Russian and English versions of which appear in *Poems and Problems*, pp. 46–47, does indeed end with a similar enumeration: "Russia, the stars, the night of execution / and full of racemosas the ravine."

59

Your hand in Russian is absolutely Russian—I almost am inclined to doubt that you wrote out those lines yourself. (A closer examination, however, revealed that you had forgotten the «ъ» which gives a tender ending to «любовь»).

January 12, 1943

No, fellow magician,—yours is one of the few legs which I have never pulled nor ever intend pulling. I hope you will believe me now. I am glad that you are studying Blok—but be careful: he is one of those poets that get into one's system—and everything seems unblokish and flat. I, as most Russians, went through that stage some twenty-five years ago. You are absolutely right about that formula—as a matter of fact I have been speaking of it in one of my Stanford lectures. *И прощаніе и слезы и заря, заря (Фетъ);*[1] *твои скалы, твои заливы, и блескъ и тѣнь и говоръ волнъ (Пушкинъ)*[2]—and many others.

Pierce is quite enthusiastic about the entomological poem.[3] Véra is almost quite well by now, but it has been a very exhausting illness. Typeplodding through Gogol. Laughlin is very patient. I shall be a full fledged American citizen in 2½ years.

Many thanks for the translator. I shall "contact" her.

The Californian *Lycaeides anna* Edw. has proved to be a subspecies of *L. argyrognomon* Bergstr. of the Palaearctic region; and an unnamed subspecies of *cleobis* Brem., a Siberian butterfly, is distributed through Saskatchewan, Alberta, Idaho, Wyoming and Colorado. These are two of the many remarkable discoveries I am making by examining hundreds of ♂ genitalia. *Lycaeides melissa* Edw. is of course quite a separate species.[4]

I am longing to see you!

V. Nabokov

Véra sends her love to both of you.

[In margin]
Романъ Николаевичъ[5] visited us yesterday. I like him very much. (Do see him in N.Y.)

1. "And farewell and tears and the dawn, the dawn (Fet)." Nabokov misremembers the widely-quoted last lines from Afanasy Fet's famous "verbless" poem "Whispers, timid breathing . . . (1850). The cited line actually begins with the words «И лобзания» ("And kisses") instead of «И прощание» ("And farewell").

2. "Your cliffs, your coves, and the glitter and the shadow and the colloquy of your waves (Pushkin)." The last two lines from Pushkin's "To the Sea" (1824).

3. "On Discovering a Butterfly," *The New Yorker*, May 15, 1943.

4. Nabokov's research on the genus Lycaeides resulted in three published papers: "The Nearctic Forms of *Lycaeides Hüb[ner]*," *Psyche, Journal of Entomology*, Vol. 50, nos. 3–4, 1943, "Notes on the Morphology of the Genus *Lycaeides*," *ibid.*, Vol. 51, nos. 3–4, 1944, and "The Nearctic Members of the Genus *Lycaeides Hübner*," *Bulletin of the Museum of Comparative Zoology of Harvard College*, Vol. 101, no. 4, 1949.

5. Roman Nikolaevich (Roman Grynberg).

60

March 7, 1943
230 E 15th St.
New York

Dear Vladimir: How are you? We miss seeing you. Helen Muchnic at Smith wrote me what seemed to me a very appreciative and intelligent letter about your *Подвиг*.[1] I meant to send it to you but can't find it. Do give her a chance sometimes to translate something of yours. I met the other day a very pretty Russian woman who writes for *Новоселье*:[2] Irina Kunina. Do you know anything about her? She invited us to an entertainment, which we went to last night—we came away with the overwhelming impression that the *Новоселье* group were a lot of Stalinist fellow-travellers organized in a more or less "innocent front." Practically the whole performance consisted of papers and poems glorifying the defense of Leningrad. A "directive" had evidently gone out, because the orations were almost identical and so simple and crude that even Mary understood what they were saying, merely from the proper names and the emphasis. Everybody quoted *Медный Всадник*[3] like mad, sometimes quite mal à propos. The keynote of Mme Kunina's speech was the oft-reiterated phrase: «Петербург тире Ленинград.»[4] I came away thoroughly depressed.

Have you heard anything about the Guggenheim? Are you teaching at Wellesley now? Do drop us a line.

I have been reading Tyutchev through. It is certainly very remarkable—not like any other poet I know. He doesn't have much range though, does he? I have read all Pushkin's longer pieces in verse. I was disappointed in the patriotic *Полтава*,[5] though I can see it is finely written. I thought things like *Братья*

Разбойники[6] and the unfinished *Тазит*[7] were more interesting and more truly Pushkin. Best to Vera,

As ever,
Edmund W.

1. *Glory.*
2. *The New Abode (Novoselye)*, a somewhat pro-Soviet Russian literary journal published in New York from 1942 to 1950.
3. "The Bronze Horseman."
4. "Petersburg hyphen Leningrad."
5. "Poltava."
6. "The Robber Brothers."
7. "Tazit."

61

ca. March 10, 1943[1]

Dear Bunny,

Your description of that little *soirée littéraire* is awfully good. That's why I have never gone near any of our Poetical Fraternities, in Paris or elsewhere. You are quite right about "Poltava." Incidentally, "Poltava" in Pushkin's output is on the same level as *Podvig*[2] in mine. I wrote it twenty years ago—and you know how one feels about one's блевотина.[3]

But I do want very much Miss Muchnic to translate my *Gift*, but I shall send her a short story first. Lovely that bit about «тире Ленинград.»[4] In Paris it would have been «мірь пусть тире Прусть.»[5] I still cannot get over your handwriting in Russian.

Oh, I am having great fun teaching 100 girls Russian. The first thing I told them was that in pronouncing the vowels «а, э, ы, о, у» ("please take out your mirrors, girls, and see what happens inside your mouths"—but there was only one little looking glass to the 25 girls in that particular class), your tongue keeps back—independent and aloof—whereas in «я, е, и, ё, ю»—the squashed vowels—it rushes and crushes itself against your lower teeth—a prisoner dashing himself at the bars of his cell. And then, Bunny, I told them something that you certainly know: that in Russian *all* the vowels, in comparison to the English ones, are *short*. («бой,»[6] for instance, is a puny, brisk little fellow in comparison to the long, indolent English or American "boy"). And so on.

I hope you will enjoy reading my new paper on Lepidoptera, which I am appending. Try reading it *between* the descriptions—though there are some fine bits in them too. I have just finished writing a story for the *Atlantic* (Weeks rang me up 4 times to get another one after "Mlle O"—and I got a letter from an Institution called "Better Speech" something, asking me the permission to use a paragraph from "Mlle O" in their manual. My pigeon-English is developing feathered feet and a primadonna's bosom).

Véra has typed about 130 pages of my Gogol book. In the middle of April I shall spend a day in New York on my way to or from a lecture at "Sweet Briar," Virginia and I simply must see you both. I miss you a lot.

I have no news from Guggenheim—and little hope. If I had, I would not have plunged into those Russian classes—though, in a way, it *is* fun. I go there twice a week, after lunch and come back at midnight. Every girl pays 10 dollars for the term. "I want to tell you, Mr Nabokov, how I enjoyed your article on Shostakovich in *Harper's Magazine*." I do hope Nicholas is getting some wrong-address compliments too.

Pushkin is a sea, but Tyutchev is a well. Slick but true. Blok is the winged boat that the child in Rimbaud's "Bateau Ivre" lets float in the gutter-stream. The other day I found an old play of mine, which was translated in England some years ago.[7] Will you read it please. Perhaps something may be done with it. The English is very stilted—it is not mine.

Съ душевнымъ привѣтомъ

В. Набоковъ[8]

1. The original is dated March 7, but it must be a mistake because this letter is a reply to Wilson's letter of March 7. The postmark on the envelope reads March 11.

2. *Glory.*

3. "Vomit." Actually *Glory* was written in 1930 (see the Foreword to the 1971 English translation).

4. "Hyphen Leningrad."

5. "The world is empty hyphen Proust" (a rhyming game in Russian).

6. Either the Russian word for "battle" or the English loan word *boy,* meaning "serving boy" or "messenger boy."

7. *The Waltz Invention.*

8. "With affectionate regards, V. Nabokov."

62

March 29, 1943

Dear Bunny,

I got that Guggenheim Fellowship. Thanks, dear friend. У тебя удивительно легкая рука.[1] I have noticed that whenever you are involved in any of my affairs they are always successful.

At the same time I got a piece of very sad news from N.Y.: I think I told you of a great friend of mine—and one of my father's соратниковъ[2]—who had just managed to escape from France,—I. V. Hessen.[3] Well, he died. I am sending you a little thing I wrote about him in Russian for the *N. R. Slovo*.[4]

I shall pass through N.Y. on Wednesday and Thursday, 14th and 15 of April. I shall ring you up Wednesday afternoon if you tell me your 'phone-number.

Weeks is working up (amid a staccato of short "ha-ha's") a good deal of [. . .] enthusiasm for the new story I offered him, "The Assistant Producer." It will be in the May issue. The enthusiasm ought to be paid for, I think. I was not satisfied with his price for "Mlle O" (deaf ladies from different parts of this dear country keep writing to me, saying: Mr. Nabokov, if you knew what it means to be deaf, you would have portrayed Mlle O with more sympathy) which was 250 dollars. The new one is about the same length and with much more kick to it. I want to get at least 500. What is your opinion?

Did you see the last ("Russian") *Life*?[5] Вотъ говнюки![6] That obscene picture of Davies![7] The legend under Pushkin's portrait![8] The style! Peter the Great "single*handed, booted* Russia into progress"!

Yours
V.

1. "You bring good luck" (lit., "You have a remarkably light hand."). This was the first of Nabokov's two Guggenheim fellowships (1943 and 1952).

2. "Comrades-in-arms."

3. The prominent jurist and publisher Iosif Hessen (1865–1943) was associated with Nabokov's father as co-founder of the Constitutional Democratic party and as co-editor of several liberal periodicals, both before and after the Revolution.

4. The New York Russian émigré newspaper *Novoye Russkoye Slovo (The New Russian Word)*.

5. The March 29, 1943 "Russian Issue" of *Life* appeared at the height of Soviet-American cooperation during World War II. With a photograph of a benign Stalin by Margaret Bourke-White on the cover, it featured a eulogizing essay on Lenin ("the greatest man of modern times") and a survey of Russian history and culture that reflected Soviet propagandistic biases and distortions.

6. "What shitheads!"

7. The former ambassador to Moscow, Joseph E. Davies, was photographed holding a copy of his pro-Stalin best-seller *Mission to Moscow* against the background of a huge collection of Russian porcelain, antiques and other art objects that he had amassed during his tour of duty.

8. It read: "Pushkin, poet-aristocrat, joined officers' conspiracy against the Czar, was exiled to Caucasus, killed in duel" (which both distorts history and gets the sequence of events wrong).

63

Dear Vladimir: I was delighted to hear about the Guggenheim—though you may not like sharing it with Vladimir Pozner,[1] who also got it.

I was glad to read the play, the Hessen memoir and the butterfly paper. The last of these was a little technical for me, but I enjoyed such words as *fulvous* and *cinereous*. You have a mistake in the use of a tense toward the bottom of p. 71: *has been repeated* should be *was repeated*. About the play: Mary and I have both read it and think it not one of your best productions. I doubt whether you could get it produced. The first scenes amused me, but I don't think there is enough to the idea to make it last through three acts—also, the unreality of everything gets on the reader's nerves before he understands that it is all a fantasy in the madman's mind; when he does find that out, he feels sold.

I have seen the Greenbergs[2] a number of times lately and had a very good time with them—though I have decided that Roman is to be seen at his best when he is perfectly sober and Sonya isn't there, as was the case when I met him one day in the afternoon. When we had dinner with them in a restaurant the other night, she handed him a small pocket mirror in the middle of the festivities so that he could see how his face was degenerating—visibly, in the course of the dinner—as a result of excessive drinking. He obediently looked at himself and seemed to be profoundly depressed. I also went with them to a Russian occasion which was *tout autrement intéressant* than the Stalinist evening I described to you: the first of a series of lectures devoted to rescuing the *Slovo o Polku Igorebe*[3] from the aspersions of André Mazon—a matter, I gathered, of patriotic duty. The discussion had many humors which would have amused you. Vernadsky[4] said that the French, not content with having burned the manuscript in Moscow, were now trying to deprive them of the poem itself.[5] The French Byzantologist Grégoire, who presided, seemed to get a little nettled by the Russians and the session ended with a debate which became, I thought, rather acrimonious.[6]

I am soon going to do a disappearing act and may go up alone to the Cape to get some writing done—in which case I'll whisk through Boston and look you up. Otherwise I'll be in New York or nearby and shall expect to see you the middle of April. Would you like me to get you a card to the Princeton Club, where you can get an excellent room for $2.50 and a lot of conveniences for nothing?

By the way, you will probably soon be hearing from a man named Weldon Kees, who is getting out an anthology of satire and wants to include two of your

New Yorker poems. You should charge him an anthology fee of *$10* apiece for them.

Best regards from all the family to you both.

As ever,
Edmund W.

I have never been able to get out of Weeks any higher price than $350 for a single article, and he says he does not pay any more. You certainly ought to try to get this, however.

1. A member of the Soviet writers' group "The Serapion Brothers" in the early 1920s, Pozner later emigrated to France where he joined the French Communist party and became a French writer. The principal theme of his French writings is the glorification of the Soviet Union and justification of Stalin. Pozner lived in the United States during World War II.

2. *I.e.,* the Grynbergs.

3. *The Song of Igor's Campaign,* often called *The Igor Tale* in English (Wilson's transcription of the Russian title reflects a confusion between the Cyrillic *в [v]* and the Latin *b*). Since the time its manuscript was discovered at the end of the eighteenth century, the authenticity of this great epic poem, claimed to date from the end of the twelfth century, has been one of the most vexing and fascinating problems of Russian literary historiography. The generally accepted view—that an unknown bard composed the poem around 1187 A.D.—has been challenged throughout the nineteenth and twentieth centuries by various scholars who sought to prove that the poem is an eighteenth-century forgery. In 1940, the French Slavicist André Mazon published a study that supported the forgery theory. The lecture Wilson describes was one of the series of lectures and discussions held at the École Libre des Hautes Études devoted to the study and refutation of Mazon's theory. The outcome of these discussions was the book *La Geste du Prince Igor, Épopée russe du douzième siècle,* edited by Henri Grégoire, Roman Jakobson and Marc Szeftel (New York, 1948). See also Wilson's letter of December 2, 1948 (Letter 189 of the present collection).

4. The historian George Vernadsky (1887–1973).

5. The manuscript of *The Song of Igor's Campaign* was lost in the flames when Moscow was burned during the French occupation in 1812.

6. Nabokov's contribution to *The Song of Igor's Campaign* controversy is his introductory essay and commentary to his translation of the poem into English (New York, 1960).

64

April 5, 1943

Dear Bunny,

I would like to see you so much—say, Wednesday night *the 14th*, 8:30 P.M. Thanks for suggesting the Princeton Club. I think I shall stay at the Wellington as I usually do. Do tell me your telephone number.

The Letters, 1943

Weeks paid me *300* for the story and added in an awed voice: "this is what we pay Bunny and this is the limit. (!)"

Here is a poem I sent to the editor of *Novoselye* in answer to an optimistic request for some of my stuff.

> Какимъ-бы полотномъ батальнымъ ни являлась
> советская сусальнѣйшая Русь,
> Какой бы жалостью душа ни наполнялась, —
> не поклонюсь, не примирюсь
>
> со всею мерзостью, жестокостью и скукой
> нѣмого рабства; нѣтъ, о нѣтъ —
> еще я духомъ живъ, еще не сытъ разлукой,
> — увольте, — я еще поэтъ![1]

I am delicately spreading the rumor that "Vladimir Pozner" is my pen-name.

Съ нѣжнымъ привѣтомъ
B[2]

1.   "No matter how the Soviet tinsel glitters
        Upon the canvas of a battle piece;
        No matter how the soul dissolves in pity,
        I will not bend, I will not cease

        Loathing the filth, brutality and boredom
        Of silent servitude. No, no, I shout,
        My spirit is still quick, still exile-hungry,
        I'm still a poet, count me out!"

This poem is dated 1944 in *Poems and Problems* and in Field's bibliography. The English translation was prepared by Nabokov for Vladimir Markov's anthology *Modern Russian Poetry* (1966).

2. "With affectionate regards, V."

65

7ᵗᵒ апрѣля 1943
Кэмбриджъ[1]

Dear Bunny,

as I may be in a post-prandial state when I see you Wednesday evening, please do not let Mary bother about dinner for me. Anyway I shall ring you up as soon as I arrive (часа въ четыре дня)[2]—but please pas de frais[3] on my account.

Oh yes, it was quite warm there. Sure. But my poem brings out that point nicely.[4] There is an electric note at the end which suggests the thermic paradox, if you know what I mean. Unfortunately you do.

до скорого![5]

Yours   V.

1. "April 7, 1943. Cambridge."
2. "About four in the afternoon."
3. "No expenses."
4. See the preceding letter.
5. "See you soon."

66

April 23, 1943

Dear Bunny,

You were going to tell me about a place you knew in N[ew] Mexico when something interrupted us. Do please give me some detailed information. What we want is a modest, but good boarding-house, in hilly surroundings. I remember collecting near a place which had some connection with Lawrence. We would like to spend the summer anywhere in the West,—I could not face another season of goldenrod.

I was so happy to see you and Mary. My friend Hessen[1] was very tongue-tied, I am afraid, but then it was his first outing. The weather in Virginia was perfectly dreadful and except for a few *everes comyntas* there was nothing on the wing; but Sweet Briar is a splendid place and my "contact with the audience" was absolutely perfect.

Твой,[2]

V. N.

Laughlin suggests our coming to Alta in summer. Do you know anything about that locality? He promises "moderate" terms.

1. George Hessen.
2. "Yours" (in the familiar, second-person singular form).

67

Dear Bunny,

Véra understood quite well, and we would have enjoyed coming hugely, but
we have hundreds of humdrums to do because we are leaving on the 21st for
Utah (I always want to write it «Юта»[1]—and of course all those lovely western
states will go to Russia after the war). We did not reply at once as Weeks had
told me that you were coming here this week. I want to see you very very much,
Bunny, but there is no way of cramming a visit to Cape Cod into this week
which as it is will hardly shut even if I sit upon it.

I have just sold to Weeks another story.[2] It will appear in the September issue, but I am sending you separately a copy—perhaps you may offer some созн-
дательной критики[3]—genitive, I suppose, after "some." Предложил хлеба[4]
(some bread). I shall soon begin dropping my hard signs and "yatjs"[5] if I have
another term of teaching.

At last my "Gogol through the Looking Glass" (is this title all right?) has
gone to Laughlin. It is a peach, an overripe peach with the velvet peeling off on
one buttock and a purple bruise on the other—but still a peach. A translator
called Guerney is going to do my Даръ.[6] I wonder if the "Mission to Moscow"[7]
will be shown to the public in Moscow, and if not how will our booted double-
breastpocketed friend explain things to the author.

Are you writing a lot? I liked your school recollections. I think I shall write
about my Tenishevskoe Oochilishche[8] soon—you have declenché[9] that particular sequence—the Russian teacher Vladimir Hippius (a wonderful poet of the
Bely school) at whom I threw a chair once; the terrific fist fights which I thoroughly enjoyed because, though weaker than the two or three main bullies, I
had had private lessons of boxing and savate (your Russian hits with the face
of the fist, opening his guard for the back swing and that is when a good An-
glosaxon uppercut comes in handy); and the soccer in the yard, and the nightmare exams, and the Polish boy who paraded his first clap, and the упои-
тельная синева невской весны.[10]

Kerensky is reported to have burst into tears upon being shown a copy of the
verse I sent you. I should love so much to read with you Griboyedov's Brains
Hurt.[11] Glorious stuff. The old man counting back nine months—«и по рас-
чету по моему»[12]—et pour cause.[13] And the wild cry for a carriage, for the
«Карета»[14] which took Russians to duels, foreign countries, exile and the Eka-
terininsky Kanal.[15] That and the Revizor[16] are the only great plays we have
produced.

I am sure you will understand the thrill I experienced to-day when a series of microscopic manipulations proved that *lotis* was a *scudderi* form and not a *melissa* one as had been supposed for seventy years.

I am dreadfully sorry that I shall not see you before leaving. We shall be back here at the end of August.

Yours

V.

Dear Edmund and Mary,

I am very sorry that we shall not be able to come, and also that V., who had promised to write you about it, waited so long for Edmund's coming here that now it is almost too late to write. Won't you be in Boston before we leave?

Sincerely yours,

Véra Nabokov

1. "Utah." In the Russian version of *Speak, Memory*, Nabokov transcribes it as «Ютаха.»

2. "That in Aleppo Once . . . ," which appeared in *The Atlantic Monthly* in November 1943.

3. "Constructive criticism" (in the genitive case).

4. "Offered some bread."

5. Letters in the pre-revolutionary Russian alphabet, which Nabokov used in his personal correspondence, but had to disregard in his teaching.

6. *The Gift* (which was actually translated into English only in the 1960s, by Michael Scammell).

7. A Hollywood film, based on the book by Ambassador Joseph E. Davies.

8. The Tenishev School in St. Petersburg.

9. "Unleashed."

10. "The enchanting blueness of springtime on the Neva."

11. Alexander Griboyedov's 1824 verse comedy, more usually known in English as *The Misfortune of Being Clever* or *Woe from Wit*.

12. "And according to my calculations" (the conjunction "and" should have been "but"). In the second act of Griboyedov's play, the important old bureaucrat Famusov tells his servant to note an appointment for the end of the current week: "Perhaps on Friday and perhaps on Saturday/I'll be the godfather at the christening of the doctor's widow's child./She has not yet given birth, but according to my calculations/It's about time she did."

13. "And for a good reason." The often overlooked implication of the passage is that Famusov has to have been responsible for the pregnancy of the doctor's widow. In *Ada* (p. 257), Demon Veen subtly asserts that he is the true father of Ada by citing the same Griboyedov quotation.

14. "Carriage." The play ends with the young hero's desperate cry for a carriage to take him away from the Moscow society he can no longer stand.

15. The canal in St. Petersburg, on the quai of which Sophia Perovskaya and her accomplices assassinated Alexander II.

16. *The Inspector General* by Gogol.

68

July 7, 1943
Wellfleet, Mass.

Dear Vladimir: Can you throw any light on either of the following matters?

(1) A man named V. S. Yanovsky[1] has written me asking for literary advice. He enclosed a little story from *Новоселье*,[2] which seems to me not bad, and a preposterous scenario for a novel, which sounds as if it had been written as a joke. Do you know anything about him? He tells me that «в среде русской Франции он пользовался некоторой популярностью.»[3] (Please send me back the scenario.)

(2) Dos Passos has brought in a moth that looks like this:

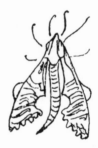

Can you tell me what it is? I couldn't find it in my little moth and butterfly book. It is evidently mimicking dead leaves.

I met last night a man named Calry,[4] who is staying with Nina Chavchavadze and who regaled me with stories of your adventures at Cambridge.

By the way, I was invited by people who had an exaggerated idea of my competence to lecture on Russian literature at Yale. I stopped off to see them on my way to New York and was presented with a mimeographed copy of Mr. Trager's Russian course, of which I had already heard from you. It is certainly something hair-raising. He has really invented an imaginary Slavic language written, like Polish, in Roman characters, to which Russian sounds are assigned, and wastes the students' time making them learn it before he teaches them the Russian alphabet. When he finally gets to the grammar, he unloads all the declensions and the verbs on them in half a dozen lessons. I don't wonder that you came back discouraged. I told them that they ought to get you to lecture on literature. They want to do a lot about Russia at Yale, but haven't the faintest idea how to go about it. Love to you all. I hope you are having a good vacation.

As ever,
Edmund W

1. V. S. (for Vasily Semyonovich) Yanovsky (1906–1989), physician and novelist, published three novels in Russian in Paris between 1930 and 1935. He emigrated to the United States in the 1940s. Here, he published several books in English, among them *Of Light and Sounding Brass* and *The Dark Fields of Venus*.

2. The émigré journal *The New Abode*.

3. "He enjoyed a certain popularity in the Russian milieu in France."

4. Count Robert Louis Magawly-Cerati de Calry, whose mother was Russian, a classmate of Nabokov's at Cambridge.

69

[Postmarked July 15, 1943]

Dear Bunny,

We had a very comfortable, cheap and wholly delightful journey. At Albany and Cleveland where we ночевали[1] we had not to bother about porters or taxis because there were not any; and there was plenty of standing room in the trains. Never in my life, not even in the wilds of Asia, have I had such good collecting as here. I climb easily to 12000 f[ee]t as our altitude is 8600 (which

incidentally has a disastrous effect on my pen). I screamed when I got my first *Cercyonis behri* Grin. What are the joys of literature compared to tracking an ovipositing *Caleophrys sheridani* Edw. to its food plant or boxing undescribed moths from the lobby windows of J. Laughlin's very pleasant though somewhat primitive hotel! The drawing you sent me is a fairly recognizable one of a Sphyngid (hawkmoth) belonging to the general genus *Smerinthus* and is probably *jamaicensis*. If so, it has eyespots on the secondaries (hind wings) which it discloses with a jerk from under its cryptic primaries (forewings) in order to frighten off such enemies as would not be taken in by its resemblance to a leaf. I liked very much Mary's criticism of Wilder's play in the *Partisan*.[3] I hated

Eastman's poem about Lot—which I think may be criticized from exactly the same point of view (juggling with anachronisms, etc.).[4]

Re Yanovsky. I have often met him in Paris and it is true that his work was appreciated by a certain coterie. He is a he-man [. . .], if you know what I mean. He cannot write. I happened to tell Aldanov that you were responsible for the facility I have in publishing my things here, and I suppose the story is going around, and you will get many more letters from my poor brethren.

Re Bobby de Calry. He is quite a character (a passive pansy, to be exact) with a pathetic fondness for titled Russians. He has haunted various nooks of my life like a mild ghost. I rather like him, although he does not really exist. I notice that his stories about me greatly improve with time. He is something out of an indifferent imitation of Proust. But still I like him.

Could you not come here? It is only an hour's drive from Salt Lake City. The tapering lines of firs on the slopes amid a greyish green haze of aspens remind me of the so-called "Russian" style in painting (Нестеровъ[5] for instance). The landlord and the poet are fiercely competing in Laughlin—with the first winning by a neck. Twenty years ago this place was a Roaring Gulch with golddiggers plugging each other in saloons, but now the Lodge stands in absolute solitude. I happened to read the other day a remarkably silly but rather charming book about a dentist who murdered his wife—written in the nineties and uncannily like a translation from Maupassant in style. It all ends in the Mohave Desert. The blurb says it is an "American classic" but I cannot believe it. Do you know it?[6]

I walk from 12 to 18 miles a day, wearing only shorts and tennis shoes. Curiously enough, in spite of the lepidoptera, my big novel is shaping out quite satisfactorily. Véra is a little disappointed with the climate here—there is *always* a cold wind blowing in this particular cañon. Dmitri has a great time catching butterflies and gophers and building dams. Weekenders come to inspect my captures and ask me whether butterflies *grow*.

Будь здоровъ, дорогой другъ[7]

В.

Best greetings from Véra to both of you.

1. "Spent the night." "The wilds of Asia" in this paragraph refers not to Nabokov's own travels (he never went to Asia) but to those of Fyodor's father in *The Gift*.

2. This spot resulted from Nabokov's spilling Carbona cleaning fluid (which he used to

put butterflies to sleep) on the page on which this letter was written. In the original, Nabokov wrote around the spot.

3. Mary McCarthy's angry review of Thornton Wilder's *The Skin of Our Teeth* in the January–February 1943 issue of *The Partisan Review* described the play as "a spoof on history" and an "anachronistic joke, a joke both provincial and self-assertive."

4. Max Eastman's narrative poem *Lot's Wife*, published as a separate book in 1942.

5. Mikhail Nesterov (1862–1942) was a portrait and landscape painter of a religious and mystical bent.

6. Nabokov must have had in mind *McTeague* by Frank Norris (1899) which served as the basis for Erich von Stroheim's famous film *Greed*.

7. "Stay well, dear friend."

70

[Postmarked August 23, 1943]

Dear Bunny

are you in New York? Because we shall spend three days there on our way back (5th–8th Sept.) and I have not got your address. We shall stay at N° 38 89th street. We want to see both of you very much. West.

I have trudged and climbed some 600 miles in the Wasatch Mts and made some superb entomological discoveries. Lovely melmoths and bread-and-butterflies.[1] A man was plugged in the diner by an envious prospector the other day. I have some good stories for you. Do drop me a note at 38 West 89th street, N.Y.

Очень дружески твой,

В. Сиринъ[2]

1. Two literary puns on entomological topics. "Melmoths" refers to the novel *Melmoth the Wanderer* (in four volumes, 1820) by Charles Maturin. It was translated into French one year after its first publication in Edinburgh and became hugely popular in France and Russia. Nabokov will have numerous occasions to comment on *Melmoth* in his annotated edition of Pushkin's *Eugene Onegin*.

The "bread-and-butter-fly" appears in Chapter III, "Looking-Glass Insects," of *Through the Looking Glass* by Lewis Carroll, where the Gnat describes it to Alice: "Its wings are thin slices of bread-and-butter, its body is a crust, and its head a lump of sugar." The Gnat explains that this insect lives on "weak tea with sugar in it" and that if it couldn't find any, "it would die, of course." To Alice's comment that this "must happen very often," the Gnat replies, "It always happens."

2. "Very amicably yours, V. Sirin."

71

November 1, 1943
Wellfleet, Mass.

Dear Vladimir: Here are proofs of my piece on Pushkin for the *Atlantic*.[1] The first one of these articles you may already have seen, as it came out in the same number with your story.[2] You may find them annoying, but they pretend to be nothing more than the first impressions of a foreigner. I hope to expand and improve them later and bring them out in a little book, and I wish you would give me the benefit of any ideas you may have about them. Please return this proof. I have written to Weeks suggesting that a group of your translations be printed with each of the pieces on the poets. I think that this is a wonderful idea.

I have been offered the book-reviewing job on the *New Yorker*, and have decided to take it for a year. (Do get out some books within the next year, so that I can write about them.) So that we are going to New York for the rest of the winter about the first of December. Now can't you people come up to see us before then? Nina Chavchavadze is staying with us, and we are all very anxious to see you. Mary is in New York looking for an apartment or would write you. How about coming for Thanksgiving—November 25th—as you did three years ago (when you conceived your great refrigerator poem)? Do try to make it. We will close our season here with a festival, and try to arrange some formidable inconvenience for you, so that you can afterwards write something that can be published in the *New Yorker*.

I have just read Gogol's "Viy," which is certainly one of the greatest stories of the kind ever written. That little wooden church out on the edge of the town with the dogs howling around it, is wonderful.

As ever,
Edmund W

[...]

1. The second installment ("Pushkin") of Wilson's three-part series "Notes on Russian Literature" which appeared in *The Atlantic Monthly* in the November and December 1943 and January 1944 issues. The series was later included, in revised form, in *A Window on Russia*.
2. The first installment appeared in the same issue (November 1943) as Nabokov's story "That in Aleppo Once . . ."

72

Dear Bunny,

I am returning your proofs. Véra and I liked both this and the other article *enormously*.[1] You will find a few mild alterations which I have made. One of them is however important. There is no metonymy or synecdoche in Pushkin's use of "volna."[2] The sea-wave is a recognised character both in Russian folklore and in Pushkin's poetry. Its glassy concavity (facing you as it is about to topple over), trimmed on top with the convex brimming of foam, breeds the armed merman, the barrel-babe[3] and the mammiferous lepidosirens of our enchanted "lookomorias."[4] Its serried multiplicity is the image of the ever recurrent human individual. With Tyutchev it is a rearing steed shattering its emerald forehoofs against the rock.[5] It is a person in the impersonal ocean. All Russian poets have it in one way or another. It is free and roving (because *gulliva* means this and n o t "indolent"—it comes from *gulyat, gulba, razgulny*[6] etc.)

Incidentally I do not believe that the staccato of the English trochee as for instance "Tiger, tiger, burning bright in the jungle of the night" (in spite of the jungle juggling in something of the jingling "gulliva")[7] really renders the corresponding Russian metre with its serpentine inflections—curves and breaks which are due to causes I have once discussed with you. I suggest therefore:

> Seawave, o seawave, o you wave,
> ever a rover and nobody's slave

or—if you mean to cling to the skeleton of the metre:

> O my seawave, roving wave,
> you that nothing can enslave

You will note that I am on the verge of a hideous pun—O my Wave, my Wave (W.A.V.E.).[8]

I am not particularly pleased with my casual effort but I am quite sure that your navy-blue "sea—free" with its rather awful suggestion of "freedom of the seas" is quite wrong.[9]

I am sending a first batch*) of translations, mainly from Tyutchev as the rest of Pushkin still needs some pruning. You will see that I have delicately toyed with one or two images—greatly improving them.

We hope to be able to come for Thanksgiving Day. You might round up some belated moths.

I am glad that you have joined the *New Yorker*.

Our love to both of you.

V.

*) on second thoughts I am sending you the whole book,[10] and will be безко-
нечно благодаренъ ежели ты внесешь кое-гдѣ необходимыя исправленія и
улучшенія. Работа была аховая, особенно Памятникъ.[11]

B.

1. *I.e.*, the first two installments of "Notes on Russian Literature."

2. In the Pushkin section of "Notes on Russian Literature," Wilson cited two lines from
Pushkin's fairy tale in verse "The Tale of Tsar Saltan": "Ty volna moya, volna!/Ty gul'liva
i vol'na," which he translated into English as "O thou, my sea, my sea/So indolent and free."
In his commentary to these lines, Wilson wrote: "Pushkin here uses metonymically the
word for *wave* for *sea* . . ."

3. In "The Tale of the Tsar Saltan" the wave is apostrophized by the baby Prince Guidon,
adrift with his mother in a barrel.

4. *Lukomorie* is an archaic and poetic word for "sea cove." It is best known in the Russian
tradition through its use in the opening line of Pushkin's "Ruslan and Ludmila."

5. Reference to Tyutchev's poem "The Sea Horse" (1830).

6. "To carouse, revelry, [one] leading a wild life."

7. The "jungle juggling" is, of course, Nabokov's own contribution, since Blake's poem
has "forest" rather than "jungle."

8. "Waves" were members of the Women's Appointed Volunteer Emergency Service
during World War II.

9. For all of Nabokov's eloquence on the subject of the wave vs. the sea, Wilson left his
translation and commentary without change when he included the article in *A Window on
Russia* (1972).

10. *Three Russian Poets.*

11. "Boundlessly grateful if you will enter the necessary corrections and improvements
here and there. It was a formidable task, especially in 'Exegi Monumentum' [by Push-
kin]. V."

73

November 10, 1943
Wellfleet, Mass.

Dear Vladimir: We are absolutely counting on you for Thanksgiving. To let us
down would be inexcusable, because we are going to order a turkey of a size
based on the assumption that you will all be here. It is also very important for
us to be able to sit down and take time to go over these translations. What I have

read of them so far are wonderful—it is only occasionally that your English goes off the track.

I am afraid that it is too late to do anything about the Pushkin piece—though I am writing Weeks to try to at least to get the *Chestnoy* and *да ведь*[1] corrected. I quite agree that my translation of the *Ty volna moya, volna* passage is lousy. Thank you for your trouble going through it.

I have an idea that I would like to discuss with you. How would it be if we collaborated on a book on Russian literature—I contributing these essays (somewhat expanded), you contributing translations. Since you haven't signed a contract with [. . .] Laughlin, you are free to dispose otherwise of these verse translations, and perhaps you could do a few in prose. I find for example that "Viy," which seems to me a masterpiece, has only appeared in translation in a collection done years ago in England and probably impossible to get. We could split the proceeds, and have something, I am convinced, that, with the mounting interest in Russian, would have a certain sale. There would be nothing like it in English. It may be that you would rather do your own book, but do think about the idea a little.

I have discovered two wonderful Russian verbs: *примелькаться* and *приедаться*. How would you translate them?[2]

As ever,
Edmund W

1. "Of honorable" and "and what a . . ." which occur in the extended passage from Pushkin's "Count Nulin," quoted at length and translated into English by Wilson.
2. See the second paragraph of the next letter for Nabokov's translation of and commentary on these two verbs. Wilson must have been reading the fifth section, "Mutiny at Sea," of Boris Pasternak's historical narrative poem "Year 1905" ("Deviat'sot piatyi god," 1926–1927), where these verbs occur in the first line.

74

Dear Bunny,

Please, don't order the turkey of extra bulk because Dmitri has a bad cold again, with fever, and we should hate to have to wire at the last moment "not coming."

Èto mne prielos' means I am fed up with it, or in a more literal sense it jades my palate. *Èto primel'kalos'*—I have had enough of this sight, or it has become familiar (to the eye) through repetition. I have seen so much of it that I have stopped noticing it.

I should love to launch that book together with you. I have mailed Laughlin the same batch of poems that I sent you and am expecting him to ask me to add a little life of each poet. This will give me a good excuse to back out. Are you sure that we shall find a publisher? If you are quite serious about this project let me know at once [. . .].

Please, do send me your corrections.

I am enclosing the remarkable agreement (which I have not yet signed) between L. and me. The *Sebastian Knight* agreement (which I have signed by now) (Russians hate signing anything) contains two amusing clauses, too.

I remain, dear Sir, very truly your obedient servant

V.

November 12, 1943

75

November 12, 1943
Wellfleet, Mass.

Dear Vladimir: There is a chance that Weeks will use some of your translations with my Tyutchev article in January;[1] but I should like to have a chance to go over them with you first. I am sending a proof of my article. Please be sure to send it back. I dare say that I get a little beyond myself in my remarks on Russian eighteenth century poetry, which are mainly at second hand, and I am reading up Derzhavin[2] in an effort to know what I am talking about.

Since I wrote you before, I have been thinking more about the project I wrote you about. Do think seriously about undertaking a book with me. We could get a considerable advance for it right down. Don't say anything about it in the meantime, though—and leave your affairs with Laughlin where they are. I believe I could sell the idea to Doubleday and perhaps get them to take your novel, too. All these matters will absolutely necessitate your coming up here for Thanksgiving.

I am sorry that it is too late to do anything about my godawful translation of the *Tsar Saltan*—in the book I will use yours.

As ever,
Edmund W.

1. The third installment of "Notes on Russian Literature" ("Tyutchev").
2. Gavriil Derzhavin (1743–1816), usually considered Russia's finest eighteenth-century poet.

76

November 23, 1943
Кембриджъ Бостонскій[1]

Dear Bunny,

some of them had little red cherries—abscesses—and the man in white was pleased when they came out whole, together with the crimson ivory. My tongue feels like somebody coming home and finding his furniture gone. The plate will only be ready next week—and I am orally a cripple. He said there could be no question of my going to Cape Cod. It is a bitter disappointment.

I was lying on my bed groaning as the frost of the drug gradually gave way to the heat of pain[2]—and as I could not work, I lay there yearning for a good detective story—and at that very moment the *Taste for Honey*[3] sailed in. Mary was right, I enjoyed it hugely—though the entomological part is of course all wrong (in one passage he confuses the Purple Emperor, a butterfly, with the Emperor moth). But it is very nicely written. Did Mary see the point of the detective's *name* at the very end? I did.

I was so upset and in such pain that I am afraid the notes I scribbled on your proofs are somewhat peevish. It is wonderful that anybody could write about Russian letters as you do. Still, I somehow did not like Tyutchev quite as much as I liked the others. You talked to him as he was on his way to the post office, or at a "five o'clock tea" *chez la petite princesse N-sky,* or beneath the pink chestnut trees of a European spa,—but you did not visit him at his house and did not spend the night talking.

Housman *has* affinities with him—you are quite right,—but why that stucco de Vigny? Housman had got something about a dead man whose over-coat is now the terrestrial globe,—quite literally—a huge wrapper. That's another link with Tewtchev.

Good old Laughlin writes me he has written to you suggesting you write a few words for the poems. I still hope you will arrange the other business.

Please send me your corrections of my stuff.

When my face is reflected by some spherical surface, I have often noticed a curious resemblance with the Angel (you know—the wrestler); but now an ordinary mirror produces this effect.

Best love from both of us to both of you,

Did you notice in the papers the way the two Turkeys got rather mixed up in the headlines?

The Letters, 1943

1. "The Bostonian Cambridge."

2. Nabokov's ordeal by dentistry was eventually transmuted into literary art in *Pnin* (Chapter Two, section 4). The following lines in the novel make for a particularly revealing comparison to this letter:

> A warm flow of pain was gradually replacing the ice and wood of the anesthetic in his thawing, still half-dead, abominably martyred mouth. [...] His tongue, a fat sleek seal, used to flop and slide so happily among the familiar rocks, checking the contours of a battered but still secure kingdom, plunging from cave to cove, climbing this jag; nuzzling that notch, finding a shred of sweet seaweed in the same old cleft; but now not a landmark remained and all there existed was a great dark wound, a terra incognita of gums which dread and disgust forbade one to investigate.

3. A detective novel by Gerald Heard (Henry Fitzgerald Heard), first published in 1941 and later retitled *A Taste for Murder.*

77

[After] November 23, 1943[1]
Wellfleet, Mass.

Dear Vladimir: We are terribly sorry to hear about your crisis of dentistry. Don't let them pull out too many—they tend to overdo this in America. I have several teeth that are functioning perfectly that the dentists told me I ought to have out years ago. Everybody is extremely disappointed that you are not coming up for Thanksgiving. Couldn't you come up some day next week before we go (Sunday)? I think that you and I really ought to have a talk about (1) your Tyutchev translations; (2) strategy in handling Laughlin and our projected book.

He has written me, buttering me up and asking about a foreword. He is going to be furious with me if I induce you not to give him your translations, and may refuse to publish the Fitzgerald book[2]—so I want to get this latter matter settled first. He may refuse to publish it anyway, however, in which case the coast will be clear. You will simply pay him back the sum he has advanced out of the advance you get from some other publisher.

Thank you very much for your commentary on my article. I have profited by it and made corrections. Weeks writes me that he wants the whole thing this week, so I am sending off to him all your Tyutchev translations. He says he may be able to use two pages of them, and I hope he can use them all. There are a few lines that I think might be bettered—where the English is a little off—

but you could attend to that in proof. Otherwise, they are very fine, and ought to give to English-speaking readers for the first time some idea of what Tyutchev is really like.

I have just read *Shinel*,[3] and want to see your translation of this, too. (See other side of sheet.) Have also read a little book of essays on Russian poetry by your friend Hodasevich[4]—excellent. There is one in which he traces the relation between *Domik v Kolomne, Pikovaya Dama*, and *Medny Vsadnik*,[5] and a story that Pushkin told at Karamzin's and that somebody else wrote and published, which is a masterpiece in its kind—the sort of literary detective work that I like to do myself.[6]

I have a lot of ideas about our proposed book—but shall hope to see you to discuss them. If you are hard up, with all that dentistry, I wish you would let me lend you the money to come up here. I am rich for the first time in my life.

As ever,
Edmund W

[Verso]

I don't think that *даже* exactly means *even* in Gogol, but, as we should say, *in fact*, or as a *matter of fact*. Dickens, too, has this kind of thing. And isn't his use of *тут же* and *словом*[7] a part of the same tone? Micawber and other characters in Dickens talk rather like the man who is telling the story of Captain Kopeikin.[8] These phrases of Gogol's are the author's equivalent for the *так сказать*'s,[9] etc. of the comic narrator. So Dickens' own style has a good deal in common with Micawber's. Gogol himself wants to give an impression of his being himself close to the slow-witted and long-winded people that he likes to write about.

1. The letter is dated November 23, but since it is a reply to Nabokov's letter of the same date, it must have been written a few days later.
2. *The Crack-Up* (see Letter 125, note 1).
3. "The Overcoat" (by Gogol).
4. Vladislav Khodasevich, *Essays on Russian Poetry* (1922).
5. "The Little House in Kolomna," "The Queen of Spades," and "The Bronze Horseman."
6. The origin of this story was later treated by Wilson in the third section of his "Notes on Pushkin," initially published in the *New York Review of Books* of December 3, 1970, and subsequently included in *A Window on Russia*.
7. "Right there" and "in a word."
8. *I.e.*, the postmaster in *Dead Souls*.
9. "So to speak."

78

Dear Bunny,

I should like to come Friday evening (I am now armed orally with a tip-top plap-plopping plate) if possible.

Upon Weeks' request I had sent him my stuff before you did. I am lunching with our gentle friend on Tuesday and want to know in advance whether you have suggested to him any special fee for the verses. Could you tell me?

You are absolutely right about the «даже» business,—those possibilities had not occurred to me—but there is one little methodological hitch in this respect which I shall discuss with you.

I am so glad you enjoyed Ходасевичъ.[1] He was a splendid personality. You must read his *Державинъ*[2] one day.

A summary of part of my scientific work on the Blues (the *Lycaeides* genus—"Silver studded Blues" in English) in which I correlate the nearctic and palaearctic representatives, is due to appear in a week or two.[3] The labour involved has been immense; the number of my index cards exceeds a thousand references—for half a dozen (very polytypic) species; I have dissected and drawn the genitalia of 360 specimens and unraveled taxonomic adventures that read like a novel. This has been a wonderful bit of training in the use of our (if I may say so) wise, precise, plastic, beautiful English language.

Let me know by Tuesday morning if possible whether Friday is all right and what afternoon train to take. Thanks for your sweet offer, but I think I can just manage it.

V.

1. Khodasevich. See his essay "On Sirin" in *Tri-Quarterly* (No. 17), 1970 and the essays on Khodasevich by Nabokov and Robert P. Hughes in *The Bitter Air of Exile,* Simon Karlinsky and Alfred Appel, Jr., editors, 1977.

2. *Derzhavin,* a brilliant critical biography of the eighteenth-century poet, published in Paris in 1931.

3. "The Nearctic Forms of *Lycaeides Hüb[ner]*" (see Letter 59, note 4).

79

Dear Bunny,

Many thanks. I shall take the 2 o'clock train and shall bring Gog[ol] and Tyut[chev].

I hope you will recognise me—I shall carry your telegram in my hand. Love from both of us to both of you.

Tvoi[1]
V.

1. "Yours V." (in the familiar, second-person singular form).

80

8 Craigie Circle
Cambridge

December 10, 1943

Dear Mary and Bunny,

I hope that you are in New York by now. That was a most enjoyable weekend, but I am quite sure that the Laughlin contract has remained lying in your study (or in the other—more suitable—place) because I did not bring it back with me and cannot remember your having given it to me. This is not very important, but still ought to be noted. [. . .] I shall write another letter saying that after all I prefer not to include *Shinel*[1] in the Gogol book. Thus we shall be able to use it for our classic—because really, you know, I have reread «Вий»[2] and cannot work up any enthusiasm for it—it is one of Gogol's weakest efforts, повѣрь мнѣ![3] I think some of the details of the Teheran meeting are delightful, for instance: "Stalin talked *freely* to his guests through an *interpreter*," or "Stalin raised his glass and looked *soberly* around." Judging by the photographs it is quite obvious that it is not the real Stalin, but one of his many duplicates— a stroke of genius on the part of the Soviets. I am not even sure whether this tussaudesque figure is real at all since the so-called interpreter, a Mr. Pavlovsk (?), who appears in all the pictures as a kind of Puppenmeister,[4] is obviously the man responsible for the uniformed doll's movements. Note the crease of the false Joe's trousers in exhibit No 3. Only wax figures have that kind of trouser leg. I am thinking of writing a full account of the business, because it was really beautifully ingenious—especially when the dummy circulated and jerkily drank 34 toasts. Mr. Pavlovsk is a great conjuror.

I got a letter from the *New Republic* asking me to review a couple of books. One of them is all about Russian humour, by Cournos,—I have not read it yet—and the other is a collection by Guerney. I am in a bilious mood and so hope that both books are comfortably bad.[5]

I did not think much of the "Judas Window," Mary. It is not your best effort.

Gogol's mother used to be quite, quite sure that her son had written *every* book that appeared during his lifetime and that he was also responsible for the invention of steamers, locomotives and mills. It made him frantic and his letters of (detailed) denial to her are most amusing. Still that lucky shot through the keyhole is not quite convincing and you ought to have found something better.[6]

We had an awful storm yesterday. I hope your house on Cape Cod is not wrecked as then the Laughlin contract would be hopelessly lost.

Give my warmest привѣтъ[7] to the Grynbergs if you see them. I hope you are not stranded in Poughkeepsie.

Affectionately yours,

V.

1. "The Overcoat."

2. "Viy."

3. "Believe me."

4. "Puppeteer."

5. Nabokov's review of *A Treasury of Russian Life and Humor*, edited by John Cournos, and of *A Treasury of Russian Literature*, edited by B. G. Guerney, appeared in *The New Republic* of January 17, 1944 under the title "Cabbage Soup and Caviar."

6. Although the context seems to indicate that "Judas Window" is a work by Mary McCarthy, she wrote nothing bearing this title. *Judas Window* is the title of the mystery novel by John Dickson Carr, published in 1938 under his pseudonym Carter Dickson. The novel contains the situation described in this paragraph. (Information courtesy of Professor Francis M. Nevins, Jr.)

7. "Regards."

81

THE NEW YORKER

No. 25 West 43rd Street

December 15, 1943

Dear Vladimir: Here is the fatal contract. The man at Doubleday is ill, so that I shan't be able to see him till the first of next week, and can't tell you anything definite. If, as I hope, you can disengage these two other books from Laughlin, you ought to get from him a new contract relating only to the Gogol book. This contract, of course, shouldn't have the option clause. I think you can let the rest of the contract go, for the purposes of the Gogol book.

I have been thinking about our projected book; and it seems to me now that it would perhaps be better for you to do merely a set of translations of verse.

Shinel[1] really belongs in your Gogol book, and we both probably have better things to do than sweating over translating Gogol. (There is a translation of *Shinel* in the Cournos anthology, which I looked at in a book-store the other day, and it seemed to me rather on the "broken English" side.) I forgot to mention to you at Wellfleet my idea that it might be a good thing to translate the Repetilov scene of *Gore ot Uma*,[2] but I believe that this, too, would be more trouble than it would be worth. I will write you more about all this when I have talked to Doubleday.

Yes: the Teheran conference was wonderful—especially when Roosevelt lifted the sword and said, "Truly, a heart of steel!" Obviously nothing came out of it except some kind of old-fashioned deal which is being concealed from the public.

It was wonderful to see you up in the country. Since we have come down here and are settled in a comfortable and quiet but rather vacuous apartment, I have been missing my base at Wellfleet, and everything around me seems of an emptiness that opens right out on the interstellar spaces. I think that airplanes, in changing our point of view on the permanence and authority of human habitations, are also damaging our intellectual and imaginative constructions. The city doesn't mean to me any more what it did when I first came to work here after the last war, and I really get along better in my house on the Cape which we at least have the illusion of filling ourselves. Etc.

As ever,

EW

We arrived in New York all ill after a trip that went on for three days, and had an element of picaresque adventure.

1. "The Overcoat."
2. *The Misfortune of Being Clever* by Griboyedov (see Letter 67).

82

8 Craigie Circle
Cambridge 38, Mass.

December 21st 1943.

Dear Bunny,

Here is the Howl:

"Dear Nabokov—

I would like to oblige you in the matter of the translations but I don't

see how I can. Your volume is part of the series and I have nothing to substitute. The book was promised to the subscribers for some months ago
and I really can't do anything but give it to them. If only we had known
of this six months ago it would have been feasible because then something else would have been prepared to put in its place.

It occurs to me that if this publisher offers so much money (I did not
tell him how much) he must be thinking of a large sale. Therefore our
small edition would hardly stand in his way. I would be willing to let him
use the poems in *his* book after a lapse of time had allowed us a normal
sale in ours. Why don't you have him write to me about this.

I do hate to stand in your way for a good sum of money but I just can't
stop the publication at this last moment.

Terribly sorry!
J. L."

What shall I do now? Can he consider me legally tied? Does his letter make
any sense? *Na vsyakyi sloochay*[1] I have just sent him a nightletter: "Please do
not start printing poems stop I dont agree with your standpoint am writing."

But I shall not write until I hear from you. Véra will be for one day in New
York, on the 28th of December. If you think you have more to discuss than you
can put into the soliloquy of a letter she could talk it over with you. In the
meanwhile, should I not better return his 75 pieces of silver straightaway as
there are some convenient aspen-poplars around his house?

Embracing you
V

1. "Just in case."

83

THE NEW YORKER
No. 25 West 43rd Street

December 30, 1943

Dear Vladimir: The man I do business with at Doubleday has had a relapse and
taken to his bed again, so that I shan't be able to see him again till he recovers.
In the meantime, we can be sure of getting $1500 from them, which we can
split between us. I think that your ideal arrangement with Laughlin would be

to make him publish the Gogol and let you keep the advance (being sure to sign a new contract for this book), but to get the other two books away from him, and pay him back his advances on them. I think you can make him do this if you are firm with him. There is no reason why you should give him the Gogol, as he suggests, with no advance on his part. If he insists on keeping the translations, that doesn't matter, if he will allow them to be reprinted a year afterwards—the understanding being, of course, that the new publisher is not to pay him anything for them.

The editor of Pocket Books has just asked me to do them an anthology of Russian short stories. I referred him to you. He wanted to know whether your political point of view was such that you would be unwilling to include Soviet stories, and I told him I didn't think so. If you do it, you ought to get at least $1000.

Happy New Year to you all!

Edmund W

[Added at top]
That letter of Laughlin's that you read to me was just what was to be expected.

1944

84

THE PRINCETON CLUB
OF NEW YORK

January 1, 1944

Dear Vladimir: I saw Lionel Trilling last night and asked him what his arrangements with Laughlin had been for his E. M. Forster book. He said that L. had given him $200 down, but that he had had a terrible time getting L. to pay him any royalties—I am not sure that he has ever been able to collect any. He remarked that the letters he had had from L. were incredible. So I don't think you ought to let him bring out the Gogol without hanging on to your advance: you may never get any money at all otherwise.

Happy New Year!

E. W.

85

V. Nabokov
8 Craigie Circle
Cambridge 38, Mass.

January 3rd, 1944

Dear Bunny,

You seem to have done a marvelous job with the selling of our book. Spas-sibo.[1] You will find enclosed a copy of my letter to [Laughlin]. Véra has had a serious conversation with me in regard to my novel. Having sulkily pulled it out from under my butterfly manuscripts I discovered two things, first that it was good, and second that the beginning some twenty pages at least could be typed and submitted. This will be done speedily. I have lain with my Russian muse after a long period of adultery and am sending you the big poem she bore.[2] It will probably go to the *Novyi Journal*.[3] You will find it much easier to read than some of my former stuff. Please, do read it. I have also almost finished a story in English.

An obscure paper on some obscure butterflies in an obscure scientific journal is another sample of Nabokoviana which will soon be in your hands.

The right procedure is to have your hero while on a visit to Spain at the close of the 15th century, *not* meet there a certain Genoese navigator. Aldanov keeps doing the opposite thing. This is my only grudge against a dear friend and a gifted writer.

I envied Véra immensely when she told me about seeing you.

We both wish you and Mary a perfect year.

V.

Papilio bunnyi

I was just about to mail this letter when I got yours. I have already sent the прилагаемое письмо[4] to [Laughlin], but I think I have been firm enough. Или нѣтъ?[5] Thanks for suggesting me to the publisher of Russian stories. From the literary material produced during 25 years of the Soviet rule I could select about a dozen readable shorts (Zoshchenko, Kaverin, Babel, Olesha, Prishvin,

Zamiatin, Leonov—и обчелся[6]). I think that my main grudge against the good old Soviets is that they produce such execrable literature, but, as I say, with a little tact I could choose a few eatable plums out of the rot—although I shall feel like a beggar rummaging in a garbage can.

1. "Thank you."
2. "The Paris Poem."
3. *The New Review,* where "The Paris Poem" was published (No. 7, 1944). It was later included, with an English translation, in *Poems and Problems.*
4. "Enclosed letter."
5. "Or haven't I?"
6. "And that's all there is."

86

THE NEW YORKER
No. 25 West 43rd Street

January 4, 1944

Dear Vladimir: Doubleday wants to get it perfectly clear what your understanding with Laughlin is about the poems before any agreement is signed; so do try to get something definite out of him sometime fairly soon.

As ever,

EW

They also insist that the book shall be titled "*So and So* by E. W., with translations by V. N.," so that people will not think we collaborated on the prose. Do you mind? I am not particularly in favor of it, and have stipulated that both our names should appear in the same size of type. I have extorted truly terrific terms from them. You will see when you sign the contract. Elder is going to write you about your novel.

87

January 7, 1944

Dear Bunny,

I expect him to reply soon, but anyway if there is *any* trouble with the poems, I am quite ready to *make lots of new translations for our book*. For instance a scene from *Boris Godunov* and perhaps a passage from One-gin and of course some more Pushkin lyrics. *And* other poets.

It was nice of you to worry about the nomenclatorial aspect, but I think D. D. are quite right.

[. . .]

I, or rather Véra, have-has typed out already ten pages of the *Person from Porlock*.

Some People[1] has always been a favorite of mine, but in the Russian chapter he confuses the Moscow restaurant "Hermitage" with the Hermitage museum in Petersburg.[2] I shall discuss the gnoseological problem of when is a mob a mob when I see you.

Yours,

V.

1. By Harold Nicolson.
2. See Letter 238, note 6.

88

[Early January 1944]

Dear Bunny,

I am sending you the socks you lent me and a sample of my translation of You-gin One-gin. I made a hole in one of them and Véra was not sure that her rather simple patching methods would satisfy you, but then she noticed that Mary had used the same Pied Piper idea when doing *her* bit, so she thinks it will be all right.

No answer from [Laughlin] yet, but as I told you in my last letter it does not much matter whether he agrees or not. I wrote a nice letter to Doubleday and Doran in reply to a similar one from Elder. I have already more than twenty pages of my novel nicely typed and will send them some thirty in all next week. To you first, if you have time.

I heard the other day at the Faculty club (at a meeting of the Entomological Society) the funniest story I have ever heard in my life. I shall enjoy telling it you.

The appended translation is a sample of a new method I have found after some scientific thinking—and it seems to me that it is the right one for translating Onegin. It is just a sample, but if you approve of it I shall translate some more passages—tell me which ones you would like to have.

Yours,

V.

89

January 15, 1944

Dear Vladimir: ① [...]

② The *Onegin* fragment is good.[1] The first of the Tyutchevs in the *Atlantic*[2] is particularly good: you make charming use of the rhyming device *(prism, is m-)* that you exploit with more virtuosity in your Russian poem. Did you invent this?

③ The Russian poem I have carefully read, and appreciated the urinal, the moon and (other) happy strokes; but I am partly in the dark as to what it is all about. Who is the похлость[3]—Stalin? I tried to get Aldanov, whom I saw the other night, to explain it to me, but I couldn't get much out of him except that you were scoring off certain Russians in Paris.

④ Katharine White,[4] one of the creators of the *New Yorker*, who has been living for some years in Maine, has come back to work in the paper. One of the ideas she came back with was to get you to do stories for them. She had torn out all your things in the *Atlantic*—is very anxious to meet you when you come on. When I go to the office, I will send you her memorandum to me on the subject. It might possibly be worth while to try them with "Spring in Fialta."

⑤ I have just had a letter from Nikolai announcing his descent on New York next week.

⑥ You torture me by not writing this entomological story.

⑦ Thanks for returning the socks, which you needn't have bothered about.

⑧ Don't you think you ought to come in to New York sometime soon for a further conference about our project?

⑨ I am beginning to get enraged letters from old subscribers to the *New Yorker*. One lady, who was indignant about my treatment of Kay Boyle's novel this week,[5] wrote me a terrible letter beginning, "I do not like thee, Dr. Fell!" (I suppose you know that rhyme out of *Tom Brown's School Days*.)[6]

Love to Vera,

as ever,

Edmund W

1. Nabokov's rhymed translation of three stanzas from Pushkin's *Eugene Onegin* subsequently appeared in the Spring 1945 issue of *The Russian Review*.

2. Nabokov's translation of three poems by Tyutchev accompanied the third installment of Wilson's "Notes on Russian Literature" (devoted to Tyutchev) in the January 1944 issue of *The Atlantic Monthly*.

3. Lines 3 and 4 of "The Paris Poem" read (in Nabokov's own translation into English): "Give some thought to the needs of that scoundrel:/He was once an angel like you." Wilson misread the word for scoundrel (in the prepositional case), *prokhvoste*, as *poshlost'* (see Letter 92, note 1); he spelled it *pokhlost'*, however, either through a contamination from *prokhvoste* or through a possible confusion between the Russian *x* and the Greek *chi*.

4. "My friendship with Catharine *[sic]* White and Bill Maxwell of *The New Yorker* is something the most arrogant author cannot evoke without gratitude and delight." Nabokov's interview with Herbert Gold, *Strong Opinions*, p. 99.

5. Wilson's review of Kay Boyle's novel *Avalanche* appeared in *The New Yorker* on January 15, 1944 and was later reprinted in *Classics and Commercials*.

6. This is either an elaborate trap for Nabokov or a case of curious confusion on Wilson's part. The saying "I do not love you, Dr. Fell" does not come from the once popular novel about English schoolboys by Thomas Hughes mentioned by Wilson. It is rather the first line of the English adaptation of the Roman poet Martial's epigram "Non amo te, Sabidi" (*Epigrams* I, xxxii) by Thomas Brown (1663–1704). The adaptation reads:

> I do not love you, Dr. Fell,
> But why I cannot tell.
> But this I know full well,
> I do not love you, Dr. Fell.

90

January 18, 1944

Dear Bunny,

1) I am sending you a grand letter from good old J. I think we were wrong in our harsh condemnation of that pure and noble soul. What a guy! (a fellow-passenger in the wilds of Virginia once made an unconscious pun during a literary conversation we had in the gentlemen's lounge: "that guy Maupassant...")

2) I am also sending you a) the poem I mailed some time ago to the *New Yorker;* b) another bit of *Onegin* (the first line of the first song was Véra's trouvaille—you will note that "best tradition" echoes «честныхъ правилъ»[1] and c) thirty seven (37) pages of my novel *The Person from Porlock* which, if you think it feasible, please pass on to Doubleday (and of course to Doran, too) after perusal. There are lots of little things which I shall weed out eventually, but generally speaking these first chapters of *The Person from Porlock* will stand as they are. Towards the end of the book, which will contain 315 pages, there will be the looming and development of an idea which has *never* been treated before.

3) I am applying for a renewal of the Guggenheim grant and am sending Moe[2] samples of work done during this year. I have had lately a rather ex-

hausting burst of literary activity and am now reverting with relief to my *Ly-caenidae*. The novel will be completed by the end of June before a collecting trip I am contemplating to make to Mendocino Co[unty], Cal. where I want to look for *Lycaeides scudderi lotis* which, so far, is known only in two speci-mens—the ♀ holotype and what I have fixed in my paper as the ♂ neotype.

4) Give my love to Nicholas and tell him that he never answered a long letter which I wrote, or meant to write, him.

5) I invented the rhyme combining a dactylic and a feminine ending—and many other minor tricks. I am sorry that you discussed my poem with friend Aldanov who for twenty years has been eyeing my literature with a kind of suspicious awe under the impression that my chief business was to demolish brother-writers. There is of course nothing of the kind in my poem nor any-thing about Stalin, but of course Aldanov regards literature as a sort of enor-mous Pen Club or Masonic Lodge binding talented and *talentlos* writers alike to a smug contract of mutual good-will, consideration, assistance and favorable reviews. *Never* discuss Khodasevich with him.

6) "Fell" rhymes with the inability to "tell." If you ever tackle Pomialovsky's *Bursaki*[3] you will find a curious parallel to "Tom Brown's School Days."

7) I may come to New York for a couple of days later on. I would dearly love to see you as I always do.

8) Some years ago Doubleday and Doran published Holland's *Butterfly Book*.[4] I have been saying nasty things about the terrific blunders in that book in my last entomological papers. But the plates are good—and I intend—this is serious—suggesting to D. D. that I make complete revision of the last (1931) edition—practically rewriting the text and bringing the whole thing up to date. It first appeared in 1898 and sixty-five thousand copies were sold. The long-winded, misleading and hopelessly inadequate text consists of some 400 unnecessary pages—but it is the only comparatively inexpensive work (15 dol-lars, I think) which illustrates (although often under the wrong names) at least 90% of the butterfly-fauna of North America. Barbour, or Banks, or Comstock[5] of the Am[erican] Mus[eum of] Nat[ural] Hist[ory] N.Y. would tell them, if they do not know, that I am well qualified for this work. What do you think of this idea?

Yours very much

V.

[In margin]
Don't tell Aldan[ov] what the novel is about—he might think I was scoring off someone or other.

[At top, upside down]

Yes, of course—I shall send the N[ew] Y[orker] a story when you tell me—it is ready but must be typed etc.

[In margin, crossed out, are several sets of figures]

1. *Best* echoes the first syllable of *chestnykh pravil,* a phrase from the opening line of *Eugene Onegin,* which Nabokov rendered in his annotated edition as "most honest principles."

2. For a vivid description of Henry Allen Moe's role in the distribution of the Guggenheim Foundation awards, see Wilson's letter to Robert Coates of August 20, 1938 in his *Letters on Literature and Politics, 1912–1972,* pp. 304–306.

3. "Seminarians." Nabokov has in mind Nikolai Pomialovsky's *Seminary Sketches (Ocherki bursy).* Published in 1863, this colorful exposé of brutal life at a provincial divinity school has remained a minor classic of Russian literature.

4. William Jacob Holland, *The Butterfly Book.*

5. Thomas Barbour (1884–1946) and Nathan Banks (1868–1953) were noted American entomologists. The Comstock mentioned here was not John Adams Comstock, Jr., the author of *Butterflies of California,* but W. P. Comstock of the American Museum of Natural History.

91

THE NEW YORKER
No. 25 West 43rd Street

January 24, 1944

Dear Vladimir: ① I have just seen Donald Elder and handed him your MS. You will soon get the contract for the Russian book. I hope you will appreciate its many beauties. You ought to come on and talk to Elder. He says that they are planning to remodel their nature books (after the war) and might be interested in your suggestions.

② I like the novel very much—am eager to see the rest of it. I have made some suggestions on the MS. I think that there are three English verbs that you do not handle with quite a sure touch: *discern, reach* and *shun* (which you sometimes confuse with *shirk*). Otherwise, it is very well written. My only possible criticism would be that you sometimes write slightly involved sentences—as in the case of the iron beetle—that don't exactly go with the rest of the prose. Poem also excellent.

③ About *Евгений Онегин:*[1] you are doing remarkably well with it; but don't you think perhaps shorter things are more in order? We can't have the whole thing, which has, besides, been several times, though badly enough, translated lately.

④ Nikolai did not materialize, but is threatening to turn up this weekend.

⑤ Yes: I have been rather disconcerted to find that Aldanov is the complete European literary man. I wonder whether his residence in Paris did this for him. He amused us much by telling us with horror of your, in his opinion, hideously ill-advised criticisms of certain American writers, and of his efforts to remonstrate with you. He thinks that J. P. Marquand is wonderful. His opinions about certain things seem to me very unintelligent; yet, in other ways, as *The Fifth Seal* shows, he must be really intelligent.

⑥ Mary wants me to call your attention to the fact that the sum you were doing in the margin of your letter is not correctly worked.[2]

As ever,

EW

1. *Eugene Onegin.*
2. Reference to the set of figures in the margin of Nabokov's letter of January 18, 1944.

92

February 7, 1944

Dear Bunny,

I have received from *The American Poet* a request for translations of Russian poets ("especially soldier poets of to-day") and an offer from the Browning Society to speak to them on Russia's "cause" as "illustrated by literature." I was down with the flu and wrote a rather irritated letter to the *American Poet* saying that I did not know any soldiers' verse, except casual bits which are even inferior to the kind of war stuff written by soldiers of other countries. I feel that somehow I have committed a *gaffe*,[1]—but anyway they do not seem to pay anything so that all the same I could not have contributed anything. Do you know those people? The Browning Society sent me their program of German studies which ends like this: ". . . in the last plaintive notes (of Schubert's "Gretchen am Spinnrode" as sung by Miss Henrietta Green who should have known better in view of the racial aspect of her name) of that fresh, youthful voice (Gretchen's, not Henrietta's), in the words "Mein <u>hertz</u> is sehr" (sic! for "ist schwer"!) one could fancy that one heard the pathetic cry of the submerged, tortured Germany, the gentle, kindly, friendly Germany, pleading for a chance to survive. That it be given a chance is as important for the rest of the world as it is for Germany. To that end, we must hope that there may preside at the peace table, not the spirit of hate and revenge, but the spirit of wisdom, understanding, charity—yes, and of enlightened self-interest."

I wrote them that Gretchen has been consoled by the frocks that her soldier friend brought her from the Polish ghettos—and that neither gelding, nor mendelism, nor domestication could turn a hyena into a soft purring cat, etc. I may have committed another tactless blunder—but I do not know all those people and do not seem to like them. Please, tell me something about them if you happen to know anything.

I have reread our contract carefully and really it is a masterpiece on your part. I also received a check (750) from D.D. I must say this solves a lot of financial worries. I want to thank you very sincerely, dear Bunny, for your arranging this matter. It was grand of you—and I really keep feeling that my contribution does not quite live up to my share. Would you perhaps like *Египетскія ночи?*[2] Do send me a list of titles (but no prose if possible).

Did you like my offrande? It is an illustration to a line in a poem of mine (in *Возвращ[ение] Чорба*[3] vol[ume]) Къ Музѣ,[4] I think) «Гроздь винограда, груша, пол арбуза»[5]

I shall see you in March.

Yours.

V.

1. "Blunder."
2. "Egyptian Nights" (by Pushkin).
3. *The Return of Chorb*, a collection of Nabokov's stories and poems published in Berlin in 1930.
4. "To the Muse," translated into English in *Poems and Problems* as "The Muse." This poem was not included in *The Return of Chorb*.
5. "A cluster of grapes, a pear, half-a-watermelon." In the printed text of the poem, the first two words of this line are «лист виноградный» ("a grape leaf").

93

THE NEW YORKER
No. 25 West 43rd Street

February 14, 1944

Dear Vladimir: We were much touched by the offrande, with its rich and suggestive symbolism. I heard from those *American Poet* people, too, and sent them a copy of the enclosed card,[1] which I commend to you as a model. It would also be appropriate for your Browning Society people. It's amusing to know that a Browning Society still exists in Boston. They used to have them in the last generation in all the more serious centers of the United States, but I had thought they were obsolete. Best regards to all. You narrowly escaped a comic valentine from us. Let's not worry about the Russian translations until sometime next summer—unless you are moved to do something.

As ever,
Edmund W

Let me know what you hear about your novel.

1. See *Letters on Literature and Politics, 1912–1972*, p. 690, for a reproduction of a printed card with the heading: "Edmund Wilson regrets that it is impossible for him to:" followed by a list of literary activities and situations.

94

THE NEW YORKER
No. 25 West 43rd Street

March 1, 1944

Дорогой Вий![1] I just saw Donald Elder and he seemed worried at not having heard from you about your novel. I gather that they are favorably disposed toward it. I think you ought to strike while the iron's hot. When are you coming to New York? Nikolai is bringing his family here for a week this month.

As ever,
EW

1. "Dear Viy!" (Viy is the earth-spirit monster in Gogol's horror story of that name). The form of address is also a pun on Nabokov's usual signature V.

95

Nice rhyme: Note-books of Night—
        Sebastian Knight.

March 26, 1944

Дорогой другъ,[1]
    I am sending you a copy of a preliminary paper on the classification of the holarctic Lycaeides forms.[2] It has produced a tremendous stir in the butterfly-

man world since it completely upsets the system of old conceptions. I am now busy preparing for publication my main work on this group, and as hundreds of drawings must be made, this takes a good deal of my time. It will be a monograph of some 250 pages.[3] The taxonomic part reads like a *roman d'aventures* because it involves terrific feuds between entomologists and all kinds of interesting psychological matters. In 1938 there were five (5) people in the whole world who knew anything of the particular group I am discussing: one of them is dead by now and another, an Alsatian, has vanished. So that's that.

I loved your article on magic[4] though I really think you might have mentioned the leading Russian Wizard who so completely mystified the Cape Cod Enchanter. Re Cape Cod: having no money to go to Colorado or California as we intended, we thought it would be a good idea to spend July–August on the Cape. Véra and the boy might even go there in the middle of June. Could you suggest a method of finding a cottage there? Do you know of any agency or of any private person (not far from you) who would like to rent for the season? Or a boarding house? (not expensive). I want to finish my novel this summer. There was a *lovely* poem about snow and Sherlock Holmes in one of the last *New Yorkers*.[5]

I am correcting the proofs of *Gogol* and would have sent them [to] you for a critical examination had I not known how busy you were reading books. I have sent Elder an account of what happens in my novel. Good old Guggenheim has not renewed his grant and financially I am rather dejected. In a fortnight or so I shall offer the *New Yorker* a story. Last week I delivered a 150 dollar lecture at Yale on Russian literature. Laughlin refunded the one dollar seventy which I spent on mailing him *Gogol* and paying for a photostat.

I rather liked the phallic implications of the pistol with which Joan toyed, in between her "act of intimacy" with the "completely disrobed" Charles Chaplin.[6] Apparently the "white haired comedian" had to choose between himself and the pistol going off and wisely selected the least lethal course. Or perhaps the gun acted as an aphrodisiac? One never knows with these great lovers . . .

My little impromptu Russian poem about «Совѣтская сусальнѣйшая Русь»[7] has kept "secretly" circulating in copied and recopied MSS among Russian Socialists of the Kerensky *entourage* affording them the exquisite long-lost thrill of spreading «запрещенные стихи»,[8] as they did under the Czars,—until finally one of these Socialists published it anonymously in the Социал[истический] Вестник,[9] introducing it (at the end of an anti-Stalin article) with the special ritualistic cautious manner of reference which was used in the case of MS revolutionary poems half a century ago. The two beautiful points are: 1) such noble civic poems are public property and 2) the poet's name is not divulged because otherwise he would be exiled to Siberia (or Labrador)—by president Roosevelt. If you are familiar with the habitus, *milieu* and style of the Russian left-wing publicist 1845–1945 you will appreciate the delicate fun of the thing.

Want to see you badly.

V.

1. "Dear friend."

2. "The Nearctic Forms of *Lycaeides Hüb[ner]*" (see Letter 59, note 4).

3. "Notes on the Morphology of the Genus *Lycaeides*" and "The Nearctic Members of the Genus *Lycaeides Hübner*"(see Letter 59, note 4). The two together come to one hundred pages.

4. "John Mulholland and the Art of Illusion," *The New Yorker*, March 11, 1944. It was later included in Wilson's book *Classics and Commercials*.

5. "Sherlock Spends a Day in the Country," by Kenneth Fearing, was in the same issue as Wilson's article on magic.

6. Joan Barry's paternity suit against Chaplin was very much in the news at the time. During the trial, an earlier episode was revealed in which Miss Barry had threatened Chaplin with a pistol and he disarmed her by "wooing and winning her then and there."

7. "Most tinseled Soviet Russia." From Nabokov's poem "No Matter How" (see Letter 54).

8. "Forbidden verse."

9. "The Socialist Herald."

96

THE NEW YORKER

No. 25 West 43rd Street

March 31, 1944

Dear Volodya: I'll be glad to see your butterfly paper. Do send me the Gogol proofs, too, if it isn't too late. I'll have plenty of time to read them. It is very amusing about the underground circulation of your poem. We are all well, except that I have developed gout and am obliged to lay off liquor. We had been hoping to see you in March. Nikolai and his wife were here and seemed in very good spirits. I had a feeling that he had been prospering, though I don't know precisely how. His face is certainly better. We discussed your personality in a searching way. Love to Vera and Dmitri,

As ever,

EW

97

THE NEW YORKER
No. 25 West 43rd Street

March 31, 1944

Dear V.: I forgot to tell you that the real estate agent at Wellfleet is Miss Eliza-beth Freeman, a sister-in-law of Admiral Nimitz and an eccentric and wonder-ful old lady. We bought our house from her—it belonged to her family. We're delighted at the idea of your coming up here, and if you can wait till after the 1ˢᵗ of May, which is when we hope to get back, we'll help you look for a place. Vera could come up and stay with us. By the way, your compatriot Chelichev[1] was also likely to be in Wellfleet, but I hope this won't keep you away.

EW

1. The painter and stage designer Pavel Tchelitchew (more correctly, Chelishchev), who at one time shared an apartment with Nabokov's brother Sergei. Parker Tyler's biography of the painter, *The Divine Comedy of Pavel Tchelitchev* (New York, 1967), speaks briefly of Tchelitchew's friendship with Mary McCarthy, Edmund Wilson and the Chavchavadzes during his summer in Wellfleet in 1944. Tchelitchew may have served as the prototype of the painter Vsevolod Romanov in *The Gift;* his art also has recognizable parallels with the paintings of the hero of Nabokov's play *The Event* (1938).

98

May 4, 1944
Wellfleet, Mass.

Dear Vladimir: We are back up here now. Do try to come here. You could all come and stay with us while looking for a house. I hope you addressed your *New Yorker* story to Mrs. White direct. If you haven't sent it off yet, send it straight to her in the country: Mrs. E. B. White, Brooklin, Maine.

I skipped a week in *The New Yorker*, because there was nothing that inter-ested me except a book on Daniel Home the medium (who had such a sensa-tional success in Russia), and as I had just done an article on spiritualism and magic, I dealt with it in a short anonymous note. I have just had a brilliant idea, by the way. The last volume of Thomas Mann's Joseph series is soon to appear and has been hanging over me like a great cloud of dough. I am going to ar-range to have my assistant do it or even perhaps to get it done by Fadiman, who is a tremendous admirer of Mann—pleading complete incompetence in this field.

The Letters, 1944

Love to the family. I hope we shall see you soon.

As ever,
Edmund W.

99

Dear Bunny,

We have written to Cape Cod, but with one thing and another, are still un-certain about going there.

Have you noticed that the wrist represents Mexico, the goatie and face the States, the east corner of the necktie Florida, the east eye Hudson Bay and the top hat the Arctic with the Polar star. I am alluding to that poster of Uncle Sam pressing a warning index to his lips: "Do not discuss . . ." which soldiers and sailors (by means of a judicious erasion) turn into "do not cuss."

I know, however, quite well that the appalling condition of my purse (a few hundred dollars melting in the bank, my miserable museal salary and some 800 which I shall earn next semester at Wellesley) is my own fault i.e., I am devoting too much time to entomology (up to 14 hours per day) and although I am doing in this line something of far-reaching scientific importance I some-times feel like a drunkard who in his moments of lucidity realizes that he is missing all sorts of wonderful opportunities.

Plan: to retire from butterflies to a cottage on the Atlantic O[cean] for at least a couple of months and finish my novel (incidentally, Doubleday Doran tell me that they cannot make up their minds on the basis of those first chap-ters. I sent them a rather poor account of the rest, *mais ils ne marchent pas*).[1] Apart from financial doubts, there is the trouble of Dmitri's health. We had decided to have him examined and, if necessary operated, at the Children's Hospital here, by Dr. Gross who was "highly recommended." After an exami-nation that was mainly based on the photographs taken in New York and on a general account supplied by Véra, Gross telephoned to say that he would like to "explore" Dmitri i.e., perform a serious operation (wholly unwarranted) on a large scale and to remove the appendix en passant. We could not agree to this and after corresponding with our N.Y. doctor (who took the photos, etc.) have decided to either try and limit Gross' surgical urge to a simple removal of the appendix, or to have it done in N.Y. It seems that this question must be settled before deciding the Cape Cod matter; on the other hand a couple of months there would be far better for his general health, etc., than staying in Cambridge where he has absolutely nowhere to play out of doors and lives in a neighborhood full of impossible little hooligans. Complicated.

I did not send you the Gogol proofs because I got bored by the book and sent them back to Laughlin.

I shall be going to Cornell for a speech at a banquet (the Book and the Bowl) around the 25th of this month and will visit N.Y. if a Russian выступленіе[2] can be arranged there on the 27th.

A little story which I have been composing on and off for a number of months is being typed and will be sent to the *New Yorker* at the end of next week.

Ужасно хочется тебя повидать, душевный privet вамъ обоимъ отъ насъ обоихъ.[3]

V

I missed your article in the last *N.Y.* Why?

1. "But nothing doing."
2. "Reading."
3. "I want terribly to see you, cordial regards to both of you from both of us" (incorporating a possible pun on the Russian word for "regards," *privet*, and the English name of a plant—as Nabokov had done in some earlier letters).

100

[Postmarked June 9, 1944 p.m.][1]

Dear Bunny,

I got your letter at the hospital where I landed owing to the following curious circumstances:

On the day of the invasion[2] certain bacilli mistook my innards for a beachhead. I had lunched on some Virginia ham in a little *Wursthaus*[3] near Harvard Square and was happily, happily examining the genitalia of a specimen from Havilah, Kern Co[unty], Calif. at the museum, when suddenly I felt a strange wave of nausea. Mind you, I had been most extravagantly well up to that point and had actually brought my tennis racket in order to play with my friend Clark[4] (echinoderms—if you know what I mean) in the late afternoon. Suddenly, as I say, my stomach rose with an awful whoop. I managed somehow to reach the outside steps of the museum, but before attaining the grass plot which was my pathetic goal, I threw up, or rather down, i.e., right on the steps, such sundry items as: pieces of ham, some spinach, a little mashed potatoes, a squirt of beer—in all 80 cents worth of food. Excruciating cramps racked me and I had just the strength to reach the toilet where a flow of brown blood rushed out of me from the opposite part of my miserable body. Since I have in me a heroic strain, I forced myself to climb the stairs, lock my lab, and leave a note in Clark's office cancelling the tennis game. Then, vomiting every three steps, I proceeded to stagger home much to the amusement of passers by who thought I had been overcelebrating the invasion.

Now, you should note, dear Bunny and Mary, that the day before, Vera and Dmitri had gone to New York for the appendicitis operation (it was scheduled to take place today,—Wednesday the 7th, today is Thursday and I feel awfully worried not being able to get any news), so that when I finally crawled into my flat I was quite alone and helpless. I have a hazy recollection: of undressing, in between monstrous distal and proximal discharges; of lying on the floor of my room and issuing a torrent of ham and blood into my waste paper basket; of progressing by spasmodic stages to the telephone which seemed unattainable, standing as it did on the incredibly lofty piano. I managed to sweep the instrument down upon the floor and bracing myself for this last achievement, dialed Karpovich's number.

Another point: that morning Mrs. Karpovich[5] had rung me up to tell me that she had just brought her husband back from their farm in Vermont where they had spent the weekend and where he had been taken seriously ill. Moreover when they came back they realized that they had quite forgotten Dobuzhinsky[6] (the painter) and his wife who were to come from N.Y. and spend the night at their house. She wanted to know whether I knew anything about them and kept dwelling on the wretched vision of D. and his wife trying to rouse an empty house. I had told her that after my tennis game with Clark I would drop in.

When she heard me gasping into the telephone and pleading for help she said: please do not play the fool (не валяйте дурака[7])—this is the usual thing that happens to humorists,—and I had quite a time persuading her that I was dying. Incidentally I vomited into the telephone which I think has never been done before. Realising at last that something was wrong, she jumped into her car and some ten minutes later found me in a state of collapse in a corner of the room. Never in my whole life have I experienced such impossible and humiliating pains. She called an ambulance and in a twinkle two policemen appeared. They wanted to know 1) who the lady was—and 2) what poison I had taken. This romantic touch was too much for me, and I swore at them roundly. Then they proceeded to carry me down. The stretcher was not made to negotiate our type of staircase (American efficiency), so I was carried downstairs, squirming and whooping, by the two men and Mrs. Karpovich. A few minutes later I was sitting on a hard chair, in a horrible room, with a negro baby howling on a table—this was the Cambridge City Hospital—of all places. A young medical student (i.e. had been studying medicine for 3 months only) attempted the ridiculous and medieval procedure of pumping my stomach by means of a rubber hose which he inserted into my nose. It so happens that my left nostril is so narrow inside that nothing can pass, while my right one is S-shaped (this is the result of a boxing competition in Cambridge Univ[ersity], 1920, where I reached the semifinals and then was K.O.'ed—a cartilage was badly damaged). Thus it is hardly surprising that the hose could not pass—and all the while of course I was suffering most hellish pains. When the utter ineptitude of the unfortunate youth dawned upon me, I firmly asked Mrs. Karpovich to take me away—anywhere, and actually signed a document to the effect that I had refused assistance. After this I had my greatest attack of vomiting and *le rest[e]*,—the funny thing being that you cannot do the two things at one time in the W.C. so I kept rolling off and squirting by turns from either end.

Mrs. Karpovich remembered that at 6 p.m. (it was about that time now) a doctor was to visit her sick husband. I was carried by a reluctant and meagre staff to a taxi and after incredible sufferings found myself shivering under five blankets on the drawing room couch at the K's. By then, I was in a state of *complete* collapse and when the doctor (a nice fellow) turned up he could find neither my pulse, nor my blood pressure. He started telephoning and I heard him saying "extremely grave" and "not a minute to be lost." Five minutes later (with poor Mr. Karpovich quite forgotten, and with the lost Dobuzhinskys wandering though unknown nightmare streets) he had arranged the matter and—lo!—I was at the Mt. Aubrey[8] hospital (where Vera had been last year, with pneumonia) in a semi-private ward—the "semi" being represented by an old man dying from acute cardiac trouble (I could not sleep all night owing to his groans and *ahannement*[9]—he died towards dawn after telling some unknown "Henry" such things as "My little boy, you can't do that to me. Use me right" etc.,—all very interesting and useful to me). At the hospital two or three quarts of some saline stuff were injected into my veins—and I lay with that needle in my forearm all night and most of yesterday. The doctor said it was a case of food poisoning and called it "hemor. collitis."[10] At the same time Dmitri was being operated in N.Y. and as I had asked Vera to let me know at once I wonder what she thought upon not reaching me. Perhaps the telephone does not work at all if Mrs. Karpovich (I forgot to ask her) who fetched my correspondence yesterday did not retrieve it (it lay on the floor, dismembered). I have just written Vera in detail, as set down here, as I thought she had better know so [as] to avoid endless misunderstandings and muddles. After those injections, in the afternoon, yesterday, the doctor found me in a good state and I told him that I was hungry. At 5 p.m. I was brought the following dinner: glass of pineapple juice, thick soup, rissoto (if I spell it right), bacon (bacon!) and canned pears floating in canned cream. This is also an aspect of American (hospital) efficiency—and although I felt that this meal was the last thing that a man who had almost died of poisoning the day before—and who was still oozing blood into the bedpan—ought to partake of, I was so hungry that I ate it all up. In the meantime I had been transferred (in spite of my protests) to the general ward, where the radio kept emitting hot music, cigarette ads (in a juicy voice from the heart) and gags without interruption until (at 10 p.m.) I bellowed to the nurse to have the bloody thing stopped (much to the annoyance and surprise of the staff and of the patients. This is a curious detail of American life—they did not actually listen to the radio, in fact everybody was talking, retching, guffawing, wisecracking, flirting with the (very charming) nurses— all the time—but apparently the impossible sounds coming from the apparatus {it is really the first time that I have heard the radio, except for very brief spasms in other people's houses and, in the saloon cars during my travels} somehow acted as a "life-background" for the occupants of the ward, for as soon as it was stopped complete quiet ensued and I soon fell asleep). This morning (Thursday 8th) I felt perfectly well,—had a good breakfast (egg was hardboiled, of course) and attempted to take a bath, but was caught in the corridor and bundled back into bed. At present I have been wheeled on to the porch where I can smoke and enjoy my воскресеніе изъ мертвыхъ.[11] I hope to go home by tomorrow.

Well, that's that. Thanks, дорогой,[12] for arranging the 500 business. I am writing Mrs. White. I have sent (three or four days ago) a story to her.[13] This story I read aloud at Cornell at a "banquet" on the 25th of May, and it was an extraordinary success. This money comes at *un moment très propice*.[14] I had to borrow 200 from the society for *помощи писателямъ*,[15]—[a] Russian affair in N.Y. Good old Aldanov arranged it, and Zenzinov.[16] I wrote Aldanov some critical remarks about his last instalment in the *Nov[yi] Russk[ii] Journal*,[17] and he took it very handsomely.

I am again in full swing writing my novel and hope to finish it in two months. I liked *very much* your account of the Russian woman's book (though neither you nor she can get over the illusion that Lenin was rather a dear).[18] There has been some excellent Perelman stuff in the latest *N[ew] Yorkers*— and that wonderful poem about Sherlock Holmes and snow.[19] I feel very much like Verlaine these days—"Mes Hôpitaux"[20] and that kind of stuff. ~~But Vera is apt to get very nervous about these matters so that if you could get in touch with her and prevent her from dashing back to Cambridge—which is perfectly unnecessary, because I am quite well—it would mean a lot to her. The Karpovichs will probably arrange about my food for the next two or three days.~~

[Crossed out by Nabokov]

[In the margin]
No, I see your letter is from Wellfleet. I thought you were back in N.Y.

My love to both of you. We have not quite settled our summer plans but I have a hunch that we shall see you soon. How is *your* health? Are you still divorced from wine, wine, wine? Some time ago I got worried about your health, but then I got your letter and assumed you were well. Are you?

Yours tenderly   V

~~Vera is staying at Anna Feigin 250 W. 104~~

[Crossed out by Nabokov]

1. This letter was misfiled at the Beinecke Library at the time of the first edition of this book. It was found by Brian Boyd, who published it (with a few deletions) in his *Vladimir Nabokov: The American Years,* pp. 73–75.

2. The Allied landing in France, which decided the outcome of World War II, took place on June 6, 1944.

3. The restaurant still exists at the same location.

4. George Clark, professor of zoology at Harvard, did research at the Museum of Comparative Zoology in 1944.

5. Tatiana Karpovich, the wife of Harvard professor Michael Karpovich.

6. Mstislav Dobuzhinsky (1875–1957), artist and stage designer, who gave the teen-aged Nabokov lessons in drawing. Dobuzhinsky designed productions for, among others, the Moscow Art Theater, New York's Metropolitan Opera and the American Ballet Theater. Nabokov had occasion to renew his acquaintance with Dobuzhinsky when the latter designed the sets for the New York production of Nabokov's play *The Event* (in Russian) in April 1941.

7. "Don't play the fool."

8. Mount Auburn Hospital in Cambridge.

9. "Panting."

10. Hemorrhaging colitis (bleeding diarrhea).

11. "Resurrection from the dead."

12. "My dear."

13. Apparently, "A Forgotten Poet," written in May 1944.

14. "Just the right moment."

15. "Aiding the writers."

16. On Vladimir Zenzinov, see Letter 182, note 7.

17. *Novyi zhurnal (The New Review)* is meant. Nabokov conflated the name of this literary journal with that of the New York daily *Novoe russkoe slovo (The New Russian Word)*. Aldanov's novel being serialized in *Novyi zhurnal* at the time was *Istoki (The Origins)*, which dealt with the assassination of Tsar Alexander II in 1881. It was later published in English as *Before the Deluge*.

18. Wilson's review of *My Lives in Russia* by Markoosha Fischer in *The New Yorker* of May 13, 1944.

19. "Sleepy-Time Extra" by S. J. Perelman, a parody of a survey of the sleeping habits of American husbands and wives (what percentage wears pajamas, what percentage eats in bed, etc.), appeared in *The New Yorker* of May 20, 1944. On the poem about Sherlock Holmes and snow, see Letter 95, note 5.

20. Paul Verlaine's memoir, written at the end of his life, of the hospitals where he had stayed.

101

[Postmarked June 15, 1944]

Dear Bunny,

I am out of the hospital after my dreadful experience and am still very weak. I scribbled you a letter from that place, but I doubt whether it was mailed. Mrs. White's plan is very acceptable,—many thanks!

My flutterbys have lost their grip during my illness and I am working again at my novel. Dmitri's operation was very successful. I may go to N.Y. for this weekend if I can muster sufficient energy.

Greetings to both of you.

Yours   V. N.

102

June 29, 1944

Дорогой другъ,[1]

as usually happens to me after seeing the Wilsons (Dmitri is still chuckling over your postcard—he especially appreciated the absence of the definite article) I have been blessed with a flow of inspiration and have composed another tremendous chapter of my novel. I think it will be finished by September. I have also translated three Pushkin poems (1. Морозъ и солнце—день чудесный 2. Что въ имени тебѣ моемъ and 3. Недаромъ вы приснились мнѣ (подражаніе Корану)).[2] The last one might have been written to-day, with allusions to commandoes and to certain small European states. A severe cold contracted while we were waiting for the taxi at S[outh] Station (and now shared by Véra and Dmitri) helped to segregate me from my bugs. You do not tell me how much you enjoyed my paper on the *Lycaeides*. Here is what they look like

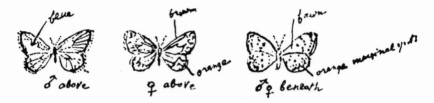

(about natural size)

I received the *N[ew] Y[orker]* cheque (300 + 200) and have thanked Mrs. White. We hope to see you both soon. I am almost sure now that my novel will be called "Game to Gunm." Weeks snapped up my story with a spasm of delight.[3] Veuillez agréer, cher Maître, l'expression de mes sentiments dévoués.[4]

V.

1. "Dear friend."

2. 1. "Frost and sunshine—a lovely day . . ." 2. "What is my name to you . . ." and 3. "Not for nothing did I dream of you . . . (Imitation of the Koran)." There is no record of publication of Nabokov's translations of these poems by Pushkin.

3. Apparently "A Forgotten Poet," which appeared in *The Atlantic Monthly* in October 1944.

4. "Please accept, dear master, the expression of my devotion" (a parodistic use of French epistolary etiquette).

103

[From Edward Weeks to Edmund Wilson,
with marginal notes from Wilson to Nabokov]

THE ATLANTIC MONTHLY

June 30, 1944

Dear Wilson:—

Nabokov has just sent us a short story which will make you grin when you read it. It is in his best vein—deft, beautifully natural, and shot through with those little arrows of satire and wisdom which make him the original he is.

I saw Nabokov yesterday at the Agassiz Museum and we talked about some new translations of Pushkin which I think he will let me see next week. Is there any hope that we can resume your series now that the summer is here? If so, I might begin to point him toward some of the poets you have in mind.

Yours sincerely,
Edward Weeks

Mr. Edmund Wilson
Wellfleet,
Massachusetts.

[In upper left-hand margin, with an arrow drawn to "point him toward"]
I thought you would enjoy seeing this graceful little letter. I like the way he assumes that he can play the role of gentle intermediary between us.

[At the bottom of Weeks' letter]
Wellfleet, Mass.
July 4, 1944
day of our never-to-be forgotten liberation from the damned British

The Pushkin translations have arrived. I like them very much—though there are a few holes I should like to talk to you about getting filled up. I have just read *Египетские Ночи,*[1] and it seems to me rather disappointing. I don't think the poem is a particularly good one to translate, as you once suggested doing. He has a situation there, as we say, but doesn't develop it. Your butterfly paper is too technical for me to get out of it all that I am sure is there.

As ever,
EW

1. "Egyptian Nights."

104

July 16, 1944

Dear Bunny and Mary,
Dmitri is in a camp in N[orth] Vermont and we have spent a week with my brother Pavel[1] who teaches horsemanship at a place in Maine. Now we would like to spend a weekend at the Cape. Could we come this week, Friday evening

and stay till Sunday evening? Could you put us up? If not perhaps we could get a room somewhere in your vicinity? We intend to look around and see whether there is something suitable for a longer stay—for a month or so.

Yes. I enjoyed Weeks' little epistle. I got one very similarly worded except that he used the word "shafts" instead of "arrows" (*re* humour). You must bear in mind that 1) the "Egyptian Nights" represent only the beginning of the thing—the idea was to have the queen fall for the youngest of the three lovers and spare his life, and 2) that the whole thing is supposed to be the facile improvisation of an Italian rhymster (see the story). I admit, however, that it is not quite worth translating.

I am working hard at my novel. It is terribly hot—I mean the weather. Pavel has married an American girl who was together with Mary at the convent. Funny—those little coincidences.

Hoping to see you soon.

V.

1. This is a leg-pull. Nabokov did not have a brother or a close cousin (who can also be referred to in Russian as "brother") named Pavel. The reference is to the possibly non-existent uncle of the heroine and to his American wife in Nabokov's story "That in Aleppo Once . . ."

105

July 23, 1944

Dear Bunny,

if it is quite convenient we shall come with our butterfly nets this Friday. Please be frank about it. I am sorry to have timed my letter so badly. I am sending this one by very special delivery.

I dreamt to-night that together with Khodasevich and Wyndham Lewis (the author of a dreadful dull and flat thing called *The Apes of God*) I was inspecting a battered town in Normandy and then I saw you and you were somehow simultaneously you and Churchill.

When we come we want to look for a boarding-house with private bathroom so as to eventually spend a fortnight or so at the seaside. Do you know of any such place in your vicinity?

I shake your hand.

Your   V.

106

Cambridge, Mass.
August 16, 1944

Dear Bunny,

I have never heard of the man Heiseler and I doubt whether he ever existed. The whole thing smacks of V-columnism, and ought to be turned over to the F. B. I. The sentence anent the "synthesis" of the "rich literary heritage" of Russia and Germany is an insult to the former. Very fishy.[1]

Thanks for giving us such a nice time. It was good to see you both. I have written another glorious chapter and have also composed a little poem which I append.[2] I have also sent it to Mrs. White. My Gogol book is out, and I have asked good old Jay to mail you a copy. Its brilliancy is due to a dewy multitude of charming little solecisms.

Allen Tate has written me asking for a review of Kaun's book. I answered no. Immediately afterwards I discovered that poor Kaun had died.[3] Il fait diablement chaud, ce qui n'est pas *khorochaud*.[4] Greeting from V. and V. to all of you including Wracky.[5]

V.

I too enjoyed Wellfleet very much. I would like to add that I regret not having had the opportunity to tell you in more detail how much I enjoyed many things in *Daisy*,[6] such as, f[or] i[nstance], the precarious balance of her snug little rural house with the cold *already* irresistibly creeping in on all sides or the heartrending story of her *only* happy day.

Véra

1. King's Crown Press, a division of Columbia University Press, had announced in August 1944 the publication of *Henry von Heiseler, A Russo-German Writer* by André von Gronicka, an assistant professor of German and Russian at Columbia. In promotional copy, the little-known Heiseler was touted as "one of the greatest intermediaries between Russian and German cultures," whose writings "represent a unique synthesis of the rich literary heritage of the two countries." (Information kindly provided by Gennady Barabtarlo)

2. "Dream," later published in *Atlantic Monthly* (September, 1946).

3. Alexander Kaun (1889–1944), professor of Slavic Languages and Literatures at the University of California. He wrote extensively on Russian and Soviet literature and was a friend and correspondent of many important Russian writers. His last book was a four-volume *Advanced Russian Reader*, brought out by the University of California Press in 1943–1944.

4. "It is hot as hell, which is not good"—a pun on the French *chaud*, hot, and the Russian *khorosho*, good.

5. Racky was the name of Wilson's dog.

6. Wilson's earlier novel *I Thought of Daisy*, first published in 1929.

107

THE NEW YORKER
No. 25 West 43rd Street

Wellfleet, Mass.
August 31, 1944

Dear Vladimir: We've enjoyed your book on Gogol. The best parts are brilliant (the exposition of пошлость[1] perfect and valuable). It does seem to me, though, that in some connections you've gone out of your way to be rather silly and perverse about the subject. I've done a review for the *New Yorker* in which (since I haven't received that large basket of fruit which I've daily been expecting) I've sharply taken you to task.[2] It isn't a real review, however—which would have been impossible in the *New Yorker*. I want to go through this book with you sometime and discuss it in detail. One thing I didn't mention, for which I think you really ought to do some kind of penance, is your extraordinary statement that Pushkin could have done nothing to help or encourage Gogol, because it is not precisely a question of *influencing*—*influence* is the word you use. Even if it were not true that Pushkin—contrary to what you say—is sometimes very close to Gogol (in *Медный Всадник*, *Пиковая Дама* and—as I think you admitted when we were talking up here—in *История Села Горюхина*),[3] one of the outstanding things about Pushkin is surely the variety and range of his literary interests. Surely he would have been just the man to suggest ideas to Gogol. His relations with other writers—like Mickiewicz—show the readiness of his sympathies. Also, isn't there something more than two dimensions to *Le Misanthrope* and the *Don Juan* of Molière? Of course, Molière isn't a poet like Gogol, but these pieces aren't exactly hot dogs.[4] You cleared up for me a number of passages that I hadn't quite appreciated—the nicknames for the playing cards, for example, and the lieutenant trying on the new boots.[5] I was puzzled by this lieutenant at first. Then [I] realized that he was purely gratuitous; but I didn't feel the full beauty of this touch till I read your discussion of the passage.

We have been having a very good time with Chelishchev, of whom we have seen something lately and whom we have gotten to like. He is very good about Gogol and says about him more or less the same kind of things that you do. He told me, however, that he considered *Вий*[6] one of Gogol's greatest things—and

I agree. It does seem to me that you rather arbitrarily neglect large areas of Gogol's work. I am reading the *Вечера*[7] etc., and expect to disagree with you about them. Love to Vera. We miss you,

As ever,

Edmund W

1. *Poshlost.* Nabokov's detailed discussion of this Russian concept of the trite and the banal in *Nikolai Gogol* helped popularize both the word (sometimes spelled "poshlust" in English) and the concept. It can be considered by now to have entered the vocabulary of American and British literary criticism. For an updated version of Nabokov's view of *poshlost* and a demonstration of how the term may be misunderstood, see the interview with Herbert Gold in *Strong Opinions*, pp. 100–101.

2. "Nikolai Gogol—Greek Paideia," *The New Yorker,* September 9, 1944. Parts of this review were later included in *Classics and Commercials* ("Vladimir Nabokov on Gogol"). The "large basket of fruit" may refer to the habit Nabokov's friend Mark Aldanov allegedly had of sending such baskets to prospective American reviewers of his books.

3. "The Bronze Horseman," "The Queen of Spades" and "History of the Goriukhino Manor."

4. Reference to the following statement about Molière in Nabokov's *Nikolai Gogol:*

> A bad play is more apt to be good comedy or good tragedy than the incredibly complicated creations of such men as Shakespeare or Gogol. In this sense Molière's stuff (for what it is worth) is "comedy," i.e. something as readily assimilated as a hot dog at a football game, something of one dimension and absolutely devoid of the huge, seething, prodigiously poetic background that makes true drama. (p. 55)

5. At the very end of Chapter Seven of *Dead Souls.*
6. "Viy."
7. *Evenings [on a Farm near Dikanka].*

108

September 10, 1944

Dear Bunny,

following Mary's example, I retired a fortnight ago to another town (Wellesley, in my case) in order to write a story.[1] I have sent a copy of it to the *New Yorker* (the cover of the latest issue with the Versailles Treaty dream is quite superb) and am sending you another for your private delectation. It is a very intricate piece of work despite its apparent simplicity. You will note that my old man remembers several little things wrong.

This has been a kind of prolongation of our Cape Cod holiday, with the addition of Dmitri who has come to us from his camp very brown and tough. We have been bathing and playing tennis. I have 18 students and they have already mastered the pronunciation. Birkett,[2] who is otherwise good, renders the pronunciation of «ы» in, say, «былъ»[3] as "b_wyl," which is disastrous—and which explains why Russian-speaking Englishmen purse their lips in order to pronounce that unfortunate letter. On the 11th we shall all go back to Cambridge. Are you going overseas? Will you be in Boston soon?

Yours,

V.

1. "Time and Ebb."

2. George Arthur Birkett, *A Modern Russian Course,* 2nd edition, London, Methuen and Co., Ltd, 1942.

3. "Was."

109

THE NEW YORKER

No. 25 West 43rd Street

September 29, 1944

Dear Vladimir: I liked your story very much (also the one about the museum in *Lettres Françaises*),[1] and I'm sorry to learn here that they rejected it. I was afraid that they would think it was over the heads of the *New Yorker* readers because it was over the heads of some of the editors. Weeks certainly ought to take it, though.[2]

We've come to town and have taken a small home way over on the East River, where I hope we shall see you eventually. We can't move in till Oct. 10 and are going back to Wellfleet for a few days in the meantime. Love to Vera.

As ever,

EW

1. "La visite au musée," the French translation of Nabokov's originally Russian story "The Visit to the Museum," appeared in *Les Lettres françaises,* Buenos Aires, issue of July 1, 1944.

2. See next letter, note 9.

110

Dear Bunny,

I have spent a month in arranging Part I of my butterfly work for publication and have had a good deal of trouble with the drawings.[1] It goes to the printers to-day and the trees are green and rusty brown, stepwise, like gobelins. Enfin—c'est fait.[2] It is going to remain a wonderful and indispensable thing for some 25 years, after which another fellow will show how wrong I was in this and that. Herein lies the difference between science and art.

Le *New Yorker* a eu le toupet de me renvoyer mon conte accompagné d'une lettre pleine d'un fatras d'inepties. Étant de mauvaise humeur ce jour-là, j'ai assez rudement engueulé la pauvre Mrs. White.[3] In a copy of an amazing periodical called *Writer* or something, which I happened to pick up in the Wellesley reading room the other day there is an absolutely stunning passage in an article about "Making the Post"[4] where the author discusses the sad plight of a writer who could not "make" it and "got so discouraged that he seriously thought of giving up writing." I liked very much your article on detective stories. Of course, Agatha is unreadable—but Sayers, whom you do not mention, writes well. Try *Crime Advertises*.[5] Your attitude towards detective writing is curiously like my attitude towards Soviet literature, so that you are on the whole absolutely right. I hope that one day you will tackle the quarter of a century-old literature *sovetskovo molodnyaka*[6]—and then I shall have the exquisite pleasure of seeing you reel and vomit—instead of the slight nausea you experienced with:

"His face was composed, with that vague expression it always took on when his interest was very much awakened (or "keenly aroused")." "For a moment the girl stared at the lanky man with the pipe" (R. T. M. Scott, "Bombay Duck"). "The tall investigator shrugged his shoulders slightly" (ibid.) "To-morrow, at 9, we are going to have a little inquest, quite informal, you know . . . it might amuse you to come, Mr. Robb." "He leaned back in his chair, fingertips together, frowning in a concentration of thought beyond my guesses." "No, said Robb quickly, the murder was committed exactly 22 minutes later." "I have Uncle Louis' voice?" she divined readily. "The niece of his voice, so to speak, he admitted" (Ernest Bramah). " 'Evening, Mr Kelton' the police captain said. 'A bad business I'm afraid.' " (Richard Connell, "The Sting of a Wasp") " 'What about your other pistol?' 'That is an ordinary five-shot automatic of a well-known American make. It is in the hip-pocket of the gray suit hanging in my closet.' " (ibid.) (And now comes the gem of my collection,—note the beautiful coincidences)

"I stared at him in complete bewilderment. 'Do you mean to say'—I began. 'That she'd never been murdered' he supplied."

(J. D. Beresford, "The Artificial Mole")

"He whipped out the photograph in question and confronted the astounded Chief Inspector with it. '*Beresford*, man! Beresford's the murderer, of his own wife.' "

(Anthony Berkeley, "The Avenging Chance")[7]

I have corrected and returned the proofs of Pushkin-Lermontov-Tyutchev to Laughlin.[8] "Time and Ebb" has been sold to Weeks.[9] Would like to see you awfully.

V.

1. "Notes on the Morphology of the Genus Lycaeides."

2. "Finally, it's done."

3. "The *New Yorker* had the gall to send me back my story, accompanied by a letter filled with a farrago of nonsense. Being in a bad mood that day, I told poor Mrs. White off rather rudely."

4. Dorothy B. Quick, "So You Want to Make the Post," *Writer*, August 1944.

5. Nabokov means *Crime Must Advertise* by Dorothy L. Sayers (1933).

6. "Of the Soviet younger generation."

7. The cited detective stories were all included in the anthology *The World's Best One Hundred Detective Stories*, Eugene Thwing, editor, published in 1929. Wilson's distaste for detective novels by Agatha Christie, Rex Stout and Dashiell Hammett was expressed in his *New Yorker* (October 14, 1944) essay "Why Do People Read Detective Stories?" later included in *Classics and Commercials*.

8. *Three Russian Poets.*

9. It appeared in *The Atlantic Monthly*, January 1945.

111

THE NEW YORKER
No. 25 West 43rd Street

October 26, 1944

Dear Vladimir: I am sending you, under separate cover, a remarkable little book which may perhaps represent the way out for modern literature. You ought to know, in reading it, that Sara Haardt was the wife of H. L. Mencken—with this explanation, I think you will find it all clear.[1]

Did I tell you we were settled in a dandy little house on East 86th St.? 10 Henderson Place. I hope you will be coming to town soon, as we miss you. I enjoyed your gleanings from detective fiction. I have been getting dozens of letters from addicts protesting against my article and only three so far approving of it. I've been pretty well swamped with work lately, what with my book, the Scott Fitzgerald proofs,[2] plus the *New Yorker* job.

Love to Sonya[3]

EW

1. Apparently, *Southern Album* by Sara Haardt, edited and with a preface by H. L. Mencken (New York, 1936). The book is a collection of short stories and memoirs, described in Mencken's preface as "an amalgam of fiction and fact."
2. *The Crack-Up* (see Letter 125, note 1).
3. Through a slip of the pen, Wilson used the first name of Roman Grynberg's wife instead of Mrs. Nabokov's.

112

"I can speak English, lord, as well as you,
for I was train'd up in the English court;
where, being but young, I framed to the harp
many an English ditty lovely well,
and gave the tongue an helpful ornament."[1]

↑

(sic!)   King Henry IV

3 (1) 121–125

December 2, 1944

Dear Bunny,

I have not written to you for ages, and now I am sending you a longish poem.[2] It is so unlikely that the *New Yorker* would take it that I am not sending them a separate copy, but as they must see it, will you please show it to them. Incidentally, if you like it, we might include it in our Doubleday book; and you might write one too, on the English aspect, and have it in *pendant*. We might dedicate them to each other!

I greatly enjoyed the little studbook you sent me. Let us imagine that owing to some tremendous desastre *all* our books were destroyed except that one, and then let us imagine its discovery in 2572. The sole monument of a vanished civilization. And a huge library of scholarly works gradually growing around it. The Rhind papyrus, so called because Rhind bought it in 1858 from some Arabs, who said they found it among the ruins of small buildings near Ramesseum, begins with the promise: "all the secrets, all the mysteries . . ." but really turns out to be a school book with, in the blank spaces of the scroll, the petty calculations of some unknown Egyptian bookkeeper or farmer in the seventeenth century B.C. Some people, however, were luckier. Plinius Caecilius Secundus, a pushing barrister (who could speak *seven* hours at a stretch), absolutely lacking any literary talent, all his life worked like a rat to build up his own fame in the minds of posterity, and succeeded. The perfect *poshliak*.[3]

I never told you how I loved your little article on Davies' style[4] (in the *Partisan*, I think),—perfectly admirable, one of your very best *morceaux*.[5]

I work a lot. Have financial troubles. Am looking for a good solid professorship somewhere. Ipse quid audes? Quae circumvolitas agilis thyma?[6] Have you ever read the "Sea-Serpent" by the zoologist Ondemann?[7]

Yours
V.

1. Nabokov's capitalization and punctuation have been retained in this citation of Owen Glendower's speech from *Henry IV,* Part I. Most modern editions of Shakespeare spell "an helpful" as "a helpful."

2. "An Evening of Russian Poetry." The reaction of *The New Yorker* was quite different from what Nabokov had expected, as Letters 117 and 118 show.

3. "Vulgarian" or "exponent of *poshlost."*

4. "Mr. Joseph E. Davies as a Master of Prose Style," *Partisan Review,* XI (Winter 1944), later included in *Classics and Commercials* under the title "Mr. Joseph E. Davies as a Stylist."

5. "Pieces."

6. "And what are you yourself attempting? Around what beds of thyme are you flitting?" Horace, *Epistles,* 1, 3, 20–21.

7. *I.e.,* Merman, from French *onde,* wave, and German *Mann,* man. This form of Nabokovian humor is familiar to the readers of his fiction from such instances as the bantering conversation between Fyodor's father and Uncle Oleg in Chapter Two of *The Gift* ("Did you never see Popovsky's horse stung by Popov's fly," where the reference is to Przhevalsky's horse, *Equus przewalskii,* on whose discoverer's books and travels the character of the father is partly based). Another similar example occurs in Chapter Two of *Pnin:* "A small job at the Aksakov Institute, rue Vert-Vert, combined with another at Saul Bagrov's Russian book shop, rue Gresset, supplied him with a livelihood." Here, allusions to Sergei Aksakov's two books about the Bagrov family (*The Family Chronicle* and *The Childhood Years of Bagrov's Grandson,* which are also featured in *Ada* and provide that novel's subtitle) are mingled with a popular eighteenth-century novella about the adventures of an escaped parrot, "Vert-Vert" by Gresset, to suggest the Franco-Russian ambience of Pnin's émigré existence.

THE NEW YORKER
No. 25 West 43rd Street

December 18, 1944

Dear Valdemar: I'm awfully glad your poem has gone through. I just got back last night. Reuel[1] was delighted with the little car that Dmitri sent him—he has been in bed with a cold, and it cheered him up. I have introduced you into my book[2] as a friend of Mr. Chernokhvostov's (you knew him in Europe and your relations are rather ambiguous), who gives a misleading explanation of the origin of his name.

Merry Christmas to you all,
EW

1. Reuel Wilson, the son of Mary McCarthy and Edmund Wilson.
2. *Memoirs of Hecate County*. In the last section of the novel, "Mr. and Mrs. Blackburn at Home," the narrator describes his polyglot neighbor Ed Blackburn (who might be the Devil himself). Blackburn has many national identities and is called Schwarzkopf by Germans and Chernokhvostov ("black tail") by Russians. The narrator says: "I was told by a clever Russian novelist who seemed to have known him in Europe but whom I did not necessarily believe, that he was a fur dealer who traded with the Soviets, that he belonged to an old Moscow merchant family and had left after the Revolution, and that his name had to do with the skins of some kind of Siberian animal on which the family fortune had been based."

1945

Mrs. Edmund Wilson
36 Vista Place
Red Bank, New Jersey

January 19, 1945

Dear Vladimir: You will be enormously excited to know that I have set out to read your Russian writings and am now very much enjoying *Машенька*.[1] Some of the images are very good: the first scene, where they are stuck in the lift, and the passage about his seeing himself in the movie. But do I understand that

Ganin and Ludmilla are supposed to have had their first *étreinte*[2] on the *floor* of a taxicab? I don't think you can have had any actual experience of this kind or you would know that it is not done that way.

The New Yorker is sending me to England and France and I'll be getting off in a month or more. I've just been shot full of inoculations against countless diseases.

Love to Vera,
Edmund W

1. *Mary.*
2. "Embrace."

115

January 20, 1945

My dear Bunny,

it could be done, and in fact was done, in Berlin taxi-cabs, models 1920. I remember having interviewed numerous Russian taxi-drivers, fine White Russians all of them, and they all said yes, that was the correct way. I am afraid I am quite ignorant of the American technique. A man called Piotrovsky,[1] a poet *à ses heures*,[2] told me that one night his fare happened to be a well-known film star and her escort; wishing to be exquisitely polite (exiled nobleman, etc.), he briskly opened the door when they arrived at their destination, and the pair *in copula* shot out heads first and sailed past him, like a "double backed" dragon he said (he had read *Othello*).

Remember, while enjoying my *Mashenka*,[3] that I wrote the book *21* years ago,—it was my first experience in prose. The girl really existed.

Laughlin writes he is doing his best to have the book of poems out, но у метранпажа запоръ.[4] In my contract with him there is one clause saying that if the book is not out by the 1st of January 1945, he loses his right to publish it— and the moneys he paid me. I shall wait till the 1st of February. In what stage is our Doubleday book?

I want to see you before you leave. I shall be in New York Saturday evening and Sunday 10−11th February. How did you like the grand old man[5] laying the blame on the Trotskyists in Greece?

Yours
V.

How *could* you name that quack Mann in one breath with P. and J.?[6]

1. Nabokov's friend, the émigré poet Vladimir Korvin-Piotrovsky.
2. "An occasional poet."
3. *Mary.*
4. "But the man in charge of the [typographical] make-up is constipated."
5. Stalin.
6. *I.e.,* Proust and Joyce.

116

February, 1945

Dear Bunny,

that was a very nice evening we spent. I limped back to Cambridge in the throes of a hideous neuralgia intercostalis on a background of 'flu, and have spent a week in bed. The effect produced by the pain is a cross between pneumonia and heart trouble with the addition of an iron finger prodding you in the ribs *all* the time. It is a rare illness, as is everything about me, and I have had it already twice in my life. I am quite well now.

You will arrive in Europe *къ шапочному разбору*[1] (a term based on the *шапки*[2] which people *разбираютъ* i.e. sort out, when leaving church in Russia—a heap of peasant caps in a corner, that sort of thing. We use the term in the sense of "pour la curée," "to the end of the show"), otherwise I would probably not let you go [...].

Àpropos of dollars, did you say anything to the *New Yorker* as you so very kindly suggested? Do, if it is quite convenient.

First class—the Sherlock Holmes article.[3]

Yours
V.

1. "At closing time" (lit., "In time for sorting of caps").
2. "Caps."
3. "Mr. Holmes, They Were the Footprints of a Gigantic Hound," originally in *The New Yorker,* February 17, 1945 and later included in *Classics and Commercials.*

117

March 6, 1945[1]

Dear Bunny,

I am enclosing a piece of the *London Times Literary Supplement* January 27, 1945 which may amuse you.[2]

Thanks for bothering about the *N.Y.* money. They added 30 dollars. I have an uncomfortable feeling that I told you the wrong sum—I had quite forgotten what it was or what I told you, being an utter imbecile in money matters. I have now found out that it was around 245.

My poem is enjoying a great and deserved success.[3] When are you going abroad? Will you flit through Boston?

Do give me some news about yourself. I like you very much.

V

1. The date on the original reads 6 III I.

2. The issue was a collection of essays on Russian topics. It is not clear which of them Nabokov selected for Wilson.

3. "An Evening of Russian Poetry" was finally published in *The New Yorker* of March 3, 1945.

118

THE NEW YORKER

No. 25 West 43rd Street

March 12, 1945

Dear Volodya:

Along with tremendous enthusiasm for your poem[1] here, there seems to operate a frustrating force. When I first brought the matter of payment up, both Ross and Mrs. White said that they thought you had not been paid enough, and Ross told me that he would send you sixty some dollars more. Then it turned out that they had sent you only thirty, and an additional check had to be made out. You should have received the second one by this time.

I get aboard my boat Wednesday—a little Norwegian steamer that lands me in England. I'll be away from four to six months. Good luck in the meantime. By the way, if you really want an academic job, you might write to Lewis Jones, president of Bennington and say that you are the person I mentioned to him a couple of years ago. I'm sorry I haven't had a chance to see more of you this winter. Our conversations have been among the few consolations of my literary life through these last years—when my old friends have been dying, petering out or getting more and more neurotic, and the general state of the world has been so discouraging for what used to be called the humanities. Love to Véra and Dmitri. I hope to see you all in the fall.

As ever,

Bunny W

Mr. Vladimir Nabokov
8 Craigie Circle
Cambridge, Massachusetts
ew-f

1. "An Evening of Russian Poetry," *The New Yorker*, March 3, 1945.

119

> May 31, 1945
> Albergo della Città
> Via Sistina,
> Rome
>
> But letters should be
> addressed to: AFHQ, PRO,
> Detachment A, APO 512

Dear Volodya: I was walking the other day in this little street on the Pincian where my hotel is and eying with curiosity the row of *hôtels borgnes*[1] the blind doorways of which open up at night to let in the soldiers with their girls when what was my astonishment to see on one of the façades (though it belongs, I guess, to a relatively respectable apartment house) a marble plaque with a bronze bas-relief of Gogol's head and an inscription which explained that he «здѣсь писалъ Мертвыя Души»[2]—put up by the Russian colony in 1901. I had already discovered that I had D'Annunzio's house right across the street, Stendhal's house in the next street, and the house in which Keats died at the bottom of the Spanish steps that go down at the end of the Via Sistina—nor is the house of the немецкий пошляк[3] Goethe very far away. I do not believe, however, that I have as yet written anything here that is as good as *Dead Souls* or the best of Keats—though (all at the expense and by the benevolent arrangement of the Allied occupying forces) I have a wonderful room on the next to top floor with a balcony on which I can spend part of the day and a splendid view of Rome.

There would be so much to say about everybody and everything that I shouldn't be able to do it justice in a letter, and shall instead transcribe a passage from a letter from Polly Boyden[4] at Truro which I have just received from the States—a passage which will, I am sure, be gratifying to your insatiable and narcissistic vanity: "I read Nabokov's *Gogol*," she says, "by accident and liked it so much I bought the *Sebastian Knight*. I think Nabokov is more inescapably the artist than anyone I have ever met personally and it chilled my blood, while

I was reading those remarkable books, to realize I actually *had* met him—like 'seeing Shelley plain.' And this in spite of the fact that I thought he became too explicit in the very last paragraph of *The Real Life*. It seemed to me he suddenly threw up the sponge and *only one paragraph to go!*" It will suffice for you perhaps as a bulletin from Rome to tell you, also, that Mario Praz, the erudite and slightly eccentric author of *La Carne, la Morte & il Diavolo nella Letteratura Romantica*,[5] who is engaged in studying Russian and has just got through Шинель,[6] talked to me enthusiastically about your Gogol book which he had somehow or other got hold of and that I have even seen a copy of it in a book store. Aside from this, I'm afraid that Europe, as you must already have gathered, is at present in pretty bad shape. The ruined parts of Italy affect me with more repugnance than anything else, I think, that I have ever seen, and when I am in them my principal feeling is that I want to get away from them as far as possible. The inhabitants constantly beg you to have them all taken to America (where a lot of their friends and relations have already gone) or to arrange to have Italy somehow annexed as one of the United States. Rome is almost untouched and delightful—though I found a cousin of Nina's whom she told me to look up living in a section that *had* been bombed, with the house across the street destroyed and the poor old lady's panes all broken and replaced either by opaque glass or not at all.[7] The mixture here of all nationalities over the grave of Italian fascism is fascinating, and I am going to try to do something about it—perhaps in the form of fiction in the *New Yorker*.

I hope that your affairs are prospering. Give my love to Vera and Dmitri. It really is awfully queer to think that Chichikov was выдуманный[8] by Gogol in this pleasant little street in the clear Italian light—all that world of *Dead Souls* seems so far away. How are your butterflies and how is your novel?

Regards as ever,

EW

1. "Shady hotels."

2. "Wrote *Dead Souls* here." Gogol's Roman apartment was located in what is now 126 Via Sistina.

3. "German vulgarian." Reference to Nabokov's statement in *Nikolai Gogol* that "there is a streak of *poshlost* running through Goethe's *Faust*."

4. Polly Boyden and her husband Preston ("Bud"), a wealthy Chicago lawyer, owned a large house in Truro. She was the author of a novel called *The Pink Egg*, which a contemporary describes as "vaguely surrealistic and vaguely Communist" and "read only by her friends."

5. This book is known in English as *The Romantic Agony*.

6. "The Overcoat."

7. For a more detailed description, see Chapter Six of Wilson's book *Europe Without Baedeker.*

8. "Invented." The short form of this participle would have been more idiomatic and conveyed Wilson's meaning better. The long form he uses suggests the negative connotations of "contrived" or "concocted."

120

Army address: AFHQ, PRO, Det. A, APO 512

> June 3, 1945
> Albergo della Città
> Via Sistina,
> Rome

Dear Volodya: This is a postscript to my letter of the other day. I found an edition of Parny in a bookshop here and bought it because Pushkin is supposed to have imitated him and I have been reading *Les Galanteries de la Bible,* which evidently inspired the *Gavriiliad.* Here is the germ of it, I suppose:

> "Le galant et beau Gabriel,
> Feignant toujours quelque message,
> Allait de village en village
> Parler d'amour au nom du ciel.
> Voyez sa complaisance extrême:
> Il annonce avec un souris
> A l'épouse, à la vierge, un fils
> Qu'obligeamment il fait lui-même."[1]

Some of it is quite well-turned and funny, but Parny hasn't a trace of Pushkin's feeling or humanity or color. There is a wonderful biographical notice about him written not long after his death. It seems that he fell in love and had a brief affair with a young girl who was made to marry some richer or nobler man, and he addressed to her the four books of elegies which caused him to be known as "Le Tibulle français."[2] Later the lady's husband died, and she wrote to Parny offering to spend with him "les derniers jours qui lui seraient comptés sur la terre;"[3] but the poet, though "sensible à ce souvenir de sa maîtresse, s'écria, 'Ce n'est plus Eléonore!' et ne répondit point (isn't that *point* perfect?) à la femme tendre et dévouée qui revenait à lui."[4] Later he got a pension of 3000 francs and so, in his last days, was able to "goûter une douce médiocrité."[5] He also wrote a long poem called *Goddam* about the English.

I was looking the other day, after reading a lot of Italian, at one of the Russian books I had brought with me. There's no question that the Russian inflections give the language a kind of close-knit syntactical strength—like Latin—which, along with the idiomatic richness, have made it a marvelous literary medium. Italian really is degraded Latin, and the only really great Italian poets are people like Dante and Leopardi who were full of and close to classical Latin. I don't believe there is an Italian of the 19th century (except Leopardi) who could have written anything comparable to the least of Tyutchev's lyrics—which have such a rare combination of subtlety and toughness of style. Sometimes, by the way, over here, I've been visited by an awful suspicion that the classical English language is doomed eventually to go down in the general western débâcle, and that a basic or pigeon form of American will emerge, as Italian did from the decadence of Latin. If mass propaganda and mechanical warfare go much further, that will be all there will be left—perhaps with a few Russian words like *сейчас, пятилетка*[6] and *allrightnik* (do you know this wonderful word, used on the New York East Side?). Already the little grammar still remaining in English seems to be going by the board in the American public schools, where I am told the children are sometimes taught that it is all right to say, "He took she and I to the movies;" and the hair-raising conjugations in Mencken's *American Language*—*I was, you was, he was; we was, you was, they was*—may come to be the standard thing. So that people like you and me will turn out to have been just old forlorn academics, like Ausonius putting together poems out of lines from Virgil.

Best regards as ever,

EW

1. "The gallant and handsome Gabriel, always pretending he had a message, went from village to village to speak of love in the name of heaven. Consider how very obliging he is: he announces with a smile to the wife, the virgin, a son that he will helpfully give her himself." This passage in Parny's poem has indeed been long recognized in Pushkin scholarship as the source of "The Gabrieliad." Evariste Parny (1753–1814) is far better known in the Russian literary tradition than he is in his native France due to the fondness of Pushkin and other Russian poets of the early nineteenth century for his work. Parny's other claim to fame is his book of forged African folklore, *Chansons Madécasses*, excerpts from which have been set to music by Maurice Ravel.

2. "The French Tibullus."

3. "The last days that will be allotted her on earth."

4. "Responsive to this remembrance of his mistress, exclaimed: 'This is no longer Eléonore!' and answered nothing to the tender and devoted woman who was returning to him."

5. "Enjoy sweet mediocrity."

6. "Now," "Five Year Plan."

121

8 Craigie Circle
Cambridge, Mass.

June 17, 1945

Dear Bunny,

I received your two nice letters just as I was beginning to get worried about you. I did know, however (from Mrs. White) that you were in Italy. «*Адри-атическія волны ... О, Брента! ... »*[1] And Ходасевич's wonderful reply «*Брента—рыжая рѣчонка, etc.*"[2] Блок and Бунин[3] have some remarkable poems on Italy too.

Италія Италіей[4]—but when are you coming back? Incidentally—Nikolai is also in Europe,—has been sent on a mission to Germany in the rank of Colonel. *Чудеса.*[5]

Two or three weeks ago I sold a story to the *New Yorker*—was paid very handsomely for it.[6] Unfortunately a man called Ross started to "edit" it, and I wrote to Mrs. White telling her that I could not accept *any* of those ridiculous and exasperating alterations (odds and ends inserted in order to "link up" ideas and make them clear to the "average reader"). Nothing like it has ever happened to me in my life and I was on the point of calling the deal off when they suddenly yielded and, except for one little "bridge" which Mrs. White asked as a personal favour, the story is more or less intact. I am always quite willing to have my grammar corrected—but have now made it quite clear to the *New Yorker* that there will be no "revising" and "editing" of my stories *dorénavant.* Я ужасно былъ золъ.[7] Mrs. White wrote me several letters and telephoned twice, and finally came to see me here (on her way to Maine). We have made it up now.[8]

I liked your account of the unsponsored Scot.[9] Our friend Laughlin is getting married to Kaiser's daughter—according to the Levins. I have given up smoking and am feeling very miserable. We may go to some place in New Hampshire in July. The correspondence we have had in this respect has proved quite instructive. "Modern comfort" means that there is a water-closet, but no bath. "Christian clientèle" is still more amusing,—and about as tempting.

Do write to me again, *друже*[10] (this is the *звательный падежъ* of *другъ*[11]). Вѣра шлётъ привѣтъ[12] and Dmitri has chicken-pox.

Yours
B.

1. "Adriatic waves ... O Brenta!" *Eugene Onegin*, Chapter One, Stanza XLIX.

2. "Brenta—rusty little stream." The first line of a poem by Vladislav Khodasevich describing the real appearance of this unprepossessing Italian river, sung by many poets because of its sonorous name.

3. Blok and Bunin.

4. "Italy is all very well and good . . ."

5. "[What] miracles."

6. "Double Talk," later re-titled "Conversation Piece, 1945."

7. "Henceforth" (French). "I was terribly angry" (Russian).

8. When the next story Nabokov sold to *The New Yorker* two years later, "Signs and Symbols," ran into the same kind of trouble, Wilson wrote Katharine White a vehement letter (*Letters on Literature and Politics, 1912–1972*, pp. 409–411), asserting the importance and originality of Nabokov's writings and defending him from needless editorial meddling.

9. Dr. Robert McIntyre, the M.P. from Scotland, whose difficulties with getting himself accredited at the House of Commons were described by Wilson in his *New Yorker* June 2, 1945 piece "Notes on London at the End of the War," which later became Chapter One of *Europe Without Baedeker.*

10. "O my friend."

11. "Vocative case of friend."

12. "Véra sends regards."

122

THE NEW YORKER
No. 25 West 43rd Street

September 27, 1945

Dear Volodya:

I have been back about a month. Will you be coming to New York any time soon? I want very much to see you. I may be going up to the Cape and have a chance to stop off in Boston, but I am not sure about it.

I have been having, as you probably know, a great deal of domestic agony,[1] and am now living alone in my New York house, where I'd be delighted to put you and the whole family up.

Don't be alarmed by your experience with *The New Yorker.* That is their regular procedure. You don't have to accept any of their suggestions. They are really very decent with their writers and, unlike many editors, won't change anything without the author's permission.

I was never so glad to get away from anywhere as I was to leave Europe. We are all very fortunate to be living in the United States, though I don't think our cultural life over here is anything to be very proud of at present.

I lent some of your novels, in Rome, to some old Russian ladies, relatives and

friends of Nina's. I think they were rather puzzled by them, though they remarked that they were very well written.

Love to Vera and Dmitri.

As ever,

Bunny W

1. Reference to Wilson's impending divorce from Mary McCarthy.

123

8 Craigie Circle

Cambridge

[After] September 27, 1945[1]

Dear Bunny,

We were very happy to learn you were *de retour*.[2] It has been awfully dull
without you. Thanks for inviting us. We would love to come but could manage
to do so only on the Columbus weekend and even that is not certain. It would
be wonderful if you came to Boston.

I heard about your domestic affairs soon after our last meeting in N.Y. (when
we had that conversation anent Nika's matrimonial difficulties; he is Colonel
Nabokov now, on a cultural mission in Germany), from an eager mutual friend.
I hoped the whole thing somehow *утрясётся*[3] but from what you write I de-
duce that it has not. I do not know what to say to you except that I have been
feeling 'very much' upset about the whole matter—especially as I did not hear
from you directly and had to sift and combine various rumours.

We spent most of the summer in Wellesley. I have given up smoking and
have grown tremendously fat. A cinematographic firm in Paris has acquired
the rights on a novel of mine (*Camera Obscura* alias *Laughter in the Dark*). Of
my two European brothers the youngest[4] has turned out to be interpreter with
the American forces in Germany; he traced me through my story in the *New
Yorker*. My other brother[5] was placed by the Germans in one of the worst concentration camps (near Hamburg) and perished there. This news gave me a
horrible shock because Sergei was the last person I could imagine being arrested (for "Anglo-Saxon sympathies"): he was a harmless, indolent, pathetic
person who spent his life vaguely shuttling between the Quartier Latin and a
castle in Austria which he shared with a friend.

I am doing the same things I was doing last year: dissecting butterflies at the Museum and teaching Russian to girls in Wellesley. I have forgotten much, Cynara. The urge to write is something terrific but as I cannot do it in Russian I do not do it at all. Cynara is the Russian tongue, not a woman.

We have passed our citizenship examinations. I know all the amendments.

Your article about Greece was most enjoyable especially in regard to the landscape.[6] But where on earth did you see *firs?* I spent a couple of months there in 1919 collecting butterflies in Kephisia and elsewhere. All those marble pillars and statues when painted must have looked atrociously garish. I feel Greece in terms of olives, but that is all.

Well, Bunny, I do hope I shall see you very soon. Please write some more.

V.

[At top upside down]
So glad you are back safe! Come and see us soon.

Véra

1. Since this letter is a reply to Wilson's letter dated September 27, 1945, it must have been written later.

2. "Back."

3. "Would be settled." Reference to Wilson's impending divorce from Mary McCarthy.

4. Kirill Nabokov (1911–1964).

5. Sergei Nabokov (1900–1945) had, like his father, a passionate interest in music, especially Wagner, an interest his brother Vladimir could not share. He was, between the two world wars, a well-known figure in European musical and theatrical circles. At the beginning of World War II, he lived in Austria with his Austrian partner Hermann Thieme at the castle Schloss Weissenstein near Innsbruck (owned by Hermann's family). He was arrested for homosexuality during a visit to Berlin in 1943. Sergei's (and Vladimir's) cousin Sophia Fasolt (née Nabokov) used her contacts to secure Sergei's release five months after his arrest. He found an office job, where he openly expressed his contempt for Hitler and his doubts about the chances for German victory. His co-workers turned him in; he was re-arrested and sent to the concentration camp Neuengamme near Hamburg. There, Sergei Nabokov died of untreated food poisoning on January 10, 1945. There is a moving tribute to him in *Speak, Memory* (pp. 257–258) which concludes: "It is one of those lives that hopelessly claim a belated something—compassion, understanding, no matter what—which the mere recognition of such a want can neither replace nor redeem."

6. The first installment in *The New Yorker* of September 15, 1945 of Wilson's "Greek Diary" ("Notes on Liberated Athens"), which later became Chapter Eleven of *Europe Without Baedeker*.

124

THE NEW YORKER
No. 25 West 43rd Street

October 3, 1945

Dear Volodya:

I've just read your story[1]—didn't know it had come out till you told me. It is awfully funny and so like the kind of situation that one is likely to find oneself in nowadays.

I'm very sorry about your brother's death.[2] Human life means absolutely nothing in Europe today. In Greece and Italy they are still shooting each other at a great rate. I think that what the Allies ought to do is announce that nobody else is to be killed—even Ribbentrop, Goering and Company. Otherwise, there will be no end to it.

Do let's effect a combination soon. I'm eager to see you.

As ever,

EW

1. Apparently, "Double Talk," written in March and April 1945 and published in *The New Yorker* of June 23, 1945. Later re-titled "Conversation Piece, 1945."
2. Sergei Nabokov's. See the preceding letter.

125

October 30, 1945

Dear Bunny,

I happened to read *The Crack Up*[1] the other night. It is first rate healthy literature. I enjoyed it hugely—as well as your poem. I should love to have a copy of the book, as a Christmas present say, with your autograph. Rich stuff, sane real stuff.

How are you? Are you coming to Boston?

I have translated some Lermontov and written quite a chunk of my novel. There are lots of things I want to tell you, show you, discuss with you.

V.

The Simonov book[2] is neither much better nor much worse than the trash published in Russia during the last 26 years (always excepting Olesha, Pasternak, and Ilf-Petrov).

1. F. Scott Fitzgerald, *The Crack-Up: With Other Uncollected Pieces, Note-Books and Unpublished Letters to Fitzgerald from Gertrude Stein, Edith Wharton, T. S. Eliot, Thomas*

Wolfe, and Essays and Poems by Paul Rosenfeld, Glenway Wescott, John Dos Passos, John Peale Bishop and Edmund Wilson. Edited by Edmund Wilson, New York, 1945. On Wilson's experiences with editing *The Crack-Up,* see *Letters on Literature and Politics, 1912–1972,* pp. 344–351.

2. Konstantin Simonov's novel about the siege of Stalingrad, *Days and Nights,* was much written about at the time.

126

THE NEW YORKER
No. 25 West 43rd Street

November 17, 1945

Dear Volodya: I want to use this passage from "Вий"[1] as an epigraph for my book. What do you think of this for a translation? I've amplified мертвец[2] in order to make it clear that the corpse was a girl.

I was very much disappointed on missing you in Boston. I wish I had some excuse for going there again.

As ever

EW

You haven't sent me the Mayakovsky parody.[3] I can't seem to find *Новый Журнал.*[4]

1. An excerpt from Nikolai Gogol's tale of the supernatural, "Viy," which Wilson used as an epigraph for *Memoirs of Hecate County* (see Letter 140 below).
2. "Corpse." In the English translation of the epigraph, Wilson had amplified Gogol's *mertvets* (corpse, masculine gender) to "the corpse of the dead girl."
3. Nabokov's poem "О правителях" ("On Rulers") couched in the form of a parody on Vladimir Mayakovsky's style. It was published in *Новый хурнал (The New Review),* No. 10, 1945, and reprinted in *Poems and Problems,* pp. 128–133.
4. *The New Review.*

127

November 17, 1945[1]

Dear Bunny,

Your Candian article is quite *superb;* but I think you are wrong in your bovine shape theory.[2] I do not know what is the highest altitude on the island but it certainly does not exceed 8500 feet—judging by the labels on my series of *Aricia psilorita,* etc. 1) no summit is high enough to afford a complete view of the island; 2) no matter how high it were, other adjacent mountains would interfere with the view; and 3) even if one could rise high enough to see the whole of Crete it would be totally unlike its outline on a modern map (where the likeness to a bull is really remarkable—I grant you that). The bull came from Assyria and Egypt. The asphodel has always seemed to me to be a pallid relative of the daffodil and not the *Asphodelus* of botanists, but possibly I am mistaken.[3] On looking up the other day some papers on Colored Thinking (*audition colorée*, etc.) I discovered that I and my likes are termed "colored thinkers" (negro philo[so]phers).[4]

It was a very great disappointment not to have seen you on your way to Cape Cod.

I am surprised at your not having written about Aldanov's new book yourself. Try to find out whether Basso received a letter of gratitude and a pineapple + sullen grapes + nuts.[5] Your European articles ought to make a fine book.[...]

Yours   V.

[Added at top]
Just got your Вий[6] letter as I was sending this. I shall send you my Russian poem next time, cannot find the book.

1. Since Nabokov had already received Wilson's letter of November 17 about "Viy," the actual date of the writing must have been later.

2. In the fourth installment of his "Greek Diary," "Views of Bull-Headed Crete" (*The New Yorker*, November 17, 1945, later Chapter Fourteen of *Europe Without Baedeker*), Wilson speculated that the fascination of the Minoan civilization with bulls might be attributable to the resemblance between the shape of the island of Crete on modern maps and the bulls in ancient frescoes. The passage Nabokov is arguing against reads: "I do not know what the state of map-making may have been in Minoan days, but I imagine that it would only have been necessary to ascend the highest mountain on Crete to get a pretty good idea of its shape."

3. Response to Wilson's brief mention of this plant: "A curious little plant with a purple stem and pale waxy perfumeless flowers turns out to be asphodel."

4. Wilson had written about the difference in perception of colors between the ancient Greeks and modern man in the first installment of "Greek Diary" (the same section that mentioned the fir trees to which Nabokov objected). Nabokov has described his ability to hear the letters of the alphabet in terms of colors in *Speak, Memory* and has also attributed this ability to the hero of his novel *The Gift*.

5. Hamilton Basso's somewhat lukewarm review of Mark Aldanov's historical novel about Byron and the Congress of Verona, *The Warrior's Grave*, translated into English under the title *For Thee the Best*, appeared in *The New Yorker* on November 17, 1945. On Aldanov and baskets of fruit, see Letter 107, note 2.

6. "Viy."

128

THE NEW YORKER
No. 25 West 43rd Street

December 4, 1945

Dear Vladimir: I seem to be in a mood to communicate with you. Tell me: Why do you think that *Hamlet* has always been so popular on the stage in the English-speaking countries? (One can understand much more easily its former popularity in Russia.) Of course it's good, but this can't be the reason. Several of Shakespeare's other plays ought to be more dramatically effective. It's true that it gives the star a fat part, but there must be something more to it than this. I asked people about it in England last spring, but never got any satisfactory answer. Hamlet is introspective, an intellectual, not successful as a man of action—there's no other such favorite character in English fiction (Tom Jones, Robinson Crusoe, Gulliver, Elizabeth Bennet,[1] Alice in Wonderland, the Canterbury Pilgrims, Mr. Pickwick are the usual kind of thing). Do give me the benefit of your opinion on this matter.

EW

1. The heroine of *Pride and Prejudice* by Jane Austen.

129

THE NEW YORKER
No. 25 West 43rd Street

December 10, 1945

Dear Vladimir: ① Thank you for your revision of my translated Gogol passage.[1] I'm adopting most of your suggestions.

② I enjoyed the Stalin poem, but don't get it all—perhaps because I haven't read Mayakovsky.[2] You must read it to me when I see you again.

③ I'm sending Dmitri a copy of the new translation of Afanasiev's[3] fairy stories—though I'm not sure it's not at an age when he's too old and not old enough for them. The publisher sent me a number of copies because I'd requested his doing it.

④ About Crete: I think that a good idea of its contours could have been gained by combining a number of views from high spots. In driving along the north coast at some distance above the sea, you can see the shoreline—its indentations and promontories—quite clearly.

⑤ The Aldanov book[4] slipped by me when I was preoccupied with doing the Greek articles, though I had meant to read it. Did you see, in the *Herald-Tribune* book supplement, that Charles A. Beard (I think) said that it was the greatest book of the year or something?[5]

⑥ The point about the asphodel is that the Greeks assigned it to the other world because it is such a waxen and dead-looking little plant. It is one of a great many things I discovered when I was in Greece, that have been turned into literary properties that have no real connection with the original objects. "Fields of asphodel" suggest flowers with attractive qualities like lilies or daffodils.

Best regards,

EW

1. See Letter 126, note 1.

2. "On Rulers." See Letter 126, note 3.

3. *Russian Fairy Tales*, collected by the folklorist Alexander Afanasiev (1826–1871). Wilson's piece on H. P. Lovecraft in the November 24, 1945 issue of *The New Yorker*, "Tales of the Marvellous and Ridiculous," concluded with a section on the English translation of *Russian Fairy Tales*, collected by Afanasiev (dubbed by Wilson the Russian Grimm). When this article was later included in *Classics and Commercials*, the section on Afanasiev was deleted. On the remarkable parallels between Afanasiev's folklore collections and Nabokov's novel *Glory*, see Edythe C. Haber, "Nabokov's *Glory* and the Fairy Tale," *Slavic and East European Journal*, Vol. 21, no. 2, Summer 1977.

4. The novel by Mark Aldanov in question first appeared in Russian in France as *Mogila voina (The Warrior's Grave)*, 1939. It was published in an English translation by Nicholas Wreden in the fall of 1945 under the title *For Thee the Best* (Scribner).

5. *For Thee the Best* was reviewed in the November 4, 1945, issue of *The New York Herald Tribune Weekly Book Review* by George Whicher. Wilson has in mind the publication's Special Christmas Number of December 2, 1945, where, under the rubric "Books I Have Liked," various prominent people were asked to name three books they have enjoyed most during the past year. The response by Charles A. Beard read, "Three votes for one masterpiece—*For Thee the Best*, by Mark Aldanov." (Information kindly provided by John E. Malmstad)

130

THE NEW YORKER

No. 25 West 43rd Street

December 18, 1945

Dear Volodya: It might interest you, as an entomologist, to look up the definition of *nigger bug* in the big Webster dictionary.[1]

Merry Christmas to you all!

Edmund W

1. The 1937 edition of *Webster's New International Dictionary of the English Language* defines "nigger bug" as "a negro bug." The definition of "negro bug" is "any of numerous minute convex black bugs of the family Thyreocoridae, especially *Corimelaena pulicaria*, common on the blackberry and raspberry."

131

December 24, 1945

Dear Bunny,

there are several reasons why *Hamlet* (even in the hideous garbled versions current on the stage) should be attractive both to the caviary-eater and to the groundling. 1) Everybody likes to see a ghost on the stage; 2) kings and queens are also attractive; 3) the number and variety of lethal arrangements are unsurpassed and thus most pleasing: a) murder by mistake b) poison (in dumb show) c) suicide d) bathing and tree climbing casualty e) duel f) again poison—and other attractions backstage. Incidentally it has never occurred to critics to note that Hamlet *does* kill the king in the middle of the play; that it turns out to be Polonius does not alter the fact of Hamlet having gone and done it. Anthology of murder.

We somehow hoped that you would come here these days. [...] I am working furiously at my novel (and very anxious to show you a couple of new chapters). I detest Plato, I loathe Lacedaemon and all Perfect States. I weigh 195 pounds.

Душевно твой,
В. Набоковъ[1]

Thanks for the *delightful* Afanasiev!

Merry Christmas and loads of luck!

Véra

1. "Cordially yours, V. Nabokov."

1946

132

Dear Bunny,

many thanks for *The Crack-Up!*[1] I am sending you seven Lermontov poems for criticism and punctuation. Please inspect them *as soon as possible*—a publisher in England is impatient to have them.

Why do all these English humorists or semi-humorists turn Catholic?

Yours, V.

1. See Letter 125, note 1.

133

THE NEW YORKER
No. 25 West 43rd Street

January 14, 1946

Dear Vladimir: I don't think these Lermontov translations are quite as success-ful as your Pushkin and Tyutchev. Lermontov's actual imagery is probably harder to make effective in English because vaguer and more conventional, but I think that the epigrammatic beat of something like *Белеет парусь одинакий*[1] ought to be possible to get. *The Angel* seems to me the least successful—you oughtn't to write *world of sorrow and strife*, especially rhyming with *life*, which would have been considered banal even for English poetry of the thirties. The little two-stanza poems are better. I have made a few corrections and sugges-tions. I wish I could talk to you about the poems in detail.

I hear from people who have seen you that you are becoming stout, optimis-tic and genial—in other words, Americanized. I believe that I had already no-ticed traces of this in your letters, and I'm not sure that I entirely approve.

As ever, EW

1. "The solitary white sail," the first line from "The Sail," an early poem by Mikhail Lermontov. This first line, one of the most famous lines in all Russian poetry, is actually

a quotation from an obscure poem by Alexander Bestuzhev-Marlinsky (see Letter 187, note 1).

Wilson garbled the line, adding a pointless palatalization at the end of the word for sail (*parus*), and spelling *odinokii* (solitary) as *odinakii*, an obsolete form of "identical."

134

Dear Bunny,

Thanks for your remarks (though I did not understand the one about my "americanization"). Lermontov *is* banal, мірь печали и слезь[1] *is* trite (and tautological to boot), and as I am rather indifferent to him, I did not go out of my way to debanalize the passages you question. You are quite right, however, in everything you have noted. Incidentally, I actually had the jet-black-maned horse in a preliminary version.

On the tenth of this month I am supposed to take part (with Ernest Simmons[2] and a playwright) in a broadcast (Columbian) discussion about Gogol's *Revizor*,[3] in a series called Invitation to Learning (I think). For this purpose I must go to N.Y. and thus will have the great pleasure of seeing you. I shall come on the 9th in the afternoon. I do not know where I shall find *un gîte*.[4] Two nights. I have to be back Monday.

When I see you I shall tell you many things; shall unfold the mists of my academic career: my position in the college where I teach is so insecure and I am so poorly paid, that with one thing and another, I am extremely anxious to find something more permanent and profitable. I have heard for instance that there is a vague vacancy at Princeton. Financially, I am very depressed. Especially as I hardly expect my novel (which will be finished in a couple of months) to sell; I mean, I dare not rely on any literary earnings. The idiotic popularity that my Russian books seem to be having in Europe according to 14 agents who are clamoring for rights, is extremely irritating since it is all in francs or lyres, etc., and the translations are hideous.

Your article on Chaykovsky was fine. But you should have given him and his brother a kick in the pants for the librettos of the operas. A *good flying kick*.[5]

Hoping to see you soon.

V.

1. "The world of sadness and tears."
2. Ernest J. Simmons (1903–1972), the noted American Slavicist, author of books on Tolstoy, Dostoevsky and Chekhov.

3. *The Inspector General.*

4. "A lodging."

5. Wilson's review of *The Diaries of Tchaikovsky* ("Mice, Headaches, Rehearsals: Tchaikovsky's Diaries," *The New Yorker*, January 19, 1946) discusses the relationship between the libretto of *The Queen of Spades* and Pushkin's story on which it was based. Like most literate Russians, Nabokov considered the libretti of *Eugene Onegin* and *The Queen of Spades* to be vulgarizations and betrayals of the Pushkin originals.

135

THE NEW YORKER
No. 25 West 43rd Street

February 4, 1946

Dear Volodya: I'd be delighted to put you up while you're here, if you have no better place to stay. Just wire me or drop me a line. I have no telephone at home. The address is 10 Henderson Place, a little street off East 86th St., just beside the Misericordia Hospital, between York and East End Avenues. It will be wonderful to see you.

When I saw the Meyerhold production of *Пиковая Дама*[1] in Leningrad, they had rearranged the opera and had a new libretto that was more like Pushkin.[2]

As ever,

EW

1. *The Queen of Spades.*

2. Vsevolod Meyerhold's staging of *The Queen of Spades* at the Maly Theater in Leningrad premiered on January 2, 1935. It was one of his last productions prior to the closing of his theater in 1938 and his arrest and eventual death under torture.

Striving to bring the opera closer to the Pushkin novella on which it was based, Meyerhold commissioned a new libretto from the poet and translator Valentin Stenich, which did away with the distortions and vulgarizations of Modest Tchaikovsky's original libretto. In Pushkin, Liza was a defenseless, abused ward of the wealthy Countess, and Hermann a selfish fortune seeker, who feigned love for Liza to get from the Countess the secret of three magic cards. The Tchaikovsky brothers made Liza a wealthy heiress and the granddaughter of the Countess and turned Hermann into a cardboard operatic lover. They moved the action to the eighteenth century because the management of the Imperial Theaters had some new eighteenth-century costumes and wanted to use them.

The Stenich-Meyerhold libretto returned the action to the 1830s, the time depicted in Pushkin. It also did away with the final suicides of Liza and Hermann. After being cheated by the ghost of the Countess (whose death he had caused), Hermann was last seen where he was placed at the end of Pushkin's story—in an insane asylum. The basso role of Liza's aristocratic fiancé, Prince Yeletsky, invented by Modest Tchaikovsky, was deleted and other characters sang his music to a new text.

The production and the new libretto were a huge success. Dmitri Shostakovich declared that Meyerhold's was the first production of the opera that was worthy of Tchaikovsky's music. But Meyerhold was arrested, he became a non-person, and the libretto by Stenich (who perished in the purges in 1939) was no longer acceptable. Therefore, Tchaikovsky's greatest opera is still being performed with the distorted and cheapened original text.

136

> I am taking the 11 a.m. train Saturday
> from here so shall be at your place
> around 4, I guess.

February 7, 1946

Dear Bunny,

I see that my broad hint worked! Thank you very much. I have sent you a telegram but discovered that there is a "strike" or something on, and so the telegram may be delayed or lost.

Oh, but you should have seen *Пиков[ую] Даму*[1] in the old days, at the Mariinsky Theatre! The costumes, etc., were *early 18th century* (so that the retrospective attitude of the old lady aged 80 towards the court of Versailles and Marie Antoinette was somewhat grotesque to say the least!) and the libretto was an abomination. Around 1912, however, the *Музыкальная Драма*[2] introduced a number of changes in this and other operas (I remember in the last scene of *Carmen* a couple of British tourists, in loud checks, very well done, who took snapshots, and an authentic *Corrida de toros* poster on the wall).

> Very happy to see you soon,
> V.

Man in February issue of Ellery Queen's magazine attacked you.[3]

[In margin]
Mystery: a perfect translation in French of Pushkin's song from "The Gypsies" in Halévy's libretto of *Carmen*[4] (? possibly found among Mérimée's papers).

---

1. *The Queen of Spades.*

2. "Music Drama." Nabokov has in mind the Theater of Music Drama, an innovative opera company that was active in St. Petersburg from 1912 to 1919.

3. In the February 1946 issue of *Ellery Queen's Mystery Magazine*, the detective writer Howard Haycraft devoted his column "Speaking of Crime" to refuting Edmund Wilson's

essays in *The New Yorker* in which Wilson dismissed the genre of detective fiction (see Letter 110 above). Haycraft's main point was that since Wilson admitted that he not only disliked this sort of literature but also never read any of it, he was not qualified to pass judgment.

4. The text of Carmen's song "Coupe-moi, brûle-moi, je ne te dirai rien" in Act One of Bizet's opera (No. 9 in the score) is a translation of a portion of Zemfira's song from Pushkin's "The Gypsies." In Chapter Two of *Speak, Memory* Nabokov mentions that he was frequently exposed to opera in his youth, including numerous performances of *The Queen of Spades*, but was able to take an interest only in the visual side of operatic productions.

137

[Telegram, marked received February 7, 1946   11:42 A.M.]

WESTERN UNION

BB2 12 6=TDB CAMBRIDGE MASS 7 1134A

EDMUND WILSON=

10 HENDERSON PLACE NYK=

DELIGHTED THANKS ARRIVING SATURDAY AT FOUR=
VLADIMIR NABOKOV.

138

February 16, 1946

Dear Bunny,

I am still in bed, "resting comfortably." My temperature was around 102 when I arrived.

It was good to see you. "It is always a joy to meet an American, for I am one of those who believe that the folly of a monarch and the blundering of a minister in far gone years will not prevent our children from being some day citizens of the same world-wide country under a flag which shall be a quartering of the Union Jack with the Stars and Stripes" ("Noble Bachelor": 341).[1]

Incidentally, I was wrong in saying that there were no Russians in "Sherlock." Except for two or three stories from the "Case Book" I had read them all, and it is queer that I should have forgotten the lady nihilist who lost her pince-nez or the lovely sentence: ". . . he was an elderly man, thin, demure, and commonplace—by no means the conception one forms of a Russian nobleman" (:493). "Students of criminology will remember the analogous incidents in Godno (Grodno?), in Little Russia." This comes from the *H[ound] of the Baskervilles* (:884) and you may be amused to know that I have named a new but-

terfly *vandeleuri* in honour of Vandeleur alias Stapleton the villainous entomologist of the story. "I learn at the British Museum that he was a recognized
authority upon the subject, and that the name Vandeleur has been perma-
nently attached to a certain moth which he had, in his Yorkshire days, been the
first to describe" (say—*Luperina berylae* Vand.) (:893–894).

I note the following pearl (:271): ". . . a sudden ejaculation caused me to wake
up." Cp.[2] ". . . qui tordent sur leurs lits les bruns adolescents" (Baudelaire,—the
one about the pink and green frock of shivering dawn).[3]

This fat volume has been a good companion—but the editing is a little care-
less; for instance, it is quite clear that the "Case of Identity" ought to *precede*
(and not follow as it does in the volume) the "Red-Headed League" (see ref. to
the heroine of the former: 195).

People do not turn pale nowadays as often as they did, and still do, in fiction.
When the criminal is not really a bad egg but technically must face a charge of
murder, then he is generally dispatched to America and as often as not his ship
is lost with all hands. A bad heart comes in handy in the case of especially lovable killers.

In reviewing various details of my very pleasant stay I notice with horror
that when speaking to Auden I confused him with *Aiken* and said flattering
things about the latter's verse in the second person. I understand now the wild
look that passed in his eyes. Stupid, but has happened to me before.

It was very nice of you to make those little corrections. I shall soon send you
the rest of the thing, but in a more or less final form so that you will not be
annoyed by such slips and solecisms or at least there will be less of them.

The egg and the crimson bag had a huge success with Dmitri. We—all
three of us—send you our love,

1. "A Noble Bachelor" is a Sherlock Holmes short story by Sir Arthur Conan Doyle, as
are "The Case of Identity" and "The Red-Headed League" mentioned later on in this letter.
The famed short novel *The Hound of the Baskervilles*, by the same author, presumably
needs no identification.

2. Cp. (in Cyrillic letters) is Russian for "cf."

3. ". . . which cause dark-haired adolescents to writhe in their beds." A misquoted line
from Charles Baudelaire's poem "Le Crépuscule du Matin" ("The Dawn"). A favorite of
Nabokov's, this poem is also evoked elsewhere in his writings, most notably in *Lolita* and
Ada, where it is the source of a minor character named Dawn. The wording of the quotation

and its context in Baudelaire's poem are: "l'essaim des rêves malfaisants/Tord sur leurs oreillers les bruns adolescents" ("the swarm of unwholesome dreams/Causes dark-haired adolescents to writhe on their pillows").

139

8 Craigie Circle
Cambridge, Mass.

March 2, 1946

Dear Bunny,

Thanks for acting so promptly. I am sorry that I shall not be in N.Y. in the near future, and therefore will not be able to visit Princeton and meet your friend.[1] Of course I would come for that purpose *спеціально*[2] if you thought something tangible would be likely to come of it. I am in very low spirits because there does not seem to be any prospect of a permanent appointment in Wellesley and I am sick of being a badly underpaid instructor. The next year (and they have stressed that it is a *one-year* appointment) I have been offered 3000 dollars for ten hours a week—and 37 weeks of it. My chief anxiety is the complete lack of security.

This is all very confidential as I would hate any of my friends to hear of it.

I hope to finish my novel this spring. One of the Lermontovs and the nightmare poem returned last year by the *N[ew] Y[orker]* are to appear in the *Atlantic*,[3] and the rest of the Lerm[ontovs] have gone to the *Russian Rev[iew]*.[4]

Still feel a pleasant tingle from the good time you gave me in New York.

Будь здоровъ[5]

1. In a letter to Christian Gauss of February 12, 1946 (*The Papers of Christian Gauss*, New York, 1957, pp. 346–347), Wilson expressed his concern for the financial situation of Nabokov ("one of my closest friends"), who was paid $2,000 a year for teaching Russian at Wellesley and "considerably less" for his second job with the "butterfly collection at the Peabody Museum." Wilson thought that Nabokov's political position, which he described as being both anti-tsarist and anti-Soviet (and thus incomprehensible within the American political climate of the time), "made his advancement difficult in some circles." He then recommended Nabokov to Gauss as a candidate for a possible opening in Russian language or literature at Princeton.

2. "Specially."

3. Nabokov's poem "Dream" and his translation of Lermontov's poem "Thanksgiving" appeared in the September and November 1946 issues respectively.

4. *Russian Review*, Vol. 5, no. 2, Spring 1946.

5. "Stay well."

140

March 8, 1946

Dear Bunny,

I have read your book[1] *d'un trait.*[2] There are lots of wonderful things in it (by the way, you often use the word "wonderful," as you do in real life). You have given your "I" 's copulation-mates such formidable defences—leather and steel, gonorrhea, horse-gums—that the reader (or at least one reader, for I would have been absolutely impotent in your singular little harem) derives no kick from the hero's love-making. I should have as soon tried to open a sardine can with my penis. The result is remarkably chaste, despite the frankness.

I was sorry to notice that nothing has been done about the misprint *от-крыл.*[3] *Открыл* means "opened" but Gogol has *от крыл* = "from (or of) wings" (*крыло* has two plur[al] genit[ives]: *крылъ* and *крыльевъ*). Another thing: *чистка* is *not* a diminutive.[4] It is the same kind of action-noun as *выставка* (exhibition), *выпивка* (drinking-bout), *покупка* (thing bought), etc. It is *not* a diminutive as for instance *картинка*[5] or, in fact, *чисточка*[6] are. But since my theory is that the devil has *always* a chink in his armour this linguistic blunder is very welcome.

I think my favourites are the Ellen Terhune one (with the little wooden babas each smaller than the other)[7] and the last one (with a splendid open-air passage).[8]

At the same time I have been reading some J. Latimer (who has also a capital description of a rubhouse)[9] and *Brideshead Revisited* which is very amusing and charming here and there, but is, on the whole, trash (and terribly *voulu*[10] at the end). Your criticism of it was extremely to the point (and your prediction correct).[11]

When shall I see you again? Will you be coming to Boston?

V

[In Véra Nabokov's handwriting]
A thousand thanks for the book. I am very fond of Wilbur![12]

1. *Memoirs of Hecate County.*
2. "In one gulp."
3. In the Russian epigraph from Gogol's "Viy" that opens *Memoirs of Hecate County,*

the words *ot kryl* ("from the wings") were run together in the first edition, resulting in *otkryl* ("opened" or "discovered").

4. The long passage in French in the last section of Wilson's book ("Mr. and Mrs. Blackburn at Home") mentions the Russian term for political purge, *chistka*, as a euphemism and a diminutive, neither of which it is.

5. "Little picture."

6. "Nice little purge." In later editions of the novel, Wilson added a footnote, blaming this confusion about Russian diminutives on his character, Ed Blackburn.

7. The second episode of *Memoirs of Hecate County*, "Ellen Terhune," concludes with glimpses of Ellen and her mother that keep receding ever further into their past.

8. The beginning of "Mr. and Mrs. Blackburn at Home."

9. Jonathan Latimer was an author of detective novels, three of which were brought out in one volume by Sun Dial Press, New York, in 1940, under the title *The Latimer Big Three*. "Rub house" is mentioned in *Memoirs of Hecate County* as a slang term of the 1920s, meaning "a cheap dance hall."

10. "Contrived."

11. In his review of Evelyn Waugh's novel (*The New Yorker*, January 5, 1946, later included as "Splendors and Miseries of Evelyn Waugh" in *Classics and Commercials*), Wilson outlined his reasons for thinking the book an artistic failure and then predicted that it would be the most successful of its author's works and a best-seller.

12. According to Mrs. Nabokov this refers to the poet Richard Wilbur rather than to the hero of the third episode in *Memoirs of Hecate County*, "Glimpses of Wilbur Flick."

141

THE NEW YORKER
No. 25 West 43rd Street

March 13, 1946

Dear √2̅:

Thanks for your letter. But you sound as if I had made an unsuccessful attempt to write something like *Fanny Hill*. The frozen and unsatisfactory character of the sexual relations is a very important part of the central theme of the book—indicated by the title—which I'm not sure that you have grasped. I'm sorry about the Russian mistake. *Открыл*[1] was a mistake of the Russian printer who set the passage up, and, six months later, when I had forgotten how it read, I tried to translate the error, and didn't understand your attempt to correct me. I'm going to get it changed in future editions. I hope to be getting to the Cape and seeing you by the end of next month.

As ever,
EW

1. "Opened" (instead of "from the wings").

142

Dear Bunny,

many thanks for the lepidoptera:[1] most of them belong to *Ebriosus ebrius*[2] but there is a good sprinkling of the form *vinolentus.*[3] At least one seems to be an authentic *A. luna* seen through a glass (of gin) darkly; the person who drew these insects possessed the following attributes:

1) was not an entomologist;

2) was vaguely aware of the fact that a lepidopteron has four, and not two, wings;

3) in the same vague groping way was more familiar (very comparatively, of course) with moths (Heterocera) than butterflies (Rhopalocera);

4) the latter suggests that at one time he may have spent the month of June (for the *luna* lurking at the back of his mind occurs only in early summer) in a country-house in New York state; warm dark fluffy nights.

5) He was not a smoker since the empty Regent cigarette box with the sketches would have contained a few crumbs of tobacco if he had been using its contents just before; it had been lying about and he just picked it up. [In margin] The reasoning here is uh-uh.

6) May have been together with a lady: she lent him the scissors to cut out of the cigarette wrapping paper the specimen of *Vino gravis;*[4] the scissors were small pointed scissors (because an attempt was made, but not pursued, to cut out one of the moths on the paper napkin).

7) There is a faint smudge of lipstick on the lid of the box.

8) He had not been eating when he started to sketch—because the first one (the *pseudo luna*) was drawn on the paper napkin when it was still folded.

9) He was not a painter but may have been a writer; this is however not suggested by the presence of a fountain pen; quite possibly he borrowed the pen from the lady.

10) The whole thing may have started from a curlicue; but the further development was conscious.

11) There is a *cherteniata* or *diablotins*[5] strain in the general aspect of the moths.

12) Was under the impression that a moth's body is all belly: he segmented it from tip to top; this *may* mean that he believed in the stomach rather more than in the heart: e.g., he would be apt to explain this or that action on material, and not sentimental, grounds.

13) The lady was doing the talking.

Well, Watson, that's about all. I am eagerly looking forward to seeing you!

Your book is causing quite a "sensation" among my literary friends here. Neither am I attracted by Marion Bloom's "smellow melons" or Albertine's *"bonnes grosses joues"*; but I gladly follow Rodolphe *("Avançons! Du courage!")* as he leads Emma to her golden doom in the bracken.[6] I mean, it was in that purely physiological sense that I criticized your hero's *prouesses*.[7]

Lovingly yours,
V.

1. Most of this letter is about some drawings of butterflies which Wilson had sent to Nabokov. Their description is a parody of a Sherlock Holmes investigation.

2. "Inebriated drunkard."

3. "Full of wine."

4. "Heavy with wine."

5. "Little devils," in Russian and French.

6. *I.e.,* Nabokov prefers the erotic descriptions in Flaubert's *Madame Bovary* to those in Joyce's *Ulysses* and Proust's *Sodom and Gomorrah*. The first French quote means "nice fat cheeks" and the second one "Forward! Take heart!"

7. "Feats."

143

THE NEW YORKER
No. 25 West 43rd Street

April 6, 1946

Dear Vladimir: The man who drew the butterflies was not a painter, but a sculptor—which you ought perhaps to have guessed from the fact that he cut one of them out. The explanation is that Dawn Powell and Louise Conner[1] went to some Greenwich Village bar that night after they left my house and fell in with this man, who drew butterflies while they were talking about you and your researches. Hope to be seeing you soon.

EW

1. On the novelist Dawn Powell, who was a friend of Wilson's and whose novels he admired, see the essay "Dawn Powell: Greenwich Village in the Fifties" in his collection *The Bit Between My Teeth* (1962) and his letters to her in his *Letters on Literature and Politics (1912–1972)*. On Louise Conner, née Fort, a longtime friend of Wilson's, see Wilson, *The Forties. From Notebooks and Diaries of the Period*, Leon Edel, editor (New York, 1983), pp. 298 ff.

144

8 Craigie Circle
Cambridge 38, Mass.
Kirkland 24–58

May 25, 1946

Дорогой мой Эдмундъ,

Что-же это—надѣялся что ты залетишь въ Бостонъ, а тебя все нѣтъ да нѣтъ . . . Когда-же мы увидимся?

Я кончилъ романъ.[1] I have just finished the novel.[2] I have revised and partly rewritten the chapters you have seen, and shall spend a week or two in removing extraneous matter, etc. It has taken four years to compose and I am now resting comfortably with the rubber-red infant at my side. As I think I told you I got the first part (with your wonderfully useful corrections) back from Doubleday. My intention is now to send the typescript to them and see what happens. I do not know whether the thing is likeable but at any rate it is honest i.e., it comes as close as humanly possible to the image I had of it all along. I do hope Doubleday or somebody will buy it because I am horribly short of money—in fact cannot take a much needed vacation for this reason. But I *am* glad the obsession and burden are gone. It also means that I shall be able to write something for *The New Yorker* (who has been really very sweet with impotent me).

I have cut out (or rather Miss Kelly[3] has sent it to me) a cartoon depicting two people wondering why you have such nasty friends. Have you seen it?[4]

Somebody told me that *Hecate* is number 13 in a best-seller list.

How are you? How is everything? I liked the one about Trotsky[5] though I do not think many people will know the difference between a duma and the Duma. The latter, of course, was a free and perfectly outspoken Parliament. One reader, however, misunderstood your remark.[6]

Sebastian is doing rather well in England, with the assistance of your delightful blurb. I have discovered a new butterfly among material (sent from Oxford!) collected in the Cayman group of islands (W.I.)[7]

Напиши мнѣ,[8]
Very much yours
V.

1. "My dear Edmund, what is going on—I had hoped that you would pay a flying visit to Boston, but there is no sign of you . . . When shall we see each other? I finished the novel."

2. *Bend Sinister*, mentioned earlier as *The Person from Porlock* and also temporarily

given the provisional title *Solus Rex* (not to be confused with the earlier Russian fragment called "Solus Rex").

3. Amy Kelly, Nabokov's colleague at Wellesley, author of *Eleanor of Aquitaine*.

4. For a reproduction of this cartoon, see *Letters on Literature and Politics, 1912–1972*, p. 434.

5. Wilson's review of Leon Trotsky's *Stalin* in *The New Yorker*, May 4, 1946.

6. In his review of Trotsky's book, Wilson wrote: "Now, what democracy really depends on, the only thing that can make the word real, is distribution of responsibility, and the soviets (councils) of a Socialist state in a country where this is unknown can no more be democratic than the dumas of the czardom could." The word *duma*, when not capitalized, may refer to the councils at the courts of the pre-Petrine Muscovite tsars; in its capitalized form, it means the freely elected parliament, the State Duma of the period 1905–1917.

7. This butterfly is described and illustrated in Nabokov's article "A New Species of Cyclargus Nabokov (Lycaenidae, Lepidoptera)," in *The Entomologist*, London, Vol. 81, No. 1027, December 1948.

8. "Write me."

145

THE NEW YORKER
No. 25 West 43rd Street

June 4, 1946

Dear Vladimir: I wasn't able to go up to Wellfleet as early as I expected because my mother had to go to the hospital to have more operations on her eye and I couldn't leave until she was out. By that time it was so late that I went straight up through Providence instead of stopping off in Boston. Friday I'm going back, but I'll have Reuel and shall be driving so that I can't go to Boston then either. (I've just purchased a remarkable car, a 1931 Cadillac, which belonged to an old lady in California and was in storage for countless years, so that it has been absolutely perfectly preserved like that Siberian mammoth in the ice. It is enormous and looks slightly comic, because it has one of those straight up-and-down store-window fronts that they do not make any more. You sit or recline in back on a high and much-upholstered seat, from which you look down on the driver and the passing world, and the whole thing gives the impression that Aldanov would think appropriate for a prosperous man of letters with a *réputation mondiale*.[1] *Hecate County*, by the way, is about to be translated into French, Italian, Spanish, Danish, Swedish and Dutch. Hitherto the only language that I have ever been translated into was Japanese.)

I'm sorry that your book has reached Doubleday at a time when Donald Elder is abroad. I've talked to Ken McCormick[2] about it and shall try to impress him with your importance. Let me know what happens about it.

I'll undoubtedly get to Boston sometime, but in the meantime couldn't you come up to the Cape to visit me? I think that you and I ought to ride around together in my Cadillac. (It has just been pointed out to me that it is the kind of thing that always gets stuck in those sandy roads up there.)

Love to the family,
EW

1. "Worldwide reputation."
2. Kenneth McCormick, editor-in-chief with Doubleday and Co.

146

8 Craigie Circle
Cambridge, 38, Mass.
Kirkland 24–58

June 21, 1946

Dear Bunny,

I should dearly like to see you driving up—sitting very straight—in that ancient automobile. Thanks for inviting me to C[ape] C[od]. I have mailed my novel to Doubleday. It is called (provisionally) *"Solus Rex"* (The [Black] King Alone)—a chess-problem term. Thanks for preparing them for the shock. I suppose you also mentioned the matter to Tate. Question: can I send a second copy to Holt *before* getting a reply from Doubleday? Is it *bien vu*[1] in literary circles? Or is it not done? My books have been handled by seedy agents, and I know little about these things.

With the feeling I had 1. some serious heart trouble, 2. ulcers, 3. cancer in the gullet and 4. stones everywhere, I had myself thoroughly examined at a good hospital. The doctor (a Prof. Siegfried Tannhäuser) found that I was constitutionally in fine shape but was suffering from acute nervous exhaustion due to the entomology-Wellesley-novel combination, and suggested my taking a two months vacation. So we have rented a bungalow in the middle of New Hampshire (Newfound Lake) and are going there in the middle of next week. I got some advance money from Weeks.

I am feeling decidedly anti-British. Do suggest some good books for Dmitri.

Yours
V.

Laughlin asks me "what's the future on *(sic)* the *Three Russian Poets?*" He has apparently sold out the ed[ition] and anyway the time limit I set him is up. What are our plans in regard to our Doubleday book? I shall do *whatever you decide*. If there is 1'/₂–2 years before our Doubleday volume can appear Laughlin might want to reprint *The 3 Poets*.

1. "Well-regarded."

147

I had a pretty little moth in my room that looked like this:

all black except white spots. What is the medium-sized yellow moth with owl-eyes that appears at this time of year: Emperor?

THE NEW YORKER
No. 25 West 43rd Street

June 25, 1946

Dear Vladimir: No: you ought to send your MS to only one publisher at a time. Have you got an extra copy of the part I haven't read? I'd like to see it. Do get a rest. I'm sorry you're not coming to the Cape, but we must arrange something in September. Yes: let Laughlin reprint the Russian poets. About Dmitri: I don't know what he has already read—will talk to him about it when I see him. Has he read *Tom Sawyer* and *Huckleberry Finn?* Isn't he old enough to read Dickens? I'm writing this in a hurry. Am in New York for three days, trying to get a lot of things done. Love to the family. Let me know what happens about the book.

As ever,
EW

148

8 Craigie Circle
Cambridge 38, Mass.
Kirkland 24–58

July 18, 1946

Dear Bunny,

I am "recuperating" (from what was practically a "nervous breakdown") in New Hampshire. The place is terrible (highway, shopkeepers, *bourgeois en goguette*,[1] advertisements with "gentile clientèle",—made a row in one such place) but we have paid in advance and cannot get out until August 18 when we shall go to Wellesley for a month.

Doubleday has not yet answered. I do not think they will want my novel and as soon as they send the manuscript back I shall forward it to you and send the second copy to Holt.

As usual I want to see you very much.

Yours
V.

1. "Bourgeoisie on a spree"; Véra Nabokov pointed out that the word "bourgeoisie" was used by Nabokov in a Flaubertian rather than a Marxist sense. For an account of the "row" Nabokov mentions, see *The Annotated Lolita*, Alfred Appel, Jr., ed., pp. 423–424.

149

THE NEW YORKER
No. 25 West 43rd Street

September 10, 1946
Wellfleet

Dear Volodya: Where are you now? There's just a chance I might be stopping off sometime in Boston. And what about your coming up here. I called McCormick up when I was in New York a couple of weeks ago—he said he was just about to read your novel. I've had my hands full this summer with a number of things that I'll explain to you when I see you. This is just to get in touch with you. I'm sorry that you wore yourself out so—hope you're fully restored now. I hope you've been seeing the good reviews that *Sebastian Knight* has been getting in England—it seems to have gone much better there than here.

As ever,

EW

150

Dear Bunny,

Thanks for your nice letter. I am quite well again,—better, in fact, than I ever was. Before I forget: if anybody accuses you of writing "immoral" stuff, please direct their attention to the following:

> "Island Interlude," *The Readers' Digest*
> September 1946,
> *25: 123*

and

> "Where the High Winds Blow," *International Digest*
> September 1946,
> *3 (2): 95*

This is real filth. Have your lawyers produce them in court. The "Island" story is about sailors looking through a telescope at nurses having showerbaths and the point of the story is a mole on one of the girls' fanny. The "High Winds" is mainly about the way Eskimos copulate (see especially: 106–107) and their children "imitating the actions of their parents, who chuckle at their youngsters' realism." There is an illustration: 108 depicting two youngsters trying to copulate while their parents "chuckle." These "Digests" are eagerly read at all schools. Perhaps these two examples might come in handy.[1]

I want to see you very badly. I am at the museum from 9 to 12 A.M. daily and go to Wellesley (till 5:30 P.M.) on Monday, Wednesday and Friday. It would be wonderful if you came on Tuesday or Thursday or Saturday.

Laughlin wants to reprint my *Three Poets* but also wants a five year "protection." I shall give it [to] him provided you are sure we shall not need this material for our Doubleday book before 1951. As he is going to Europe soon, could you, please, drop me a line straight away.

I have written Doubleday (Bradbury)[2] to hurry up: they have been reading my novel since May, must know it by heart. You have not seen the whole thing yet and I am very eager to have you read it. I went to New York the other day and saw Roman: we sunbathed on his roof and then I played chess with Yanovsky.

Have been re-reading Tolstoy and Dostoevsky. The latter is a third rate writer and his fame is incomprehensible.

Крѣпко жму твою руку,[3]

V.

1. Nabokov offers Wilson these examples to use as ammunition in the campaign to protect *Memoirs of Hecate County* from being banned as obscene. "Island Interlude" is, of course, a chapter from Thomas Heggen's extremely popular novel *Mr. Roberts.*

2. Walter Bradbury, senior editor at Doubleday at the time.

3. "I firmly clasp your hand."

151

[Postmarked September 23, 1946]

Dear Bunny,

Yesterday I had the visit of McCormick. He told me that novels about "dictators" have no appeal at present, that the public wants "escapist" books and that therefore my novel would come out at the "wrong" moment. However, he was interested to know whether I would be interested in signing a contract of the kind a man called Stone[1] did (a certain sum per year supporting the writer while he writes). You know how sick I am of the drudgery of teaching (or rather of the inability to combine this with writing). I said I would be glad to accept such an offer. He asked me how much I was getting at Wellesley (3000) and I told him (3000). Of course, since giving up Wellesley would mean giving up all chances of an "associate professorship," etc., the sum I would require would be somewhat higher. We all spoke of a possible revision of the Holland's *Butterfly Book*[2] which they had published (last edition in 1931). McC[ormick] asked me what I was writing or going to write but I found it difficult to explain to him *tout de go*[3] the new kind of novel I had in mind and have instead written him today about it (giving him a very general idea of it).

I must repeat that I am very very eager to have all this arranged, but I am also anxious to have my Krug novel[4] published as soon as possible. Do you think something will come of all this?

There is something else. Tate to whom I showed the MS as one private individual to another (I mean with the clear understanding that I was *not* submitting it to his firm Holt) is sending me letters and telegrams asking me to come to N.Y. (expenses paid). I am telling him that I can do nothing before Doubleday gives me a definite answer.

We agreed, I and McCormick, that he would see "his directors" Tuesday 1st Oct[ober] when they have a meeting and that they will then decide things—with the knowledge of my approval of their plan.

Do please write me. I am sure you have been helpful in this business as you always are, but I feel I still need your advice.

Yours

V.

I am very anxious to know more about your "trial." Did the material I suggested fit into the plan of defense? Those ("Digests," "Winks," "Peeps," etc.) are the real offenders. *Hecate Co[unty]* is as pure as a block of ice in a surgical laboratory.

1. Irving Stone, who was under contract with Doubleday from 1940 on.
2. See Letter 90, item 8 and note 4.
3. "Right off."
4. *I.e., Bend Sinister.*

152

THE NEW YORKER
No. 25 West 43rd Street

September 24, 1946
Wellfleet

Dear Volodya: I saw McCormick when I was in New York last week and talked to him about your book. They seem to think that it will be hard, at this time, to sell a book that deals with the life of fascism; but McCormick says he is going to look you up when he comes to Boston and see whether he can't make some arrangement with you. This is vague, but he will probably propose giving you an advance on some other book. It might be better if you kept the whole thing in abeyance till Donald Elder comes back the first of November. If Doubleday definitively won't publish the present book, I think you ought to send it to Allen Tate at Holt. *Don't sign any agreement with Doubleday if they won't publish the present book.* Insist that they will have to take it if they want further work of yours. If they refuse, see what you can do elsewhere. If you don't come to terms with some other publisher, take the whole thing up later with Elder.

I hope that you have not arranged to give Laughlin a volume of your stories as one of his advertisements seemed to indicate. As for the poets, give Laughlin only a two-year protection. I'm going to drop my *New Yorker* job entirely and perhaps do only one article a month after the first of the year and shall be able to get back to my other work.

I was glad to hear from Roman that you were reading Dostoevsky for the first time.

I got a letter from the State Department asking me to report on your abilities and character, which I shall do with no mention of your puns and practical-joking proclivities.[1]

The Letters, 1946

I hope to drive down to Boston with Rosalind sometime after the fifth, when Reuel will have gone back to his mother, and will call up and let you know. I have a telephone now, by the way: Wellfleet 172 Ring 11. I'm extremely anxious to see you.

As ever,

EW

1. Nabokov's teaching position at Wellesley was temporary, subject to yearly renewal. In search of a more secure job, he had applied to the Department of State for work as the head of the Russian section at the newly created Voice of America. In the Edmund Wilson holdings at the Beinecke Library, there is a letter (dated September 20, 1946) to Wilson from Special Agent R. D. Clark asking for a letter evaluating Nabokov's "family and education background, marital status, general reputation, personality, loyalty, ability, etc." There is also Wilson's highly laudatory letter of recommendation.

As Brian Boyd put it, "But the opening closed when Nicolas Nabokov, whom he [Vladimir Nabokov] had also approached for a reference, secured the job for himself instead." See Boyd, *Vladimir Nabokov: The American Years*, p. 113.

153

8 Craigie Circle

Cambridge 38, Mass.

Kirkland 24–58

November 1, 1946

Dear Bunny,

I do not know where you are. How did the N.Y. trial come out? I was in N.Y. just before you came (*teste* Tate). My novel is going to the better bidder—Holt.

I have at last compared Wilson's "City of the Plague" with the *Пир во время чумы*.[1] The latter *is* a wonderfully close translation of the former except for the two songs which are quite different (and much finer in Pushkin). My own translation of the *пир* into English is uncomfortably like the Wilson original in part but, on the whole, superior to it.

Please, drop me a note.

Yours

V.

Holt advances 2000, Doubleday offered only 1000. Holt loved the book. Doubleday was cool.

1. *Feast during the Plague* (by Pushkin). See Letter 21, note 3, and Letter 22, note 4.

154

November 17, 1946
The Minden Inn
Minden, Nevada

Dear Volodya: I was awfully glad to hear about your book. Did you make any arrangement with them for subsidizing you while you write another?

I am out here in a small but excellent country hotel, leading a quiet, industrious and healthful life. Have been reading up the early books of Malraux and deciding that he is probably the greatest contemporary writer. Did you ever read *La Condition Humaine?*[1] I should be curious to know how you reacted to it.

I'm going to get married out here, go to San Francisco for a few days, and then back to the East—leaving Nevada December 10 and arriving in New York the 18th. Then up to Wellfleet for Christmas and the rest of the winter. I do hope you people can get up to see us. I am marrying a girl named Elena Thornton—née Mumm and the daughter of a man who made champagne. Her mother was Russian—named Struve. She is a friend of Nina's and Nicholas', and you may know about her. It is all such a fortunate affair that I am afraid something dreadful will happen—an earthquake in San Francisco, perhaps.

My case was heard early in November, and the decision is to be handed down the 27th. Do drop me a line out here. I'm anxious to read the end of your novel. Love to Vera.

As ever,
Edmund W

1. *Man's Fate.*

155

November 27, 1946

Dear Bunny,

I was tremendously glad to receive your Nevada letter. Véra joins me in wishing you and your wife mnogo, mnogo samovo luchezarnovo shchast'ia.[1] We are looking forward to seeing both of you soon.

My novel, the final title of which is *Bend Sinister*, has gone to the printers. The second copy of the MS is more or less dismembered (parts will be published in magazines, I think), so I still cannot show you *B. S.* Somewhere inside me there is something insisting that I would like you to judge of the thing only in its final, or at least page proof, form, especially as I have altered considerably the first chapters so that you have not seen the novel at all yet. I want it to come to you *whole*, as a nice solid surprise, a kind of wedding present.

Et maintenant—en garde![2] I am at a loss to understand your liking Malraux's books (or are you just kidding me? or is literary taste so subjective a matter that two persons of discrimination can be at odds in such a simple case as this?). He is quite a third-rate writer (but a good kind man, a very decent fellow). *J'ai dressé*[3] a little list of questions (regarding *La Condition Humaine*)[4] which I suggest you answer.

1. What are those interesting *couvertures* in which the *femmes, enfants et vieillards* (God, what a combination—what a 10,000th combination!) are *enveloppés*,[5] and where the hell has the author seen people *sneezing* when exposed to frost?

2. What is the *grand silence de la nuit chinoise* (try and substitute: *de la nuit americaine, de la nuit belge,*[6] etc., and see what happens—and please note that China consists of a great number of different biotic regions). From childhood I remember a golden inscription that fascinated me: "Compagnie Internationale des Wagons-Lits et des Grands Express Européens." Malraux's work belongs to the *Compagnie Internationale des Grands Clichés.*

3. Do crickets (the cricket—the Goddamned couleur locale pet cricket—that was *éveillé*[7] by one of the characters' arrival, p. 20) and mosquitoes (p. 348) occur, in the imaginal stage, *in early spring*, in Shanghai? I doubt it.

4. Have you never noticed the way bad writers attempt to give individuality to their (hopelessly amorphous) characters by inflicting upon them some trick of speech (rather like the dog that Galsworthy or Hugh Walpole or some other English *seredniak*[8] gave to one of his characters and h a d to keep on referring to e v e r y t i m e the man appeared)? I simply cannot believe that you are able to stomach the recurrent *bong* of Tchen, the *'bsolument*[9] of Katow and other *soi disant*[10] mannerisms that make me squirm (all typical in an author who like Malraux is intrinsically devoid of humor). This particular trick has been extensively used by Russian (Soviet) writers in a pathetic effort to give some originality or attractive quaintness to the staunch pig iron strong-silent communists they depicted; and detective story writers do the same in regard to their sleuths.

5. Why on earth has he given his Russian *bonhomme*[11] a name ending in "w" and derived—which of course he did not know (*la vengeance du Verbe,*[12] I call it)—from the old Russian word *kat* which happens to mean executioner? Perhaps he took "Schatow" from a German translation (or a French translation

employing German transliteration) of Dostoevsky's novel and replaced the first consonants by the K of Kaliaev.[13] *La vengeance pure du Verbe bafouillé.*[14]

6. What exactly (racially? politically? visually? in any other terms?) is a *Russe du Caucase*[15] (p. 101) (as referring to the highly irritating maitresse of the capitalisto-individualisto-lotiesque-decobratique[16] Frenchman) and how do you like the *beau visage d'Américain un peu* (say 3%) *Sioux*[17] (p. 197)?

7. The *quand j'étais encore socialiste-révolutionnaire*[18] casually mentioned by the communist Katow (as a frog would say: when I was still a tadpole) is of course all wrong both phylogenetically and ontogenetically, but is probably necessary for the poor purpose of explaining his leaning towards terroristic tactics.

8. Do you really mean to say that you do not see that *La Condition Humaine* (as well as his *Temps du Mépris*[19]) is one solid mass of clichés? Analyze the impossibly trite rhythms of such sentences as *jamais il n'eut cru*, etc. (p. 202) or *il fallait revenir parmi les hommes*[20] and countless other platitudes (dark, crisp, staccato platitudes in the best machine gun-order-of-the-day-*simplicité héroique-qu'il mourut*[21] modern style).

9. *A chevo stoiat odni èti zagolovki: Minuit, Trois Heures du Matin,*[22] etc.!

10. Have you read Pilniak, Lidin, Vsevolod Ivanov and other descendants of Savinkov and Andreyev, i.e., writers of the first Soviet decade who loved using Chinese backgrounds and did this kind of thing better?

11. Have you tried asking a cultured Chinese about the howlers in *La Condition Humaine*? (of course the worst howler is the (wrong) stressing of a (correct) local feature. The dying Britisher who recalls the white cliffs of Dover. He might, but would he?

This about sums up my position. The longer I live the more I become convinced that the o n l y thing that matters in literature, is the (more or less irrational) *shamanstvo*[23] of a book, i.e., that the good writer is first of all an enchanter.

But one must not let things tumble out of one's sleeves all the time as Malraux does.

Krepko zhmu tvoiu ruku, drug moi.

Tvoi[24]

V

1. "Lots and lots of the most radiant happiness" (partly in phonetic transcription).
2. "And now—watch out!"
3. "I have compiled."
4. See the second paragraph of Letter 154.

5. "Blankets" in which the "women, children and old men" [. . .] are "wrapped."

6. "Great silence of Chinese night" [. . .] "of American night," "of Belgian night."

7. "Awakened."

8. "Mediocrity."

9. " 'bsolutely."

10. "Would be" or "so called."

11. "Fellow."

12. "The vengeance of the Word."

13. Shatov is a character in Dostoevsky's *The Possessed;* Ivan Kaliaev was a Socialist Revolutionary terrorist who was executed during the 1905 revolution for his part in several political assassinations. Nabokov's paternal uncle Konstantin narrowly escaped being blown up by one of Kaliaev's bombs when he turned down a ride offered to him by the Grand Duke Sergei Alexandrovich a few minutes before the duke was assassinated (*Speak, Memory,* p. 60).

14. "The pure vengeance of the mumbled Word."

15. "Russian from the Caucasus."

16. That is, suggesting the trashy French best sellers by Pierre Loti and Maurice Dekobra.

17. "American's handsome face which was slightly [. . .] Sioux."

18. "When I was still a Socialist Revolutionary."

19. American edition called *Days of Wrath.*

20. "He would have never believed" or "one had to go back among men."

21. "Heroic simplicity—that he died."

22. "To say nothing of those priceless headings: Midnight, Three O'Clock in the Morning, etc.!"

23. "Shamanism" (*i.e.,* magic).

24. "I firmly clasp your hand, my friend. Yours, V."

156

THE NEW YORKER
No. 25 West 43rd Street

December 1, 1946
The Minden Inn
Minden, Nevada

Dear Volodya: I knew that I would get a rise—but I am perfectly sincere about Malraux. Some of your points against *La Condition Humaine* seem to me badly taken, the others of little importance. As for enchantment, he has always enchanted me since I read *Les Conquérants*[1] (though I don't care for *Le Temps du Mépris*). *La Condition Humaine* seems to me the novel I have read which has best expressed the crises and emotions of its period—and the first installment of *La Lutte avec l'Ange,*[2] written during the war, in some ways even more remarkable. (I admit that he has no sense of humor: *La Voie Royale*,[3] though an exciting book, has its unintentionally humorous aspects.) He is surely the only first-rate imaginative genius that the French have produced since Proust. Inaccuracies, clichés and clumsiness do not in themselves invalidate a writer. You and I, besides, differ completely, not only about Malraux, but also about Dostoevsky, Greek drama, Lenin, Freud, and a lot of other things—about which, I'm sure, [we] will never be reconciled; so that we'd better, I suppose, stick to the more profitable discussion of Pushkin, Flaubert, Proust, Joyce, etc. (Your enthusiasm for *South Wind*,[4] by the way, seems to me an extravagant example of the betrayal of a man of taste by his enjoyment of a special kind of thing—in this case, malicious humor—which hasn't necessarily anything to do with first-rate literature.)

Do you know Silone at all? I've also been reading out here the books of his I hadn't read. He and Malraux now emerge, I think, as the masters of this political-social-moral semi-Marxist school of fiction that is the great development in its field since the analytical psychological novel; but their points of view are entirely different. You might like Silone's better—though he's not really so great a man as Malraux.[5]

I'm very eager to see your own book. Do have them send me the proofs. *Hecate County* was convicted in New York by a vote of two to one. Doubleday is going to appeal it. The dissenting judge wrote a very intelligent opinion; the other two—what is rather unusual—voted *Guilty* without explanation. It is all an awful nuisance and is putting a crimp in my income.

I have been having a very quiet and not unpleasant, rather purgatorial, time out here. It is a queer and desolate country—less romantic than prehistoric and spooky. I made some money one night at roulette, and then threw it all away. Gambling, however, is a weakness of the great Russian writers that is incomprehensible to me. As an amateur magician, I can more or less see how the roulette wheels, the dice and the *vingt-et-un* (Black Jack) deals are being manipulated. The pretty girls they get out here to do the dealing in the card games are simply wonderful with their fingers and must have had months of preliminary practice. I like to go in to watch them.

I'm looking forward to getting back to Wellfleet and hope you people can get up to see us. [...]

As ever,

EW

1. *The Conquerors.*
2. *Wrestling with the Angel.*
3. *The Royal Way.*

4. By Norman Douglas. *In Strong Opinions* (1973), Nabokov named *South Wind* among the books he had liked in his youth and still continued to like. Wilson's negative opinion of this book covers three pages (pp. 212–214) in *Europe Without Baedeker*.

5. Wilson develops the parallel between Malraux and Silone in the chapter "Two Survivors: Malraux and Silone" in *Europe Without Baedeker*.

157

8 Craigie Circle
Cambridge 38, Mass.
Kirkland 24–58

December 19, 1946

Dear Bunny,

are you back East? Shall we see you soon?

I have been reading a good deal of Henry James lately and am intending to write a piece called "The King (H.J. in this case) is Naked." So is T.S.E.[1]

It was not quite fair to bring out *South Wind* but I cannot be cross with you. Nong.

We are in fine shape, all three and send you our love.

Bong.[2]

Yours   V

1. T. S. Eliot.

2. "Nong" and "bong" are how Chinese characters pronounce the French words *non* and *bon* in *Man's Fate* by Malraux. See Letter 155.

1947

158

THE NEW YORKER
No. 25 West 43rd Street

January 9, 1947

Dear Vladimir: We spent Christmas in the Cape, are now in New York for a few days, and are going back to Wellfleet tomorrow to spend the rest of winter there. When we get settled, I hope that you can come up to see us. At present Nina and Rosalind[1] are living with us.

At a Russian Christmas party the other evening, I met your old roommate Kalashnikov,[2] with an apparently Spanish wife. He said he wanted to get in touch with you. I tried to draw him out about your career at Cambridge, but all I could get out of him was that you were a queer fellow and that you had impressed him by writing English verse.

About Henry James: it's possible, as Ezra Pound says, to get no impression of him at all if you begin by reading the wrong things. But once you have read him at his best and got an idea of his literary development, almost everything he wrote becomes interesting. I think that almost all his long novels tend to run into the sands in the second volume, and that some of the shorter ones are more satisfactory. Be sure to read, in the New York edition, the volume that contains *What Maisie Knew, In The Café,* and *The Pupil.* These stories are among my favorites.

Allen Tate seems to be dazzled by your novel. I am anxious to read it in proof. But why on earth did you sign with them, as he says you did, a contract with an option clause and no advance on your next book? This is something that must *never* be done.

As ever,

EW

1. Wilson's daughter by his first wife, Mary Blair.
2. See next letter, note 4.

159

Dear Bunny,

nakonetz-to[1] I am sending you my novel. The 'author's copy' has already gone back to the printers. I have transferred from it only the major corrections so do not bother about the missing commas before subord[inate] clauses and other trifles. But if you find some real howlers, please *prishcholkni ikh.*[2] Although you have seen the first chapters, do start from the beginning again since I have introduced some subtle improvements and, incidentally, a remarkable moon. Needless to say, your opinion of *Bend Sinister*—*no vprochem ty vsio znaesh sam.*[3] And little by little, I hope, you and I shall shift to Russian altogether.

Your running into yet another dead fish [out] of my past is very amusing, especially as you seem to be trying to reconstruct me much in the same way as I did in regard to Sebastian. The man K. was—and probably has remained—a typical Russian fascist of the old school, *chernosotenetz i durak.*[4] He was my roommate only for one term, thank God, for he failed in his exam at the end of the first year and had to leave Cambridge Univ[ersity]. He considered himself extraordinarily well-read but the only two books he *had* read were *Sionskie Protokoly*[5] and *L'homme qui assassina* by Farrère.[6] Later he added to this list the *Island of San Michele.*[7] We shared a shabby sitting-room and he used to throw things at me or drown the fire in the fireplace when I attempted to do some reading. His examination paper was on Democracy and he started it with a sentence which *instantly* settled his fate. The sentence was: "Democracy is a Latin word." He was moreover a most disgusting snob, but ladies thought him witty and most attractive (do not tell Nina Chavch[avadze] about all this, she is quite sure we used to be boon companions. We did play a lot of lawn-tennis together, etc., and in the early twenties I almost married a cousin of his, but that's about all).

I want to ask you something in connection with the book-reviewing in *The New Yorker*. It is a delicate question since I should not like to seem to be butting into your own arrangements in any way and from any angle. If you again took the whole thing into your hands, it would be, of course, wonderful. *But, if* the inter-Wilsonian gaps are supposed to remain, I was wondering whether I could not attempt to fill them with some reviewing. Would you care to *nashchupat' pochvu*[8] in *The New Yorker*, or should I write about it to Mrs. White? I mean, tell me absolutely frankly what you think of this rather desperate plan of mine (for I *must* do something to improve my finances). I am giving up my museum curatorship in the fall,—it interferes too much with my literary work. I have re-written, with Véra's help, thirty or so lectures on Russian literature, and am delivering them twice a week in Wellesley. I had hopes that, with Cross dead, some arrangement might have come my way in Harvard, *en fait de*[9] Russian Department. But apparently I am not their type. Nothing came either of the Russian Broadcasting plan. Good old Nika got the job which had been promised me. [...]

Well, it is time to allow you to settle down comfortably to the reading of *Bend Sinister.* We both are very anxious to see both of you but we cannot leave Cambridge, unfortunately. I may be coming to N.Y. some time in spring.

What are you writing now? I have read (or rather re-read) *What Maisie Knew.* It is terrible. Perhaps there is some *other* Henry James and I am continuously hitting upon the wrong one?

V

1. "At last."
2. "Knock them out."
3. "But you in any case know all that."
4. "Anti-Semite [lit., "member of the Black Hundreds"] and idiot." On Nabokov's Cambridge University roommate Mikhail ("Mishka") Kalashnikov, see Brian Boyd, *Vladimir Nabokov: The Russian Years,* especially pp. 169–179. As Boyd points out, Nabokov shared lodgings with "Mishka" not for one term but for two years.
5. *Protocols of the Elders of Zion.*
6. In *The Gift,* Nabokov made Claude Farrère's trashy novel *(The Man Who Killed)* and *Protocols of the Elders of Zion* the favorite reading of the disagreeable stepfather of the novel's half-Jewish heroine, Zina Mertz. The Russian version of *Speak, Memory* briefly mentions the same two books in connection with Nabokov's temporary Russian roommate at Cambridge (*Drugie berega,* p. 221).
7. *I.e., The Story of San Michele* (original title, *Mont San Michele*) by Axel Munthe.
8. "Explore the ground."
9. "With regard to." Samuel Hazzard Cross (1891–1946) was one of the pioneers of Slavic literary studies in America.

160

January 30, 1947
Wellfleet, Mass.

Dear Vladimir:

I was rather disappointed in *Bend Sinister,* about which I had had some doubts when I was reading the parts you showed me, and I will give you my opinion, for what it is worth. Other people may very well think otherwise: I know, for example, that Allen Tate is tremendously excited about it—he told me that he considered it "a great book." But I feel that, though it is crammed with good things—brilliant writing and amusing satire—it is not one of your greatest successes. First of all, it seems to me that it suffers from the same weakness as that play about the dictator.[1] You aren't good at this kind of subject, which involves questions of politics and social change, because you are totally uninterested in these matters and have never taken the trouble to understand them. For you, a dictator like the Toad is simply a vulgar and odious person who bullies serious and superior people like Krug. You have no idea why or how the Toad was able to put himself over, or what his revolution implies. And this makes your picture of such happenings rather unsatisfactory. Now don't tell me that the real artist has nothing to do with the issues of politics. An artist may not take politics seriously, but, if he deals with such matters at all, he ought to know what it is all about. Nobody could be more contemplative or cooler or more intent on pure art than Walter Pater, whose *Gaston de Latour* I have just been reading; but I declare that he has a great deal more insight into the struggle between Catholicism and Protestantism that was raging in the sixteenth century than you have into the conflicts of the twentieth.

I think, too, that your invented country has not served you particularly well. Your strength lies so much in precise observation that, in combining Germanic and Slavic, you have produced something that does not seem real—especially as one has always to compare it with the hideous contemporary reality. Beside the actual Nazi Germany and the actual Stalinist Russia, the adventures of your unfortunate professor have the air of an unpleasant burlesque. I never believed in him much from the beginning, was never moved by the wife and the son; but I thought you were going eventually to turn him inside out, take the whole thing apart and show that our ideas of injustice and tragedy were purely subjective or something of the sort. (I'm sorry that you gave up the idea of having your hero confront his maker.) As it is, what you are left with on your hands is a satire on events so terrible that they really can't be satirized—because in order to satirize anything you have to make it worse than it is.

Another thing, *Bend Sinister* is (with the exception of that play) the only thing of yours that has seemed to me to have longueurs. It doesn't move with the Pushkinian rapidity that I have always admired in your writing. I know that you have been aiming here at a denser texture of prose than in a thing like *Sebastian Knight,* and some of the writing is very remarkable, but there are moments,—don't send me an infernal machine!—when I am reminded of Thomas Mann.

You have certainly improved it a lot, though, since the manuscript I saw. I expect to reread it when I get the book and find much that I didn't appreciate.

By the way I see that I was wrong in changing the gender of *derrière* in the proof—for some reason, I always think of it as feminine. One thing I believe I forgot to correct is the girl's saying that the man has "a regular sense of humor."[2] This is impossible. She would have to say either that he had a wonderful sense of humor or that he was a regular card (I don't believe you want *regular* here at all).

About the *New Yorker*: I'll take it up with them. William Shawn, not Mrs. White, is the person to talk to about it. The thing to do is for you to write him a letter, and I'll speak to him about it when I call him up again. I think it is a good idea. Hamilton Basso and I now do one review apiece a month, but I still owe them several from my last year's contract, so for awhile things won't look much different.

Is it Nicholas who is doing the broadcasting? I didn't know he was back from Europe.

Before giving up Henry James, try the long novel called *The Princess Casamassima* and the first volume of his autobiography, *A Small Boy and Others*. These represent two departments of his work which you may not yet have sampled.

We are living up here in Wellfleet. The days become rather monotonous, but we are quietly working for civilization. Nina is staying in the house with us till Paul gets back from China. We don't expect to get to New York till sometime late in March. I'm still working on my book about my trip to Europe. By the time it comes out next fall, it will be deliriously out of date.

Yes: I'm completely finished with Laughlin—wrote him long ago, when he asked me to do some favor, telling him what I thought of his practices. I regard it as a calamity that he is bringing out a book of your stories.[3] Do try to have Holt take it over.

I wish that, when you write me, you wouldn't transliterate your Russian, as it is more trouble for me that way. I always have to put it back before I can make out what it is.

Love to Vera. I hope she will forgive me for not liking Professor Krug as well as some of your other creations.

As ever,

EW

1. *The Waltz Invention.*

2. In Chapter Sixteen of *Bend Sinister*, Mariette says to her sister Linda: "I must say, your new steady has a regular sense of humor." Despite Wilson's stricture, Nabokov retained this wording in later editions of the novel.

3. *Nine Stories*, published by New Directions in 1947.

161

Dear Bunny,

Spasibo za pismo i zamechania[1]—sorry, I thought I was giving you little informal lessons of Russian by inserting those Russian words—but apparently my method was wrong.

The point of *L'égorgerai-je ou non* (To be or not to be) is, of course, the well-known hypothesis that what Hamlet meant by the first words of his soliloquy was: "Is my killing of the king to be or not to be?"[2]

"Cries on havoc" is correct—it is so in Shakespeare.

"Ghostly apes," etc., is of course not supposed to sound like Shakespeare. The meter is not of his time.

"Lower and belowed" is meant to illustrate a common German mistake ("w" for "v") when printing propaganda in English.[3]

"Recurved" is extensively used in zoological works ("Krug in the larval stage . . ."). Look up, for instance, "ibex" in Webster.

"Froonerism" is a combination of a Freudian *lapsus lingui* and a spoonerism.

I too had my doubts as to whether you would appreciate the atmosphere of my book,—especially when you praised Malraux. In historical and political matters you are partisan of a certain interpretation which you regard as absolute. This means that we will have many a pleasant tussle and that neither will ever yield a thumb (inch) of *terrain* (ground).

I am writing another book which, I hope, you will like better.

Véra joins me in sending you our love.

Yours

V.

[Scribbled at the top]
Thanks for your valuable corrections.

1. "Thank you for your letter and comments." Wilson must have sent Nabokov another letter with stylistic comments on *Bend Sinister,* a letter that was not preserved and which Nabokov is here answering.

2. Chapter Seven of *Bend Sinister* contains a detailed exegesis of Shakespeare's *Hamlet,* occasioned by a translation of the play by Adam Krug's friend Ember into a language that is primarily Russian but containing some odd admixtures ("Cries on havoc" and "ghostly apes," mentioned further on, are a part of that exegesis). The first three lines of Hamlet's soliloquy are rendered by Ember as:

Ubit' il' ne ubit'? Vot est' oprosen.
Vto bude edler: v razume tzerpieren
Ogneprashchi i strely zlovo roka—

(or as a Frenchman might have it:)

L'égorgerai-je ou non? Voici le vrai problème.
Est-il plus noble en soi de supporter quand même
Et les dards et le feu d'un accablant destin—

The usual Russian version of "To be or not to be?" is *Byt' ili ne byt'?* Nabokov's punning transformation of these words, *Ubit' il' ne ubit'?*, means "To kill or not to kill?" The rest of the quotation is standard Russian except that *oprosen* is a non-existent noun derived from the verb *oprosit'*, "to canvass," "to take a poll"; *vto bude* is a rather transparent distortion of *chto budet*, "which would be" (*bude* is the Ukrainian equivalent of the Russian *budet*); *edler* is German for "nobler"; and *tzerpieren* is a quasi-Yiddish infinitive derived from the Russian *terpet'*, "to endure," "to tolerate." The whole can be re-translated back into English as: "To kill or not to kill? Here is a question./ Which would be nobler: in the mind to endure/ the fiery slings and arrows of evil fate . . ."

The French version turns Ember's Russian rendering of Hamlet's question into: "Shall I slit his throat or not?" and then continues with a reasonably faithful translation of Shakespeare's original English.

3. In the 1964 edition of *Bend Sinister*, Nabokov changed "lower and belowed" to "lover and beloved." The words occur in one of the passages that parody Lenin's speeches, Stalin's constitution and Nazi propaganda in Chapter Thirteen of the novel.

162

THE NEW YORKER
No. 25 West 43rd Street

February 12, 1947
Wellfleet, Mass.

Dear Volodya: I have talked to Shawn about reviewing for the *New Yorker*. He says that nothing can be done this year, as he has already made agreements with several people to do a review or two apiece every month or so. But he seemed favorably disposed—he has read your *Gogol*. If I should drop out completely before the end of the year, I'll take it up with him again—though I'm afraid it will be a long time now before *Hecate County* is reprinted, if it ever is at all. I'm going to try to get a good review for your book—I don't want to do it myself because I don't want to say that you're a great writer but that I don't think *Bend Sinister* shows you at your best. (I've been hoping to do eventually, for the *Atlantic*, an article about your work as a whole.)

You misunderstood what I said about your dropping into Russian: it's not the Russian that I object to but your writing it in Roman characters, уич из джуст аз муч овь а нюсанс аз иф ай константли дид т'ис.[1]

I think that some of those tricks you expound are ƎLS∀L ᗡ∀ᗺ ʎ7IS ʎ7ᗺ∀ -ꓘ∀ƎdSNᑎ NI, but I suppose it is useless to remonstrate. I wish you were here so that we could talk—should be curious to see whether you could persuade me to like Professor O better.[2] This little дворянское гнездо[3] is leading a strange self-contained and highly creative life among the bleak winds and alcoholic neighbors. Elena is quietly transforming the house so that parts of it look already like Turgenev and I have had to rope off an American Wing. Nina has retired into her winter life, which has elements of hibernation. They alternate in getting dinner and vie with one another in cookery while I play the phonograph. It is all a great relief to me, and I am going to send everybody Valentines.

As ever,

EW

1. The English phrase "which is just as much of a nuisance as if I constantly did this" in a somewhat shaky Cyrillic transcription.
2. The name of the protagonist of *Bend Sinister*, Krug, means "circle" in Russian.
3. "Nest of Gentlefolk" (the title of a Turgenev novel).

163

February 22, 1947

Dear Bunny,

It was very nice of you to find out about that book reviewing business. And in general I liked your letter very much and was dreadfully sorry I did not see you when you passed through here.

I am sending you a Russian poem which I have composed recently.[1] The very full translation with notes, which I append, helped me, incidentally, to find out the degree of accuracy and completeness I had reached in rendering what I wanted to render. About 97%.

Yours ever,

1. Very probably "To Prince S. M. Kachurin."

164

Dear Bunny,

I have not had a word from you for ages. How are you? Did you get my Russian poem? Roman visited us recently and thought highly of it. He flew over with my friend George Hessen for the week-end and we had a delightful time—which would have been still more delightful if you had been there.

My novel is due to appear in the beginning of June. Someday you will read it again. They sent me a most absurd blurb and after an exchange of telegrams Tate wrote a new one. He has been awfully nice throughout. I have reached Tolstoy in my Wellesley course; it is going to be repeated next year, but my position is still insecure and the salary meagre—and I have little hope that *Bend Sinister* brings me any money. I am writing two things now 1. a short novel about a man who liked little girls—and it's going to be called *The Kingdom by the Sea*[1]—and 2. a new type of autobiography—a scientific attempt to unravel and trace back all the tangled threads of one's personality—and the provisional title is *The Person in Question*.[2]

I have finished my main entomological paper,[3] and butterflies will be more or less shelved for a year or so. We are thinking of going to Colorado or somewhere this summer, if luck lays an egg. Dmitri is doing very well at school this season, getting wonderful reports, and we hope he gets a scholarship at a good boarding school. He is 6 feet tall. French lovers of literature do not love the author of *bong* and *'bsolument*, I learn. I have reread your *Wound and the Bow*, and the one on Hemingway is excellent—except when you explain fluctuations in his work by fluctuations in the market. I have also read *Homeward, Angel* which I had always been afraid to touch—and how right I was! There are kingfisher-flashes here and there but on the whole it is very poor stuff. I have reread *The Amer[ican] Tragedy*—no special comment.

Spring is coming on rollerskates. When shall we see both of you?

Yours ever,

V.

---

1. The working title of *Lolita* (from Edgar Allan Poe's "Annabel Lee").
2. The future *Speak, Memory*.
3. "The Nearctic Members of the Genus *Lycaeides Hübner*" (see Letter 59, note 4).

165

A. [Inscribed on a typescript of Wilson's cycle of poems "Easy Exercises in the Use of Difficult Words"[1]]

Would there be no chance of getting you up here the weekend of May 16? We were planning a little party for then and would love to have you. Elena is writing Vera.

E.W.

B. [Inscribed on a typescript of the poem "Brief Comments on Curious Words"[2]]

This is a sample of the intellectual brilliance with which you will be entertained, if you come up here the weekend of the 16th.

E.W.

1. *Night Thoughts,* pp. 202–204.
2. *Ibid.,* pp. 205–206.

166

THE NEW YORKER
No. 25 West 43rd Street

July 18, 1947

Dear Vladimir:

I have evolved the following idea for the next phase of our Russian project. I have been making arrangements with the Oxford Press to bring out two of my old critical books and a new one, and a man named Vaudrin there—who reads Russian and knows something about Russia—mentioned to me that he had had the idea of trying to persuade you to do for them a volume of translations of Blok's poetry. I should be just as glad to get out of doing the Russian book, because so much has been coming out on Russian subjects and I have in the meantime become more interested in doing something about certain areas of American writing that have not been properly explored. So I have asked Oxford Press whether they would care to pay Doubleday the advance they gave us and sign with us two new contracts: mine for a book of miscellaneous essays, in which my *Atlantic* articles would be included, yours for a book such as you suggested our doing together but to be done by yourself alone: a translation of selected poems through the whole history of Russian poetry, with introduction and perhaps commentary. Vaudrin is eager to do this, and Doubleday has been induced to consent. The question is whether you want to undertake such a book. I have made it clear to Vaudrin that we should both expect further advances beyond the $750 apiece that we got for what was to be a joint production. Please let me know—writing to Wellfleet—how you react to this.

We are tremendously settled at Wellfleet with our large and complicated family. Everybody but me plays chess like mad, and Elena's son the other day beat the local expert after a game that lasted for hours and made them miss their dinners. Now they are clamoring for you, of whose brilliance they have heard from Rosalind.

I hope you're having a "rewarding" time out there. Geoffrey Hellman of the *New Yorker*, an amateur of lepidoptera, has come to the Cape this summer, but finds it disappointing, as you did.

Love to Vera and Dmitri.

As ever,

EW

Mr. Vladimir Nabokov
8 Craigie Circle
Cambridge, Mass.

EW:pf

167

Columbine Lodge
Rocky Mountain National Park
Estes Park, Colo.

July 24, 1947

Dear Bunny,

I am sorry to sever our Siamese connection, but otherwise your scheme is highly acceptable, and I am very grateful to you for having so neatly arranged my side of the transaction.

I have a certain number of translations ready. Tell me, how big should the volume be: 80 pages? 100 pages? The less, the better. And when do you think I could get the additional money? The sooner the better, as I am rather in a fix at the moment (as always in summer).

I am having a wonderful, though somewhat strenuous time collecting butterflies here. We have a most comfortable cabin all to ourselves. The flora is simply magnificent, some part of me must have been born in Colorado, for I am constantly recognizing things with a delicious pang. You forgot Olesha in your interesting list (*re* Muchnic's book).[1]

Will you be in New York in the first week of September? We shall stop there for three or four days on our way back.

I should love to have a chess tussle with your family!

Ever yours,
Vladimir

1. Wilson's review of *An Introduction to Russian Literature* by Helen Muchnic ("Helen Muchnic: A Teacher Turned Critic," *The New Yorker*, June 21, 1947) concludes with the suggestion that someone write a survey of all contemporary Russian writers "wherever living and of whatever party, who have flourished since 1917" and lists Trotsky, Sholokhov, Simonov, Aldanov, Nabokov and the "extinguished" Pasternak among the major writers who should be included.

168

THE NEW YORKER
No. 25 West 43rd Street

August 10, 1947
Lenox, Mass.

Dear Volodya: If you are going to be in New York in September, be sure to call Vaudrin at Oxford Press and see him about the book of translations. If you want to get a further advance, I think that you will have to promise something on a bigger scale than a hundred pages: specimens of all the principal poets with commentary and introduction. I probably shan't be in New York the first week in September, but we get to Boston fairly often, and I'll hope to see you there.

We've come over here to Lenox, on a week's vacation from the family, for the Berkshire Music Festival. If you were interested in music, I'd tell you about it.

As ever,

EW

I saw Elder when I was in New York Wednesday, and he told me frankly that I "had no future with Doubleday" and that he would advise me to transfer my two contracts that I have with them (one of them for the Russian book) to some publisher who would take more interest in marketing my work. He had just been served notice, two weeks before, that Doubleday was no longer interested in having him scout for the more serious kind of talent, and that thenceforth he was to occupy himself only with books that would have very large sales. This means that we don't have to worry about our book, but can wait while we run into some other publisher who really thinks he wants it.

Love to Vera,

EW

169

Columbine Lodge
Rocky Mountain National Park
Estes Park, Colo.

August 29, 1947

Dear Bunny,

I am sorry I shall not find you in New York, where we intend to stop a week or so (5–10 September) before returning to Cambridge. We hope to see both of you there soon.

Many thanks for not telling me about the music at Tanglewood. I have just had a terrible evening here with a Mr. Mitropoulos, a conductor of an orchestra somewhere in the Middle West,[1] who was under the impression (at the beginning at least) that I knew music as well as Nicholas does.

As many as four lepidopterists have visited me here to pay their respects and take me to distant collecting grounds. I have sold two stories to *The New Yorker*. The second (an autobiographical essay dealing with an uncle of mine)[2] underwent some "editing," which upset me so much that I almost decided to stop trying to earn my living that way. This is strictly *entre nous* as I would not like to hurt Mrs. White's feelings. She did her best.[3]

I liked your Kafka and Sartre articles.[4]

Yours,

V.

1. *I.e.*, Dimitri Mitropoulos, the conductor of the Minneapolis Symphony Orchestra.

2. "Portrait of My Uncle," later Chapter Three of *Speak, Memory*.

3. For Wilson's subsequent reaction to this information, see his letter to Katharine White in *Letters on Literature and Politics, 1912–1972*, pp. 409–411.

4. "A Dissenting Opinion on Kafka" (*The New Yorker,* July 26, 1947) and "Jean-Paul Sartre: The Novelist and the Existentialist" (*ibid.,* August 2, 1947). Both essays are included in *Classics and Commercials.*

170

THE NEW YORKER
No. 25 West 43rd Street

October 15, 1947
Wellfleet, Mass.

Dear Volodya: Maybe the thing is just to let the Russian book alone for the time being. The publishers are all in a panic, trying to cut royalties, etc., and Oxford doesn't seem to be disposed to give us very good terms. If we wait awhile we may do better. Sorry to have missed you Monday, but will have a chance to see you later. We expect to be in Boston through a large part of January, February and March (Elena is having a baby about the middle of Feb[ruary]).[1]

As ever,

EW

1. Helen Miranda Wilson, born February 19, 1948.

171

November 7, 1947

Дорогой другъ,[1]

I see with dismay that I have not thanked you yet (Véra joining) for your book,[2] which I enjoyed—though I emphatically disagree with some of your politico-historical generalizations.

We both congratulate you both on the предстоящее прибавленіе къ семейству[3] and are looking forward to having you in our vicinity soon.

A question: Laughlin is ready to sell me the plates of *Laughter in the Dark* for 75 dollars. Holt wants to buy them but does not know that I can get them so cheap from Laughlin. Would it be cricket if I sold them to Holt for 200–300 dollars?

My new book is developing nicely. I think the *N[ew] Y[orker]* is going to print bits of it—there is one coming this month.[4]

The Letters, 1947

My girls and my bugs are as usual taking a lot of my time.

Yours
V.

1. "Dear friend."

2. *Europe Without Baedeker.*

3. "Forthcoming addition to your family."

4. Various sections of *Speak, Memory*, originally published under the title *Conclusive Evidence* in 1951, were serialized in *The New Yorker* between January 1948 and June 1950.

1948

172

February 23, 1948

Dear Bunny,

You naively compare my (and the "old Liberals' ") attitude towards the Soviet regime *(sensu lato)*[1] to that of a "ruined and humiliated" American Southerner towards the "wicked" North. You must know me and "Russian Liberals" very little if you fail to realize the amusement and contempt with which I regard Russian émigrés whose "hatred" of the Bolsheviks is based on a sense of financial loss or class *degringolade.*[2] It is preposterous (though quite in line with Soviet writings on the subject) to postulate any material interest at the bottom of a Russian Liberal's (or Democrat's or Socialist's) rejection of the Soviet regime. I really must draw your attention to the fact that my position in regard to Lenin's or Stalin's regime is shared not only by Constitutional Democrats, but also by the Social[ist] Revolutionaries and various socialist groupings, and that Russian culture was built by liberal thinkers and writers which I think rather spoils your neat simile of "North and South." To spoil it completely I may add that the rather local and special difference between the North and South is much more comparable to that between first cousins, between, say, Hitlerism (Southern race prejudice) and the Soviet regime, than it is to the gap existing between fundamentally different systems of thought (totalitarianism and liberalism).

Incidental but very important: the term "intelligentsia" as used in America (for instance, by Rahv in *The Partisan [Review]*) is not used in the same sense as it was used in Russia. Intelligentsia is curiously restricted here to avant-garde writers and artists. In old Russia it also included doctors, lawyers, scientists, etc., as well as people belonging to any class or profession. In fact a typical Russian *intelligent* would look askance at an avant-garde poet. The main features of the Russian intelligentsia (from Belinsky to Bunakov[3]) were: the spirit of self-sacrifice, intense participation in political causes or political thought, intense sympathy for the underdog of any nationality, fanatical integrity, tragic inability to sink to compromise, true spirit of international responsibility . . . But of course people who read Trotsky for information anent Russian culture cannot be expected to know all this. I have also a hunch that the general idea that avant-garde literature and art were having a wonderful time under Lenin and Trotsky is mainly due to Eisenstadt[4] films—"montage"—things like that—and great big drops of sweat rolling down rough cheeks.[5] The fact that pre-Revolution Futurists joined the party has also contributed to the kind of (quite false) avant-garde atmosphere which the American intellectual associates with the Bolshevik Revolution.

I do not want to be personal, but here is how I explain y o u r attitude: in the ardent period of life you and other American intellectuals of the twenties regarded with enthusiasm and sympathy Lenin's regime which seemed to you from afar an exciting fulfillment of your progressive dreams. Quite possibly, had the position been reversed, Russian avant-garde young writers (living, say, in an Americoid Russia) would have regarded the burning of the White House with similar enthusiasm and sympathy. Your concept of pre-Soviet Russia, of her history and social development came to you through a pro-Soviet prism. When later on (i.e., at a time coinciding with Stalin's ascension) improved information, a more mature judgment and the pressure of inescapable facts dampened your enthusiasm and dried your sympathy, you somehow did not bother to check your preconceived notions in regard to old Russia while, on the other hand, the glamor of Lenin's reign retained for you the emotional iridescence which your optimism, idealism and youth had provided. What you now see as a change for the worse ("Stalinism") in the regime is really a change for the better in knowledge on your part. The thunderclap of administrative purges woke you up (something that the moans in Solovki or at the Lubianka[6] had not been able to do) since they affected men on whose shoulders St. Lenin's hand had lain. You (or Dos Passos, or Rahv) will mention with horror the names of Ezhov and Yagoda—but what about Uritsky and Dzerzhinsky?[7]

I am now going to state a few things which I think are true and which I don't think you can refute. Under the Tsars (despite the inept and barbarous character of their rule) a freedom-loving Russian had incomparably more possibility and means of expressing himself than at any time during Lenin's and

The Letters, 1948

Stalin's regime. He was protected by law. There were fearless and independent judges in Russia. The Russian *sud*[8] after the Alexander reforms was a magnificent institution, not only on paper. Periodicals of various tendencies and political parties of all possible kinds, legally or illegally, flourished and all parties were represented in the Dumas. Public opinion was always liberal and progressive.

Under the Soviets, from the very start, the only protection a dissenter could hope for was dependent on governmental whims, not laws. No parties except the one in power could exist. Your Alymovs[9] are specters bobbing in the wake of a foreign tourist. Bureaucracy, a direct descendant of party discipline, took over immediately. Public opinion disintegrated. The intelligentsia ceased to exist. Any changes that took place between November 1919[10] and now have been changes in the decor which more or less screens an unchanging black abyss of oppression and terror.

I think I shall eventually polish this letter and publish it somewhere.[11]

Yours,

V

1. "In a broad sense." While this letter may well be a reply to a now lost Wilson letter or a response to things said during a personal discussion between the two writers, the mention of Wilson's name in conjunction with those of Philip Rahv and John Dos Passos later on in the letter suggests that Nabokov may be reacting to the book *Discovery of Europe* (New York, 1947), edited by Rahv and with contributions by, *inter alios*, Wilson and Dos Passos. The book is a collection of impressions of Europe written by Americans between the eighteenth century and the beginning of World War II.

The entries on Russia are Andrew D. White's account of his conversations with Tolstoy, the astonishingly bland and uninformed letters on the Russian scene of 1901 by Henry Adams (who saw the country as frozen in the early Middle Ages), impressions of Lenin and the October Revolution by John Reed and Lincoln Steffens, and Edmund Wilson's "On the Margin of Moscow" (an excerpt from his travel account which appeared in *Travels in Two Democracies* in 1936 and was later included, in an expanded version, in *Red, Black, Blond and Olive*, 1956). The three selections on post-revolutionary Russia are overwhelmingly sympathetic to the Lenin-Trotsky takeover of power, while Rahv's introductory material is careful to draw the distinction between the heroic and liberating October Revolution and the Stalinist regime that supposedly reversed and betrayed it.

2. "Loss of class position." The most frustrating experience of Russian writers who lived in the West during the 1920s and 1930s was their inability to make their Western colleagues see that their opposition to the Soviet system was based on its suppression of human rights and on its practicing enslavement while preaching liberation, rather than on loss of property or social status, as was invariably assumed in the West. For a good account of this entire phenomenon, see Nina Berberova's autobiography *The Italics Are Mine*, New York, 1969, pp. 229–237.

3. Vissarion Belinsky (1811–1848), often called "the father of the Russian intelligentsia," was a radical literary critic of the Romantic period. Ilya Bunakov (1880–1942), whose real name was Fondaminsky, was one of the leaders of the Socialist Revolutionary party before the Revolution. After the Revolution, Bunakov edited the excellent literary journal *Contemporary Annals (Sovremennye zapiski)*, published in Paris, in which much of Nabokov's early work appeared. He died in a German concentration camp.

4. *I.e.*, Sergei Eisenstein.

5. In Chapter Two of *The Gift*, when Fyodor's mother came to see him in Berlin, they "visited a cinema where a Russian film was being shown which conveyed with particular *brio* the globules of sweat rolling down the glistening faces of the factory workers—while the factory owner smoked a cigar all the time."

6. Solovki was a concentration camp on the site of the famed old monastery on Solovetsky Island in the far North, where several hundred Socialists and non-Leninist Marxists were deported in 1923. Lubianka is the name given to a one-time insurance company building in the center of Moscow, which was converted into a detention house by Felix Dzerzhinsky during the terror of 1918 and has remained the most dreaded place in the city throughout much of Soviet history.

7. Nikolai Ezhov (also spelled Yezhov) and Heinrich Yagoda carried out Stalin's purges during the 1930s and later themselves fell victims of these purges. Moses Uritsky was in charge of the mass terror ordered by Lenin in 1918; Uritsky's assassination by the young poet Leonid Kannegiser unleashed a further wave of retaliatory terror. Felix Dzerzhinsky established the *Cheka* ("Extraordinary Commission") in December 1917, setting the pattern for later political police repression.

8. "Legal system."

9. Sergei Alymov (1892–1948) wrote lyrics for patriotic and propagandistic popular songs. Because of his good knowledge of English—he lived abroad between 1911 and 1926—Alymov was often attached as an escort to visiting American writers during the 1930s (and was occasionally mentioned in their accounts as a major Russian literary figure). Wilson got to know Alymov during his stay in the Soviet Union.

10. Nabokov is speaking of the revolution of November 7, 1917; this must have been a slip of the pen.

11. This was done when a portion of this letter was incorporated into Chapter Thirteen of *Speak, Memory*. Describing his reunion with a Cambridge classmate, disguised in the text palindromically as Nesbit (his younger self) and Ibsen (the same man in maturity), Nabokov wrote:

> In the early twenties Nesbit had mistaken his own ebullient idealism for a romantic and humane something in Lenin's ghastly rule. Ibsen, in the days of the no less ghastly Stalin, was mistaking a quantitative increase in his own knowledge for a qualitative change in the Soviet regime. The thunder-clap of purges that had affected "old Bolsheviks," the heroes of his youth, had given him a salutary shock, something that in Lenin's day all the groans coming from the Solovki forced labor camp or the Lubyanka dungeon had not been able to do. With horror he pronounced the names of Ezhov and Yagoda—but quite forgot their predecessors, Uritsky and Dzerzhinsky. While time had improved his judgement regard-

ing contemporaneous Soviet affairs, he did not bother to reconsider the preconceived notions of his youth, and still saw in Lenin's short reign a kind of *quinquennium Neronis.*

173

April 7, 1948
Wellfleet, Mass.

Dear Volodya: Those translations of yours seemed awfully good in that little English edition[1]—though your last line of *Белеет парус одинокий*[2] is a conspicuous example of your failure to master the English subjunctive.

Sartre has just got out a book called *Situations,* that has a little essay on you, apropos of *La Méprise.*[3] Have you seen it? By the way, Katharine White tells me that it was she who suggested you for Cornell—when Morris Bishop told her they were looking for somebody.[4]

Don't forget that you are coming up here, and love to Vera.

EW

1. The English edition of *Three Russian Poets* was brought out in 1947 by Lindsay Drummond, London.

2. "The solitary white sail," the first line of Lermontov's poem "The Sail" (see Letter 133 and note 1 to that letter). The last line of Nabokov's translation reads, "As if in tempests there was peace."

3. Jean-Paul Sartre's essay on *Despair* (the French edition was called *La Méprise,* i.e., *The Error*) which appeared in *Situations* was originally written in 1939. Sartre saw Nabokov as an out-and-out imitator of Dostoevsky and qualified *Despair* as "an abortive novel" *(roman-avorton).* The reason for Nabokov's failure as an artist, according to Sartre, is that he lacks roots, unlike his contemporary Yury Olesha, who has the benefit of being a useful member of Soviet society. While the comparison with Olesha is apt—he was indeed the writer closest to Nabokov in writing manner and the one Nabokov admired most among his Soviet contemporaries—it acquires an ironic meaning when one realizes that at the very time when Sartre was setting him up as an example for Nabokov, Olesha was being crushed as a man and nearly destroyed as a writer by unbearable ideological pressures. As Arkady Belinkov's detailed study *Sdacha i gibel' sovetskogo intelligenta: Yurii Olesha (The Surrender and Demise of a Soviet Intellectual: Yury Olesha,* Madrid, 1976) shows, 1937 to 1939 was a time when Olesha was driven by a series of denunciations and threats in the Soviet press to abandon his artistic integrity, to purge his writing of all originality and to produce groveling essays and trashy film scripts that extolled Stalin's benevolent rule and lamented the misery and slavery in which those not fortunate enough to be ruled by Stalin still had to live.

Nabokov's devastating views on Sartre as a novelist are to be found in his review of *Nausea*, "Sartre's First Try," first published in *The New York Times Book Review*, April 24, 1949, and later included in *Strong Opinions*.

4. The circumstances of Nabokov's hiring by Cornell University—where he taught from 1948 to 1959—have been described in Morris Bishop's genial memoir "Nabokov at Cornell" (in the Nabokov issue of *Tri-Quarterly*, Number 17, Winter 1970, later published as the book *Nabokov!*, edited by Charles Newman and Alfred Appel, Jr.).

174

April 10, 1948

Dear Bunny,

I have been in bed for a couple of weeks with a bad case of bronchitis. In view of the enormous amount of work I have to get finished at the museum before leaving Cambridge, this illness has been a most irritating set-back. Moreover, the avalanche of work I shall be under will prevent us, I am afraid, from coming to the Cape! There is a kind of *fatalité* about that visit—we wanted to come so much and see all of you—and now we have to give up the idea for the third or fourth time.

I enjoyed your lusty poem.[1] There seems to be something wrong about the French in *sera du genre humain*—does not mean anything in this combination of words.

The "was" in the last line of the "Sail"[2] was intentional as "there were" seemed cacophonic to me and sagging.

I have read *The Ides of March*[3] and found it amusing after a fashion but on the whole very flimsy. The thing is much too easy—and has been done so many times in England. Maurice Baring did it quite as well. In the last issue of *The New Yorker* Connolly has written some awful Freudian rot about "father-writers."[4]

Greetings from us to both of you,

V.

[Added at top of page]
A whole picture gallery (of X-ray phot[ographs]) has been taken of my lungs, and next week I shall have to submit to a gruesome operation called bronchoscopy.

Не было печали, такъ черти накачали.[5]
(there was no sorrow—so the devil(s) pumped up some)

1. "Cardinal Merry Del Val" (*Night Thoughts*, pp. 187–191), which contains the line *L'Internationale sera du genre humain* ... (The Internationale shall be of human kind ...).

2. See Letter 173, note 2.

3. By Thornton Wilder.

4. In his essay on the critical writings of Virginia Woolf ("The Novelist as Critic," *The New Yorker*, April 10, 1948), Cyril Connolly wrote that Henry James, James Joyce and F. Scott Fitzgerald are popular because they are archetypes, which Virginia Woolf was not: "Henry James and James Joyce were high priests, old tribal magicians—to specially selected tribes. [...] Fitzgerald is another archetype: the young man slain in his glory ..."

5. A popular Russian saying which Nabokov puts into English *verbatim*.

175

[Postcard from Véra Nabokov to Elena Wilson]

May 9, 1948

Dear Elena,

It is very charming of you and Edmund to invite us and we would have loved to see you all including little Helen. Unfortunately Vladimir is ill again. The thing is quite serious and he will have to remain in bed for quite a long time. All this is very distressing.

Please tell Edmund that Vladimir enjoyed his poems.

Cordially yours,

Véra

176

V. Nabokov
8 Craigie Circle
Cambridge 38, Mass.

May 30, 1948

Dear Bunny,

It was awfully good of you to interest *The New Yorker* in my plight. I hope to know by the end of the summer what decision to take. Their offer will help me greatly to accept whatever decision the doctor thinks best for me.

I have just sent them a sixth story[1] and, if they take it, I shall have some security during the coming two or three months, provided there is no turn for the worse in my health.

Your visit was most bracing and we do hope to have a chance of seeing both of you here again before we leave for Ithaca. We intend to go there at the end of June or the beginning of July.

Yours,

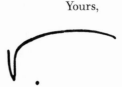

1. "Colette," later Chapter Seven of *Speak, Memory,* which appeared in *The New Yorker* of July 31, 1948.

177

June 1, 1948
Wellfleet, Mass.

Dear Volodya: I am sending you Sartre and Havelock Ellis's Russian sex masterpiece.[1] Please be sure to send them back. The Ellis doesn't belong to me.

Do you think it's really a good idea for you to spend the summer in Ithaca?—which is probably hot, crass and dull. And wouldn't the people there be sure to know about your condition? I don't know where to suggest your going except up here. I'll try to find you something, if you like. The Chavchavadzes want summer boarders.

We saw Nicholas and his bride in New York, and were struck by her close resemblance to Connie.[2] He seemed very cheerful—talked about going to Europe to attend the music festivals and rescue displaced cultural persons.

As ever,
EW

The Letters, 1948

1. "Confession sexuelle d'un Russe du Sud, né vers 1870 . . ." which Havelock Ellis included as an appendix to the sixth volume of the French edition of his collected writings (*Etudes de Psychologie Sexuelle*, VI, Paris, 1926). Written around 1912 by an anonymous Ukrainian in French—there seems to have been no English edition—this 106-page confession, with its solid command of the Russian social and cultural realities of the time, is an authentic and highly interesting document. The writer, born into a wealthy but radicalized Ukrainian family, began his highly active sex life at the age of 12, when he was seduced by several young girls of his own age as well as by several adult women. Because of his obsessive preoccupation with sex between the ages of 12 and 20, he failed at his studies and was left without any prospects for a career. Sent by his family to Italy, the narrator became celibate, resumed his studies, graduated from an engineering school and made plans to marry a well-educated young Italian woman with whom he had fallen in love. But on a business trip to Naples at the age of 32, he learned of the existence of child prostitution. Seduced by two experienced child-prostitutes aged 11 and 15, the narrator lapsed into his former obsessive pattern, except that now it took the form of compulsive searching for available girls in their early teens and of exhibiting himself to them at outdoor urinals. His marriage called off, all his earnings going to satisfy his compulsion, the narrator ends his confession on a note of despair about his inability to control his sexual urges. Because of the wide availability of eager, cooperative and sexually precocious nymphets, he sees no hope of ever mastering his drives in the future.

Nabokov alludes to this confession fleetingly in Chapter Ten of *Speak, Memory* and somewhat more explicitly in the Russian version of this memoir, *Other Shores*, where we read:

> Our innocence seems to me now almost monstrous in the light of various confessions dating from the same years and cited by Havelock Ellis, which speak of tiny tots of every imaginable sex, who practice every Graeco-Roman sin, constantly and everywhere, from the Anglo-Saxon industrial centers to the Ukraine (from where an especially lascivious report by a landowner is available).
>
> (*Drugie berega*, p. 184. Cf. *Speak, Memory*, p. 203)

The theme of the closing pages of the confession—a man obsessed by young girls, led on and seduced by his would-be victims who turn out to be far more experienced sexually than he—has an obvious bearing on certain portions of *Lolita*. In his essay "On a Book Entitled *Lolita*," Nabokov wrote that after he had destroyed the short story that contained the germ of *Lolita*, the next "throb" of inspiration for the book came to him "around 1949." While *Lolita* had already been mentioned in this correspondence in April 1947 (Letter 164), Nabokov's reading in June 1948 of the nymphet hunter's confession published by Havelock Ellis may well have provided the additional stimulus for the next stage of the book's development. Considering Wilson's subsequent dislike of *Lolita*, it is curious that it was Wilson (as we learn in *Upstate*, he had other occasions to supply Nabokov with erotic literature) who provided this stimulus.

2. Wilson notes the resemblance between Nicolas Nabokov's second wife, Constance Holladay, and his third wife, Patricia Blake.

178

Dear Bunny,

Many thanks for the books. I enjoyed the Russian's love-life hugely. It is wonderfully funny. As a boy, he seems to have been quite extraordinarily lucky in coming across girls with unusually rapid and rich reactions. The end is rather bathetic.

It is very sweet of you to suggest finding a place for us on the Cape, but for various reasons I think that the Ithaca plan will turn out all right. The house we have taken for the summer seems to be very comfortable. We shall probably leave at the very end of June.

The New Yorker has taken my sixth story.

I am "resting comfortably" and am engaged in preparing for publication a work on butterflies,[1] and then I shall ditch butterflies for at least a year.

Roman was awfully nice on the 'phone.

Do come again.

Yours

V

1. "The Nearctic Members of the Genus *Lycaeides Hübner*," Bulletin of the Museum of Comparative Zoology at Harvard College, Vol. 101, Boston, 1949.

179

June 13, 1948

Wellfleet, Mass.

Dear Volodya: Your butterfly piece in the *New Yorker* was wonderful—one of the best things you have done in English.[1] Good luck with Ithaca.

As ever,

EW

1. "Butterflies," later Chapter Six of *Speak, Memory*, appeared in *The New Yorker* of June 12, 1948.

180

Dear Volodya: I've just been doing an article on Tolstoy's sister-in-law's memoirs[1] and want to translate some passages from T's diary. There is the following sentence about his relations with the peasant mistress that he had before he was married: Уже не чувство оленя, а мужа к жене,[2]—which I thought was plain sailing as "It is no longer the feeling of a rutting stag, but of a husband for a wife." But the Chavchavadzes seem to think that *олень* here has some such special meaning as our word *stag* in a phrase like *stag-line, a stag party*—that is, a bachelor lover. Can you throw any light on this? I can't find any such meaning in any Russian dictionary.

How are you and how are you getting along in Ithaca?

As ever,

Edmund W

1. Wilson's review of *Tolstoy As I Knew Him* (original title: *My Life at Home and at Yasnaya Polyana*) by Tatyana Kuzminskaya, "The Original of Tolstoy's Natasha," *The New Yorker*, August 28, 1948, can also be found in *Classics and Commercials*.

2. "No longer the feeling of a stag, but of a husband for his wife."

181

Dear Bunny,

Yes, *олень* just means rutting stag or free roaming animal in that context. It has, of course, not a shade of the Americanism "stag dinner," etc. There may be some allusion to a harem of does, but I must see the passage.

I miss you. No tennis or butterfly-hunting for me this year. We have a very comfortable house with a lovely garden. Have reread a number of Russian books. Gorky is C+ in his fiction, but attains almost A− in his memoirs about Tolstoy, etc.

We send you and Elena our love. My health seems to be all right, but the whole business has rather upset me.

Yours

V.

182

957 E. State St.
Ithaca
(till the 10th of September)

September 3, 1948

Dear Bunny,

Many thanks for having the two Bishop books sent to me.[1] I read them with interest—because he was a friend of yours, mainly.

I got comfortably engrossed in your Tanglewood piece[2] until I came to the music part, and then dropped it like a hot cob.

Have reread Gorkiĭ's non-fiction stuff (on Tolstoĭ, etc.—incidentally note new transliteration) and, *увы* (alas), find it as poor as the rest of his output—though I remember liking the Tolstoĭ bits in my youth. I lived in the house ("Gaspra," Countess Panin's place in the Crimea) in 1918, where Gorkiĭ and Chehov *(sic)* used to visit Tolstoĭ when he was ill. Have thoroughly studied and checked the 6 volume *Academia* (Soviet) edition of Pushkin, where some of the translations from the French are utterly ridiculous. Have found a remarkable poem by Parny, in 1777, *Epitre aux Insurgents* (American). Have had some lively correspondence with the Army in regard to a hideous transl[ation] of *Bend Sinister* (a novel I published a couple of years ago,—you should read it some day) into German. My honeymoon with the *New Yorker* is still going strong—have sent them two more pieces written here. One deals with my composing my first poem (in 1914)—and I am not sure Ross will stomach it.[3] Dmitri has developed a magnificent tennis form owing to the Cornell coach but his chess is still only passable. Véra has bought a car and has learned to drive it in a very short time. I saw, but could not catch, a very rare migrant butterfly *(L. bachmanni)*. My health is good. We have rented an enormous, pleasantly furnished house (note new address beginning 10 Sept: 802 Seneca St., Ithaca). Visitors encouraged. Have you seen a book by a man called Hyman, who accuses me of borrowing from you, and you of borrowing from me (a nice case of symbiosis)?[4] Years ago I wrote a very funny piece about a fellow who combined Marxism and Freudism, and now I see it is being seriously done by some critics whom Hyman admires. Why don't we write together a scholarly prose translation of *Evgenii Onegin* with copious notes?

How are you, how is Елена?[5] Véra sends you both her love. Have you written any more poems of the bouncing "Voltairean" type (in the Russian sense)?

Yours
V.

[On top, upside down]
I wonder, would Doubleday be interested in publishing a volume of my translations (*Three Poets* and a number of new transl[ations])?

[In margin of p. 1]
In another publication (*Accent*, I think) he (Hyman) calls me a "Czarist Liberal"[6]—just as Molotov calls Zenzinov and Weinbaum[7] "White Bandits."

[In margin of p. 2]
I wish somebody would explain the thirty-year gap (1830–1860) during which
not a single great writer was born in Russia. What is your idea?

1. The two posthumous collections of writings by Wilson's friend and classmate John
Peale Bishop which were published in 1948: *The Collected Poems of John Peale Bishop*, ed-
ited with a preface and a personal memoir by Allen Tate; and *The Collected Essays of John
Peale Bishop*, edited with an introduction by Edmund Wilson.

2. Wilson's "Koussevitzky at Tanglewood." *The New Yorker*, September 4, 1948.

3. Nabokov's misgivings proved well-founded. "First Poem," later Chapter Eleven of
Speak, Memory, was rejected by *The New Yorker* and later appeared in *The Partisan Review*
in September 1949.

4. In a generally hostile evaluation of Wilson's significance as a critic in the chapter devoted to him in Stanley Edgar Hyman's book *The Armed Vision* (1948), Wilson was accused
of using other people's insights and research without giving them credit: "On Russian literature Wilson used D. S. Mirsky's two histories and his study of Pushkin, de Vogüé's *Le Roman russe* and many of the specific insights of Vladimir Nabokov, whose translations he has
been working with for several years. (Wilson is quite possibly indebted to Nabokov for the
remarkable, and quite uncharacteristic, detailed analysis of musicality in a poem by Pushkin he printed in his Pushkin article in the *Atlantic Monthly*, an analysis that seems to represent a remarkable acquaintance with the Russian language on Wilson's part and seems
at the same time very characteristic of Nabokov.)"

5. Elena.

6. In a review of several critical studies in *Accent*, Spring 1948, Hyman accused most
modern critics of extreme subjectivism and of a tendency to turn the writer they discuss
into a replica of their own selves, adding that "the worst [example] in our time may very
well be Vladimir Nabokov's émigré Czarist liberal and surrealist Nikolai Gogol." For a se-
quel, see Letter 203, note 2.

7. Vladimir Zenzinov was a prominent Socialist Revolutionary activist before the Revolution. In post-revolutionary times he was an émigré editor and commentator. According
to Nina Berberova's *The Italics Are Mine*, it was Zenzinov who prevailed on the editors of
Contemporary Annals to delete the biography of Chernyshevsky from *The Gift* when the
novel was being serialized in that journal in the 1930s (the other editors, who went along
with this unique instance of political censorship "from the left" in what was otherwise an
admirably liberal and open-minded émigré publication, were also former Socialist Revolutionaries). Mark Weinbaum was the editor of the New York Russian-language daily *Novoye russkoye slovo*.

183

September 9, 1948
Wellfleet, Mass.

Dear Volodya: I looked up the Parny poem, which rather surprised me on his part. Have you read the section called "Aphorisms and Notes" in the volume of John Bishop's prose?—which, I think, contains some of the best stuff in the book. Do you know a play called *A Game at Chess*, by Thomas Middleton, the Elizabethan dramatist? I have been reading him and think he has been fantastically overrated by Eliot, Swinburne and others. This is the only play of his I have read that interests me at all—though it seems to me that the idea had greater possibilities. It might amuse you, as the whole play is a chess-game and all the characters pieces, who act out a political allegory. It is in volume VII of Bullen's edition of Middleton, and the explanation of the allegory and the curious history of the play is in the Introduction to vol. I. It requires more explanation, though, than Bullen supplies. What worried me in reading it was that sometimes chess moves seemed to be taking place which did not represent anything I could grasp in terms of the plot. A man who is or was at Cornell is supposed to have done a better edition. Middleton was particularly interested in chess, and there is also a famous chess-game in his *Women Beware Women*.

There is a review of your translations in the *New Statesman* of August 7.[1] I haven't read Hyman's book—just looked at it in a bookstore. I know him and have a low opinion of him. All I know of Gorky are one or two of his plays and his memoirs of Tolstoy, Chekhov and Lenin, which certainly give pretty vivid impressions of the people. I am doing rather a long poem in my amphisbaenic verse, which I'll send you when I've finished it.[2]

Elena is going to Europe for a month next week to help reorganize the family business in Switzerland. She dreads seeing what was happened to Germany and talking about the war with her brother and sister, who have been there most of the time. I'll be staying up here with the baby and nurse.

I'm very much interested in a Haitian novelist, Thoby-Marcelin. I think you might like his books: *Canapé-Vert* and *La Bête de Musseau*.[3] I don't know anything like them. The first one seemed to me anthrop[olog]ically fascinating, but when I read the second one just now, I saw that he was a decidedly distinguished, perhaps even important, writer. There is a third one coming out which is said to be terrific. It is all a critique of morals from a point of view which enters into both the Voodoo and the Christian religions, and by no means of such special local interest as you may think when you first encounter it. Haiti seems to be producing quite a remarkable culture. I'm thinking of trying to get the *New Yorker* to send me there for a visit.

Vera is wonderful to learn to drive. I think the thing to do about Doubleday is to return to our original idea. I have just written Elder about it. The book might be for 1950. I have more time now to read non-contemporary stuff and am going back to Russian this fall.

Everybody sends love. I am glad that your health is all right and that you are comfortably settled in Ithaca.

As ever,

EW

1. This was Philip Toynbee's review of *Pushkin, Lermontov, Tyutchev*, the English edition of *Three Russian Poets*, in *The New Statesman and Nation* of August 7, 1948. Toynbee gave the quality of Nabokov's translations qualified praise ("Mr. Nabokov is a deft and loyal translator. He has not the dubious advantage of being himself a poet"). But since he was also highly enthusiastic about Oliver Elton's version of *Eugene Onegin*, his judgment could hardly have mattered much to Nabokov.

2. The poem is "Reversals, or *Plus ça change*" (*Night Thoughts*, pp. 185–186). Amphisbaena is a mythic serpent that has heads at both ends and can move in either direction; amphisbaenic verse features rhyming words in which syllables are reversed.

3. *La Bête de Musseau* was translated into English as *The Beast of the Haitian Hills*. On Wilson's enthusiasm for and personal involvement with Philippe Thoby-Marcelin and his brother Pierre Marcelin, who wrote as a team, see the section "Haiti and the Marcelins" in *Letters on Literature and Politics, 1912–1972*, pp. 461–470, the section on Haiti in *Red, Black, Blond and Olive* and Wilson's introductory essays to the English translations of their two later novels, *The Pencil of God* (1951) and *All Men Are Mad* (1970).

184

October 1, 1948
Wellfleet, Mass.

Dear Volodya: Was it you and Vera who were complaining to me about not finding Faulkner rewarding? I have just read his *Light in August*, which seems to me most remarkable, and, as I have an extra copy, am sending it to you. Do read it.

I thought that you and I were remarkably good in the *New Yorker* the other week.[1] Your piece was one of your best. If you haven't already seen the article about the Tolstoy Museum in the current *Atlantic*, you ought to look it up.[2] It is funny, but deeply depressed me. You will have to find some other explanation than the innate wickedness of the Bolsheviks to explain how the race that produced Tolstoy can have afterwards produced this degradation of intellectual life.[3]

1. Wilson's contribution in *The New Yorker* of September 18, 1948 was "Francis Grierson: Log House and Salon," in the "Books" section. Nabokov was represented in the same issue by "My Russian Education," later Chapter Nine of *Speak, Memory*.

2. "Tolstoy in Soviet Hands" by Mikhail Koriakov in *The Atlantic Monthly* of October 1948. Koriakov, a Soviet journalist who defected to the West, wrote of his experiences as an employee at the Tolstoy Museum in Yasnaya Polyana during the late 1930s, describing the brutalizing effect of constant governmental pressure and interference on literary research and museum activities, the hamstringing of literary studies by the continual requirement to cite Lenin and to conform all findings to Lenin's views of Tolstoy and, finally, the desperate plight of the collectivized peasants of Yasnaya Polyana, so much worse off economically than their serf ancestors had been in Tolstoy's time.

3. The rest of this letter is missing.

185

CORNELL UNIVERSITY

Department of
Russian Literature

Vladimir Nabokov
802 E. Seneca St.
Ithaca, N.Y.

Goldwin Smith Hall
Ithaca, N.Y.

November 1, 1948

Dear Bunny,

Your letter took more than a week to reach me (I mean the letter in which you tell me that you are through with Doubleday) and I wrote you my superb bit of criticism anent Faulkner before I got it.[1]

My eagerness to have that book with you is partly due to the fact that I have been translating a good deal lately. For instance, I am making a new translation of *Слово о полку И[гореве]*.[2] I shall send you a first rough draft of my version because I think you ought to like that marvellous poem written by an unknown poet in 1187.

Except for your excursions into the *экономически-соціальное*[3] (which is most perverse and distressing coming from you) I liked your Tolstoĭ piece very much.[4] But I am appalled by your approach to Faulkner. It is incredible that you should take him seriously. Or rather—it is incredible that you should be so fascinated by his message (whatever it is) as to condone his artistic mediocrity.

Some ten years ago you had an admirable story about your family[5]—most of it absolutely superb and then towards the end fatally marred by the introduction of the *соцiалэкономический*[6] factor. On the other hand the wonderful chapters about the Slav girl in *Гекатово Графство*[7] were so good because your artistic sense completely consumed and dissolved your *соцэкономический подход*.[8] Keep it down, keep it down (the *идейность*[9]), for God's sake.

I have had a very curious exchange of letters with Weeks and am sending you copies of them for your enjoyment[...].

You are one of the very few people in the world whom I keenly miss when I do not see them. I am in good health and my academic job is vastly more comfortable and less interfering than Wellesley. The very, very nice Whites[10] have been here and we spent a quite charming evening together at the Bishops— who are also most lovable people. My huge butterfly work is soon coming out— shall send you a copy.[11]

How was Elena's trip to Europe? Best love to both of you from both of us.

Yours,
V.

1. See Letter 187.

2. *The Song of Igor's Campaign.*

3. "Economic-social." Here and in the items glossed in notes 6, 8 and 9, Nabokov mocks the compulsory formulations of Soviet criticism.

4. "The Original of Tolstoy's Natasha." See Letter 180, note 1.

5. Most likely "A New Jersey Childhood: 'These Men Must Do Their Duty!'," *The New Yorker*, November 18, 1939, later reprinted under the title "At Laurelwood" in *Note-Books of Night* (which Wilson had sent to Nabokov) and in *Night Thoughts*.

6. "Social-economic."

7. "Hecate County." The reference is to the character of Anna in "The Princess with the Golden Hair" section of *Memoirs of Hecate County.*

8. "Socioeconomic approach."

9. "Ideological content."

10. Katharine Sergeant White, Nabokov's editor at *The New Yorker*, and her husband E. B. White.

11. "The Nearctic Members of the Genus *Lycaeides Hübner.*"

186

November 15, 1948
Wellfleet, Mass.

Dear Volodya: ① Here is my amphisbaenic (backward-rhyming) poem.

② Did you really write me a letter about Faulkner?[1] Some of our mail has been disappearing lately. I am curious to know whether or not you ever read

Light in August. Of course he has no message (except in the pamphlet attached to this last book) [and] is merely interested in dramatizing life. In spite of his carelessness, I should think he would be rather congenial to you. I have been reading him spellbound lately. I think he is the most remarkable contemporary American novelist.

③ I have never been able to understand how you manage, on the one hand, to study butterflies from the point of view of their habitat and, on the other, to pretend that it is possible to write about human beings and leave out of account all question of society and environment. I have come to the conclusion that you simply took over in your youth the *fin de siècle Art for Art's sake* slogan and have never thought it out. I shall soon be sending you a book of mine which may help you to straighten out these problems.[2]

④ Do send me the Weeks correspondence. Have you been reading his little memoirs in the back of the *Atlantic?*

⑤ I have been learning to play chess. It is a wonderful game and I enjoy it, but I doubt whether I shall ever be any good.

⑥ Elena has been ill ever since she got back from Europe though she is now a good deal better. She seems to have had a pretty harrowing time visiting her family in Germany, and caught flu there and had to leave before she was well to go to Switzerland and struggle with the reorganization of a business of which she is a principal stockholder.

⑦ A Russian cousin of hers in Paris who writes[3] sent me a lot of books, including many volumes by a Russian poet named Poplavsky.[4] Who is he? Ought I to read him?

⑧ Katharine White gives me a very good account of you. I am glad that you are comfortable there. We miss you when we go to Boston. Did you know that they had called upon Helen Muchnic to help them out with Russian literature at Harvard?

⑨ Do send me your *Igor* translation. I've just received an elaborate volume, *La Geste du Prince Igor,* published by the Ecole Libre des Hautes Etudes à New York, under the auspices of Jakobson and others.[5] Have you seen it? It includes translating into various languages, a vindication of the Слово authenticity, commentary, etc.

⑩ I shall try to do something about our great Russian volume when I go down to New York later on.

Love to Vera. When, if ever, will you be coming back this way again?

As ever,

EW

1. See the next letter.

2. The new and revised 1948 edition of *The Triple Thinkers* (originally published in 1938). For Nabokov's response to this book, see Letter 190.

3. Pierre Balacheff.

4. During a brief, six-year meteoric literary career as poet, novelist and literary critic, Boris Poplavsky (1903–1935) made such a momentous impression on the Russian émigré community in Paris that his name and personality still haunt the memories and memoirs of writers who knew him or read him in the 1930s. Often dubbed "the Russian Rimbaud" by émigré critics, Poplavsky combined in his poetry the tradition of Russian Symbolism derived from Blok with such French influences as those of Laforgue, Apollinaire and Breton. Edmund Wilson, who wrote so knowingly and appreciatively of Corbière, Laforgue and Rimbaud in *Axel's Castle*, would surely have liked this Russian descendant of theirs, had he but read him. In the early 1990s, with the new popularity of the formerly banned writers of the Russian emigration, there was a surge of Poplavsky publications in Russia, including his two novels, *Apollon Bezobrazov* and *Homeward from Heaven*, previously known only in serialized excerpts.

5. See the end of note 3 to Letter 63.

187

CORNELL UNIVERSITY

Department of
Russian Literature

Vladimir Nabokov
802 E. Seneca St.
Ithaca, N.Y.

Goldwin Smith Hall
Ithaca, N.Y.

November 21, 1948

This is a copy of my old letter which
logically must come before the new one.

Dear Bunny,

I have carefully read Faulkner's *Light in August*, which you so kindly sent me, and it has in no way altered the low (to put it mildly) opinion I have of his work and other (innumerable) books in the same strain. I detest these puffs of stale romanticism, coming all the way up from Marlinsky[1] and V. Hugo—you remember the latter's horrible combination of starkness and hyperbole— *l'homme regardait le gibet, le gibet regardait l'homme.*[2] Faulkner's belated romanticism and quite impossible biblical rumblings and "starkness" (which is not starkness at all but skeletonized triteness), and all the rest of the bombast seem to me so offensive that I can only explain his popularity in France by the fact that all her own popular mediocre writers (Malraux included) of recent years have also had their fling at *l'homme marchait, la nuit était sombre.*[5] The book you sent me is one of the tritest and most tedious examples of a trite and tedious genre. The plot and those extravagant "deep" conversations affect me as bad movies do, or the worst plays and stories of Leonid Andreyev, with whom Faulkner has a kind of fatal affinity. I imagine that this kind of thing (white trash, velvety Negroes, those bloodhounds out of *Uncle Tom's Cabin* melodramas, steadily baying through thousands of swampy books) may be necessary in a social sense, but it is not literature, just as the thousands of stories and novels about downtrodden peasants and fierce *ispravniki*[4] in Russia, or mystical adventures within the *narod*[5] (1850–1880), although socially effective and ethically admirable, were not literature. I simply cannot believe that you, with all your knowledge and taste, are not made to squirm by such things as the dialogues between the "positive" characters in Faulkner (and especially those absolutely ghastly italics). Do you not see that despite the difference in landscape, etc., it is essentially Jean Valjean stealing the candlesticks from the good man of God all over again? The villain is definitely Byronic. The book's pseudo-religious rhythm I simply cannot stand—a phoney gloom which also spoils Mauriac's work. Has *la grace* descended upon Faulkner too? Maybe you are just pulling my leg when you advise me to read him, or impotent Henry James, or the Rev. Eliot?

I am very much looking forward to our Russian book. We ought to plan the volume more definitely.

↓   Sincerely yours,

This was written before I got a
letter from you (strangely delayed)
telling me you had broken with
Dayday, etc.

November 21, 1948

This is my new letter to you.

Dear Bunny,

Of course I read *Light in August* and of course I wrote to you about it (see enclosure).

I was interested in Miss Muchnic's new appointment. I sometimes wonder whether the curious disinclination on Harvard's part to avail itself of my services might not have been due to my taking a crack or two at some academic shibboleth (say, Goethe's *Faust*) in my book on Gogol.

"Art for art's sake" does not mean anything unless the term "art" be defined. First give me your definition of it and then we can talk.

I also want to draw your attention to the fact that biological and ecological characters have no taxonomic value *per se*. As a systematist, I always give priority to structural characters. In other words two butterfly populations may breed in vastly different environments—one, say, in the Mexican desert and the other in a Canadian bog—and still belong to the same species. Similarly, I do not give a hoot whether a writer is writing about China or Egypt, or either of the two Georgias,—what interests me is his book. The Chinese or Georgian features are intraspecific ones. What you want me to do is to give superiority to ecology over morphology.

I know the *La Geste* volume well,—and am, as a matter of fact, reviewing it for the *American Anthropologist*. It is on the whole an admirable work, Szeftel's and Jakobson's studies being especially brilliant. There is a touch of *kvasnoï*[6] Russian patriotism about Vernadsky's essay. Cross's translation, although revised and corrected by Jakobson in regard to sense, is couched in hopelessly pedestrian English, so that many images are distorted or lost.[7] It would be nice if you wrote something about the book for the *New Yorker*.

Poplavsky was an émigré poet who died young in Paris twenty years ago (of an overdose of heroin).[8] He had a small but not unpleasant voice, a kind of provincial primitive charm. As one of the facets of émigré literature, he may be of interest to future scholars.[9]

We were sorry to hear that Elena was sick. We hope she is quite well now.

Your having taken up chess is good news. I hope you will soon be playing well enough for me to beat you.

Below is a poem.

Yours,

V

To E. W. on reading his amphisbaenic poem.

At first my brain was somewhat numbed
by your somnambulistic numbers, Edmund.
Now, having shaken off that stupor,
I find the latter anagrimes with "Proust"
while "T. S. Eliot"
goes well with "toilets."
O Emir
of the mirror-rime!
I fear your envy,
and humbly sign: V. N.

[In margin, in Véra Nabokov's hand]

We both would very much like you both to come and visit us here. Dmitri's room is free and we have an additional bed.

Véra

1. Alexander Bestuzhev-Marlinsky (1797–1837), the Romantic prose writer and poet whose tales of adventure form an important stylistic link between the Sentimentalist prose of the end of the eighteenth century and the prose writings of Pushkin and, especially, Lermontov.

2. "The man was looking at the gallows, the gallows was looking at the man."

3. "The man was walking, the night was dark."

4. "Police officials."

5. "The People."

6. "Jingoist."

7. Roman Jakobson (see Letter 189, note 5) contributed a total of six items to *La Geste du Prince Igor* and is actually the book's principal author. Marc Szeftel wrote a historical commentary on the text, George Vernadsky did an essay on the historical background of the poem and Samuel Hazzard Cross provided a translation into modern English.

8. This version of Poplavsky's death was widely circulated among the Russians in Paris. What had actually happened was that he was poisoned by a deranged friend. See Anthony Olcott, "Poplavsky: the Heir Presumptive of Montparnasse" and Simon Karlinksky, "In Search of Poplavsky: A Collage," both in *The Bitter Air of Exile: Russian Writers in the West 1922–1972,* Simon Karlinsky and Alfred Appel, Jr., eds., Berkeley-Los Angeles-London, 1977.

9. Nabokov was to write of Poplavsky with more warmth and appreciation in Chapter Fourteen of *Speak, Memory:*

> I met many other émigré authors. I did not meet Poplavsky who died young, a far violin among near balalaikas.

> Go to sleep, O Morella, how awful are aquiline lives

> His plangent tonalities I shall never forget, nor shall I ever forgive myself the ill-tempered review in which I attacked him for trivial faults in his unfledged verse.

Nabokov's review of Poplavsky's first collection of verse, *Flags (Flagi),* was published in the émigré newspaper *The Rudder (Rul')* on March 11, 1931.

188

802 E. Seneca St.
Ithaca, N.Y.

November 26, 1948

Dear Bunny,

In my last letter to you, I asked you whether you would write anything on the subject of the *Slovo.*[1] I now find that my own essay on *La Geste* is so good that it would be a pity to bury it in the *Anthropologist* (gratis). So if this does not clash with your own plans, or indeed does not interfere in any way with your program for the *New Yorker*, I would like to submit my essay to them.

I am writing to Mrs. White in the same strain.

We spent a quiet Thanksgiving pleasantly colored by the recollection of the pleasant time we spent with you and your family last year.

Yours

V.

1. *I.e., The Song of Igor's Campaign.*

189

December 2, 1948
Wellfleet, Mass.

Dear Volodya: I hope that you can persuade the *New Yorker* to let you write about the Слово.[1] I thought it was hopeless for me to suggest it for myself, but you may be able to prevail on them by making a special occasion of it. I'm calling up Shawn this afternoon and will mention it to him. Don't tell them that the book is mostly in French. I think that the whole story of the French attack on the Слово's authenticity might be made very amusing. I attended, with Roman Grynberg, one of the sessions of the Ecole Libre devoted to the discussion of this problem.[2] It was *très mouvementé*.[3] The question had evidently become a patriotic issue. Vernadsky read a paper, in which he remarked that the French, not content with having destroyed the text at the time of Napoleon's invasion, seemed now to want to deprive Russia of the honor of having produced the poem, and every time he demonstrated, writing the words upon a blackboard, that some detail of ancient warfare or dress had been confirmed by subsequent discovery, the Russians present broke into applause. He was replied to by a French or Belgian Byzantologist,[4] with a silky manner and a well-cared-for beard, who tried to show, in a patronizing way, that the Слово was a fraud. Roman Jakobson[5] could not contain himself and made tumultuous interruptions. Finally, monsieur Byzantologist said: "M. Jakobson, c'est un monstre."[6] There was a terrible silence, as the audience remembered poor Jakobson's extraordinary appearance and wondered whether the meeting would have to end in violence. But the speaker went on: "Je veux dire qu'il est un monstre de science—il est philologue, sociologue, anthropologue,"[7] etc. It was at the moment when the Russians were standing up to the Germans after the ignoble flop of the French, and I was struck by the Russian propensity for using events in the literary world as pretexts for creating issues in connection with current politics (which you seem to have reacted against by leaning in the other direction at an angle of forty-five degrees and denying that literature has anything to do with social institutions).

I wish we could visit you, but in our present circumstances it's difficult for us even to get to Boston for a night.

You haven't grasped the amphisbaenic technique: *stupor* fits, not *Proust*, but *reputes,* or better, *rope Utes*—in the sense of lassoing members of a Far Western Indian tribe.

As ever,

EW

1. "The Song" (or "The Tale").

2. Wilson forgets that he had already described this session five years earlier in his letter to Nabokov of April 1, 1943 (see Letter 63), though without some of the fascinating detail he is providing here.

3. "Very lively."

4. Henri Grégoire, one of the co-editors of the *La Geste* volume (cf. Wilson's earlier description of the meeting).

5. Roman Jakobson (1896–1982), the distinguished Russian-American literary scholar, critic, and a foremost theoretician of the Formalist method of criticism in the Soviet Union in the 1920s and more recently of Structuralism in the West, devoted much of his life and energy to establishing and demonstrating the authenticity of *The Song of Igor's Campaign*. During his stay at Cambridge and Cornell Nabokov had a cordial personal relationship with Jakobson and shared his critical approach. Later, there was a parting of the ways. In the annotations to his 1960 edition of *The Song of Igor's Campaign*, Nabokov wrote:

> I made my first attempt to translate *Slovo o Polku Igoreve* in 1952. My object was purely utilitarian—to provide my students with an English text. In that first version I followed uncritically Roman Jakobson's recension as published in *La Geste du Prince Igor.* Later, however, I grew dissatisfied not only with my own—much too "readable"—translation but also with Jakobson's views. Mimeographed copies of that obsolete version which are still in circulation at Cornell and Harvard should now be destroyed. (p. 82)

Because Nabokov's edition, while tending to accept the work's authenticity, also outlines the grounds for skepticism, Jakobson took a strongly negative attitude to it.

6. "Mr. Jakobson is a monster."

7. "I mean that he is a monster of learning—he is a philologist, a sociologist, an anthropologist."

1949

190

Dear Bunny,

I liked your book[1] very much—though not all of it. I think you are wonderful when you get down to the quiddity of the work you discuss, but your sociological forays are perfunctory and superficial. Here are a few scholia:

1. The spouting of verse at parties, etc., is not especially characteristic of the Soviet Union; it was just the same in old Russia, among all types of people.[2]

2. Your reference to Keats in regards to *Onegin* is absolutely and beautifully to the point, and you will be proud to know I had the same passage from the "Eve of Saint Agnes" in my Pushkin lecture notes.[3]

3. Your remarks on Praed[4] are likewise brilliant.

4. There is a dreadful mistake in your account of the Onegin-Lensky duel. I cannot imagine what made you think that it was a "back-to-back-march-face-about-fire" affair popularized by movies and cartoons.[5] This variant did not exist in Pushkin's Russia. The duel in Onegin is the classical *duel à volonté* of the French Code, and is fought as follows. We shall assume that a man has "called upon" (not the corrupt "called out") another for a hostile "meeting" (an English term for *rencontre*)—in other words, the cartel of defiance (termed "challenge" or "message" in England and Virginia) has been dispatched and accepted and all preliminary ceremonials have been adjusted. The seconds mark the ground at a certain number of paces. For instance, in the Onegin-Lensky duel, thirty-two paces are measured. A certain number of paces are told off between the extreme points, leaving a space of say ten paces in the center of the ground (*la barrière*, a kind of no man's land, beyond the limits of which neither can advance).

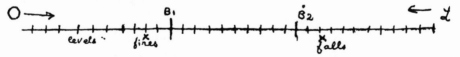

The principals take their positions at the extreme points O and L, facing each other, of course, and keeping the muzzles of their pistols pointing to the ground. At a given signal, they advance upon each other and can fire whenever they think proper. Onegin started gently leveling his pistol when both had advanced four paces. They walked another five paces, and Lensky was killed on the first fire. Now, if Onegin had discharged his pistol without effect, Lensky might have made him come up to the *barrière* limit (B_2) and taken a long, cool aim at him. This was one of the reasons why serious duelists, like Pushkin himself, preferred to have the other fellow fire first. If after the exchange the adversaries still felt bloodthirsty, they might have the pistols reloaded (or use a fresh brace) and begin all over again. This type of duel was popular in France, Russia, England and the Southern States with variations from 1800 to 1840.[6]

5. "There was for the man of imagination and moral passion a basic maladjustment to society" (in old Russia) (p. 46). Tell me please where and when was such a man ever adjusted to society?

6. The translation of the "Bronze Horseman" is first-rate and I am going to use it in my classes, telling them it is my own.

7. Why juggle with the term "bourgeois" in regard to Flaubert? You know quite well that in Flaubert's sense it was not a class category. In other words, Flaubert in the eyes of Marx was a bourgeois in the Marxist sense, while Marx in Flaubert's eyes was a bourgeois in a Flaubertian sense.[7]

8. Re p. 117. You really believe that in the first years of the Soviet regime it was laying (with blood-stained hands) the (blood-soaked *papier-maché*) foundation for a new humanity?[8]

9. You are also quite mistaken about Lenin's taste in the way of literature.[9] In this he was a perfect bourgeois (in all senses). When he says "Pushkin," he is not thinking of our (yours, mine, etc.) Pushkin, but of an average-Russian mixture of a) school manuals, b) Chaykovsky, c) hackneyed quotations, d) a kind of safe feeling about Pushkin as being "simple" and "classical." The same refers to his attitude towards Tolstoy (what he wrote on Tolstoy is quite childish).[10] Stalin also likes Pushkin, Tolstoy and Romain Rolland.

10. Have you ever read Radek on literature?[11] Very like Goebbels. I have both in my notes.

11. The "decline" of Russian literature in 1905–1917 is a Soviet invention.[12] Blok, Bely, Bunin and others wrote their best stuff in those days. And never was poetry so popular—not even in Pushkin's days. I am a product of that period, I was bred in that atmosphere.

12. Your defense of American democratic literature from Soviet critics is admirable. I go further and maintain that Soviet literature *sensu stricto* has hardly reached the level of Upton Sinclair.

Véra joins me in wishing Elena and you a splendid New Year. (I, Véra, also join Volodia in sending you my sincerest thanks for your wonderful book).

Yours,

V.

1. *The Triple Thinkers,* a collection of essays.

2. In the essay "Is Verse a Dying Technique?" Wilson wrote:

> We might perhaps see a revival of verse in a period and in a society in which music played a leading role. It has long played a great role in Russia; and in the Soviet Union at the present time you find people declaiming poetry at drinking parties or while traveling on boats and trains almost as readily as they burst into song to the accordeon or the balalaika, and flocking to poetry readings just as they do to concerts. (p. 29)

3. In "In Honor of Pushkin," Wilson juxtaposed the first stanza of "The Eve of St. Agnes" with Pushkin's description of the onset of winter in Chapter Four, stanzas xl–xlii of *Eugene Onegin*. Nabokov cited Wilson's prose version of these stanzas from *The Triple Thinkers* ("with a few minor inexactitudes, which I have italicized," as he put it) in his annotated edition of *Onegin*.

4. Winthrop Mackworth Praed (1802–1839), whose descriptions of social scenes Wilson thought closer to Pushkin's than anything in Byron.

5. Wilson later corrected his description of the Onegin-Lensky duel in subsequent editions of *The Triple Thinkers* in response to this letter (see Letter 236).

6. This passage was expanded into the numerous accounts of duels and dueling techniques in Nabokov's annotations to his four-volume edition of *Eugene Onegin*.

7. "The Politics of Flaubert" examines this writer's *oeuvre* and especially his novel *L'Education sentimentale* largely in terms of how Karl Marx might have reacted to it. The concluding sentence of the essay reads:

> The bourgeois has ceased to preach to the bourgeois: as the first big cracks begin to show in the structure of the nineteenth century, he shifts his complaints to the incompetence of humanity, for he is unable to believe in, or even conceive, any non-bourgeois way out. (p. 87)

8. Reference to the following sentence in the essay "The Ambiguity of Henry James": "It has been shown by Mr. Van Wyck Brooks in his literary history of the United States how the post-Revolutionary American had been stimulated—much like the Russian of the first years of the Soviet regime—to lay the foundations for a new humanity [...]."

9. Wilson had written ("Marxism and Literature," *The Triple Thinkers*, p. 200) that Lenin "was fond of fiction, poetry and the theater, and by no means doctrinaire in his tastes," citing Krupskaya on Lenin's preference for Pushkin over Mayakovsky and Gorky on his fondness for Tolstoy.

10. In the same essay, Wilson wrote: "In his very acute essays on Tolstoy, [Lenin] deals with him much as Engels deals with Goethe—with tremendous admiration for Tolstoy's genius, but with an analysis of his non-resistance and mysticism in terms not, it is interesting to note, of the psychology of the landed nobility, but of the patriarchal peasantry with whom Tolstoy had identified himself."

Lenin's seven brief essays on Tolstoy were all written between 1908 and 1911. They add up, when bound in one volume, to a total of 36 pages. They bear such titles as "Tolstoy as the Mirror of the Russian Revolution," "Tolstoy and the Contemporary Labor Movement" and "Tolstoy and the Proletarian Struggle." Like the overwhelming majority of Lenin's pre-revolutionary writings, these essays are in essence polemics against other Marxist groupings, the Populists or the Socialist Revolutionaries. Tolstoy's name is brought up in them as a pretext for Lenin's current topical sermon. Apart from Gorky's and Krupskaya's rather suspect testimony about his fondness for *War and Peace*, Lenin is on record as having appreciated only two pieces of writing by Tolstoy—the short stories "Master and Man" (because it documents the exploitation of poor peasants by rich ones) and "Lucerne" (for its indictment of Western parliamentary democracies).

11. Karl Radek is mentioned in "Marxism and Literature" in connection with the advent of the Stalinist attitudes in literature: "And it is probable that the death of Gorky, as well as the imprisonment of Bukharin and Radek, have removed the last brakes from the precipitate descent, in the artistic as well as the political field, into a nightmare of informing and repression."

12. This is Nabokov's response to Wilson's statement: "As for the pre-revolutionary periods in which the great new forces are fermenting, they *may* be great periods for literature—as the eighteenth century was in France and the nineteenth century in Russia (though there was a decadence after 1905)."

191

THE NEW YORKER
No. 25 West 43rd Street

January 11, 1949
Wellfleet, Mass.

Dear Volodya: Thank you for your letter. I am glad to be straightened out about the duelling technique in *Evgeni Onegin*, but what you say doesn't alter the fact that Onegin is made to take a stealthy advantage of Lensky, because he really hates him—which, as I remember, you once denied. You may say that Onegin's quietly lifting his pistol was due merely to the fact that he was more experienced, but I think it is obvious from the way in which Pushkin describes the movements of the two men that he wants to convey the idea that Onegin was out to murder Lensky.[1]

I am reading Tolstoy's *Воскресение*[2]—which, so far, seems to me better than it is usually said to be. It is a pity I had not read it when I wrote that Kuzminskaya review, as I see that it deals precisely with the theme of the tragic liaison between people of different classes that I complained of Tolstoy's having left out of his other novels.

Nothing new with us. If we're lucky, we may get to Stamford for a few months in the middle of February.

As ever,

EW

1. Wilson's assertion in *The Triple Thinkers*, reiterated here, that Onegin's killing of Lensky at the duel was a premeditated murder, motivated by his jealousy of Lensky's love for Olga and his envy of Lensky's poetic gift, must surely be based on a misreading. The view is neither borne out by a close reading of Pushkin's text, nor is there any support for it in the vast literature devoted to the exegesis of the novel in Russian.

2. *Resurrection*.

192

Do you still work upon such sets
as for example "step" and "pets,"
as "Nazitrap" and "partizan,"
"Red Wop" and "powder," "nab" and "ban"?

V. N.

February 6, 1949

Dear Bunny,

Everything all right?

I have been writing rather nicely during a fortnight vacation that ends to-morrow. The Cardinal, I think, *has* been doing a little spying, etc., but it is also true that they tortured him before his court appearances.[1] The Catholic Church, incidentally, must feel some wistful, retrospective regret that those handy drugs were not known during the Inquisition. Do write something about poor Ted Spencer[2]—some of his work has a pleasant tang of its own, and anyway онъ лучше многихъ.[3] I have invented a marvelous new transcription of Russian, but I do not dare show it [to] you.

It would be so nice if you both could come to visit us. I do not know when we shall come your way.

Yours,
V.

1. On February 3, 1949 Joseph Cardinal Mindszenty, Primate of the Catholic Church in Hungary, was put on trial in Budapest on charges of treason, espionage and plotting to overthrow the government. The Cardinal's alarming appearance in photographs taken at his trial served to confirm the reports that he was tortured and forcibly drugged to make him confess.

2. Theodore Spencer, the Boylston Professor of Rhetoric and Oratory at Harvard, a poet and the author of *Shakespeare and the Nature of Man*, had died on January 18, 1949, of a sudden heart attack in a taxi outside his Cambridge home at the age of 49.

3. "He is better than many."

193

Dear Bunny,

I have just received the following letter from Vaudrin of Oxford Univ[ersity] Press:

> As you may have heard, we have been discussing with Edmund Wilson the possibility of publishing a collection of his essays that would include some pieces on Russian literature originally intended for the Doubleday book you and he undertook to do jointly. I gather that Doubleday are not pressing you and Wilson to produce a manuscript, but of course before we could do anything about taking on this new book by Wilson his Russian material would have to be released by Doubleday. This in turn involves your commitment to Doubleday.
>
> I understand that Doubleday paid you and Wilson $750.00 each as an advance against royalties on your joint project. In considering whether or not we can proceed with a new book of Wilson's (of which the Russian essays would be a part) we must bear in mind that Doubleday will probably insist on their recovering their $1,500.00 as a condition for releasing Wilson. But while we might be able to make an advance against royalties to Wilson that would enable him to repay his share of the Doubleday advance, we do not know what we might be able to do about your obligation. I do not think that we could offer (assuming you would entertain an offer) to take on the separate publication of the translations you would have contributed to the Doubleday book, since we doubt that the market would justify such a move on straight commercial grounds. Perhaps, however, you have some other project or projects in mind or in preparation that would interest us, and against which we could provide an advance payment that would enable you to liquidate the Doubleday agreement. For one thing, I understand you are giving a course on Russian literature at Cornell, and possibly you are planning to put your lectures into book form. We might well be interested in such a project, and there may be others you would be willing to let me hear about. Anyhow, perhaps you would let me know your own thoughts about the general problem I have raised here.
>
> With all good wishes, etc.
>
> signed: Philip Vaudrin

I hate to think that our double commitment to Doubleday may interfere with your plans. On the other hand, I don't think I can offer Vaudrin anything that would induce them to buy us out jointly. I could not possibly publish my lectures for, if I did, I would not be able to go on delivering them, and anyway they are not written for publication. The only publishable material I have is a) those verse translations that were published in England and were destined, with several additions, for the Doubleday book; b) my own poems in English (too few to make a volume); c) a novel *(Otchayanie, La Méprise)* in an English translation I made some years ago and published in England (1935 or 36, I believe) under the title of DESPAIR.

I doubt that any of these could tempt the Oxford Press.

Perhaps Doubleday could be prevailed upon to release you independently from my own commitment? Or, if you think it advisable, I might write Doubleday and suggest that they publish my translations instead of my part in our Siamese book? The New Directions edition was a sell-out and I often receive inquiries as to where those translations can be obtained. (Am referring those people to the English edition.)

I would like to do anything in my power to help you get disentangled. If you have any ideas of how to manage it, do tell me.

Roman tells me you are adding weight.

We are sending you both our very best regards.

Yours
V

194

March 24, 1949
c/o Eitingon
Hillcrest Park
Stamford, Conn.

Dear Vladimir: We have come down here to Stamford to stay till sometime in May. Roman tells me that you are coming on to New York sometime in April. Couldn't you stop off here for a night? I am trying to arrange with Oxford to take over the Doubleday contract and give us both new contracts for separate books, if this is agreeable to you. Vaudrin says he is writing you. I want to discuss this with you, as well as other matters. I am making things easier for Stanley Edgar Hyman by plagiarizing *Bend Sinister* in my play.[1]

Love to Vera,
EW

1. *The Little Blue Light.*

195

March 28, 1949

Dear Volodya: Thanks for the butterfly monograph.[1] I don't know why I didn't reply to your last letters. Perhaps they weren't as brilliant as usual. (I'm not sure that one may not have gone astray. I seem to remember only a short note.) I just got your letter about the publishing problem. We can discuss it when you come on. When I wrote you before, though, I'd forgotten that you were no longer at Cambridge, so that you couldn't drop off at Stamford. Perhaps you could come out or, in any case, I could meet you in New York. Elena and I are reading Chekhov aloud in the evenings. She can pronounce the words, which I can't, but hasn't as much literary vocabulary as I. We really need somebody to coach us, and I hope you will give us a lesson when we see you again.

As ever,

EW

1. "The Nearctic Members of the Genus *Lycaeides Hübner*."

196

Cornell University
Goldwin Smith Hall
Ithaca, N.Y.

[Mid-April 1949]

Dear Bunny,

My New York lecture has been postponed—it will take place on the 7th of May. I got an invitation from Roman for the 16th of April, but this is cancelled now. Will you be in New York in May? We want to see both of you very much. Thanks for inviting us to Stamford, but this will have to be put off too.

I liked your Indian piece very much.[1] Did you see what Dos Passos has been writing about the Perons in *Life*?[2] Has he gone mad? Or is it some neo-radical fad—to praise Evita? Or is it meant to be satirical? Or—my pen trembles at the thought—has he perchance joined the True Church?

I think I told you already that we shall probably travel to Utah by car in mid-June to attend a July Writers' Conference at Salt L[ake] City.

We *must* see each other before that.

Yours

V.

1. "A Reporter in New Mexico: Shalako," *The New Yorker*, April 9 and 16, 1949, which later formed several chapters in the "Zuñi" section of *Red, Black, Blond and Olive.*

2. "Visit to Evita" by John Dos Passos appeared in *Life* on April 11, 1949. It depicted a glamorous, popular and hard-working Eva Duarte de Perón who helped her stable and fatherly husband run Argentina.

197

April 23, 1949
Hillcrest Park
Stamford, Conn.

Dear Volodya: I'm afraid we'll be gone by May 7, as we want to leave here as close to the first of the month as possible. Couldn't you get up to see us at Wellfleet? Shall write you later about publishing arrangements.

<u>EW</u>

198

Cornell University
Goldwin Smith Hall
Ithaca, N.Y.

[May 23–25, 1949][1]

Dear Bunny,

Just a couple of words between two lectures. This is the last academical week. Around the 20th of June we shall start driving westwards—first to a Writers' Conference in Utah Univ[ersity], then to Teton Nat[ional] Forest, Wyo[ming], to look for a butterfly which I have described, named, fondled—but never actually taken myself.

It is bitterly annoying never to be able to accept your kind invitations. We would like to see both of you so much! Around the 15th of June Dmitri will be coming back from his school. I am going to devote the next 20 days to some fierce writing. I have sold my book of memoirs на корню[2] to Harpers, and the arrangement is quite satisfactory. Shall have the whole thing ready in a year's time. I never got any thanks from you for the wonderful emir I gave you: partizan—Nazitrap.[3]

I suppose I shall have to offer Vaudrin a little book on *Onegin:* complete translation in prose with notes giving associations and other explanations for every line—the kind of thing I have prepared for my classes. I am quite certain

I am not going to do any *rhymed* translations any more—their dictatorship is absurd and impossible to reconcile with exactitude, etc.

Nobody wants to publish (too long or "too scholarly") a piece I have written (some 12 typed pages) on *Slovo o Polku Igoreve*. The *New Yorker* has rejected it, and I am not sure the *Partisan va marcher.*[4]

Véra drove me to N.Y. and back—beautifully, through lovely soft-bosomed scenery, and I had some highly diverting games of chess with Роман, G. Hessen, Николаевскій and Церетелли.[5] Missed you very much.

Greetings from both of us to you both,

V.

1. Erroneously dated "1945" in the original.

2. "As it stands." Nabokov uses an agricultural expression that refers to crops sold before they are reaped or harvested.

3. See Nabokov's amphisbaenic poems in Letters 187 and 192.

4. "Will work."

5. *I.e.,* Roman (Grynberg), George Hessen, (Boris) Nikolaevsky and (Irakly) Tseretelli. Nikolaevsky (1887–1966) was a one-time revolutionary, whose post-revolutionary publications documented the history of terrorism in Russia. His book *Forced Labor in Soviet Russia* (together with David J. Dallin), 1947, was the most authoritative treatment of that subject prior to Solzhenitsyn's *The GULAG Archipelago*. Tseretelli (1882–1959), the Georgian Marxist leader, was in the Menshevik faction of the Social Democratic party and was sentenced in pre-revolutionary times to ten years of hard labor for his revolutionary activities. Freed by the February Revolution, he became Minister of the Interior in the Provisional Government. After the October Revolution, he tried to establish an independent Socialist state in Georgia but was defeated by the Bolsheviks and had to emigrate. His two volumes of memoirs about the February Revolution were posthumously published in Paris in 1963.

199

[Postcard, postmarked Jackson, Wyoming, August 18, 1949   6 P.M.]

Teton Pass Ranch
Wilson, Wyoming

Dear Bunny,

We have had some wonderful adventures in Utah and Wyoming and are driving back next week. I have lost many pounds and found many butterflies. We send both of you our very best greetings. We *must* see each other somewhere, somehow.

V.

200

Wellfleet
Cape Cod, Mass.
September 28, 1949

Dear Volodya:

I was glad to get your card. We have just come to the end of a very busy summer, what with the family—the boys have just gone back to school[1]—and my
literary activities. I've finished my play,[2] which I'm now trying to get produced,
and have gotten together a volume of my articles written during the twenties.[3]

Gleb Struve[4] came up here to see us in the summer—with his odd and *farouche* girl-friend[5]—do you know her? I had a long conversation with him
about Russian and English versification, which cleared up for me the misunderstandings of our correspondence on this subject several years ago, and I propose to give you the benefit of my enlightenment. The point is, I found out from
Struve, that Russian words, however long, have actually only one stress. I had
never noticed that Russian dictionaries indicate only one accented syllable,
whereas English ones give secondary accents. Thus the emphasis in Russian
verse is different from that of English. In English, the secondary accents are
used to make the beat just as the main ones are. The sophistication of English
verse, in the hands of the great poets from Shakespeare to Yeats, consists partly
of displacing these accents. There is nothing that corresponds to this in Russian—hence your inability to grasp the reality of what I called substitutions of
feet. You can't substitute or syncopate in Russian. You can't have such lines in
blank verse as the *Never, never, never, never, never,* of *King Lear* or the *Cover
her face; mine eyes dazzle: she died young,* of *The Duchess of Malfi.* The metrical sophistication comes in another way: the number of syllables in Russian is
usually perfectly regular, as it is only rarely in English, but there are many
fewer stresses and you juggle with these. This juggling is what you were trying
to tell me about, but you made the mistake of supposing that we had the same
thing in English. You imagined, I think, that a word like *constitution* coming at
the end of an iambic pentameter was pronounced *constitúshun,* whereas actually an actor who has been trained to speak verse pronounces it *con-sti-tú-ti-őn:*
the *ti-őn* is a full iambus (in older English the *on* was *oun*). Russian, in fact, has
taken over the metrical forms of English and German verse, but has used them
for a different kind of music, and the result is a twofold misunderstanding as
between you and me. You don't understand our displacement of accent—so
that when, for example, you and I were working on *Mozart and Salieri,* it disturbed you, and seemed to you wrong, every time I suggested an emendation

The Letters, 1949

255

that would involve making an iambus a trochee. You were right in the given instance because you had made your translation in absolutely uniform iambics, but no good English poet would think of writing a long blank-verse poem in this way. On my side, I realize now, I have never, in reading Russian poetry, understood how it ought to sound. It always seemed to me too monotonously regular—as metronomic as a schoolboy's exercise—and this regularity was puzzling in poets who were brilliantly capable of every other kind of variety. I hope that you will read me some Russian poetry some day and expound to me the effects that escape me. (I also found illuminating your discussion of the poetic formulas in your story in the *Partisan Review*.)[6] On the other hand, in writing your English verse, which I think you make as regular as Russian, you do not exploit all the resources of which English verse is capable.

When shall we see you? We have wanted to make a motor-trip over to my old family place in upstate New York, which needs attention, as nobody has been there in years, and we might possibly go on further and visit you, as Mary and I did the last time I went, when Nicolas was at Wells College; but our money prospects are so poor at the moment that we are unlikely to get off. Later, we may be able to go to New York for the winter. Do you ever get down from Ithaca?

Elena sends love. How is Vera? Do write and keep me in touch with all your facts and fantasies.

How did you like my Anglo-Russian limericks?[7] They were the result of setting out one day to look up all the equivalents of the four-letter words in Dahl. To my surprise, I found them all. Some of their English opposite numbers are not included even in the big Oxford dictionary.

I read a lot of Chekhov last summer and was tremendously impressed by it—had had no idea how much ground he covered, what a large area of life he described—particularly interesting in connection with what has been going on in Soviet Russia, because a lot of the types he deals with—peasants who have bettered their position, dissatisfied and incompetent clerks—are the same people who came later to the top. Have also been reading more Faulkner. Your failure to see his genius is a mystery to me—except that you do not, in general, like tragedy. Have you tried *The Sound and the Fury?*

As ever,

Edmund W.

1. Reuel Wilson and Elena Wilson's son Henry Thornton.
2. *The Little Blue Light.*

3. The collection that was eventually expanded to *The Shores of Light: A Literary Chronicle of the Twenties and Thirties*, published in 1952.

4. The literary scholar Gleb Struve (1898–1985), Nabokov's friend since their university days, was the author of *Russian Literature Under Lenin and Stalin, 1917–1953* and of the only comprehensive survey of Russian émigré literature, *Russkaya literatura v izgnanii (Russian Literature in Exile)*. He co-edited (together with Boris Filippov) editions in the West of Osip Mandelstam, Boris Pasternak, Nikolai Gumilyov, Nikolai Klyuev, Nikolai Zabolotsky and Anna Akhmatova, issued when the work of these poets was totally or partly banned in the Soviet Union.

5. Mary Kriger, later Mrs. Gleb Struve. *Farouche* in this context means "shy."

6. "First Poem" (Chapter Eleven of *Speak, Memory*), in *Partisan Review* of September 1949.

7. These limericks are to be found in *Night Thoughts*, p. 210, under the general heading "Something for My Russian Friends." The first of them is about Nabokov and his interest in butterflies; the Russian equivalents of the "four-letter words" (three-letter in Russian) which Wilson mentions, however, were decorously replaced with dashes in the published version of the limericks.

201

November 9, 1949

Dear Bunny,

I did not write you before because my book (the autobiographic one) is taking a lot of my time. I always told you that Russian words had only one stress-accent.[1] I am sure I also mentioned in the course of our correspondence that long English words tend to double the accent (though perhaps more so in American speech than in British). I don't see the point of the "-ion" affair, but anyway it is not unlike the change of *-ie* endings to *-ьe* in corresponding Russian nouns, such as *zhelanie* to *zhelan'e*.[2] Ponder this. We shall continue the discussion—of which I seem to be getting the better—when at last I come to you or you to me.

A story about my first love adventure is going to appear soon in the *New Yorker*,[3] but another piece, on my student days, had to be withdrawn because they wanted me to revise certain passages (that readers might have found offensive or at least surprising) about Lenin and tsarist Russia. It is much the same kind of harmless stuff I once wrote you about American radicals and their attitude towards Leninism, etc.[4] Sad.

I have still about fifty pages of the book, and my little motor is running sweetly. I am afraid you will not care for the thing but I have to get it off my chest.

Down with Faulkner!

Yours,

V

1. Actually, Nabokov never did.

2. Two alternate forms of the nominative singular of the Russian word for "desire," which admits two forms of the ending, one of one and one of two syllables; these two suffixes are illustrated earlier in this sentence. Like the instrumental suffixes of feminine adjectives and nouns discussed in Letters 203 and 205, these neuter nominative endings may be chosen at random. In prose, the choice is guided by stylistic considerations, while in verse it may be determined by whether one or two syllables fits the meter.

3. "Tamara" (later Chapter Twelve of *Speak, Memory*) appeared in *The New Yorker* on December 10, 1949.

4. Chapter Thirteen of *Speak, Memory*, which drew a parallel between the Leninist and Stalinist terror and contained passages that were based in part on Nabokov's letter to Wilson of February 23, 1948 (Letter 172 of this edition), was rejected by *The New Yorker*. It eventually appeared in *Harper's Magazine* for January 1951 as "Lodgings in Trinity Lane."

1950

202

[From Véra Nabokov to Edmund Wilson]

April 8, 1950

Dear Bunny,

Vladimir is sick at the hospital and has asked me to write you. We have heard from Roman that you too have had your encounter with the grippe. I hope this is all over by now. My own bronchitis is fairly over but Vladimir's degenerated into a severe attack of intercostal neuralgia, which means excruciating pains and does not respond to treatment. The pains were so violent that the doctors at first did not believe it could be "merely" neuralgia. They ворожили надъ нимъ[1] for a whole week and are now reluctantly admitting that it must be neuralgia after all. In the meantime the pains have improved a little.

V. has asked me to thank you for the *Furioso*. He was very much amused by your wicked little parody (so was I) and found the rest of the issue rather entertaining as well.[2]

He further wants me to ask your advice for him in the following matter. Harper was going to publish his book of recollections in the fall, but now would like to put off publication until after Christmas because of the abundance of "memoirs and autobiographies scheduled for publication by other firms during the fall season." They say that the first three months of the year are "very nearly as good from the standpoint of total sales as the pre-Christmas season," etc. V. does not feel entirely convinced by these arguments. He does not believe that, after a surfeit of autobiographies in the fall, people would be likely to develop a fresh appetite for them three months later. He also feels that his book can take a chance in a race. And finally he is afraid that the post-Christmas season is not all that Harper says it is. He would be very grateful if he could have your opinion before answering Harper about it.

It was so nice to see you and Elena in New York after all this time. You both looked wonderful, and so did Raoul. I won't say anything about the baby because I don't want to "gush."

Sincerely,

Véra

[Added upside-down at top]
I am enclosing a little item for your collection of Nabokoviana. This one has again a little Wilson contribution. It also has a marvellous frontispiece. And do not miss the picture of the author on the back.

1. "Practiced their sorcery on him."
2. *Furioso* was a literary magazine published at Carleton College in Minnesota between 1939 and 1953. Its Spring 1950 issue ran Edmund Wilson's letter of rebuttal to a review by Paul Goodman of Mary McCarthy's book *The Oasis*. The "wicked little parody" consisted in Wilson's pretending that Paul Goodman did not really exist and that the review attributed to him was a hoax.

203

April 14, 1950
36 Vista Place
Red Bank, New Jersey

Dear Volodya: I have come down here to be with my mother, who has been very ill—in the hospital—but is now better. Elena has told me on the phone that a letter has come from Vera saying that you have been ill with the flu. I, too, took to my bed the day after the *New Yorker* party and completely lost my voice from laryngitis. That evening had so many disagreeable incidents and *funestes*[1] consequences that I have suggested it ought to be written about in the same way as John Hersey's *Hiroshima*. You would describe each small human unit pursuing his individual interests, passing from table to table, from ballroom to restaurant, hardly noting a discomfiture, a boredom, an irritation or an incipient drunkenness that seemed only incidental and unaware of the magnitude of the disaster that was annihilating them all.[2]

I had been just about to write you, after reading your admirable last install-ment.[3] I was reminded by your mentioning Abbazia, which I had just been reading about in Chekhov,[4] that I had been meaning to ask you about a point of Russian grammar. In reading Chekhov lately, I have been noticing that he sometimes uses the -ой form and sometimes the -ою form of the adjective in the instrumental case of the feminine singular. At first, I developed a theory that the -ою was used with the nouns that had their instrumental in -ю. I would find, for example, длинною, отборною бранью,[5] but then I would find this[6] form simply used in the predicate with a feminine subject—она[6] or some woman's name, and the -ой form used in the predicate with жизнь.[7] Finally (in the first paragraph of the section of *Моя Жизнь*),[8] I found с благотворитель*ной* целью and с благотворитель*ною* целью[9] only a few lines apart. What is the point here?[10] Is there any real principle involved? Paul Chavchavadze thought that the longer form was used when you needed another syllable, but I don't see how that can be true in this passage. (Don't bother to reply to this unless you are feeling better. I'll be here all through next week—after that, can be reached through Wellfleet, though I may not be able to go further away from here than New York.)

I have been reading the works of Genet. I suppose you know about him. His books, which are hair-raisingly indecent, are only now being brought out in editions that are sold in the regular way. He is a homosexual burglar who has spent a good deal of time in prison. Cocteau, when he was trying to get him out of jail, is supposed to have told the authorities that he was the greatest living French writer, and I think that there is something to be said for this opinion. I have read *Notre-Dame des Fleurs* and *Journal du Voleur*[11] and am very much impressed by them—especially by the former. As a writer, he is perfectly ex-traordinary—it is hard to understand how he could have educated himself so well (a boy from a foundlings' home, who spent all his early life as a thief and tramp) and cultivated so rich a talent. His vocabulary and his rhythms are unique like his queer experience. And he deals as hardly anyone else has done with the ambivalent (blessed word!) psychology of submission and domination that is so much in evidence in the present world—and with which you your-self are often occupied. I'll lend you *Notre-Dame des Fleurs* sometime if you haven't seen it. Hope you're well by now. Love to Vera.

EW

1. "Disastrous."

2. "We went to the *New Yorker* party celebrating their twenty-fifth anniversary. It was enormous—a thousand people invited—and far less attractive than the one fifteen years

ago, when there was a smaller staff and fewer contributors. The evening, in fact, was one of catastrophes, and it had been suggested that *The New Yorker* ought to write it up in the vein of Hersey's *Hiroshima*. Prominent persons whom I will not name were guilty of wholesale malignant rudeness [...] I was ill, had already lost my voice, and had a relapse the next day. Vladimir Nabokov, who had come down from Cornell for the occasion, hearing that Stanley Edgar Hyman was there, went up to him and asked what he meant by calling his father 'a tsarist liberal.' Hyman, who was evidently afraid that Nabokov was going to attack him physically, replied, 'Oh, I think you are a great writer! I admire your writing very much!' Nabokov went back with acute neuralgia and has spent a long spell in the hospital." Wilson's letter to Morton D. Zabel of April 28, 1950, in *Letters on Literature and Politics, 1912–1972*, p. 480.

3. "Perfect Past," later Chapter Ten of *Speak, Memory*, in *The New Yorker*, April 15, 1950.

4. Anton Chekhov's story "Ariadne," which Wilson cites in Letter 206, takes place in part in Abbazia (now Opatija in Croatia). That city was also the scene of one of Nabokov's earliest memories, described in Chapter One of *Speak, Memory*.

5. "With a long string of choice swearwords" (from Chekhov's story "The Murder," section IV).

6. "She."

7. "Life."

8. "My Life," by Chekhov.

9. "With charitable aim," cited with two alternate variants of the feminine adjectival suffix in the instrumental case.

10. For an explanation, see Letter 201, note 2.

11. *Our Lady of the Flowers* and *The Thief's Journal*.

204

April 15, 1950
36 Vista Place
Red Bank, N.J.

Dear Vera: I wrote to Volodya yesterday before your letter had reached me. About the publishing problem: I have never been able to take seriously the reasons that publishers give for bringing out books at this or that season. They seem to change these ideas constantly, and I don't think it really makes much difference *when* a book is published. Volodya's book, in any case, is really a work of literature, with which books of memoirs would hardly compete. If his contract calls for fall publication and he wants it to come out in the fall, he has every right to insist on it. If it isn't in his contract, he can still insist, but he may not be able to make them do what he wants.

I am sorry he has been so sick. Please thank him for the book, which I haven't yet seen, as Elena didn't forward it to me.

My son's name, by the way, is not Raoul, but Reuel. The English equivalent for Raoul is Rollo or Roland. Reuel is a Biblical name, one of the names of Moses's father-in-law Jethro. It means *friend of God* (el = God). It is rather uncommon (though there is a poet named Reuel Denney), but is an old name in my mother's family.

Best regards,

Edmund W.

205

802 E. Seneca St.

Ithaca, N.Y.

April 17, 1950

Dear Bunny,

Most Russian writers use both -ой and -ою indiscriminately, which I deplore. There seems to be something vaguely similar to this in the use of "which" and "that" in the case of some English authors. Tolstoy was the greatest offender; he often flaunts both endings in the same sequence of adjectives and nouns. «За желтою нивой и за широкою сонной рѣкою»[1] is an extreme example. I presume Chav[chavadze] thought you were speaking of verse. In my own prose, being at heart a pedant, I stuck to -ой unless there was some special "musical" reason for prolonging the whine of the instrumental.

Véra and I were very glad to get your nice letters. I spent almost two weeks in a hospital and have been howling and writhing since the end of March when the influenza I caught at that somewhat dingy but well-meant party tapered to the atrocious point of intercostal neuralgia, the symptoms of which, the wracking, unceasing pain and panic, mimic diseases of the heart and kidney, so that for days on end I was experimented upon by doctors although I told them I knew my illness by heart, had gone through exactly the same torture four times in my life before. I am not quite well yet, had a little relapse to-day and am still in bed, at home. Véra is splendidly replacing me in the lecture-hall.

I am writing the last (16th) chapter of my book. There will be only one more (chapter 15) in the *New Yorker*, a rather intricate thing I have just sold them about my son's infancy. The *New Yorker* has bought in all 12 of the 15 submitted to them. One piece was in the *Partisan*, two others, both spiced with politics, are still on my hands. I shall probably send one of them to the *Partisan*, though they pay very little.[2]

Do send me the homosexual burglar's book!! I love indecent literature! Next year I am teaching a course called "European Fiction" (XIX and XX c.[3]). What

English writers (novels or short stories) would you suggest? I must have at least two. Am going to lean heavily on the Russians, at least five broad-shouldered Russians, and shall probably choose Kafka, Flaubert and Proust to illustrate West-European fiction.

I think your poem is the most successful one you have written in that vein. I liked the pifka-pafka hugely—in fact I kept repeating it during my hours of pain at the hospital.[4] I used to be given up to three injections of morphine per night, but each kept me in a state of endurable, dulled pain only for an hour or so. Have been looking through Eliot's various works and reading that collection of critical articles about him and am now more certain than ever that he is a fraud and a fake (even worse than ridiculous Thomas Mann—and with more brains).

Do write me another interesting letter. My nerves are all warped and ragged after these weeks of pain.

Best love to all of you from both of us.

V.

1. "Beyond a yellow field of corn and a wide drowsy river." The instrumental case suffixes of the adjectives in this example are not matched with those of the nouns.

2. "Exile," later Chapter Fourteen of *Speak, Memory,* appeared in the *Partisan Review* for January–February 1951. Chapter Fifteen appeared in *The New Yorker* on June 17, 1950 as "Gardens and Parks." There is no Chapter Sixteen in any of the three versions of this book, *Conclusive Evidence* (1951), *Speak, Memory* (also 1951), and *Speak, Memory. An Autobiography Revisited* (1967). The Russian version, *Drugie berega* (Other Shores), New York, 1954, which differs in some aspects from the English ones, has only fourteen chapters.

3. A Russian way of writing "nineteenth and twentieth centuries."

4. "With a rumble-de-bum and a pifka-pafka
Came the fife-and drum corps parading for Kafka."

From Wilson's poem published in *Furioso,* IV, No. 3 (Summer 1949), as "Bulletin No. 7: The Mass in the Parking Lot" and later included in *Night Thoughts* (as "The Mass in the Parking Lot"), pp. 181–184.

206

Edmund Wilson
Wellfleet, Cape Cod
Massachusetts

April 27, 1950

Dear Volodya: ① I've just looked up the passage in *Медный Всадник*[1] that you thought I had mistranslated. My Soviet text (редакция Бонди, Томашевского,

Щеголева[2]) gives «Наш герой/ Живет в чулане.»[3] I called up Paul Chavcha-vadze and asked him to look it up in his old edition, and he found «в Коломне,»[4] as you said. The Soviet text is supposed to restore several passages that were altered under pressure from Benckendorff[5]—some sordid details, for example, about the houses of the poor washed away by the flood. I must look up and find out what else there is.

② Russian grammar: À propos of the instrumental, I used rather to resent its peculiar use to indicate a transitory or non-actual state—Когда я был маль-чиком. Она воображала себя в будущем не иначе как очень богатою и знатною;[6] but now it seems to me a charming nuance. But one thing I have not mastered is the predicative form of adjectives. I find the following in Chekhov: Вы сегодня бог знает какой скучный![7] Why isn't this скучен or скучны?[8] Is it какой[9] that makes the difference?

③ I have sent you the Genet book and am curious to know what you will think of it. I am fascinated by the language, a combination of argot, ordinary colloquialisms, very fancy literary vocabulary and precise technical terms. Huysmans, who could only do it synthetically, would have been crazy about Genet. And I suppose there is a slight element of illiteracy—what do you make of his use of one of his favorite words *sourdre*[10] (which he sometimes seems to write *soudre*)? He seems to have invented a participle for it: *sourdi*—on the analogy, I suppose, of *ourdi*,[11] just as Faulkner has produced *surviven* on the analogy of *driven*, etc. (As writers, they have something in common, and Gen-et's writing in certain passages has something in common with yours—I don't mean in the matter of these solecisms.)

④ I am sending you, also, a small package of my own writings.

⑤ About your book: I am not sure that you wouldn't do better to bring it out with several unpublished chapters and announce this fact on the jacket. It has been proved that people tend not to buy books that they think they have read all of in magazines. Make the advertising-copy writer at Harper's—or better write the blurb yourself—explain that there are new chapters *on politics* not published in the *New Yorker.* You must have fans that would buy the book to read them.

⑥ I'm sorry you've been having such a horrible time. I've never yet gotten over my own illness—have something wrong with one of my vocal cords—God's punishment for talking too much and too loud. Have also been told by the doctor that I'd have to lose fifteen pounds. So I live in a gruesome round of inhalations and sprays, dextrose and saccharin tablets, condemned to talk in a whisper and keep a weighing machine in my bathroom.

⑦ About the English novelists: in my opinion the two incomparably greatest (leaving Joyce out of account as an Irishman) are Dickens and Jane Austen. Try rereading, if you haven't done so, the later Dickens of *Bleak House* and *Little Dorrit*. Jane Austen is worth reading all through—even her fragments are remarkable.

⑧ We may still possibly get over to your part of the world—when Henry[12] graduates from school—and might possibly drive over to see you. Till how late will you be in Ithaca?

Love to Vera,

EW

1. "The Bronze Horseman."

2. "Edited by Bondi, Tomashevsky, Shchegolev" (three of the most eminent Pushkin scholars of the Soviet period).

3. "Our hero / Lodges in a small room" (Wilson's translation of this passage from "The Bronze Horseman" in *The Triple Thinkers*).

4. "In Kolomna" (rather than "in a small room"; a closer rendition of *v chulane* would have been "in a storeroom"). Since all the more recent Soviet academic editions of Pushkin have "in Kolomna," it could hardly have been a case of restoring a passage suppressed by tsarist censorship.

5. Count Alexander Benckendorff (1783–1844) headed the political police during the reign of Nicholas I.

6. "When I was a little boy. She could not imagine herself in the future as anything but very rich and distinguished." The second example comes from Chekhov's story "Ariadne."

7. "God, how boring you are today!" From Chekhov's "My Life," section VII.

8. The singular (masculine) and plural short forms of the adjective "boring." As attested elsewhere in this correspondence, Wilson had trouble understanding the difference between the long-form Russian adjectives, used attributively, and short-form ones, used as predicates. He confuses the construction used by Chekhov with an adverbial one of similar meaning, *kak vy skuchny*, which would use the plural short form he proposes (the singular short form would have to agree in number with the subject in this instance, and is thus impossible grammatically, since the subject is in the plural). A parallel in English is the difference between the forms "How boring you are" and "What a bore you are"—one can use either one, but one cannot hybridize them. Wilson is proposing the Russian equivalent of "How a bore you are."

9. "What a . . ." (translated in note 7 contextually as "how").

10. "To spring forth," "to gush."

11. Past participle of *ourdir*, "to warp" or "to plot."

12. Henry Thornton.

207

April 28, 1950

Dear Bunny,

Many thanks for lending me the book—which I read with pleasure. It is awfully good *in parts*. I have the impression that it was written by a *littérateur*[1] in the quiet of his study. The whole "tough-blood-murder" addition is poor and artificial, with Raskolnikovian echoes. The trial of N. D. des Fleurs is simply very bad, mediocre *littérature* at its best. It is a pity that the author did not limit his subject to the description of the mores of *tantes*[2]—this part is superb. I cannot understand why he called the book by the name of his least successful and convincing character. The *pièce de résistance* is, of course, Divine and she-he is beautifully done. A few other points: I liked the measurements of the penis given for the lovers. Coming to think of it, I applied the same descriptive method to my butterflies.[3] Another thing: I thought the description of the love making on the whole rather conventional—once you get the hang of it—in the sense that XVIII century pornographics with their colorless "assauts," "ébats,"[4] enumeration of orgasms, etc., are conventional. The artificial side is augmented by the fact that the perfect health of those men is somewhat suspicious (especially as some were heterosexual too), and really, Frenchmen do take baths at least *sometimes*. I was a little disappointed by there being no girls around. The only *jeune putain*[5] was sandwiched between two boys kissing each other, the idiots.

I am throwing in notes on English versification that I happened to use in one class of mine. Ponder them.

Love,
V.

[Appended to Letter 207]

The following five variations occur *within the framework of the English iambic line* (especially pentameter) with masculine or feminine ending.

1. Simple "pyrrhization" *(sic)* due to the metrical accent falling on a weakly stressed monosyllable ("to") or on a long word ("incalculable") sprawling over at least two feet of the meter.

"And to forget incalculable chance"
υ – υ ´ υ ´ υ – υ ´

This line contains both examples of simple pyrrhization. The absence of *natural* stress in a *metrically* stressed syllable is denoted by the symbol – (instead of ´).

2. Pyrrhization of a two-syllable trochaic word (generally in the first foot of the line) or "de-trochaization".

"Simply forget incalculable chance"

$$\acute{-} \; - \quad \cup \; \acute{-} \quad \cup \; \acute{-} \quad \cup \; - \; \cup \qquad \acute{-}$$

This variation is denoted by $\acute{-}\,-$, to show that the naturally stressed syllable of the *word* coincides with a *metrically* unstressed syllable (while there is simple pyrrhization in the second syllable of that word denoted, as above, by $-$ without accent).

3. "Slurring", due to local/contemporaneous (this or that period) pronunciation, of a syllable (heavn for heaven or fluttring for fluttering)

all heaven was full of flaming fluttering wings

$$\cup \; \acute{-} \; (\cup) \quad \cup \; \acute{-} \quad \cup \; \acute{-} \quad \cup \quad \acute{-} \; (\cup) \; \cup \qquad \acute{-}$$

4. De-syllabization of *the* as used by many very modern poets (in a kind of neo-Renaissance way) before a vowel

The appointed time etc.

$$(\cup) \; \cup \; \acute{-} \quad \cup \quad \acute{-}$$

5. Spondaization. This is feebly represented in English verse.

Rise! Follow me etc.

$$\acute{\underset{\cup}{}} \quad \acute{-} \; \cup \quad \acute{-}$$

This can be nicely combined with the so-called "enjambment" (for instance if a preceding line ended in "Man,").

The more variations an iambic poem contains, the richer their combinations, the more pleasing it is.

So here they are, those five variations of the typical iambic foot ($\cup\acute{-}$):

1. Simple "pyrrhization" $\cup-$
2. "De-trochaization" $\acute{\cup}-$
3. "Slurring" $\cup\acute{-}(\cup)$
4. "De-syllabization" $(\cup)\cup\acute{-}$
5. "Spondaization" $\acute{\cup}\acute{-}$

But everywhere the framework remains the same, that is, iambic.

V. Nabokov
Spring Term
1950

1. "Man of letters."
2. "Aunties."

3. Nabokov's monograph "The Nearctic Members of the Genus Lycaeides Hübner" features illustrations and descriptions of the genitalia of forty-six male butterflies.

4. "Assaults," "frolics."

5. "Young whore."

208

May 5, 1950

Dear Bunny,

Yes, the key-word is какой. The predicative would turn on как.[1] There is no difference between, say, как ты мил and какой ты милый.[2] But in some cases the meaning may suffer. For example какая она хорошая means *comme elle est bonne*[3] (I find Russian translates so much better into French) but как она хороша would mean *comme elle est belle*[4] (cp. *elle est assez bien* = она довольно хороша = she is rather good looking). *Voilà.* You are right about the я был мальчиком,[5] etc. To have been a boy is as fantastic as the dream of being some day a rich old man.

As far as I know the correct reading is в Коломне.[6] This is what the Soviet Академическій Пушкин[7] has.

Yes, I noticed what you say about good old Jean (by the way, shall I send you the book by mail to Wellfleet?). The only meaning *soudre* has for me is 'to gush.' Both he and I have read Rimbaud—Giraudoux—Proust, etc.

That is a good suggestion, about the unpublished chapters. I understand that you are *not* one of those "fans" of mine.

Thanks for the suggestion concerning my fiction course. I dislike Jane, and am prejudiced, in fact, against all women writers. They are in another class. Could never see anything in *Pride and Prejudice*. But the Dickens suggestion has *du bon*. I shall re-read both books. My father was an expert on Dickens, and at one time read to us, children, aloud, chunks of Dickens, in English, of course.

I had to interrupt this letter here and in the meantime have plunged into *Bleak House* which is admirable so far. I shall take Stevenson instead of Jane A.

I hope you have reverted to that good old voice of yours (anxious to hear it again; we shall be here till the end of May, and then may go for a fortnight to Boston—to have my dentist there extract the rest of my teeth). Our plans are vague for the summer. Possibly, we shall wing out west at the end of June. When is Henry's graduation? Would you be coming here before or after it?

Many thanks for *Furioso* (not *all* of the poem is good, I am afraid: dog-rhyme leading blind-poet), the book of stories[8] (I liked "Galahad"—but I am not sure what exactly *se passa entre eux*[9] in the sexual scene) and the play. Its dialogue is absolutely first-rate and there are some very amusing bits (I loved the Peters). There is something sirinesque about the transformations of the gardener.[10]

To Elena and you Véra and I send our love.

V.

[In margin in Véra Nabokov's handwriting]
Now *I* am going to read the play. In the meanwhile many thanks for the nice *dédicace*.[11]

V.2

1. See Letter 206, notes 8 and 9. This paragraph is a reply to Wilson's questions in paragraph 2 of that letter. Nabokov here cites some examples of the difference in the use of the short-form and long-form adjectives, but fails to tell Wilson that this is what they are both talking about or to explain how this difference works.

2. "How nice you are," in an adverbial short-form construction and in a long-form adjectival construction respectively.

3. "How good she is."

4. "How beautiful she is."

5. "I was a little boy."

6. "In Kolomna" (see the first paragraph of Letter 206).

7. "Academic [edition of] Pushkin."

8. The book of stories in which Wilson's story "Galahad" appeared was *The American Caravan: A Yearbook of American Literature*, edited by Van Wyck Brooks *et al.*, New York, 1927.

9. "What happened between them."

10. In Wilson's play *The Little Blue Light*, set in the "not-remote future," Children of Peter ("the Peters") are a fanatical right-wing Roman Catholic political organization. The mysterious gardener, who keeps changing his ethnic origins throughout the play, is revealed at the end to be Ahasuerus, the Wandering Jew. In 1923 Nabokov published a dramatic monologue *Ahasuerus* in his father's newspaper *Rul' (The Rudder)* in Berlin under his émigré pen name Sirin—hence the "sirinesque" quality of the gardener's transformation. *Ahasuerus* is the same work that Andrew Field repeatedly mentions as *Agaspher*, a title that comes from an erroneous transliteration from the Russian.

11. "Dedication."

209

Edmund Wilson
Wellfleet, Cape Cod
Massachusetts

May 9, 1950

Dear Volodya: ① Here is another problem. In Chekhov I find the following:
«В открытую дверь было видно и улицу, тихую, пустынную, и самую луну,

которая плыла по небу.»[1] I don't see why this isn't written «были видни и улица . . . и луна.»[2] In any other language I know, the moon and the street would be the subjects of the verb, but here they appear to be the objects—which is surely completely illogical. This passive construction is rather rare in Russian, isn't it?

② About Genet: the tough boy who kills and betrays and remains impenitent to the end—of the type of Notre-Dame des Fleurs—represents his ideal and appears in everything I have read of his. I agree about the pornographic passages—but they are the kind of erotic fantasies, more or less detached from reality, that people seem to cultivate in prison (like the Marquis de Sade in the Bastille). They are only carried off by the fact that the story is not really that of the author's invented characters, but that of Genet in prison trying to project himself into a novel. The men are all dream-men, and even Divine—who, I grant you, is somewhat more convincing than the others—is to some extent a dream-*tapette*.[3] Genet's life, as he tells about it in his memoirs, *Journal du Voleur*, has certainly been miserable. I believe that he was in with a life sentence when Sartre and Cocteau got him out of jail. I'm very much amused by the remark that he's reported to have made about Gide: "Il est d'une immoralité douteuse."[4] Please send the book to Wellfleet.

③ I've just been examining the early text of *Madame Bovary* that was published last year. It is impressive and to me a little surprising to see how Flaubert worked. The most marvellous passages in the finished version are often quite flat in this one, and even rather inept. It is startling to see the distance (in the scene where Charles Bovary, as a boy, looks wistfully out the window at Rouen) between, "Sous lui, en bas, la rivière, qui fait de ce quartier de Rouen comme une Venise de bas étage, coulait safran ou indigo, sous les petits ponts qui la couvrent," and, "la rivière, qui fait de ce quartier de Rouen comme une ignoble petite Venise, coulait en bas, sous lui, jaune, violette ou bleue entre ses ponts et ses grilles."[5] It is as if he first assembled his data and then at a given point turned on the music and magic. I am especially interested in this because it is more or less my own method. You, I imagine, are more likely to start with the words themselves.

④ You are mistaken about Jane Austen. I think you ought to read *Mansfield Park*. Her greatness is due precisely to the fact that her attitude toward her work is like that of a man, that is, of an artist, and quite unlike that of the typical woman novelist, who exploits her feminine day-dreams. Jane Austen approaches her material in a very objective way. Each of her books is a study of a different type of woman, whom Jane Austen can see all around. She wants, not to express her longings, but to make something perfect that will stand. She is, in my opinion, one of the half dozen greatest English writers (the others being Shakespeare, Milton, Swift, Keats and Dickens). Stevenson is second-rate. I don't know why you admire him so much—though he *has* done some rather fine short stories. I tried reading to Henry and Reuel a couple of summers ago one of the only books of Stevenson I had ever liked, *The New Arabian Nights*, but completely failed to interest them in it. It surprised me to find that these stories were the thinnest kind of verbalizing and that the characters had not even a fairy-tale existence. Sherlock Holmes, which we had just been reading and which was partly derived from *The New Arabian Nights*, seems a solid creation beside them. I didn't like *Treasure Island* even as a child.

⑤ You are all off, as usual, on English versification, but I am tired of arguing this subject.

⑥ I don't know what you mean when you say I am not one of your fans.

⑦ I am sending another package of reading matter. (a) Another *Furioso*, with another burlesque by Scott.[6] His French is no good, but the parody of Gide I thought very funny—it sounds just like the last installment of his diary. (Zane Grey was a writer of romantic Westerns, of whom you may never have heard.) (b) *The Big Con*,[7] a very curious book by an authority on the underworld. I found it more repellent than Genet, but I think it is worth reading. It throws a good deal of light on certain aspects of American life. The confidence men are, as the author says, only just over the line that divides the criminal from what is regarded as legitimate business. There are some incredibly funny stories in the book—especially about pickpockets and such people who unsuccessfully aspired to be confidence men. The author is a very strange character—a professor of linguistics whose specialty is the language of the underworld. He has recently changed to a different college—I think, Tulane in New Orleans. When the president asked him why he wanted to come there, he answered: "Frankly, sir, New Orleans has the biggest red-light district of any Southern city, and I am working now on prostitution." He does his academic stuff by day, and spends his evenings in the brothels, disguised as a pimp. (c) *Mr. Squiggles' Reward*—one of the oddest of many odd things that are sent me by unknown people.[8] (You might send this back with the Genet, but keep the other things.)

⑧ Henry's graduation is June 16. We shall start on our trip about a week before that. If you were in Boston then, we could stop off and see you there. This would be the ideal arrangement. Do keep me posted about this.

⑨ I have been having rather a rocky time, spending alternate weeks in New Jersey and here. My mother has been ill and I, at the same time, have been having this trouble with my vocal cord. I had a small operation last week, and

I hope this will be the end of it. The only advantage of our recent illnesses, yours and mine, has been that, occurring simultaneously, they have given us an opportunity to renew our literary correspondence.

As ever,

EW

1. "Through the open door one could see both the street, quiet, deserted, and the moon itself, which floated in the sky." From Chekhov's story "The Peasants," section VI.

2. "Were seen both the street ... and the moon." Wilson's form *vidni* does not exist, and it is not clear whether he meant the feminine form *vidna* or the plural form *vidny*, both of which are contextually and grammatically possible in this instance, the first one requiring the verb in the singular, however. Wilson is puzzled because Chekhov used an impersonal construction which puts "street" and "moon" in the accusative case, since they are the direct objects, rather than making them the subjects. Either possibility is quite common in Russian.

3. "Pansy."

4. "He is of a dubious immorality."

5. "Under him, below, the river, which turns this quarter of Rouen into a sort of lowly Venice, was flowing, saffron and indigo, beneath the small bridges that covered it" and "the river, which turns this quarter of Rouen into an ignoble little Venice, was flowing below, under him, yellow, violet or blue between its bridges and gratings."

6. "Gaëtan Fignole, Pages de Journal" by W. B. Scott, *Furioso*, Winter 1950. Scott not only parodies the journals of André Gide, but also cleverly satirizes the French propensity for zeroing in on peripheral or minor phenomena in American culture and blowing them up to cosmic proportions. The imaginary French writer Fignole discovers Zane Grey (and of course immediately hyphenates him into Zane-Grey). He decides that here is a literary figure of the stature of Aeschylus and Dante and just below that of Racine ("One suspects that in this strange work the American character has found a shatteringly precise statement. Ah, these savage puritans!")

For the Nabokov issue of the *TriQuarterly* in 1970, W. B. Scott contributed a parodistic letter from Professor Emeritus Timofey Pnin addressed to "Professeur Apple" (i.e., Alfred Appel, Jr.), in which Fignole's godmother Zénaïde Fleuriot, mentioned in his journal in *Furioso*, makes a brief appearance.

7. David W. Maurer, *The Big Con. The Story of the Confidence Man and the Confidence Game*, Indianapolis-New York, 1940. In his letter to Mamaine Koestler of April 3, 1950 (*Letters on Literature and Politics, 1912–1972*, p. 485), Wilson described Maurer as "a curious professor of linguistics who is probably the greatest noncriminal authority on the American underworld and whose attitude toward confidence men is almost as perversely admiring as that toward his own favorite kinds of criminal."

8. This work is not merely odd, but also extremely obscure, since it could not be located in any index or library. In 1998, the indefatigable Nabokov scholar D. Barton Johnson managed to locate a copy. The title is *Mr. P. Squiggles' Reward*. The author is Dennis McCalib, and the book was published in 1948 by the Alley Printshop in Pasadena, California.

210

May 15, 1950

Dear Bunny,

Awfully grateful to you for the books. Scott's piece is admirable. His French seemed to me quite good though Véra says she detected a few wrong tenses—but then Frenchmen make mistakes too. The whole thing is very funny and successful. For one instant I had the wild hope that the big *Con*[1] was French.

I am in the middle of *Bleak House*—going slowly because of the many notes I must make for class-discussion. Great stuff. I think I told you once that my father had read every word Dickens wrote. Perhaps his reading to us aloud, on rainy evenings in the country, *Great Expectations* (in English, of course) when I was a boy of twelve or thirteen, prevented me mentally from re-reading Dickens later on. I have obtained *Mansfield Park* and I think I shall use it too in my course. Thanks for these most useful suggestions. You approach Stevenson from the wrong side. Of course *Treasure Island* is poor stuff. The *one* masterpiece he wrote is the first-rate and permanent *Jekyll and Hyde*. I hope you have enjoyed Cardinal Spellman's poem dedicated to an Alfred E. Smith Memorial Hospital. It ends:

> ... and we
> as brothers must within these troubled waters
> protect, maintain Al's heritage and ours
> devotedly in service to our fellow men.[2]

I have to go to Boston to have six lower teeth extracted. My plan is to go thither (туда) Sunday the 28th, grunt at the dentist's (a wonderful Swiss, Dr. Favre) Monday and Tuesday and perhaps Thursday (the 31st), then mumble back, toothless, to Ithaca to correct examination papers and return to Boston by car with Véra on the 6th or 7th to have a denture put in; then we shall stay there till the 11th and fetch Dmitri in New Hampshire on the 12th to go back to Ithaca through Albany, near which, at a place called Karner, in some pine-barrens, on lupines, a little blue butterfly I have described and named ought to be out. Would it be possible to fit a meeting with you into this scheme?

Было видно in this sense should be understood as «было видно слѣдующее»[3]—a kind of collective adjectival noun is implied; thus neuter.[4] But it is a good question—as I say to my pet students.

My method of composing is quite different from Flaubert's. I shall explain it to you at length some day. Now I must go to room 178 to analyse *Даму съ Собачкой*[5] in English, translating from the Russian text and indulging in most brilliant technicalities that are quite lost on my students.

The Letters, 1950

It may just happen that I shall have to shift the whole Boston affair to after the 12th. Keeping up this exchange of letters is like keeping up a diary—you know what I mean—but *please* do not give up, I love your letters.

V.

1. In French it is the word for "cunt."

2. Cardinal Spellman's "tribute to the late Governor" was read by him at the dedication of the Alfred E. Smith Memorial Building of St. Vincent's Hospital and published in *The New York Times* of May 15, 1950.

3. "One could see" [...] "one could see the following."

4. A nice example of the difficulty for a native speaker of a language to grasp the problems of non-native speakers. Wilson was perplexed by the accusative case of the nouns, not by the gender of the verb (cf. Letter 173, note 2), as he points out in his next letter.

5. "The Lady with the Dog" (by Chekhov), with English-style capitalization.

211

Edmund Wilson
Wellfleet, Cape Cod
Massachusetts

May 25, 1950

Dear Volodya: ① Couldn't you come up to see us here after you have been to the dentist next week?—or between the 7th [and] 11th on your 2nd trip? That would be the ideal arrangement.

② What worried me in that Chekhov sentence was not that the verb was neuter—I thought it was simply impersonal—but that *улица* and *луна*[1] were put in the accusative. This is illogical. The ordinary usage seems to be exemplified by Далеко впереди еле были видны ветряные мельницы; в ясную погоду оттуда бывает виден даже город.[2] These are nominatives, aren't they? How do you explain this strange inconsistency?

③ I liked very much your *New Yorker* poem[3]—but it involves a false accent on automobile—*autómobile*[4]—which evidently betrays your mistaken ideas about English metrics.

I have just come back from another trip—New York, New Jersey and Newport (where I went to see Mary and deal with the problem of Reuel's school)—and am trying to settle down to work, so must прекратить this литературную переписку.[5] Do come to see us.

As ever,

EW

I am extraordinarily good on Dickens in *The Wound and the Bow*—I think you ought to read my essay.

1. "Street and moon."

2. "Far ahead windmills could barely be seen; in clear weather even the city could be seen from there." This is the beginning and the end, with the middle left out, of the lengthy sentence in the opening paragraph of Chekhov's story "Gooseberries."

3. "The Room" in *The New Yorker* of May 13, 1950.

4. The stanza in question reads:

> Whenever some automobile
> subliminally slit the night
> the walls and ceiling would reveal
> a wheeling skeleton of light.

5. "Stop this literary correspondence."

212

May 28, 1950

Dear Bunny,

1. Automobile. If you insist on having a primary or strong secondary accent on "au" then you are really making *two* words of it—"auto" and "mobile" and then you can *never* use "automobile" in iambic or trochaic verse unless you accent "mo" (which is vulgar—though in the iambizational tradition and tendency of English) or drop the second syllable—thus: "aut'mobile" ("Black aut-'mobiles stood waiting at her door"), a trick I dare you to find in any English poem of the classical period—in regard to similarly weighted words. My pronunciation of "automobile" being less topheavy than yours (although there is, I admit, a *slight* stress on "au"), I use it as fluently as I would use, in an iambic line, «многострада́льный» or «пу́шкиновѣ́дъ»[1] or «а́нгелолю́бъ» (lover of angels)—all of which are pronounced *exactly* as "automobile" (of Webster's second choice). «Онѣ́гинъ былъ пушкиновѣ́дъ,»[2] for instance, is an iambic tetrameter or an amphibrachic one depending on whether you stress the *былъ* or the *пуш*. Once [and] for all you should tell yourself that in these questions of prosody—no matter the language involved—you are wrong and I am right, always.

2. *Было видно* = *было возможно видѣть* = *it was possible to see*—which is followed of course by the accusative. I realize now that your question was simpler than I thought.

3. Between the 7th and the 11th of June I shall be under my dentist's supervi-

sion, alas. After that I must be back here to write a story that will pay for a vacation in the Rockies. It is probable that Harry and Lena Levin will *héberger*³ us between the 7ᵗʰ and the 11ᵗʰ. Shall write again when I know more of our movements.

Yours affectionately,

V.

[In margin]
Good line, by the way:
"Onegin was an expert on Pushkin"

     1. "Long-suffering" or "Pushkin expert."
     2. "Onegin was a Pushkin expert."
     3. "Put us up."

213

[Postmarked May 29, 1950]¹

I mean I dare you to prove that an elision in Shakespeare, say, is due to the word being stressed in common usage thus: $'\text{∪∪}'$ so that the second syllable has to be syncopated in order to usher it² into an iambic line.

V

     1. This is a completed letter, meant as a response to the third paragraph of Wilson's letter of May 25 and, it would seem, as an addendum to the first paragraph of Nabokov's letter of May 28.
     2. The original had *the* instead of *it*, which must have been a slip of the typewriter.

214

Edmund Wilson
Wellfleet, Cape Cod
Massachusetts

June 3, 1950

Dear Volodya: ① It is impossible to use *automobile* gracefully in iambic verse at all. You would have to have anapests or dactyls. The line you wrote is something that would be stumbled over by any native of the English-speaking world, and it demonstrates the fallacy of your stress theory. As I was trying to explain to you some time ago, even the last syllable of a word like *imagination* had through Milton and I don't know how much later a stress that had to be treated with respect:

> "Guiding the fiery-wheeléd throne,
> The Cherub Cóntemplátión"
> *Il Penseroso*

Today it is always slurred: "the first imagination of Christendom" is a blank-verse line of Yeats and more the kind of thing you mean, but your method of approaching such a line leads you into errors about English metrics. *Воображе́ние,*[1] I take it, has only one stress that counts, but this is not the case with the two long words of the line above. The last syllable of *Christendom* is extremely important to the structure of the line. So is the first syllable of *automobile,* and you have spoilt your line by disregarding it.

② As for the street and the moon that Chekhov, in a mood of masochism all too common in Russian literature, has made the victims of the verb instead of, as they should be, its dominators: you have given me two distinct explanations neither of which can justify the construction.[2] The truth is that this is one of the grotesque anomalies so rife in Russian grammar. I propose, when our enlightened proconsuls have to come to the rescue of that unfortunate country, in my role of Secretary for Colonial Culture, to exterminate such absurdities by making indulgence in them punishable by imprisonment.

③ About *Dr. Jekyll and Mr. Hyde:* I tried reading that to Reuel, too, and it, too, seemed to me thin. Though it is on a bigger scale, I don't really like it as well as Poe's *William Wilson,* which I imagine must have suggested it. I even prefer *Dorian Gray.* I don't know what is involved here. People sometimes have infatuations for second-rate foreign authors that mean something different to them than they do to their countrymen. I don't understand your admiring *Jekyll* and disliking *Черный Монах* and *Вий,*[3] the last of which seems to me the greatest story of the horrible supernatural I have ever read. By the way, I think *Дама с Собакой*[4] rather overrated. I think it owes its popularity—the Soviets have lately got out a special illustrated edition—to its being the only one of these later stories of Chekhov's that has any hint of a love affair not frustrated without respite or putrefying in пошлость.[5] *Архиерей,*[6] which I've just read, is a masterpiece.

I am getting rather tired of all these topics and think we ought to start something new. Let me know about your movements. Our definite plan now is to be in Boston the 15th and go on that afternoon—Elena to St. Paul's; Rosalind,

Reuel and I to Utica, on our way to Talcottville—all probably getting back Sunday. We'd love to have you anytime. Good luck with your teeth.

EW

1. "Imagination."

2. The second explanation (in Letter 212) is the correct one and should have satisfied Wilson, one feels, had Nabokov but explained to him that they are talking about an *impersonal* construction, similar to the English "one could see."

3. "The Black Monk" (by Chekhov) and "Viy" (by Gogol).

4. "The Lady with the Dog." In Chekhov's title the word for "dog" is in the diminutive. Wilson disregards this, turning the heroine's little spitz into a dog of one of the larger breeds.

5. *Poshlost* (triteness).

6. "The Bishop."

215

June 3, 1950
Ithaca

Dandelions

Moons on the lawn replace the suns
that mowers happily had missed.
Where age would stoop, a babe will squat
and rise with star-fluff in its fist.
Vladimir Nabokov

Another example of Russian rules of prosody applied to English verse. Vera and I came back yesternight (вечор[1]—not many Russians know the meaning of this word) from Boston minus my teeth and the Mass[achusetts] part of her license (we were arrested for speeding. She did not stop when a policeman in a car signaled to her and then he followed us for ten minutes and finally, at 70 m.p.[h.],[2] scrowded us to the curb) and we were again driving thither on the 7th. We stayed at the Vendôme (tall stale rooms). Yesterday morning on our way back, we drove to a certain place between Albany and Schenectady where, on a pine-scrub waste, near absolutely marvelous patches of lupines in bloom, I took a few specimens of my little *samuelis*. I am lying in bed today reading exam. papers and preparing my memoirs *("Conclusive Evidence")* for Harpers. Have written Viking Press, for whom I had agreed to translate *Karamazov Brothers*, that I cannot undertake it after all. Yours, V.

[In the margin]
Do you want *Sebastian Knight* in French and *Bend Sinister* in Dutch?

1. *Vechór* is a substandard word, meaning "last night." Many Russians do not know it and mistake it for *vécher,* "evening."
2. Crossed out by Nabokov.

216

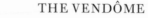

THE VENDÔME
Commonwealth Ave. & Dartmouth Street
BOSTON

June 8, 1950
Staying here till the 11th
then coming back for one night
on the 12th & going back to
Ithaca on the 13th

Dear Bunny,

When I was a little child and traveled to various European resorts, I could never resist the temptation to scribble on sheets of hotel paper. It would have been so nice if Elena and you were here with us!

Love

V

217

Dear Bunny,

have heard from Cambridge friends that the play went beautifully.[1] It is a charming thing and well worth *оглушительныхъ рукоплесканій*[2] (*oglushitel-nyh rukopleskanij*—my final idea of transliteration).

After several false starts, we did not, after all, head for Cape Cod. *Cela devient comique.*[3]

Dmitri had five weeks of courses in debating at N.W. Univ[ersity] for high schoolers and came back still taller than he was—he is now 6 f[eet] 5 inch[es]. We play tennis every morning and are both in great shape.

This is only a brief note as I am disgustingly busy: correcting the proofs of *Conclusive Evidence* (parts of which you saw in the *New Yorker*), checking the French translation (by Gide's secretary)[4] of *Sebastian Knight* and correcting the miserable Reinhart English edition of *Mme Bovary* for my (looming) course.

Best love

V.

1. Wilson's play *The Little Blue Light* opened at the Cambridge (Massachusetts) Summer Playhouse on August 14, 1950.
2. "Deafening applause."
3. "This is becoming comical."
4. *The Real Life of Sebastian Knight* was translated into French by Yvonne Davet.

218

Dear Volodya: We were sorry that you didn't get here. I suppose there's no hope of your being able to get away now?

Several New York producers, including the Theater Guild, have offered to do *The Blue Light*—so I guess that (barring a Russian bombing) it will certainly go on this winter. I had the curious inconvenience of a not extremely bright little English girl (an able and well-trained actress, though) in the role of my cynical heroine.[1] During rehearsal, she would pull up short at some speech that belittled the Christian faith and say, "I have a block against that line. Frankly, I think it's in bad taste." She flatly refused to deliver a line that said something about the Greek Liberation Movement's having been "put down by the British with American tanks"—though this is an historical fact—on the ground that it was anti-English. The last night of the run, two Catholic ladies in the audience left the theater and went to the box-office, and on the ground that their church had been insulted, demanded their money back. We think of establishing a poor-box to take care of such cases in New York.

I don't like your title for your memoirs—quite unsuitable in color and texture. It will also mislead the customers and drive the salesmen crazy.[2]

By the way, I have just been talking to Geoffrey Hellman's father, who years ago bought up a lot of unpublished Stevenson papers and letters. They contained many sensational things. He wrote a book based on them,[3] which he is going to send me, and, if it is interesting, I'll pass it on to you. Do you know how Stevenson's work was inhibited and censored by his wife, who was an absolute Tartar, and how she and some of his friends worked up for him, after his death, a bogus sentimental personality? It seems that *Dr. Jekyll and Mr. Hyde* was not originally a moral parable, but a much more detached affair, in which Mr. Hyde was presented more sympathetically. Hellman says that Stevenson was ashamed of it in the form in which it actually appeared.

Henry went to Cambridge today to start in at M.I.T.; Reuel begins school next week. Elena is exhausted from the summer. We are hoping to get to New York for a holiday next weekend. There's no chance of your being there, is there?

Have you seen the translation of *Mme Bovary* made by Karl Marx's daughter—the first in English?[4] I have an extra copy if you'd like it.

As ever,

EW

1. In the Cambridge production of *The Little Blue Light*, the role of Judith was played by Jessica Tandy.

2. Nabokov must have agreed, for he changed the title of the book from *Conclusive Evidence* to *Speak, Memory* within a year after its publication.

3. George Hellman, *The True Stevenson. A Study in Clarification*, published in 1925.

4. The translation of *Madame Bovary* into English by Eleanor Aveling, née Marx, was brought out in a limited edition in Switzerland in 1938.

219

802 E. Seneca St.

Ithaca

November 18, 1950

Dear Edmund,

it is only today that I have a moment to thank you for your book[1] (Véra joins me)—but "better late than never, as said the woman who missed her train" (an old Russian chestnut).[2] There are lots of things in it that are superb, especially the attacks and the fun. As with most good critics, your war-crying voice is better than your hymn-singing one. Some day you will recall with astonishment and regret your soft spot for Faulkner (and Eliot, and H. James). Your bit on Gogol and me contains various things (added? changed?) that I do not seem to remember having seen in the original version. I protest against the last line.[3] Conrad knew how to handle *readymade* English better than I; but I know better the other kind. He never sinks to the depths of my solecisms, but neither does he scale my verbal peaks.

I want to make my mid-term report on the two books you suggested I should discuss with my students. In connection with *Mansfield Park* I had them read the works mentioned by the characters in the novel—the two first cantos of the "Lay of the Last Minstrel," Cowper's "The Task," passages from *King Henry the Eighth*, Crabbe's tale "The Parting Hour," bits of Johnson's *The Idler*, Browne's address to "A Pipe of Tobacco" (Imitation of Pope), Sterne's *Sentimental Journey* (the whole "gate-and-no-key" passage comes from there —and the starling) and of course *Lovers' Vows* in Mrs. Inchbald's inimitable translation (a scream).[4] In discussing *Bleak House,* I completely ignored all sociological and historical implications, and unravelled a number of fascinating thematic lines (the "fog theme," the "bird theme," etc.) and the three main props of the structure—the crime-mystery theme (the weakest), the child-misery theme and the lawsuit-chancery one (the best). I think I had more fun than my class.

I am worried about Roman. I wonder whether he has quite recovered from his heart attack.

It is fairly probable that I shall visit New York some time in the beginning of next year. I want to see you very much. Véra and I send Elena and you our best love.

V.

1. *Classics and Commercials.*

2. The more familiar version of this saying, which Nabokov quotes *verbatim*, preserving the Russian word order, has a Jew rather than a woman miss the train.

3. "Aside from this, in spite of some errors, Mr. Nabokov's mastery of English almost rivals Joseph Conrad's." This sentence was not found in the text of Wilson's original review of *Nikolai Gogol* in *The New Yorker* (September 9, 1944). The rewritten and somewhat abbreviated version of the article in *Classics and Commercials* was retitled "Vladimir Nabokov on Gogol."

4. Among the literary works which are read or mentioned by the characters of Jane Austen's novel and which might require more precise identification are Sir Walter Scott's poem "The Lay of the Last Minstrel," Samuel Johnson's series of essays known collectively as *The Idler*, and Hawkins Browne's "Address to Tobacco," which is a set of imitations of six authors, among them Pope. *Lovers' Vows*, a play selected for performance by some of the novel's characters, is Elizabeth Inchbald's English adaptation of the lachrymose melodrama *Das Kind der Liebe (The Child of Love)* by August von Kotzebue.

220

[Written at the bottom of an early version of the
poem "Voluptates Tactionum"[1] (in typescript)]

[Postmarked December 29, 1950, 7 p.m.]

Dear Bunny and Elena

here's a little present for Christmas.

Véra and I hope to see you in the course of the coming year.

V

1. "Voluptates Tactionum" was published in *The New Yorker* of January 27, 1951; it was reprinted in *Poems and Problems*, p. 166. The typescript on which this message was written is close in wording to the published version, but the line breaks come at different points, so that the rhymes and meter—trochaic tetrameter—of the final version are not evident.

221

Edmund Wilson
Wellfleet, Cape Cod
Massachusetts

January 10, 1951

Dear Volodya: Thanks for the little poem.[1] I have been trying to do a clerihew[2] in Russian, and it has turned out to be an exercise in the predicative use of the instrumental. What I have produced seems to me rather dubious. Will you tell me how it ought to be, if at all?

Лев Толстой
Был писатель большой;   Can you
Но когда хотел крестьянином считаться,   rhyme
Он только слыл безумным дворянином;   infinitive
Когда притворется християнином,   with present
Он просто злючкой казатся.[3]   indicative?

I particularly liked your installment in the *Partisan Review.*[4] We are going to New York next Monday to stay the rest of the winter—address: c/o Mrs. Lloyd, 11 E 87th St.; phone Lehigh 4-6250. I hope you'll get down there some time. The Theater Guild is doing the *Blue Light.* They are now trying to cast it and get a director.

As ever,
Edmund W

1. "Voluptates Tactionum."
2. Clerihew is a form of comic poem named after its inventor Edmund C. (for Clerihew) Bentley. A standard clerihew is supposed to consist of two couplets of unequal length, which makes Wilson's Russian effort rather uncanonical.
3.   "Leo Tolstoy
Was a major writer;
But when wanted to be considered a peasant,
He was only reputed a mad nobleman;
When pretended to be a Christian
He simply to seem a nasty child."

This translation preserves the unidiomatic quality of Wilson's Russian. The non-existent word in the fifth line, *pritvoretsia,* may be either a misspelling for the infinitive *pritvoriat'-*

sia, "to pretend," or meant as the past tense form *pritvorialsia.* The verb in line six seems a misspelled infinitive; it certainly is not a present indicative form *(kazhetsia),* which was apparently what Wilson wanted it to represent.

4. "Exile," Chapter Fourteen of *Speak, Memory.*

222

CORNELL UNIVERSITY

Department of   Goldwin Smith Hall
Russian Literature   Vladimir Nabokov   Ithaca, New York

February 5, 1951

Dear Bunny,

have just read the sad news about your mother. Véra and I deeply sympathise with you.

I am *proud* of you for being "adamant" in the *Blue Light*[1] business!

Yours

V

1. See the next letter.

223

Edmund Wilson
Wellfleet, Cape Cod
Massachusetts

February 7, 1951

Dear Volodya: Thank you for your letter. My mother was nearly eighty-six, was completely deaf, nearly blind and so arthritic that she could hardly stand up. But it was impressive to see how well she kept up and how keen she still managed to be. When she died,[1] she had a moment before been having coffee and joking with Rosalind and her nurse. That morning she had asked Rosalind about her beaux and said, "I suppose they're a lot of writers. Don't marry one or you'll never have any money."

That story about the *Blue Light* in the *Times* was not entirely true. The Theater Guild denied it, but, so far as I know, the denial was not published. We had differences on several points, but there was never any question of doing the whole of the printed text. It looks now as if the original people were going to do it April 1, in conjunction with ANTA (if you know what that is). I am much better pleased, for the Guild is old and gaga.[2]

I hope that you will have the publishers send me a copy of your book. You should have them put me on the publicity list, so that you will not have to supply the copy yourself. And please have it sent to the New York address—which, it turns out, is c/o Mrs. *Moise,* instead of Mrs. Lloyd.

I have been reading with great enjoyment the earlier series of Gogol's Ukrainian *Вечера.*[3] I have the impression, from the contemptuous way in which you discuss these in your Gogol book, that you have not read them since childhood.

Did you get the Russian clerihew I sent you? If it is off the track, I wish you would let me know. Clerihews, of course, run to lines of any length and are doggerel—like Ogden Nash.

Love to Vera. Is there no chance of your getting to New York during the spring vacation?

As ever,

EW

---

1. Helen Mather Kimball Wilson, Edmund Wilson's mother, died on February 3, 1951.

2. After some reports in the press that *The Little Blue Light* was to be produced on Broadway by the Theatre Guild, the play was done by the American National Theater and Academy (ANTA), with Melvyn Douglas, Arlene Francis and Burgess Meredith in the cast. It ran for eight performances.

3. *Evenings [on a Farm Near Dikanka].*

224

March 10, 1951

Dear Bunny,

No—I conscientiously reread those Gogol tales (as explicitly stated in my book on G.) and found them exactly as I thought they were on the strength of old impressions. I also remember I had reread them in 1932 or 1933 for an article on Gogol in Russian which I still use for my Russian courses.[1]

In my European fiction class I have finished lecturing on *Anna Karenin* and "The Death of John, son of Elijah"[2] (joke) and am proceeding to draw a most fascinating comparison between *Jekyll and Hyde* and "Metamorphosis," with the latter winning. After that: Chehov, Proust and parts of Joyce. The Moncrieff translation of Proust is *awful*, almost as awful as the translations of *Anna* and *Emma* but in a way still more exasperating because Mr. Moncrieff *a son petit style à lui*[3] which he airs.

Did you get the two copies of *C[onclusive] E[vidence]*, one with a *dédicace?* Perhaps, whenever you have the occasion to bother about it, you will send the Wellfleet copy back to me. Did you get my nasty letter about your nasty Russian verse? Will you be in New York at the end of May? Véra and I will be there at that date for a reason and an event which I have been asked not to divulge until mentioned in the papers—but which, I suspect, you know of.

Yours,
V.

1. This article has apparently not been published. Véra Nabokov thought it might have been intended as a foreword to an edition of Gogol's *Evenings*.

2. *I.e., The Death of Ivan Ilyich* (by Tolstoy).

3. "Has his own little style."

225

THE NEW YORKER
No. 25 West 43rd Street

March 19, 1951

Dear Volodya:

Elena was so delighted with your book that she swore she was going to write you a letter, to which I was going to add my own comment, but as she hasn't got around to this, I must let you know my opinion; which I know you have been nervously awaiting. This is that *Conclusive Evidence* is a wonderful production. The effectiveness and beauty of the material have really been raised to a higher power (in the sense of being cubed) by the pieces appearing in a book and in the proper order. I reread the whole thing with avidity, except for the final one that deals with parks and perambulators, the only one I do not care much for (though Elena particularly likes it). I don't approve of the title, which is un-interesting in itself—and what is the conclusive evidence? Against the Bolsheviks?

I have received only the inscribed copy. The other will be in Wellfleet. I hope that you will have both of them put down to publicity, in which case you won't be charged with them. I am a practicing critic, and I want to send the other one to Mario Praz in Rome, who writes about American and English books in one of the papers there.

We're going back to Wellfleet early in May. I know nothing about the event that is bringing you on at that time. Is there no chance of your coming to the Cape?

I did not get your nasty letter and am still awaiting enlightenment—which I think you owe me in return for my inestimable services in straightening you out about English metrics.

I have been fascinated by von Frisch on bees—about whom you first told me.[1]

I have only looked into the Moncrieff translation of Proust. What struck me was that he had turned Proust's lugubriousness into something lighter and brighter and English.

As ever,

EW

1. An English translation of *Bees: Their Vision, Chemical Senses, and Language* by Karl von Frisch, the book in which he explains his decoding of the dancing language of the bees, was published in 1951 and reviewed by Wilson in *The New Yorker* of July 14, 1951.

226

March 24, 1951

Dear Bunny,

It may sound foolish (in the light of what I always have felt toward criticism of my work), but your letter did give me a twinge of pleasure. I would dearly have liked to get Elena's letter and, please, thank her for me for her kind and subtle attitude toward *Conclusive Evidence*. Title: I tried to find the most impersonal title imaginable, and as such it is a success. But I agree with you that it does not render the spirit of the book. I had toyed with, at first, *Speak, Mnemosyne* or *Rainbow Edge* but nobody knew who Mnemosyne was (or how to pronounce her), nor did *R. E.* suggest the glass edge—"The Prismatic Bezel" (of *Sebastian Knight* fame).[1]

A British publisher—Gollancz, do you know the firm?—wants the book and dislikes the title. If Green (the *first* page of his *Nothing* is *wonderful*— with your intonation, I hope) had not used so many mono $\begin{cases} \text{vocables} \\ \text{syllables} \end{cases}$ for the titles, I would have thrown him "Clues" (or "Mothing"!).[2]

Several things have happened to me recently. Karpovich, head of the Russian Department at Harvard, will be away next spring term and has suggested I replace him in the Russian Lit[erature] courses, so that we shall probably

The Letters, 1951

transfer our activities to Cambridge (of which I am thinking with great warmth at udder-conscious and udderly boring Cornell) in January. Another pleasant aspect of this is that we will be much nearer to you in space. We are terribly keen to come to the Cape.

Life, a magazine, wants to take photographs of me catching butterflies, and of rare butterflies on flowers or mud, and I am doing my best to give it a strictly scientific twist—nothing of the kind has ever been done with rare Western species, some of which I have described myself—so they are sending a photographer to be with me, for a week or so, in some productive locality in S.W. Colorado or Arizona (Dmitri is in a great singing voice today, booming French from *La Juive,* and in a minute he is driving me to the soccer field for some practice and coaching) in July—they do not quite understand what is going to happen.

I thought you had some secret influence or something, suggesting my name—*que sais-je?*[3]—in the matter of the American Academy that is giving me a ceremonious award on the 25th May. I know nothing whatsoever about that institution and at first confused it with a Mark Twain horror that almost obtained my name in the past; but I am told this is the real thing. I am asked not to divulge this news until it appears in the gazettes.

Love to both of you from us both.

V

P.S. I suppose you will find in Wellfleet my letter about your poem. I took it apart, viciously. It is a salad of mistakes.[4]

1. *The Prismatic Bezel* is the title of a novel written by the title character in *The Real Life of Sebastian Knight.*

2. The British novelist Henry Green had a considerable success in the 1950s with novels bearing such titles as *Caught, Back, Concluding* and *Nothing.* "Mothing" is the very last word in Nabokov's *Bend Sinister.*

3. "Or whatever."

4. Nabokov's critique of Wilson's clerihew about Tolstoy has unfortunately not been preserved.

227

THE NEW YORKER
No. 25 West 43rd Street

March 26, 1951

Dear Volodya: Gollancz is rather an intelligent man who knows about books and only publishes books he believes in; but his business is rather small, and he won't give you much money. He is bringing out *The Little Blue Light*, but has refused another book of mine that he said he wanted to publish because he wouldn't give me my terms, which I got from another publisher.

I didn't know about the Academy award, and am glad to hear about it. I refused to be a member when they elected me some years ago. It is chockful of mediocrities. The only good thing about it is that it does, from time to time, hand out money to writers. It may have been Allen Tate who inspired them to give you some—he has been very active there lately. I can't wait to see the *Life* feature of Nabokov catching butterflies. I am delighted that you are coming back to Cambridge.

My play is now in rehearsal—opens April 18.[1]

Yes: I read *CE* with avidity all through one day. In *Classics and Commercials*, I left what I had written in 1944 about your English almost rivalling Conrad's, because I did not want to make corrections based on later developments. The English of *CE* is at least as good as Conrad's and has qualities that Conrad could never have managed. I think you must have profited somewhat from *The New Yorker*'s (at times outrageously stupid) fine-tooth-combing of prose. I noticed only two sentences that seemed to me dubious in the least. But you have certainly, since *Bend Sinister*, made great progress in subtlety and flexibility. Your claims for the old regime didn't seem to me exaggerated, as they have sometimes done on other occasions.

Love to Vera and Dmitri,

EW

1. It actually opened on April 15.

228

802 E. Seneca Street

Ithaca

June 2, 1951

Dear Bunny,

it was a joy to see you and find you in such good shape.

Do not forget to send me your insect notes.[1]

As once before, I am writing to you in the middle of an exam (the Europ[ean] fiction affair).

On the 10th we are driving to Plymouth, N.H., for *Митюша*'s[2] graduation. We shall be in Boston on the evening of the 11th (probably see the Levins), spend the night at the Vendôme and drive back in the afternoon of the 12th to Ithaca, stopping for the night with friends at a place which begins with an R— can't remember. Then, around the 20th we shall start westward first to the San Miguel M[ountains] in S.W. Colo[rado], then in early August to the Tetons and back here, Sept[ember] 1.

My article on Klots' book appears this Sunday in the T.B.R.[3]

I notice that it begins with the kind of "to be" phrase that we discussed!

I have jotted down carefully all the little movements, curl-twining, pimple-teasing, roving eyes, etc., peculiar to exams. Will come handy some day.[4]

Love from both of us to Elena and you.

V.

1. This request was taken literally. See next letter.

2. Mitiusha, an affectionate diminutive for Dmitri.

3. Nabokov's enthusiastic review of *A Field Guide to the Butterflies of North America, East of the Great Plains,* by Alexander B. Klots, was published in *The New York Times Book Review* of June 3, 1951.

4. Nabokov made use of these notes in his description of college examinations in the interview with Alvin Toffler that appeared in *Playboy* in January 1964 and was later included in *Strong Opinions.*

229

[In margin of the corrected galley proofs of Wilson's essay
"The Intelligence of Bees, Wasps, Butterflies and Bombing Planes"][1]

Dear Volodya: This is just a piece of hackwork. You don't need to send back the proofs unless you want to make notes in them. If you don't want me to mention you by name, I won't.[2] I enjoyed our luncheon very much and am sorry we can't see you in Boston. I haven't heard anything further from the people in Colorado. I didn't grasp the seriousness of angina pectoris when you told me about Roman. Is it supposed to be fatal for him? I'll certainly look him up when I go down again. *Hecate County* is out in England, and I can see from the clippings sent me that their anti-Americanism is working against its being suppressed. They take a contemptuous tone toward what they call the American bluenoses.

EW

1. *The New Yorker* essay, which was a review of the book by Karl von Frisch on bees (see Letter 225, note 1), as well as of *Insects in Your Life* by C. H. Curran, *Dragons in Amber* by

Willy Ley and the butterfly book by Alexander B. Klots, and which included a meditation on the similarity of mass aggression patterns in twentieth-century man and collectivist insect societies.

2. The last paragraph of Wilson's essay began: "It is the opinion of Mr. Vladimir Nabokov, who is a distinguished lepidopterist as well as a novelist and a poet, that the markings of moths and butterflies, so amazing for the complex detail by which they achieve protective mimicry, have been carried to a point that suggests, on the butterfly's part, a gratuitous artistic effort." Cf. the following from Chapter Two of Nabokov's *The Gift:* "He told me about the incredible artistic wit of mimetic disguise, which was not explainable by the struggle for existence (the rough haste of evolution's unskilled forces), was too refined for the mere deceiving of accidental predators, feathered, scaled and otherwise (not very fastidious, but then not too fond of butterflies), and seemed to have been invented by some waggish artist precisely for the intelligent eyes of man [...]."

Since the English version of *The Gift* was not published until 1963 and Wilson is not known to have read the Russian edition, another possible source of his citation of Nabokov on mimicry may have been the discussion of the same subject in section 2, Chapter Six of *Speak, Memory,* which concludes: " 'Natural selection' in the Darwinian sense could not explain the miraculous coincidence of imitative aspect and imitative behavior, nor could one appeal to the theory of 'the struggle for life' when a protective device was carried to a point of mimetic subtlety, exuberance, and luxury far in excess of a predator's power of appreciation. I discovered in nature the nonutilitarian delights that I sought in art. Both were a form of magic, both were a game of intricate enchantment and deception."

Elena Wilson, however, believed that the topic had been discussed by the two writers well before the publication of *Speak, Memory.*

230

802 E. Seneca St.
Ithaca, N.Y.

June 13, 1951

Dear Bunny,

your article is lucid and limpid and I have no special comments to make (except perhaps the unlovely "creating dramatic suspense," and a repetitive introduction of "such"—but this is not what you asked me to check).[1] As a matter of fact I think it is a first-rate article.

Yes, by all means mention Mr. Vladimir.[2] I have decided to welcome all kind and manner of publicity from now on. I am sick of having my books muffled up in silence like gems in cotton wool. The letters from private individuals I get are, in their wild enthusiasm, ridiculously incommensurable with the lack of interest my inane and inept publishers take in my books. And they are so touchy, so very touchy, those fellows. After I gave Harper and Harper my candid opinion about an idiotic blurb they concocted for *Conc[lusive] Evi[dence]* they were never the same and are now taking a morbid pleasure in hushing up the book. The general result of my proud and disinterested and even contemptuous attitude toward the *fata*[3] of my books has *not* resulted in valor and honesty's obtaining the upper hand—in the long run—over mediocrity and cheapness. On the contrary—I am completely in the *dèche*,[4] am in miserable financial difficulties, see no way out of academic drudgery (ill-paid to boot) and so on. The *New Yorker* has rejected what I considered to be the best story I ever wrote, and I have no hopes whatever of seeing the one I am writing now accepted by any magazine.[5] But from now on *je vais me trémousser*,[6] and be very practical and cunning, and send my books to critics, and put in special clauses into my contracts with publishers about the money they must spend on boosting my books.

We are in the midst of packing. Next fall we shall have another house, smaller but more comfortable. We are starting westward *в двадцатых числах сего месяца*[7] and shall probably spend July near Telluride in southwestern Colorado where I want to study in the field a butterfly I described from preserved specimens. I am taking with me copious notes relating to a novel I would be able to finish in a year if I could completely concentrate upon it. "Father David's deer" is, I believe, a better name for the animal than "Milu."[8] He was a great man—David.[9]

Yours,
V.

1. In "The Intelligence of Bees, Wasps, Butterflies and Bombing Planes," Wilson had written of Willy Ley: "He has a considerable narrative gift and cannot tell about a scientific expedition or even a line of research or the development of a theory without investing it with excitement and creating dramatic suspense." Elsewhere in the same essay there is the phrase: "a combination of such curious and disconcerting facts with practical information on such subjects as . . ." The second "such" was added by Wilson in the galleys he sent Nabokov; the addition was made in order to avoid saying "on subjects like . . ."

2. See Letter 229, note 2.

3. "Fate." The reference is to the Latin saying "Habent sua fata libelli" ("Books have their fate"), which is also a Russian proverb.

4. "Completely broke."

5. "The best story I ever wrote" refers to "The Vane Sisters." "The one I am writing now" was "Lance," which Nabokov was planning at the time of this letter, but wrote only after the next letter (as pointed out by Brian Boyd).

6. "I am going to bestir myself."

7. "After the twentieth of this month."

8. The Milu deer, also known as Father David's deer, was mentioned by Wilson when he discussed the writings of Willy Ley.

9. Father Armand David (1826–1900), the French naturalist and explorer of the then little known areas of the Far East. Father David's travels and discoveries paralleled those of the Russian explorer Nikolai Przhevalsky, whom Nabokov admired and whose travel accounts inspired certain portions of *The Gift*.

231

623, Highland Rd.
Ithaca
Tel. 43109

[Early September 1951]

Dear Bunny,

I am ill. The doctor says it is a kind of sunstroke. Silly situation: after two months of climbing, shirtless, in shorts, in the Rockies, to be smitten by the insipid N.Y. sun on a dapper lawn. High temperature, pain in the temples, insomnia and an incessant, brilliant but sterile turmoil of thoughts and fancies.

I do not recall if I told [you] of some of my experiences in the San Miguel Mts. (Southwestern Colo., Telluride and vicinity) and near or in Yellowstone Park. I went to Telluride (*awful* roads, but then—endless charm, an old-fashioned, absolutely touristless mining town full of most helpful, charming people—and when you hike from there, which is 9000′, to 10000′, with the town and its tin roofs and self-conscious poplars lying toylike at the flat bottom of a *cul-de-sac* valley running into giant granite mountains, all you hear are the voices of children playing in the streets—delightful!) for the sole purpose, which my heroic wife who drove me through the floods and storms of Kansas did not oppose, of obtaining more specimens of a butterfly I had described from eight males, and of discovering its female. I was wholly successful in that quest, finding all I wanted on a steep slope high above Telluride—quite an enchanted slope, in fact, with hummingbirds and humming moths visiting the tall green gentians that grew among the clumps of a blue lupine, *Lupinus parviflorus,* which proved to be the food plant of my butterfly.

We then met some more charming people near W. Yellowstone, Mont[ana], and rented for a ridiculously small sum a ranch in the hills, which Véra and I had absolutely to ourselves,—aspens, pines, more warm-blooded animals than I have ever seen in one place, not a human for miles around, a distant gate we had to unlock when we drove through on a road with more flowers than sand— and all this for a couple of dollars per day. And provisions were much cheaper than in the dismal town I have come back to. In the meantime Dmitri was camping on Jenny Lake in the Tetons, in a small tent, and climbing mountains along their most difficult and dangerous sides. The thing with him is an extraordinary overwhelming passion. The professional alpinists there are really wonderful people, and the very physical kind of exertion supplied by the mountains somehow is transmuted into a spiritual experience.[1]

I shall get quite an adequate salary at Harvard where, in addition to two Russian courses, I shall give one dealing with European novels (from Cervantes to Flaubert); but at present I am in quite awful circumstances, despite a thousand dollars I borrowed from Roman in spring. Not a single magazine has found fit to buy, or indeed to understand (and this refers also to the *New Yorker*) my last story,[2] and as I have no intention whatever to come down to "human interest" stuff, I shall have to remain in the realm of what fools call "experimental" literature and face the consequences. I am underpaid here in a ridiculous and insulting manner. I love to complain—this is why I am telling you all this.

Around the 17th of this month, if I am well, I shall take Dmitri to Harvard. Is there *any* chance of you and Elena being in Cambridge between the 17th and the 20th? (My classes here begin on the 21st). Véra and I would enjoy so much even a fleeting glimpse of you two.

Съ душевнымъ привѣтомъ[3]

V.

1. Alfred Appel, Jr., has pointed out that portions of this letter were reworked into the final pages of *Lolita*.
2. "The Vane Sisters."
3. "With fond regards."

232

Wellfleet
Cape Cod, Mass.

September 5, 1951

Dear Volodya:

It is pleasant to hear you are ill, as it means a renewal of our correspondence. I wish you would send me your story—I'd like to read it, though I don't know whether I can be helpful in getting it printed. You can't be any more broke than I am—I have never been so badly in debt in my life.

Elena and I are both rather the worse for wear, at the end of the summer with its children and their many and long-remaining guests, and my mother's seventy-year-old housekeeper, who has been with us most of the time. We weren't able to get away, as we usually do, in August. Elena has been ill, and I have been down with gout.

We are hoping to get to New York this month, but we shan't be in Boston till later. It is cheering to have you there again. Couldn't you come up here for a weekend in October or spend Thanksgiving with us or both?

I am now going to resume my recumbent position in order to get my gouty foot up. This letter is certainly not a very brilliant contribution to our interchange. I depend on you to keep it up.

Elena sends love.

Edmund W

233

623 Highland Rd.
Ithaca

November 18, 1951

COINCIDENCE!

Dear Bunny,

it was good to see you. I am still chuckling over your account of the "Noble Prize" episode and the "Russian stooges." Anyway, a local party got it this year.[1]

I shall be in New York on the 8th of December (staying at Roman's and talking at a Russian club in the evening)—I am telling you this to find out if you will be in town. Any chance of it?

Have sold a "difficult" story to the *New Yorker*.[2] Katharine White writes that Ross did not understand it, but that she and Lobrano[3] managed to persuade him that it was worth buying. Curious situation.

We intend to move to Cambridge (where we have rented a house, 9 Maynard Place) in the first days of February, immediately after the exams here.

How's the new play?

Love from both of us to both of you.

V.

1. Wilson's name had been submitted for the Nobel Prize that year. He received an official-looking special delivery envelope from Stockholm, which he opened with trepidation. It turned out to be a hoax chain letter from a crank (Elena Wilson's recollection). The "local party" who "got it" in 1951 was Pär Lagerqvist.

2. "Lance" appeared in *The New Yorker* on February 2, 1952.

3. Gustave Stubbs ("Gus") Lobrano was for many years the head of the fiction department of *The New Yorker*, a position he at times shared unofficially with Katharine White.

234

[From Véra Nabokov]

November 19, 1951

Dear Elena and Bunny,

Vladimir was on the point of mailing his letter when your telegram arrived. We wired you yesterday and now I just want to add that we would have loved to come but V. is still trying to dig his way from under a tremendous heap of work in connection with his spring courses, and his own research. I am not sure that I can get him over to Boston for a day, as we had planned, but I am still trying.

We hope to see you often when we shall be in Cambridge, and, perhaps, you will be in NY on the 8th?

Best wishes and love from both of us.

Véra

1952

235

623 Highland Rd.
Ithaca

January 16, 1952

Dear Bunny,

I have not heard from you for ages. I should, presumably, thank you for the, presumably, nice things you said when, presumably, you answered the questions about me that the Guggenheim people, presumably, asked you. I am really very eager to turn *E.O.* into English, with all the trappings and thousands of notes. By the way, have you revised the unfortunate description of the duel in your book (has there been a second edition of it?)? Please, do—if you have not done so yet.

Are you in good health? Is the family all right? Véra and I are looking forward to seeing more of you and Elena this year. We intend to leave on the 30th of this ~~mind~~ month (curious slip). The house we have rented is 9 Maynard Place, Cambridge.

Dmitri's first term at Harvard began tempestuously and we are awaiting with some interest the results of his exams. I have been to New York and stayed with the Grynbergs. I thought Roman looked much better. He has translated the "Exile" chapter of *Concl[usive] Evi[dence]* into Russian, but I now see with horror and dismay that his labour is lost—it all sounds impossibly brutal in Russian, and cannot appear while the people I allude to, through my American veils (which the translation tears away, of course), are alive.

Some months ago Aldanov (who is awfully decent in these matters) tipped me off in regard to the possibility of trying the Ford people for the publication of my big Russian novel *Dar*[1] (that never appeared completely, in book form), and to my amazement they have now acquired the rights.[2]

As usual, I am atrociously busy, but hope that at Cambridge I shall have some timespace for certain pleasurable labors that I contemplate—a novel (in English) that I have been palpating in my mind for a couple of years.

Do write me a word.

Véra and I send Elena and you our very best love and greetings.

V.

1. *The Gift.*
2. The Chekhov Publishing House in New York, which specialized in the publication (in Russian) of works of Russian literature unavailable or banned in the Soviet Union and was supported by the Ford Foundation, brought out the first complete version of *The Gift* in 1952 (including the Chernyshevsky chapter censored at the time of the original publication by the ex-Socialist Revolutionary editors of *Contemporary Annals* in Paris).

236

Edmund Wilson
Wellfleet, Cape Cod,
Massachusetts

January 18, 1952[1]

Dear Volodya: I recommended you warmly for a Guggenheim, but I wish you had given them some other project—it seems to me a pity for you to spend a lot of time on *Onegin* when you ought to be writing your own books.

I corrected my description of the duel in the English edition of the *The T[ri-ple] T[hinker]s* which is just about to come out. It is clear, however, that Push-kin means Onegin to take a certain advantage of Lensky.

We have been leading a most monotonous but rather pleasant and produc-tive life up here. I have been working on a gigantic book containing ninety-two of my articles, mostly written in the twenties and thirties, which has been turning into a sort of volume of literary memoirs.[2] We are going to Boston to-morrow for a long-postponed holiday. At the end of this month, we hope to get to New York for February and March. We're very glad you're coming to Cam-bridge and shall see you there later on.

Nobody seems to know at *The New Yorker* what is going to happen now that Ross is dead. I am afraid it may deteriorate instead of taking a new lease on life.

What do you think of Colette? I've been reading her a little for the first time and really don't like it much. The books about Chéri repel me. Have I ex-pounded to you my theory of the role in Russian literature of the решительный шаг and the пристальный взгляд?[3] If not, I will do so sometime.

I should like to see the review that Harold Nicolson did of your book. I sup-pose you saw the thing in the *New Yorker*.

As ever,

EW

1. This letter was dated January 18, 1951 by Wilson and was printed under this date in the first edition of this book. But as Brian Boyd pointed out, the context of the letter within the other letters of January 1952 indicates that 1951 was a slip of the pen for 1952.
2. *The Shores of Light*.
3. "The decisive step and the fixed gaze."

237

THE NEW YORKER
No. 25 West 43rd Street

January 22, 1952

Dear Volodya: Isaiah Berlin gave me this[1] (he is a wonderful character—you ought to know him). The impression I get from it is that Harold Nicolson wishes he had written the book himself. Do you think the sentence in the last paragraph about being a poor mixer can be intended seriously? On rereading it, I see that he simply means that you are not a good gregarious American. I don't think he quite understands how large the United States is, and that there are fresh wide open silent spaces full of butterflies.

As ever,

EW

1. A clipping of Harold Nicolson's article "Dead Butterflies," which was a review of the English edition of *Speak, Memory* and appeared in the London *Observer* on November 4, 1951. Nicolson regretted that Nabokov had devoted so much space to moths, butterflies and childhood memories instead of concentrating on the political realities of pre-revolutionary Russia. The passage to which Wilson specifically alludes is found in the final paragraph of Nicolson's review. It reads: "Mr. Nabokov does not strike me as possessing an integrated character. It seems strange to me that a man of his sensibility should have been so bored at Cambridge and so happy in the United States. He is obviously a poor mixer, since he prefers to eat his meals on the sofa and in silence. Chess and butterflies and writing novels do not seem to accord well with the noise of the American life."

The reference to Nabokov's eating habits comes from the description of Nabokov's un-successful dinner with Ivan Bunin in Chapter Fourteen of *Speak, Memory:* "Unfortunately I happen to have a morbid dislike for restaurants and cafés, especially Parisian ones—I de-test crowds, harried waiters, Bohemians, vermouth concoctions, coffee, *zakuski*, floor shows and so forth. I like to eat and drink in a recumbent position (preferably on a couch) and in silence."

238

January 24, 1952

Dear Bunny,

Thanks for the recommendation. The *E.O.* will not take too much of my time and can be quite smoothly combined with other pleasures. But I am sick of teaching, I am sick of teaching, I am sick of teaching. One hundred and fifty exam papers to read before I leave for Cambridge.

Do not miss my story "Lance" in one of the near *New Yorker* issues. And do not miss in it a reference to you and Elena. It is introduced into the text with a watered-silk effect which is the tender point of genius, the asparagus tip of art, if you see what I mean. Katharine White, for reasons you will understand—in a soft flash of comprehension—when you come to that passage, was against the reference but I did not give in.[1] I must have put the equivalent of a dozen dis-tant thunderstorms in nervous energy into that little story.[2]

You ask me what I think of Colette. *C'est pour les gosses.*[3] Second rate vaca-tional literature. Not worth speaking about.

On the other hand I am extremely enthusiastic about the *пристальный взгляд*[4] business—you really have something there, and I am eager to hear more.

Thanks also for the Harold Nicolson article. I am vaguely under the impression that the reasons of his fastidious displeasure are really political—he was extremely pro-Soviet, etcetera, in the old days, used to wear a scarlet tie, and I am told that the governess he describes in one of the pieces of *Some People* is the same old English governess my young sisters had at one time in Petersburg.[5] I confess I liked very much that book but his later work has been trashy. Incidentally—now comes the famous Sirinian punch—he most ridiculously confused the Petersburg museum "Hermitage" and the Moscow restaurant "Hermitage" in those *Some People* of his.[6]

We are in the throes of packing. Beebe[7] has sent me a paper on some observed migrations of insects in Venezuela. They passed in a gap between two mountains—bees, flies, beetles, wasps. He sent the bees to a bee expert, the wasps to a wasp expert (to have them identified). Each wrote back—the wasp man, the beetle man, the blackfly man—that in each respective batch there were two or three *moths* admirably mimicking this or that insect. Beautiful little fellow travellers! I have just finished a paper on my finds in Southwest Colorado last summer.

Будь здоровъ[8]

V.

1. The reference in question reads: "We are here among friends, the Browns and the Bensons, the Whites and the Wilsons, and when somebody goes out for a smoke, he hears the crickets, and a distant farm dog (who waits, between barks, to listen to what we cannot hear)."

2. Within its brief span, the narrative of "Lance" combines three distinct superimposed levels of reality: inter-planetary exploration, mountain climbing and medieval romance. Like the earlier story written in English, "Time and Ebb," laid simultaneously in the present, the past and an unimaginable future, "Lance" strikes one in retrospect as a preliminary study pointing toward the literary method of *Ada*.

3. "It's for the kids."

4. "The fixed gaze" (cf. Letter 236, note 3).

5. Miss Plimsoll, the protagonist of the opening sketch in Harold Nicolson's *Some People*.

6. In "Titty," the sixth sketch in *Some People*, Nicolson describes driving across the Troitsky Bridge and "under the pencil-spire of St. Peter and St. Paul" in St. Petersburg on his way to have dinner at the Hermitage restaurant—which was one of the best-known restaurants in Moscow.

7. Apparently the naturalist and explorer William Beebe (1877–1962).

8. "Stay well."

239

[A note on the letter from Ernest J. Simmons to Wilson of January 30, 1952, inviting him to participate in a symposium commemorating the centenary of Gogol's death, to be held at Columbia University on March 6, 1952, with Nabokov, Leon Stilman and René Wellek as other participants.]

Dear Volodya: I have written him that I should be glad to celebrate the Gogol anniversary, but that his ten-minute speeches with "informal discussion"—evidently aimed at a radio audience—are a horrible idea and will do nothing for the memory of Gogol. What are you going to do? Maybe you and I ought to hold a little memorial service of our own. You will attack the Ukrainian tales and I'll defend them.

EW

240

9 Maynard Place
Cambridge, Mass.

February 21, 1952

Dear Bunny,

It was nice of you to warn me of your non-participation in that dismal Gogol affair. Simmons wrote me too, but *that* letter was addressed to Cornell and wandered for a week before reaching me, which it did after I had received your letter and just before an energetic telephone call from "Ernie" (as Harry[1] calls him) who was puzzled at my silence. Of course, you are right, and " 'tis nonsense all" (as Tatiana Larin and Fanny Price both remark).[2] I told him over the snowlined wires that only if they paid a fat fee would I consider, etc.

You never told me whether you had read my "Lance." I thought I had worked "the Whites and the Wilsons" rather neatly into my text. Shall we go to New York "to meet" the Shawns? I would like a quiet talk with you, for $4^{1}/_{2}$ hours, over a little glass of wine, after which we would have a long dinner—reclining on the left elbow.

We are having a grand time here. Twice a week I thunder against Cervantes from the pulpit, before an abyss of more than 500 students—and twist Dostoevsky's arm in a Russian Lit[erature] class.

Ghosts of a horrible experience I had in the spring of 1948, complete with endless sputum-analysis and a bronchoscopy, crept back into my life when a

routine X-ray examination here revealed a "Shadow behind the Heart"—
something that has been haunting me for more than ten years and that no doctor has been able to explain—but what a wonderful title for an old-fashioned
novel!

We have a very charming, ramshackle house, with lots of *bibelots* and a good
bibliothèque,[3] rented unto us by a charming lesbian lady, May Sarton.[4]

Véra joins me in sending Elena and you our very best love.

V.

1. Harry Levin.

2. In Chapter Forty-Four of *Mansfield Park*, " 'tis nonsense all" is the reaction of the
heroine, Fanny Price, when she reads in a letter from the man she loves that her rival for his
affections, Mary Crawford, is "very fond" of her. In his annotated translation of Pushkin's
Eugene Onegin, Nabokov utilized Fanny's phrase to translate the line from Tatiana's love
letter to Onegin *"Byt' mozhet, èto vsyo pustoe"* as "Perhaps, 'tis nonsense all," giving Jane
Austen due credit in his annotations.

3. "Trinkets" and "library."

4. In her book *The Fur Person* (1957), May Sarton described the friendship that developed between her tiger cat Tom Jones and the Nabokovs during the latter's stay at her house.

241

[A postcard]

February 25, 1952
17 E. 97, N.Y.

Dear Volodya: Do come on for the *New Yorker* party (which has its amusing
aspects)—we are anxious to see you.

E.W.

I'm sorry you told me that there was something about me in your *New
Yorker* story, because I have to make it a rule never to read anything in which I
am mentioned, for fear it will influence my judgment one way or the other.

[In margin]
Elena says to tell you to come to dinner here before going on to the W's.

[At top]
Mary's new book is very good—in some ways, the best thing she has done.[1] I
think you ought to read it.

1. *The Groves of Academe* by Mary McCarthy.

242

9 Maynard Place
Cambridge, Mass.

February 26, 1952

Dear Bunny,

I do not think you should have made that remark—to me.[1]

Many thanks to Elena for her kind invitation. Alas, we shall not be able to come to New York after all.

I have read Mary's book. It is very amusing and quite brilliant in parts; but "Domna,"[2] with its *popovski*[3] implications, is an impossible name for a Russian woman of the "upper classes" (as she oddly calls herself); *kïssel*[4] should be *kissel*, or even better, *kisel* (there is no ы in the Russian for which the *ï* presumably stands); *narodnika* is *not* the feminine of *narodnik*[5] but the $\begin{cases} \text{accusative} \\ \text{genitive} \end{cases}$ singular masculine; and *boxe*[6] (French) is not *le boxe*, but *la boxe*.

Yours.

V.

1. The one about never reading anything in which he is mentioned and thus being prevented from reading "Lance" (cf. Letter 241).

2. Domna Rejnev, the Russian-born college instructor, is one of the principal characters of *The Groves of Academe*.

3. "Priestly." Domna Rejnev's background is described in the novel as follows: "Her grandfather had been a famous Liberal, one of the leaders of the Cadet party in the Duma; her father, a well-educated man, a friend of Cocteau and Diaghilev . . ." Given this kind of family background, the name Domna (from the Latin *Domina*), usual only among the Orthodox clergy—a separate caste in pre-revolutionary Russia—and the peasants, is indeed a highly unlikely choice. Western authors who describe Russian characters often fail to realize that names might be associated with a particular social or cultural background. In a novel by Rebecca West *(The Birds Fall Down)*, there appears a Count Diakonov (*i.e.,* "son of a deacon"), which is about as likely in Russia as an Earl of Parish-Priest would have been in England.

4. *Kisel'* is a Russian puréed fruit dessert. The doubling of the *s* in order to make sure it has an unvoiced sound is quite usual when Russian words and names are transcribed into English or French (as in "Moussorgsky"); the *i* with a dieresis which stands in certain transliteration systems (including the one Nabokov used in his *Onegin* commentary) for a completely different Russian vowel, usually transcribed as *y*, makes no sense at all.

5. "Populist." The context of the word in the novel is: "As Mulcahy had more than once said to her, she had the temperament and the vocation of a *narodnika.*" If the last word is intended to mean "a female populist," it is quite wrong, since the feminine form of *narodnik* would be *narodnitsa*, if it existed. It might, however, represent an incursion of Russian

grammar into the English context, with the meaning "the vocation of a Populist (gender unspecified)," in which case the genitive form would be the appropriate one.

6. "Boxing," "prize fighting."

243

9 Maynard Place
Cambridge

April 19, 1952

Dear Bunny,

Moe[1] *vient de*[2] inform me that I am getting a grant for the translation of "You Gin? One Gin" (I think I have already communicated to you the gist of that little play: *First Tippler* to *Second Tippler:* "You gin?" (Second Tippler nods assent). *First Tippler* to *Barman:* "One gin."). It is a pun on the title of Pushkin's novel in verse. "Pushkin" himself is a good example of nepotism (to "push" one's "kin").

I am writing you this hasty note to thank you for helping me in getting that grant.

Yours.
V.

1. Henry Allen Moe of the Guggenheim Foundation.
2. "Has just."

244

Edmund Wilson
Wellfleet, Cape Cod,
Massachusetts

May 19, 1952

Dear Nabokovs: We expect to be going through Boston Sunday June 1 and hope to see you. I assume that you'll still be there. Do save Sunday evening if you can.

As ever,
EW

The Letters, 1952

305

245

[From Véra Nabokov to Elena Wilson]

9 Maynard Place

Cambridge 38, Mass.   May 22, 1952

Dear Elena,

We shall be delighted to see you and Bunny on June 1st. Can you come to dinner to our place, at around 7? Please drop me a line, and tell me also if you two would feel like having a few people come in later. We thought of asking the Shorers, possibly Lena Levin (if she does not accompany Harry to Syracuse where he will go to get an honorary degree),[1] and perhaps one or two others.

Vladimir has finished his lectures to-day. So we shall go butterfly-hunting this weekend, but shall be back by Sunday afternoon (the 25th).

We are looking forward to your visit very much.

Cordially,
Véra Nabokov

1. Elena Levin and Mark and Ruth Shorer. Mark Shorer (1908–1977) was a scholar, writer and biographer of Sinclair Lewis and D. H. Lawrence. He worked at U.C. Berkeley in the final decades of his life.

246

Edmund Wilson
Wellfleet, Cape Cod
Massachusetts

May 27, 1952

Dear Vera: We'd love to come to dinner Sunday—and see the Levins and anybody else. Have just received Volodya's Дар.[1] I think that the time is approaching when I am going to read his complete works and write an essay on them that will somewhat annoy him.

As ever,
Edmund W

1. *The Gift.*

247

THE VENDÔME
Boston

June 3, 1952

Dear Volodya: I always enjoy writing to you when I am in Boston and you are in Cambridge. I think the name you want is Pompey. Negro slaves used sometimes to be called that. I don't see how you can keep the Negro element out of it.[1] About coming up to see us: I didn't understand last night that you would be free all next week. The weekend wouldn't be so good, because Reuel and Ilyin[2] are both arriving then; but we'd love to have you sometime earlier. The best from our point of view would be if you could drive up with me Friday or Saturday, relieving the boredom of my trip. I'll call you up when I'm leaving Talcottville. As ever,

EW

[Added at top]
We enjoyed last night extremely, though we were both in rather battered condition.

1. This might possibly be a reference to Nabokov's investigation of the circumstances of the enslavement of Pushkin's African ancestor Abram Gannibal, which later formed a separate appendix in his edition of *Eugene Onegin*.
2. Nikolai Dmitrievich Ilyin, who, according to the recollections of Elena Wilson, "spent six rather confused weeks here that summer going over Russian grammar and reading Russian with Edmund."

248

Our address will be until further notice:

Goldwin Smith Hall
Cornell Univ[ersity]
Ithaca, N.Y.

June 14, 1952

Dear Bunny,

We are really very much disappointed at not being able to come—and feel very "crabby." Besides the car trouble we wired you about, there are lots of other hindrances. We are leaving for the West (probably some mountain range in Wyoming) Monday or Tuesday and there are thousands of things to be settled, etc. We think it is very sweet of you both to keep on inviting us, and sooner or later we shall come to stay with you for weeks if not months.*)

We enjoyed seeing Elena and you. Are you reading *Dar*?[1] I have more or less completed my academical labors for the time being and am going to work on something of my very own. What was that job you spoke of?

Let us keep in touch, cher ami.

Yours,

V.

*) <u>In any case</u> we shall visit you for 1 or 2 days in September.

1. *The Gift.*

249

Afton, Wyo[ming]

Corral Log Cabins

August 10, 1952

Dear Bunny,

this is a lovely little place in southwest Wyoming. We have made it our headquarters, Véra and I, for collecting butterflies in the neighbouring National Forests while Dmitri is climbing the Tetons from Jenny Lake where he camps.

I have not read a book (save for a collection of Henry James' short stories—miserable stuff, a complete fake, you ought to debunk that pale porpoise and his plush vulgarities some day) nor written a word since I left Cambridge. How are you and Elena? Our last meeting was much too brief. You never told me about that job you mysteriously mentioned—what was it? There is no greater pleasure in life than exploring entomologically some alpine bog—but I have discussed all that in *Dar*.

Yours,

V.

250

August 26, 1952

Talcottville

New York

Dear Volodya: Princeton has just had a handout from one of the millionaire foundations which enables them to invite outside people for rather a queer-sounding series of lectures. You deliver six lectures (on anything you like), one a week, and that is all, except that you have to live there a whole semester and attend, once a week, a lecture given by somebody else—which, as Mario Praz says, sounds sado-masochistic. There are supposed to be discussions after the lectures, in the course of which I suppose you will be heckled by "New Critics" and Roman Catholic converts. For this you get $5000. I have urged them to ask you, Cyril Connolly and Praz and a number of other people; if they really wanted to, they could have a brilliant series; but the trouble is, I fear, that they will prefer to invite a lot of semi-academic mediocrities with whom they will feel more at home.

I have been having a wonderful time up here. It is a house that belonged to my mother's family and that she left me when she died—built about 1805. Talcottville is a very old-fashioned and rather strange place. It is fascinating to me—though more or less of a bore to Elena. I hope that you will come to see me here when we have got the place in better shape.

We're leaving here Labor Day and during September my address will be Wellfleet.

Love to Vera,

EW

251

Goldwin Smith [Hall]
Cornell Univ[ersity]

October 21, 1952

Dear Bunny,

Thanks from both of us for your new collection, *Брега Лучезарные*.[1] I think I am going to read—or reread—these pieces with great pleasure—with some nasty bit of criticism popping out of me at the least expected moment.

I must also thank you for your nice Princetonian letter. Alas, no offer yet.

If you open *Webster's New Collegiate Dictionary,* 1949 (and, probably, earlier editions under other titles), you will find in the "Biographical Names" section the following adorable definition of your man.[2] "Sade, de . . . . . . Fr. soldier and pervert." Ponder these two professions, with that "dirty" epithet ("French") and the dignified rhythm of the phrase (amphibrachic and prim).

Yours,

V.

1. *The Shores of Light.*

2. Reference to Wilson's essay "The Vogue of the Marquis de Sade" in *The New Yorker,* October 18, 1952.

252

PRINCETON UNIVERSITY
Princeton, New Jersey

November 3, 1952
MANSGROVE
Princeton, New Jersey

Dear Volodya: I was delighted by the Webster description of Sade. I have had more than a dozen letters from enthusiastic sadists—some of them in curiously crabbed and wobbly handwriting.

Have you ever read Chekhov's уголовный роман, *Драма на Охоте,*[1] which came out as a serial in 1884–85, but was never reprinted by him? It seems to me a very remarkable thing, and I don't know why more fuss hasn't been made about it (though there has been a Hollywood film based on it).[2] Do read it if you haven't. It is in the new Soviet edition—Vol. 3—and in at least one of the older ones.

We are very comfortably settled here. This job of mine is a dream. I have urged them to invite you, and they talk as if they would, but they have a list of about seventy names, and the man who runs it—half-Belgian, half-South Carolinian, and doesn't coordinate—is excessively vague, always misses trains and loses keys. I wish you could come down here and meet him and his associates.

Love to Vera,
E.W.

1. "Crime novel, *Drama During a Hunt.*" Wilson cites the original Russian title of this production of Chekhov's student days. It is better known in English as *The Shooting Party.*

2. *Summer Storm* with George Sanders and Linda Darnell, 1944. It was directed by Douglas Sirk, who developed it while he was still known as Detlef Sirk and worked at the Ufa Studios in Berlin. The film was Sirk's first successful film in Hollywood.

The Letters, 1952

1953

253

Portal, Arizona

May 3, 1953

Dear Bunny,

This is a magnificent place, near Paradise (a ghost town), sixty miles from civilization (Douglas), a ten-minute drive from cactus to pine; and then a short climb to aspen. The word "portal" is rather dreadfully associated in my mind (which has always contained more associations than thoughts) with a certain euphemism in your *Hecate*.

We all but visited you on our way here. I was, however, on the verge of a breakdown and not fit for company. For two months in Cambridge I did nothing (from 9 A.M. to 2 A.M.) but work on my commentaries to *E.O.* The Harvard libraries are wonderful. I even found the dream book that Tatiana used to explain her prophetic dream.[1] It is going to be a work of some 600 pages, including the (rhythmic) translation of *all* known lines (even those he crossed out). When the time came to leave Cambridge I was so joggy and jittery and buzzy with insomnia and so forth that I decided to lay aside Pushkin for a few months and start copying out my new novel (of which I shall tell you more in the fall). I spend several hours daily collecting butterflies. It struck me I might shift from Sterne to Fielding in my lectures but *Tom Jones* is awfully drab (with rather helpless references to Hogarth).

We had a wonderful time with your charming daughter in Boston.[2] I played an unforgettable game of chess (no, two games) with her. I saw also Tate, tight as a drum, tight Tate reading his, Ransom's, Cummings' and Bishop's poems to a Radcliffe audience. A very dear fellow.

Write me a letter, please. We (Véra and I, and, eventually, Dmitri, until he goes climbing in Brit[ish] Columbia in July—and we may drift north, too) may stay here till midsummer at least. We have a nice cottage on a ranch, with nobody in the main house but a mining engineer (whose lifetime hobby is computing the frequency of words used in crossword puzzles) and his ninety-four-year old father (who has founded 106 churches—and knew the Fox sisters[3]).

Love from both of us to both of you.

V.

1. *Martyn Zadeka*, the manual on interpreting dreams which Tatiana consulted in Chapter Five of *Eugene Onegin*. Nabokov points out in his *Onegin* commentary that the

title of the book comes from the name of a possibly spurious seer and sage, Martin Zadeck, who supposedly lived in Switzerland in the eighteenth century.

2. Rosalind Wilson.

3. Margaretta, Leah and Kate Fox, the founders and originators of modern spiritualism and table-turning.

254

May 16, 1953
Wellfleet, Mass.

Dear Volodya: I was glad to hear from you. Where are you going when you get back from Arizona? We are going to be in Talcottville (N.Y. State) in the latter part of the summer, and if you are going to be in Ithaca, we might arrange a visit one way or the other.

Is there any chance of your publishing a book any time before the fall after next? I hope so, for it would give me a pretext to do a long *New Yorker* article about you and include it in a book that is supposed to come out in 1954. For my purpose, a novel would be better than the *Eugeni Onegin*, but I suppose that this could be made to serve. I have been aiming to make you my next Russian subject after Turgenev. (I have arranged to do an article for the *New Yorker* on the *Pentateuch*, read for the first time.[1])

About Fielding: I have always found him wooden. *Tom Jones* is an enormously overrated book. In general, I think that the English are seen at their best in their literature, but what they seem to admire in Fielding are the solid English qualities in their more uninteresting form: commonsense, good humor, heartiness and honest manliness. You are quite right to stick to Sterne.

We are back here in the Cape. It is always a relief, as you know, to get away from an academic community.

I am about to embark on a project—a novel—that has been hanging over me for years, and that fills me with trepidation.[2]

Keep me in touch with your movements and your literary plans. Elena and Rosalind send love to all of you.

As ever,

EW

1. In connection with Wilson's investigation of the Dead Sea Scrolls.

2. This novel was left unfinished at the time of Wilson's death; to date, it has not been published.

255

General Delivery
Ashland, Oregon

June 20, 1953

Dear Bunny,

Véra and I drove from Arizona to Oregon through the lake region of California, collecting en route. In the meanwhile, Dmitri, in an old Buick he had put together, was making his way west from Harvard Square. We met in Ashland, a lovely place. From here he will go to British Columbia in July—to climb with his club; and his parents intend to stay on till the end of August here: we have rented the house of a professor (Ashland is a college town) who has gone east for the summer. The collecting is good.

Yes, I will have *koe-shto*—sorry, *кое что*[1]—published by the fall [of] 1954. I am writing nicely. In an atmosphere of great secrecy, I shall show you—when I return east—an amazing book that will be quite ready by then.[2] I think I told you that the notes to *E.O.* will also form a book. Finally I have started a series of stories about a creature of mine, a Professor Pnin, which I hope the *New Yorker* will be interested in. I am enclosing two poems. I had more but don't know where they are. The first was rejected by the *New Yorker* as too obscure; the second has just been sent to K[atharine] White and, probably, will be rejected, too.[3]

I have been reading—after Fielding—a very curious fat book, with incredible Victorian coils of coyness about it—*Daniel Deronda* by G. Eliot.

It is rather sad we see each other so very seldom. Next year we shall stay east and go to the seaside. We shall return to Ithaca in September this autumn, and hope you will be still around.

I am absolutely against capital punishment. *Anything* is better, even an unjust pardon.[4]

Greetings from all of us to all of you.

1. Nabokov defers to Wilson's request not to transliterate Russian in Latin letters and supplies the Cyrillic original of *koe-shto* (spelled phonetically), "a thing or two."

2. *Lolita.*

3. "Lines Written in Oregon" and "The Poplar."

4. In England, a royal commission was about to produce a report recommending the abolition of the death penalty, while in America the Rosenberg case was still widely discussed in the press.

256

October 15, 1953

957 E. State Street
Ithaca, N.Y.

Dear Bunny,

Where are you? Is everything all right? Are you anywhere near us? We would love to see you.

I would like to show you a ballad[1] I wrote some time ago. And quite soon I may show you a monster.[2]

The summer passed in such intense work that I find academic duties positively relaxing. But I have still a lot of literary work to complete.

Do give me some information of yourself. And tell me, if you know of a place that will publish poetry—and pay for it.

Love from both of us to both of you.

V.

I am going to send this letter via *The New Yorker.*

1. "Ballad of Longwood Glen," which was turned down by *The New Yorker* in 1953. Nabokov worked on it on and off for four more years, and *The New Yorker* finally accepted it and published it in its edition of July 6, 1957.

2. *Lolita*, on which Nabokov had worked steadily since 1951 and which he had almost completed at the time of this letter.

257

October 23, 1953
Wellfleet, Mass.

Dear Volodya:

I had been wondering what you were up to. We are no longer at Talcottville but back here. After Christmas, we are going to that old Europe, where I have been asked to perform during February at the Seminar of American Studies at Salzburg—expect to take in London and Paris on the way.

Here is a story that you ought to be told. Paul Brooks, the head of Houghton Mifflin, is an enthusiastic amateur naturalist. One day he opened his door and found a Polyphemus moth on his doorstep, a male. He was surprised, because, according to him, it was irregular to see one in Boston at that time of year. The moth came into the house, flew through some of the rooms and then departed. The same thing happened the next day and the day after that. After the third visit, Brooks remembered that he had a Polyphemus cocoon. When he went to the box in the drawer where he kept it, he found that a female had emerged. He put her outside on the sundial, and the male at once came and got her. They left him a little note saying that if at any time he should get into trouble with dragons or ogres, he had only to call upon them.

I have had a horrible two weeks of gout, but am over it and am otherwise prospering. I have been working on three major literary projects, but won't describe them, since the results will inevitably reach you.

The only publication that will pay anything much for poetry is the *New Yorker*. You know about the *Atlantic* and *Harper's*. Or do you mean that you want, as you ought, to publish a book of poems? If you do, I'm afraid that you'd have to engage to give them a novel or something, too. Love to Vera. Elena sends love.

E W

258

November 23, 1953

Dear Bunny,

I hear you had *podagra*[1]—how are you now?

We are going to Cambridge for Thanksgiving and staying at the Levins.

And Dec[ember] 12 I have to be in New York. Is there any hope that we might coincide at one of these space-time points?

I think I am finishing my book. Do write me "a pair of words."

Yours
V.

1. Gout.

259

December 3, 1953

Dear Volodya: I'm afraid we are going to miss you again. We are going to be in Boston Monday–Wednesday of next week, and in New York Dec[ember] 27–30. We are sailing on the 30th. We have all been rather wretched here: gout and flu. Elena is not even yet recovered. Did I tell you that I was going for a month to Salzburg to disseminate American culture—then afterward, if I am not worn out, to Israel for *The New Yorker?* Elena
[Continued on top of the card]
loved your last short story,² said she was going to write you. I liked it, too, but expected more of a wow at the end.

Love, Edmund W.

1. This postcard was found by Jeffrey Meyers among the Wilson papers at the University of Delaware Library. Gratitude is expressed to Professor Meyers for sharing his discovery and to the library for the permission to publish it.

2. The beginning of the novel *Pnin*, published as a story in *The New Yorker* of November 28, 1953.

1954

260

Taos, NM
Gen[eral] Del[ivery]

July 30, 1954

Dear Bunny,

I have been wanting to write you for months but this has been, and still is, and will be for a long while yet, a time of great labors with me. First of all I want to thank you for your book of plays. I still think the *Siniy Ogonyochek*¹ your best one in the way of harmony and multiple sense. I thought the Diabolic Play² extraordinarily amusing and well done. Véra joins me in sending you her thanks and tokens of appreciation. Next, let me tell you I enjoyed hugely your Biblical Essay in the *N[ew] Y[orker]*³ and hope there is more to come.

I am now collecting butterflies in New Mexico. A dull series of events led us to rent by wire from Ithaca a house here. We are near a superb canyon where I go for my hunting, and twelve miles from Taos which is a dismal hole full of third-rate painters and faded pansies. The house cost only 250 dollars for the whole summer, and an orchard was thrown in. Unfortunately our Spanish neighbors take all the fruit and a colorful smell of drains pervades what is euphemistically called the patio. The mountains around us, though high enough for my purposes, are not interesting enough for Dmitri to climb. He is with us this summer but may go to the Tetons a little later. How are you spending the summer? Give us news about all of you. Will you be in New York in Mid-September? I have to deliver there on the 14th of Sept[ember] a lecture on the Art of Translation at the English Institute.

I have had to lay aside my *Eugene Onegin* work for other things. One of them is an edition of *Anna Karenin* in English with my notes, commentaries, introductions, etc., for Simon and Schuster. They wanted a revision with notes for Part One first, and this I have just completed.⁴ With Viking I have signed a contract for my book on Pnin, but will not be able to finish it before the end of the winter.

The novel⁵ I had been working at for almost five years has been promptly turned down by the two publishers (Viking and S. & S.) I showed it to. They say it will strike readers as pornographic. I have now sent it to New Directions but it is unlikely they will take it. I consider this novel to be my best thing in English, and though the theme and situation are decidedly sensuous, its art is pure and its fun riotous. I would love you to glance at it some time. Pat Covici⁶ said we would all go to jail if the thing were published. I feel rather depressed about this fiasco. Another thing that has left me quite limp and hysterical is my Russian version of *Conclusive Evidence* which is appearing serially in the *Novyi Zhurnal* and will be published by the Chekhov firm in the fall.⁷ Please, write me. Best love from both of us to Elena.

> all this is a secret

Yours,

V.

1. *The Little Blue Light.*

2. Wilson's play *Cyprian's Prayer*, which was included, together with *The Little Blue Light*, in his volume *Five Plays*, published in 1954.

3. "On First Reading Genesis," *The New Yorker*, May 15, 1954. There was indeed "more

to come," since this essay led to the section on Israel in *Red, Black, Blond and Olive* and to both *The Scrolls from the Dead Sea* and its later version, *The Dead Sea Scrolls.*

4. The project was never realized, but the completed portions were included in the section on Tolstoy in Nabokov's *Lectures on Russian Literature*, Fredson Bowers, editor; 1981.

5. *Lolita.*

6. Pascal Covici (1888–1964), senior editor at Viking Press.

7. The Russian version of *Speak, Memory,* called *Other Shores,* was brought out by the Chekhov Publishing House in 1954, after portions of it were serialized in the émigré journals *Opyty (Experiments)*, No. 3, and *Novyi Zhurnal (The New Review)*, Nos. 37 and 38, during the same year.

261

August 9, 1954
Talcottville
Boonville RFD
New York

Dear Volodya: By all means, send me your book. I'd love to see it, and if nobody else is doing it, I'll try to get my publisher, Straus, to. I agree about Taos, but used to love the Jemez mountains—have you been there? I expect to go to New York rather early in September, but don't expect to be there as late as the 14th. Isn't there any chance that you could come over here? It isn't so terribly far from Ithaca—about an hour's drive north of Utica. Elena and the children will leave on the 3rd, but I'll probably stay here till the Tuesday after Labor Day. It's been far too long since we've seen you.

I read your note to the Russian version of your memoirs and made some comparisons with the English text. There was something about it I was going to say to you, but haven't the book here and can't remember what it was. I'm still going to read your complete works, but thought I might not see them in perspective without some more intimate knowledge of the Bible. There are going to be two more of those articles.

Love from all our family to yours. Do try to come to see us here.

As ever,
EW

262

September 5, 1954

Dear Bunny,

We had to leave Taos very suddenly. Véra fell ill (liver trouble)—and the diagnosis reached by an Albuquerque doctor was so frightening that we all three made a dash for New York. The doctors there, however, after a thorough examination, pronounced Véra well—and we are now back in Ithaca.

Thanks for your nice letter—and for writing F. & S. about the thing. It is still in Laughlin's large hands. I am very anxious for you to read it, it is *by far* my best English work.

I shall be in N.Y.C. on the 14th of this month—to talk on Problems of Translation (*Onegin* in English)[1] at the English Institute, Columbia Univ[ersity]. This has been a hectic hash of a summer. Véra's illness and some other unexpected expenses have left me in a pitiful state of destitution and debt.

Yours,

V

1. The lecture was later published as "Problems of Translation: *Onegin* in English" in *The Partisan Review*, Vol. 22, No. 4, 1955.

263

Wellfleet
Cape Cod, Mass.

November 30, 1954

Dear Volodya:

Roger Straus lent me the MS of your book, and I read it when I was in New York—though rather hastily, because I had to give it back, and I have waited to write you about it till I could get some other opinions. I also had Elena and Mary read it. I enclose Mary's reactions from a letter to me, which she says I may quote to you. Elena seems to have liked the book better than either Mary or I—partly, I think, because she has seen America from the foreigner's point of view and understands how it looks to your hero. The little girl, for example, seems quite all right to her, though rather implausible to me.

I am afraid that you will never get the book published by anybody except perhaps Laughlin. I have, however, written about it to a man named Weldon

Kees, a poet, who has just written me that he is associated with a new publishing venture in California, and that they want to bring out books of a kind that might otherwise not be published. I have also talked about it to Jason Epstein at Doubleday. It seems that, when they wiped out your part of the advance on that Russian book we were going to do, there was some sort of understanding that you would eventually submit a novel. Did you ever send them anything? I also suggested that he might be interested in your translation of *Onegin* for his paperback Anchor series. This has been a huge success, and I have been making money out of the two books of mine they have published. They would give you a big advance, but, as a paperback, the book might never get reviewed. To me, this doesn't matter a bit, and I am going to give them a collection of my essays on Russian subjects. If I were you, I'd send Epstein the *Onegin* when you finish it. He's a highly intelligent boy, very well read and with a good deal of taste.

Now, about your novel: I like it less than anything else of yours I have read. The short story that it grew out of was interesting, but I don't think the subject can stand this very extended treatment. Nasty subjects may make fine books; but I don't feel you have got away with this. It isn't merely that the characters and the situation are repulsive in themselves, but that, presented on this scale, they seem quite unreal. The various goings-on and the climax at the end have, for me, the same fault as the climaxes of *Bend Sinister* and *Laughter in the Dark:* they become too absurd to be horrible or tragic, yet remain too unpleasant to be funny. I think, too, that in this book there is—what is unusual with you—too much background, description of places, etc. This is one thing that makes me agree with Roger Straus in feeling that the second half drags. I agree with Mary that the cleverness sometimes becomes tiresome, though I don't think I agree with her about the "haziness." (I have suggested a few minor corrections on the MS.)

I wish I could like the book better. I am sorry that we see so little of you. We're going to be in New York for a week beginning December 15. If you're coming on for the holidays, let us know. We'll probably be staying at the Algonquin, but if we're not, you can reach me at the *New Yorker* office.

As ever,

EW

[Enclosed extract from Mary McCarthy's letter to Wilson]

About Vladimir's book—I think I have a midway position. I say think because I didn't quite finish it; I was three-quarters through the second volume when we had to leave. At Roger Straus' instructions, I left it at the Chelsea for

Philip Rahv to pick up—he may run some of the first part in PR.[1] I don't agree with you that the second volume was boring. Mystifying, rather, it seemed to me; I felt it had escaped into some elaborate allegory or series of symbols that I couldn't grasp. Bowden[2] suggests that the nymphet is a symbol of America, in the clutches of the middle-aged European (Vladimir); hence all the descriptions of motels and other U.S. phenomenology (I liked this part, by the way). But there seems to be some more concrete symbolism, in the second volume; you felt all the characters had a kite of meaning tugging at them from above, in Vladimir's enigmatic empyrean. What about that pursuer, for instance? I thought maybe I'd find the answer if I finished it—is there one?

On the other hand, I thought the writing was terribly sloppy all through, perhaps worse in the second volume. It was full of what teachers call *haziness*, and all Vladimir's hollowest jokes and puns. I almost wondered whether this wasn't deliberate—part of the idea.

[Elena Wilson's letter to Nabokov]

Wellfleet
Cape Cod, Mass.

November 30, 1954

Dear Vladimir:

The little girl seems very real and accurate and her attractiveness and seductiveness are absolutely plausible. The hero's disgust of grown-up women is not very different, for example, from Gide's, the difference being that Gide is smug about it and your hero is made to go through hell. The suburban, hotel, motel descriptions are just terribly funny.

I don't see why the novel should be any more shocking than all the now commonplace "études of other unpleasant moeurs." These peculiar tastes are surely as prevalent even if they haven't been written about as often. Why shouldn't the book be published in England, or certainly in France and then come back here in a somewhat expurgated form and be read greedily?

Unfortunately, my opinion is very unimportant. We would love to see you soon. Please give my love to Véra.

Elena

In other words, I couldn't put the book down and think it is very important.

1. *The Partisan Review.*
2. Bowden Broadwater, Mary McCarthy's new husband.

264

CORNELL UNIVERSITY

Vladimir Nabokov

Goldwin Smith Hall

Ithaca, New York

February 19, 1955

Dear Elena and Bunny,

Belatedly but with perfectly preserved warmth I now want to thank you for your letters—Elena's was especially charming.

Doubleday has of course returned the MS and I have now shipped it to France. I suppose it will be finally published by some shady firm with a Viennese-Dream name—e.g., "Silo."

(I did show Doubleday not one book but at least two or three—the last I can remember was *Bend Sinister* for Permabooks, on their request, when a man of the name of McKay[1] or something like it was in charge; before Epstein took over.)

I have been completely immersed in *Onegin* during these last months. I have finished the translation of the text and of *all* variants I could find, but the commentaries are voluminous and their arrangement in readable form will take me many months. Doubleday was not interested in publishing the thing in the form I want it to appear [in], with the notes running to at least 400 pages, and the Russian text *en regard*. I have found all kinds of sensational analogies, etc., in English and French literatures, and have solved the mystery of the master motto.[2]

Bunny, I liked *very much* your Palestine essay.[3] It is one of your best pieces.

This has been, and still is, a difficult winter for us. My financial woes have not been allayed by my concentrating on *Lolita* and *Onegin*. My novel about the Russian professor Pnin is progressing very slowly. Another chapter has been bought by the *New Yorker*.

Dmitri is finishing Harvard this spring. Our plans for the summer are extremely hazy. I am taking a semi-sabbatical next spring semester. Véra and I miss you.

V

P.S. A gifted young playwright has turned my *Bend Sinister* into a rather good play.[4] I would be grateful if you could tell me whom to show it.

1. George de Kay, who was an editor at the Permabooks division of Doubleday during the 1950s.

2. See the next two letters.

3. The "Israel" section of *Red, Black, Blond and Olive*, a large portion of which appeared in *The New Yorker* on December 4, 1954.

4. The playwright was Evan Jones; his dramatization of *Bend Sinister* was never published or produced on the stage.

265

THE NEW YORKER
No. 25 West 43rd Street

March 1, 1955

Dear Volodya: Sending plays around to producers is an endless and hopeless job. I suggest that you get your dramatist to send the play to Harold Friedman, c/o Brandt & Brandt, 101 Park Ave., N.Y. He is the best play agent in New York for serious plays—has done a lot for Thornton Wilder and others. He is very intelligent and understands drama as a department of literature. You might mention that I suggested your sending him the play.

For the *Onegin* I should think you would have to fall back on a university press—Harvard?

I am glad you are doing a novel about Pnin. As for money, do you know that the *New Yorker* has raised its regular rate 10%, and that you get a further raise of 25% if you contribute, in a single year, more than a certain wordage? I was astounded at how much I was paid for my two Palestine articles (one of them still to appear).

What *is* the master motto of *Onegin*—"O rus! O Русь!"?[1] I am eager to see your edition.

As ever,

EW

1. This, as Nabokov points out in his reply, is not the master motto that opens the novel, but the epigraph to Chapter Two. The pun is on the Latin vocative form *rus* (countryside) and the archaic and poetic Russian word for Russia, *Rus'*.

266

March 10, 1955

Dear Bunny,

I thank you for your kind advice anent the agent. It does seem to be the very best plan. I have also written to a man called E. Kazan whom I once met in Cambridge, Mass.

Yes, the *New Yorker* paid me very generously for my Pnin piece. I hope to finish the book—which I have already sold to Viking—sometime in June.

No, I was thinking of the "Pétri de vanité"[1]—the motto heading the whole novel. The one which you mention is the Chapter Two epigraph. The first *rus*, countryside, comes, of course, from Horace, Satire VI. The pun is found in *Bièvriana*, an insipid collection of *jeux de mots*[2] attributed to the Marquis de Bièvre. I have also found it in Stendhal's Journal, Appendix II, ed. 1888. The entry (1838) reads: "En 1791 ... le parti aristocrate attendait les Russes à Grenoble (Suvorov was in Switzerland); ils s'écriaient: O Rus quando ego te aspiciam."[3] In regard to the master motto ("Pétri de vanité") I have found a whole system of fountainheads in: 1. Voltaire's "La Guerre Civile de Genève"; 2. Malebranche's "De la Recherche de la Vérité"; and, last but not least, 3. "Lettre de M. Burke (Edmund Burke) à un Membre de l'Assemblée Nationale de France" (!)[4]

I have greatly enjoyed all that tremendous research. One of the most difficult clues to pursue proved to be the origin of Pushkin's Abyssinian ancestor. I do not know how many old and new maps of that country I have examined, and how many travels (Jesuits, Protestants, Bruce, Salt, etc.) I have studied in order to find "Lagon" (Logo), a town mentioned by "Gannibal" (that great-grandfather)—who in a certain fascinating sense was a descendant of Rasselas![5]

We shall see each other this year. Véra joins me in sending you and Elena our very best love.

V

---

1. "Full of vanity ..."—the beginning of the French master motto that opens *Eugene Onegin*.

2. "Play on words."

3. "In 1791 ... the aristocratic party was expecting the Russians in Grenoble [...]; they exclaimed: O Russia, when shall I behold you" (the capitalization changes Horace's "countryside" to "Russia"). For another example of this line in Stendhal and a more detailed discussion, see the beginning of Nabokov's commentary to Chapter Two of *Eugene Onegin*.

4. For a detailed explanation and discussion, see the section on the master motto in Nabokov's edition of *Onegin*.

5. See Appendix One, "Abram Gannibal," in Volume 3 of Nabokov's edition of *Eugene Onegin*. "Bruce, Salt, etc." refer to travel accounts by James Bruce (1790) and Henry Salt (1811), which Nabokov utilized in his research on Pushkin's Abyssinian ancestor.

267

Véra Nabokov
700 Stewart Ave.

April 24, 1955

Dear Elena and Bunny,

We were extremely sorry to learn from Katharine White of your two "separate accidents." She does not say what it is, but adds that you "also have a cat with a broken leg." We hope you are all recovering and will make your trip to New York. To our regret we cannot make a trip there at the same time with you and attend the Whites' party, since Vladimir is up to his chin in *Pnin*. For the same reason he is not writing you, but wants me to join his very best wishes to mine.

Love,
Véra

268

Vladimir Nabokov
Goldwin Smith Hall
Cornell University
Ithaca, N.Y.

July 2, 1955

Dear Bunny,

The very *sympathique* Jason Epstein has visited me here. I am going to do a translation for them (Russian author and work not yet quite settled).[1] They offer me 7½% royalty and an advance of $1000 on it. Epstein suggests that I find out from you if this is all right. Are there any other points I should raise? It is going to be an Anchor book.

I have sold my LOLITA and it will probably come out this summer.[2] I would like you to read it some day.

We are not going west this summer. I cannot leave Ithaca until I finish my Pnin book. I have sold the *New Yorker* yet another instalment.

Véra and I send you and Elena our very best love.

P.S. Where are you exactly? Epstein says you are at Talcottville, but a man called Roberto Fasola[3] says you are in Wellfleet. So I am sending out two copies of this note.

1. It turned out to be *A Hero of Our Time* by Mikhail Lermontov.
2. After being rejected by four leading American publishing houses, *Lolita* was brought out by the Olympia Press in Paris in a two-volume edition.
3. This man proved impossible to identify.

269

July 7, 1955
Talcottville
Boonville RFD 1
New York

Dear Volodya: I have enjoyed both copies of your letter. Since you're at Ithaca, why don't you come over to see us? You may not find on the map this little village of eighty people; but look for Boonville in Oneida County about forty miles north of Utica. We'd be delighted to see you.

About the Anchor book: you should perhaps ask for $1500—especially if you're doing an introduction.

Our telephone here is Boonville 418K.

We both are enjoying *Pnin*.

As ever,
Edmund W

270

Dear Bunny,

Thank you for your letter.

We shall be driving to Middlebury College, where I am to give a lecture, and would like to stop on our way, on July 18th, at Talcottville to see you and Elena. Will you be there in the afternoon on the 18th? We cannot stop for long but shall have a few hours at our disposal. It would be nice if we could see you both. I think we could manage to arrive between two and three. We would have to leave about 6 or so.

Yours,

V.

270a

July 16, 1955

Sorry to have confused dates. My lecture at Middlebury College is Wednesday. We shall visit you on the way back Thursday afternoon July 21, unless you object.[1]

1. A telegram from Nabokov to Wilson.

271

[Véra Nabokov to Elena Wilson]

August 6, 1955

Dear Elena,

You must be back on the Cape by now, so I am going to send this letter there. I want to tell you how much we enjoyed seeing you both and your adorable Helen'очка.[1]

Two days after we got home, and just after finishing the last proofs, Vladimir sprained his back; he suffered terrible pains and had to be taken to the hospital as soon as a room became available. It looked terrible, they had to take him there by ambulance. It was a whole week before he felt well enough to go home, and even now he still is

Volodia's contribution

not quite well and has to have massage and diathermy every other day. While he was away, Dmitri arrived for a short stay and we moved to a new house.

I hope you have a nice cool breeze (though not a hurricane) on the Cape. The heat here is appalling.

Our best wishes to all of you.

Sincerely,
Véra Nabokov

1. The Russian diminutive suffix -ochka added to the name of Elena and Edmund Wilson's daughter Helen.

272

August 18, 1955
Talcottville

Dear Volodya and Vera: Here is Larousse's definition of *fastidieux:* "(*Lat. fastidiosus* de *fastidium*, ennui). Fade. Qui cause de l'ennui, du dégoût: *lecture fastidieuse.* Ant. Amusant, divertissant."[1] I am sure that I have never seen it used with the meaning you think it has.

I thoroughly enjoyed my visit. You must return it at Wellfleet. Elena was delighted at the prospect of your coming.

I had a heavy trip home with my driver. He not only speaks French, Polish and Italian, but has a smattering of German, Spanish and modern Greek, which he illustrated copiously, and can intone the Catholic mass in Latin. He plays the cello, violin and flute. He was professionally an osteopath, so able that at one time he was admitted to practice in one of the New York hospitals, from which osteopaths are supposed to be debarred. When his patients did not respond to his treatment, he would send for a preacher to pray with them, and this would sometimes work. Later, he retired and drove a taxi. One of the prodigies he performed in this line was driving a man who was mentally deranged on a trip of four hundred miles from Boonville to somewhere in Maine in one day. The doctors had given him a bottle of whisky and a hypodermic needle in case the patient showed signs of going off the handle; but nothing more than one swig of the whisky was needed, because the driver patted his head and talked to him in Canadian French—the patient was also a Canuck—about his (the patient's) mother and sister, who had been dead twenty-eight years. He talked to him all the way.

Well, aufwiedersehen, as he said to me in parting. I shall always remember Ithaca in terms of our magnum of Piper-Heidsieck, Volodya's translation of Pushkin, Morris Bishop's excellent dinner and Vera's excellent breakfast. The swans and ducks in the lake and Volodya's conception of the character of Lenin, and discovery of the worthlessness of Stendhal[2] and his account of the sexual habits of the younger generation.

As ever,

E.W.

1. "*Fastidieux:* (Lat. *fastidiosus,* from *fastidium,* boredom). Insipid. That which causes boredom or disgust: *boring reading.* Ant[onym]: amusing, diverting." "[Nabokov] and Vera would not believe me two summers ago, when I told them that *fastidieux* in French meant *tiresome* and not *fastidious* . . ." (Edmund Wilson, *Upstate,* p. 160).

2. "Nabokov has just discovered that Stendhal is a complete fraud, and is about to break the news to his class" (Wilson's letter to Helen Muchnic of August 18, 1955, *Letters on Literature and Politics, 1912–1972,* p. 578).

273

August 31, 1955
808 Hanshaw Rd.
Ithaca N.Y.

Dear Bunny,

it was a joy to see you. Thanks for the amusing letter.

Alas, my accursed lumbago has crept back, and we shall not go to the seaside as we had hoped. Littré[1] (in Supplement) gives under *fastidieux: dégouté, difficile à satisfaire*[2]—which as I said is fairly close to *брезгливый*[3] in such locutions as *с брезгливым видом* = *d'un petit air dégouté.*[4] I have finished *My Poor Pnin* but the book is much shorter than my publisher thought and I am afraid he will not be pleased. Love to both of you from both of us.

In pain
V.

1. The standard French dictionary, compiled by Emile Littré (1801–1881).

2. See the preceding letter and its note 1. The definition of *fastidieux* quoted here means "fastidious, hard to please."

3. "Squeamish."

4. "With a squeamish air" (Russian), "with a fastidious air" (French).

274

Dear Bunny,

It was a pleasure seeing you but our meeting was much too brief.

Rahv, who had offered to print parts of my little *Lolita* in the *Partisan,* has changed his mind upon the advice of a lawyer. It depresses me to think that this pure and austere work may be treated by some flippant critic as a pornographic stunt. This danger is the more real to me since I realize that *even* you neither understand nor wish to understand the texture of this intricate and unusual production.

Our plans are to spend some six weeks of my sabbatical half-year in Cambridge, arriving there early in February, after which we shall probably drive to California, and return to Cornell in September. We are looking forward to seeing you and Elena in Cambridge.

We regret so much not having been able to join you in Boston for Thanksgiving.

Yours ever,

V.

275

December 17, 1955

Dear Bunny,

Many thanks for the British edition of THE TRIPLE THINKERS, with the revised duel. Now, at least, they have something to shoot at.

I have finished reading the other book, and Véra is half through. We like your little introductions very much. I find most of the selections are fine. There is too much, however, of Lawrence and Anderson, both of whom are complete mediocrities artistically.[1]

I have almost finished the whole ONEGIN book. I still have to put in a couple of months more work at libraries. And then comes the gigantic index on which I have not even started and which I intend to make as complete and detailed as possible. We shall spend February and March in Cambridge, with Dmitri and the Widener.[2] We hope to see you and Elena there.

Véra joins me in wishing all of you a wonderful Christmas.

Love,

V.

1. The book in question is the 1955 reissue of *The Shock of Recognition: The Development of Literature in the United States Recorded by the Men Who Made It*, an anthology edited by Edmund Wilson and containing his introductory pieces on the writers included, among whom are D. H. Lawrence and Sherwood Anderson.

2. The Widener Library at Harvard.

1956

276

16 Chauncy Street
Cambridge, Mass.

February 29, 1956

Dear Bunny,

Thanks for my predecessor's book.[1] I am sure his ghost is appalled by the boners in the dreadful translations[2] you have graced with your preface. You can well imagine how strongly I disapprove of your preface.[3] Do you really think that Chehov is Chehov because he wrote about "social phenomena," "readjustments of a new industrial middle class," "kulaks" and "rising serfs" (which sounds like the seas)? I thought he wrote of the kind of things that gentle King Lear proposed to discuss in prison with his daughter. I also think that at a time when American readers are taught from high school on to seek in books "general ideas" a critic's duty should be to draw their attention to the specific detail, to the unique image, without which—as you know as well as I do—there can be no art, no genius, no Chehov, no terror, no tenderness, and no surprise.

We are going to New York on the 6th of March for two or three days.

A foul little flurry in the London papers concerning LOLITA has been demurely alluded to by Harvey Breit in his column. When you do read LOLITA, please mark that it is a highly moral affair and does not portray American kulaks. In the same issue of the *Book Review* there is a nice advertisement of Books on Sex, with patients "telling their case histories in their own words." I am extremely irritated by the turn my nymphet's destiny is taking, but although I foreglimpsed the situation, I have no inkling how to act, nor do I know even what kind of assistance or defense I can expect in our times when crusades are definitely *vieux jeu*.[4] Shall we see you and Elena in New York?

Yours,

V

1. Anton Chekhov, *Peasants and Other Stories*, selected and with a preface by Edmund Wilson, Garden City, New York, 1956. In "Anniversary Notes" Nabokov wrote: "I do love Chekhov dearly [...] it is *his* works which I would take on a trip to another planet" (*Strong Opinions*, p. 286). On the affinities between Chekhov ("my predecessor") and Nabokov, see Simon Karlinsky, "Nabokov and Chekhov: the Lesser Russian Tradition," *TriQuarterly*, No. 17 (Winter 1970); also reprinted in *Nabokov!*, Alfred Appel, Jr. and Charles Newman, eds.; also, same author, "Nabokov and Chekhov," in *The Garland Companion to Vladimir Nabokov*, Vladimir Alexandrov, ed., New York & London, 1995, pp. 389–402.

2. The uncredited translations of Chekhov's stories in *Peasants and Other Stories* contain a number of misreadings of Russian idioms.

3. Wilson's brief, four-page introduction is almost entirely devoted to sociological analysis of the class origins of Chekhov's characters.

4. "Old hat."

277

[Véra Nabokov to Elena Wilson]

April 20, 1956

Dear Elena,

It was delightful to see you and Bunny in your charming Cape-Cod *усадьба*.[1]

A surprise was awaiting us here: the MG is about to be sold, it proved not good enough for racing after all. What a relief.

Volodia wants you both to look up his poem "Rain"[2] in *The New Yorker* of April 21. He still feels invigorated and refreshed by the mental sea breeze. And we both have the kindest memories of your charming hospitality.

Last night we saw Dos Passos, mellow and merry, at dinner at the Levins. In another twelve days we shall be on our way.

Don't forget that you promised to come and see us in Ithaca.

Love from both of us to you all.

Véra

1. Country estate.
2. Reprinted in *Poems and Problems*.

278

Edmund Wilson
Wellfleet, Cape Cod
Massachusetts

April 24, 1956

Dear Volodya and Vera: We enjoyed your visit so much that we feel that we ought to be writing the bread-and-butter letter.

I hope that you will read my article on Cabell in last week's *New Yorker*.[1] He has certain things in common with Volodya, of whom I was sometimes reminded in reading him. I'd be interested to see how you would react to his writings.

I have consulted Dahl, and I find that he gives самодур[2] the same derivation as дурак.[3] Самодурить is defined: дурить в свою голову, упрямиться[4]—play the fool in an obstinate way.

As ever,

EW

1. "The James Branch Cabell Case Reopened," *The New Yorker*, April 21, 1956.

2. "Petty tyrant," usually with reference to the head of a Russian merchant-class family; the term was made popular by mid-nineteenth-century critics, who used it to describe a frequent type in Alexander Ostrovsky's melodramas about parental tyranny in merchant families. "Volodya declared with emphasis—contrary to the authority of Dahl, the great Russian lexicographer—that *samodur* had anything [*sic*] to do with the root of *durak*." (*Upstate*, p. 160)

3. "Fool."

4. "To be stubborn" (Wilson provides the translation of the words that precede the comma).

279

V. Nabokov
Goldwin Smith Hall
Cornell University
Ithaca, N.Y.

August 14, 1956

Dear Bunny,

Véra and I have just returned from a marvelous trip to the Rockies. We stayed first at Mt. Carmel, a village in southern Utah where we had hired a house. We collected butterflies in the Grand Canyon, Arizona, and in other national parks in the vicinity. Pink, terra-cotta and lilac mountains formed a sympathetic background to the Caucasus of Lermontov in *A Hero of Our Time* which is now ready to be mailed to Doubleday, with commentaries and a map. In July we moved on to higher altitudes in Wyoming and Montana. Incidentally, in one of his letters to Fliess the Viennese Sage[1] mentions a young patient who masturbated in the w.c. of an Interlaken hotel in a special contracted position so as to be able to glimpse (now comes the Viennese Sage's curative explanation) the Jungfrau. He should have been a young Frenchman in a Wyoming motel with a view of the Tetons.

I notice with pleasure that your scrolls are still on the bestseller list.[2] How are you? Where are you? Only now have I had the opportunity to read carefully something you showed me one day during our wonderful session at Wellfleet in spring, namely Struve on Nabokov.[3] The book is excellent but I was a little surprised to see that while raking up some scurvy remarks Georgy Ivanov made about me twenty-five years ago, Struve did not take the trouble to say that these were exclusively prompted by an article in which I had demolished a novel by Odoevtseva, Ivanov's wife.[4]

We have a nice house with a guest room. Dmitri is staying with us, between an engagement in Kennebunk Port and going back to school in September. He has assisted Véra and me very ably in our Lermontov translation. I do not recall if I told you that after some mental teetering I decided not to translate Turgenev's memoirs after all. The agreement Straus sent me contained certain impossible clauses, and, moreover, he adopted in his letters a paternal tone that I could not stomach. In the meantime Doubleday has acquired PNIN, and I plan to go to New York to discuss with Epstein, who is a charming and subtle person, some other projects.

Will you be back from Europe by the beginning of September? Is there any chance of our getting together in New York?

Véra joins me in sending Elena and you our best regards.

V

1. Sigmund Freud's letter of December 9, 1899 to Wilhelm Fliess.
2. Wilson's *The Scrolls from the Dead Sea.*
3. Gleb Struve's book on Russian émigré literature, published in 1956, contained what was probably the first comprehensive survey of Nabokov's Russian period. It remains to this day the best available account of Nabokov's reception in Russian émigré criticism.
4. Struve's book outlined the controversy in the émigré press occasioned by the poet Georgy Ivanov's savage denunciation of Nabokov's novels in the first issue of the literary journal *Chisla (Numbers)* in 1930. Nabokov was to remember the incident, 34 years after it happened, in his *Playboy* interview of 1964, where he attributed Ivanov's enmity, as he does here, to his own adverse review of Irina Odoevtseva's novel (see *Strong Opinions,* p. 39). On Georgy Ivanov and his literary significance, see Vladimir Markov, "Georgy Ivanov: Nihilist as Light-Bearer," *The Bitter Air of Exile: Russian Writers in the West 1922–1972,* Simon Karlinsky and Alfred Appel, Jr., eds., Berkeley-Los Angeles-London, 1977.

280

HOTEL VIER JAHRESZEITEN
RESTAURANT WALTERSPIEL

September 1, 1956
München
Maximilianstrasse 4

Dear Volodya: Your letter has just reached me. I had been thinking about you lately—trying to imagine you in Germany. Elena is back in Wellfleet—Helen had been left with friends and had to be collected. I have a sailing for October 2, but may break down and leave earlier. Try me at the Princeton Club if you are going to be in New York.

I am leading a peaceful and pleasant life alone in this excellent hotel—going to the excellent opera at night and trying to finish *Die Leiden des Jungen Werthers,* which I began in 1933 and have never been able to get through. It seems appalling that young men all over Europe should have been killing themselves on account of this book.[1]

I saw Nicholas last night on his way to Salzburg for some of his eternal cultural liaison work,[2] and we saw him a number of times in Paris and went out to his country place, which is terrific. Splendid flower and vegetable gardens, a pretty little blue-eyed boy, a not remarkably pretty but young and well-informed blue-eyed wife. His mother-in-law lives in a large château—the father-in-law just having died—with medieval towers and a slimy green moat. Nicholas and his wife inhabit a smaller house near it. Nicholas loves to take people around the château and has a regular guide's patter, including at certain points, as he says, typical guide's jokes. I have never seen him so comfortable and happy. His son Ivan by his first wife is about to marry the daughter of some highly-regarded French diplomat. But I can't help having the feeling that he (Nicholas) might suddenly become disgusted with the whole thing and drop it. He is writing an opera about Rasputin, with a libretto by Stephen Spender. He makes it sound dramatically marvellous but hasn't done much toward the music.[3]

Nicholas has a strange story about our Embassy's calling him up under the impression that he was the author of *Lolita* and asking how they could get twenty copies. The book is prominently displayed in several shops along the Rue de Rivoli.

Knowing my interest in Genet, Nicholas tried to arrange for me to meet him through neighbors of his who know him. Genet, he says, said, "Un Américain?

Est-ce qu'il a de l'argent pour me donner? Est-ce qu'il tape?"[4] When told probably not, he said that he had no interest in meeting me. He has had a great vogue
lately, the slightly expurgated edition of his works brought out by Gallimard
has sold about 10,000 a volume, and he has become a sort of public figure. When
Cocteau was received into the Academy, he sat beside the Queen of Belgium. I
read two more of his books last summer, which were better than the one I gave
you. I think you ought to look into them. He is really a formidable writer when
he gets the *bitte*[5] in his teeth.

I expect to go to Talcottville early in the spring next year and have every
intention of visiting Ithaca. But I hope we can arrange something in the meantime.

Another book you ought to read is Angus Wilson's *Anglo-Saxon Attitudes*.
En Attendant Godot[6]—which we saw in Paris—turns out to be a wonderful
play, though it didn't impress me so much when I read the text. In Germany
they are mad about Thomas Wolfe, a writer I have never been able to read, and
have dug up a play of his, written by him in his early twenties and never published or performed, the première of which I have been invited by the translator to attend.[7]

This will keep you abreast of literary developments in the Old World.

Love to Vera.

As ever,

EW

1. On the same day, Wilson also wrote to Morton D. Zabel about completing Goethe's
novel *The Sorrows of Young Werther*, which he had begun reading when he was learning
German "for Marxist purposes." See *Letters on Literature and Politics, 1912–1972*, p. 536.

2. Nicolas Nabokov spent much of the fifties and the early sixties arranging musical and
cultural festivals and conferences in Paris, Berlin, Rome, Tokyo and New Delhi.

3. *Rasputin's End*, known earlier as *The Holy Devil*, was eventually completed and performed in Louisville, Kentucky, and Cologne, Germany.

4. "An American? Does he have any money to give me? Does he borrow money?"

5. A pun on the French slang term for "cock" (penis) and the English locution that was
to provide the title of Wilson's 1965 book *The Bit Between My Teeth: A Literary Chronicle
of 1950–1965*.

6. *Waiting for Godot* by Samuel Beckett.

7. Wolfe's play *Mannerhouse* was widely performed in West Germany in 1953 in a translation by Peter Sandberg.

281

September 18, 1956
Cunard Line
R.M.S. "Queen Mary"

Dear Volodya: I have been reading the correspondence of Mérimée and Turgenev—*Une Amitié Littéraire* (Hachette, 1952). It turns out that you were mistaken in assuming that Mérimée knew no Russian, had his translations fed him by some lady. He was coached by Turgenev for over ten years. He translated a number of Turgenev's stories and checked on the translating of most of them. The dictionaries he used were inadequate, and he was always having to call on Turgenev. His deficiencies appear in these letters, but he does deserve a good deal of credit for pioneering in this field in France. I found the book very interesting and think that you ought to look into it. Mérimée on Pushkin is curious. He appreciates him in certain ways, but admits that he is no judge of poetry. What he really admires in Pushkin is the *côté* Mérimée.[1] I had forgotten how prudish and Victorian the Second Empire was. Turgenev is always being expurgated by the editor of *La Revue des Deux Mondes;* and Mérimée himself protests about the cruelty of Turgenev's stories.

I was able to get an earlier sailing, so am coming back earlier than I expected—landing today and shall be in Wellfleet by the end of the week.

As ever,

EW

1. "His Mérimée aspect."

282

October 22, 1956

Dear Bunny,

I enjoyed your letter about Mérimée. Yes, I will look at that book.

It was a pity not to find you in N.Y.C. where we spent a couple of days last week. I rang up the Princeton Club—and slowly put down the receiver as they do in the movies.

We participated in a little council with Epstein, Dupee, and Lasky to decide what part or parts of *Lolita* to publish in the *Anchor* magazine of which they want to devote one-fourth to her.[1] I am writing to you while supervising an examination on the *Slovo.*[2]

Véra (who supervises it too) joins me in sending Elena and you our very best love.

V.

Getting sick of teaching, wasting so much time.

1. The first appearance of *Lolita* in print in the United States was in the form of an excerpt in *Anchor Review*, No. 2, June 1957, with an introduction by F. W. Dupee. Melvin J. Lasky edited *Anchor Review* at the time.
2. *The [Igor] Tale.*

283

December 13, 1956

Dear Bunny,

I have not thanked you sooner for your book[1] because I wanted to read it first, but a busy spell interfered. We have both read it now and want to thank you very cordially for your charming inscription.

There are some delightful, first-rate pieces in it, such as the one about your father and the first of the two about the Jews, but I am as always distressed by your conception of Russian history,[2] which is all wrong, being based on the stale Bolshevist propaganda which you imbibed in your youth. I cannot understand how you, who appreciate so much Russian writers of the Nineteenth Century, can combine this appreciation with a complete ignorance of the *obshchestvennoe dvizhenie* (liberal movement)[3] that started in the time of Alexander I, was conspicuously present throughout the century (despite absolutism), and was deliberately played down by the Leninists and Trotskyists for propaganda reasons.

I also think that some of your zoological and biological considerations are unsound scientifically.[4]

We have been always frank with each other, and I know that you will find my criticism exhilarating.

Wonderful Jason Epstein flew over for lunch with an Englishwoman from Heineman's. I shall always be tremendously grateful to you for having put me in touch with Doubleday.

Véra and I would like to know about little Helen's operation—has she completely recovered by now? Are you all back in Wellfleet?

Our love to Elena and you, we wish you all a wonderful Christmas.

V

1. *A Piece of My Mind: Reflections at Sixty.*

2. In Section V of the book, "Russia," Wilson draws on the impressions of Melchior de Vogüé (who visited Russia in the 1880s) in order to compare that period with the post-Stalinist era and concludes that the country had always remained backward, oppressive and "Byzantine."

3. More precisely, the civic-protest movement which was responsible for the gradual liberalization of Russian society between the reforms of the 1860s and the October Revolution.

4. Reference to Section VIII of *A Piece of My Mind*, "Science," which is couched in the form of a dialogue between a zoologist and an iguana on the principles of evolution.

284

Edmund Wilson
Wellfleet, Cape Cod
Massachusetts

December 20, 1956

Dear Volodya: Of course I know about the liberal movement in Russia, and—though it failed—do not undervalue it. But the subject did not have any relevance to what I was writing about in *Piece of My Mind*. I'm doing a long essay on Turgenev—a liberal, but one who became more and more pessimistic.[1]

I'm looking forward to the spring, when I hope to be able to come to Ithaca from Talcottville—about the beginning of June. In the meantime, we've taken a home in Cambridge and are moving there Jan. 18: 16 Farrar St.; Kirkland 7-3445. Is there any chance of your coming to Cambridge during the spring vacation?

I am enclosing an American primitive appropriate to upstate New York. I have been given a collection of them, and am using them for Christmas cards.

Поклонитесь от меня всем Вашим—крепко и дружески жму Вашу руку (как написал Толстому Тургенев).[2]

E.W.

Yes: Helen has recovered from her operation—she went back to school today.

1. "Turgenev and the Life-Giving Drop," which appeared in *The New Yorker* on October 19, 1957 and was later included in *A Window on Russia*.

2. "Give my regards to your entire family—I firmly and amicably clasp your hand (as Turgenev wrote to Tolstoy)." The slightly inappropriate choice of the perfective form of "wrote" mars this otherwise elegant and idiomatic Russian salutation.

1957

285

Dear Bunny,

Yes, Monarchists and Bolsheviks are united in abominating Liberals (from Mensheviks to Oktyabrists,[1]—including, of course, the *Partiya Narodnoy Svobodï*,[2] to which my father and Milyukov belonged). And you are also right in assuming nobody paid much attention to these attacks: Monarchists and Fascists were culturally of no significance whatsoever in the history of Russian emigration, though politically they were, and still are, extremely active. They derive their financial support from American snobs. *D'ailleurs*,[3] if you turn to Chapter 13 of my CONCLUSIVE EVIDENCE, you will find all the information you need on the question.

It might also interest you to know, perhaps, that the British government has requested the French Government to ban the books of American authors, written in English and published in Paris (including my LOLITA), and the French Government was glad to oblige. The indignation of the French press does not seem to have been reflected in the American press.

We are very eager to see both of you. We may come to Cambridge on a warm day in spring. How long are you going to be there?

I would like you so much to see Dmitri who is a marvelous fellow with a Shalyapinesque voice.[4]

I am finishing a long discussion of English and Russian prosodies (mainly in connection with the iambic tetrameter).[5]

> Дружески жму (zhmu)
> руку. Мы оба шлем вам
> обоим сердечнейший привет.[6]
> V

1. The Mensheviks were the Marxist Social Democrats who dissented from Lenin's totalitarian program; the "Oktyabrists," better known in English as the Octobrist Party, split off from the Constitutional Democrats after the Revolution of 1905 due to their support of the October Manifesto of Nicholas II, which most of the other moderate and radical parties did not consider sufficiently democratic. Nabokov sets these two parties up as the opposite extremes of the political spectrum that stood for democratization and political freedom in pre-revolutionary Russia.

2. "The Party of the People's Freedom," otherwise known as the Constitutional Democratic party, of which Pavel Milyukov and Nabokov's father were co-founders. It was in protecting Milyukov from an assassination attempt that the senior Nabokov lost his life.

3. "Besides."

4. Dmitri Nabokov was beginning his career as an operatic basso and his father is comparing him to his illustrious predecessor Fyodor Chaliapin.

5. Appendix Two to the *Onegin* commentary, "Notes on Prosody," also published later as a separate booklet.

6. "I clasp *(clasp)* your hand amicably. Both of us send both of you our most cordial regards." The transliterated word is one more humorous violation of Wilson's behest not to transcribe Russian into Latin letters.

286

Goldwin Smith Hall
Cornell, Ithaca, NY.

February 18, 1957

Dear Bunny,

Dmitri tells us in his last letter that he had a wonderful time with Elena, you and Roman. We envied him.

Tol'ko chto pereehali (только что переѣхали)[1] into another (enchanting) house. We shall stay here most of the summer. To the good apprehender, salute.

One exquisite point about PNIN is the little conversation between Pnin and Chateau about me and the blue butterflies at their feet. I actually described and named that particular Lycaenid (*Lycaeides samuelis* Nabokov, type locality Karner, near Albany, N.Y.).[2]

The British Government (Home Office) Гом Оффис[3] has asked the French Minister of the Interior to ban books in English detrimental to the morals of British and American tourists. France complied. A number of French newspapers have voiced their indignation, and "L'affaire Lolita" is in full swing.

How are you, dear *drug?*[4] I thought you looked fine in the little portrait in *The New Yorker.*[5]

Vale[6]—as Voltaire, Onegin and Pushkin used to say.

Yours,
V

1. "We have just moved" (transliterated and then in Cyrillic letters).
2. "Look, how pretty," said observant Chateau.

   A score of small butterflies, all of one kind, were settled on a damp patch of
   sand, their wings erect and closed, showing their pale undersides with dark dots

and tiny orange-rimmed peacock spots along the hindwing margins; one of Pnin's shed rubbers disturbed some of them and, revealing the celestial hue of their upper surface, they fluttered around like blue snowflakes before settling again.

"Pity Vladimir Vladimirovich is not here," remarked Chateau. "He would have told us all about these enchanting insects."

"I have always had the impression that his entomology was merely a pose."

"Oh no," said Chateau.

Pnin, Chapter Five

3. The English words "Home Office" in a slightly whimsical transcription.

4. "Friend."

5. This seems to be a humorous reference to the butterfly-ogling fop Eustace Tilley, whose likeness graced the cover of that week's issue of *The New Yorker*, as it does every February.

6. "Farewell" (in Latin).

287

February 29, 1957
16 Farrar St.
Cambridge, Mass.

Dear Volodya: I am more like a dear drug than a dear друг,[1] having been in bed with bronchitis and laryngitis for the better part of two weeks. I went on to New York to be at rehearsals of *Cyprian's Prayer*, which New York University put on, and had a relapse. It is absurd and characteristic of the British that they should take steps to ban English books in France. Have you been following the cases of book-banning before the Supreme Court now? It has just handed down a decision that one of the local Michigan laws against "indecent" books is unconstitutional. If they come to the same conclusion in the two other cases they have—one of which comes from New York—it will probably be possible to republish *Hecate County*, and, I should think, bring out *Lolita* over here. Here is another one of these monarchist curiosities. They amaze me.

As ever,

<u>EW</u>

We had a very pleasant evening with Roman and Dmitri—think Dmitri is a fine boy.

1. The Russian word for friend happens to be *drug*.

The Letters, 1957

288

Dear Volodya: The arrival of *Pnin* has done something to cheer up this rather desolated household—we have had nothing but miseries since we came here: everybody has been more or less ill, and I lost my voice again—to say nothing of other troubles. On top of everything else, our old dog Bambi died. *Pnin*, then, was especially welcome. I think it is very good, and also that you may at last have made contact with the great American public. My reason for thinking this is that the reviews I have so far seen all say exactly the same thing: this shows that no one is puzzled, they know how they are meant to react. By some miracle, the picture on the jacket is excellent. I enclose some corrections and suggestions. There are the usual Doubleday misprints, but not quite so bad as usual. Perhaps this may lead to an interest in *Lolita*. Another of the books in that series, *The Ginger Man*[1]—which was sent me with *Lolita* and which I thought was garbage—has been published in the regular way in England and is getting respectful reviews. It is certainly the height of absurdity that the British government should ask the French to protect British tourists from naughty books, and that the French should accede to this request.

William James,[2] who lives at the end of this street, has asked me to send you his regards. I suppose you know that his wife has had a stroke and does not seem to improve. We hobnob back and forth, having drinks at one another's houses.

Love to Vera. Elena says be sure to tell you how she likes *Pnin*.

As ever,

EW

52　have not the least intention *of being* (not *to be*) dropped . . .

63　*Choosy* is vulgar and not used quite right here. *Fastidious* would be better.

96　*kidnapped*—two p's

110　*brought down the house* is incorrect in this context. A fine performance on the stage brings down the house.

116　An irrelevant i has got into *prosperous*.

122　Why do you follow Constance Garnett's foolish idea of leaving the a off Anna Karenina?

124　*In the half a dozen rooms* is incorrect: in this case, you have to say *half dozen*.

130   *Teamed* is amusingly misspelled.

132   The pronunciation of tsh *(tshay)* is no different from ch in English.

164   *three hundred sixty-five* is vulgar—there should be an *and*.

188   We arrived at last to . . . This is impossible: should be *arrived at*.

177   *Grandaunt* doesn't exist—should be *great aunt*.

190   *Crenulated* should be *crenellated.*[3]

1. By J. P. Donleavy. Like *Lolita*, it was originally brought out by the Olympia Press in Paris.

2. William (Billy) James (1882–1961), painter and art teacher, was the second son of the philosopher William James.

3. Except for the correction of the spelling of "prosperous," none of these suggestions was heeded and the passages Wilson indicated were allowed to stand in later editions of *Pnin*—including "Pnin, who teemed with Madame Bolotov." The last of Wilson's corrections is erroneous, since "crenulated" and not "crenellated" is clearly indicated by the context.

289

March 24, 1957

Dear Bunny,

With a dense glaucous cold in my head, and as hoarse as a лошадь,[1] I lectured the other day through the fog of my throat on Dostoevsky's *Memoirs from a Mousehole*,[2] and so can well sympathize with you and your family. Do take care of yourself, друже[3] (hope you know this wonderful vocative case).

I am a little disturbed about your peripatetic tippling with Billy James. As the younger and sturdier boy you should be aware of his not being supposed to drink. I hope you like him as well as I do. My father considered his father's works as one of the greatest and most brilliant contributions to psychology and had me read him when I was twelve or thirteen. Billy is a dear soul with an admirable delicacy of string-tone.

I am completely engrossed in my *Onegin*, and *must* finish him this year. I have at last discovered the right way to translate *Onegin*. This is the fifth or sixth complete version that I have made. I am now breaking it up, banishing everything that honesty might deem verbal velvet and, in fact, welcoming the awkward turn, the fish bone of the meager truth. You, who have Greek, could you tell me (I need this badly) if "nor the storm-wind with its swirl of shingle, shall buffet and sweep away/ a treasure house of songs/" is a literal translation of a passage (around lines 11–13) in Pindar's ode for Xenocrates, or is it just a fancy British paraphrase (by Sir John Something, a "fain-doth" fellow, in the Loeb classical library, p. 249),[4] that most exasperating of all forms of belles-lettres in the world: how I loathe the elegant scholar!

I keep fretting at the space and time element that keeps preventing us from seeing more of each other.

Regards from Véra and me to Elena and you.

Yours,

V

[In Wilson's handwriting at top]
treasure house mentioned in strophe before thunder cloud

1. "Horse."

2. *I.e., Notes from the Underground.* A closer rendition of the Russian title would be *Diary* (or *Memoirs*) *Written in a Basement.*

3. "Friend" (in the vocative case).

4. "Sir John Something" was Sir John Edwin Sandys, the translator and editor of Pindarus, *Greek and English Odes,* London, 1919, to which edition Nabokov refers.

290

March 26, 1957
Widener Library

Dear Volodya: *The Treasure house of songs* is in the strophe before. This strophe begins: "This neither the wintry storm," etc. Is this Sir Somebody's translation of the whole passage? There is quite a lot more in it. Here is a literal translation from the notes of a class-room text (*Pindar: The Olympian & Pythian Odes, with notes, etc., etc.,* by C. A. M. Fennell, Cambridge University Press):

"Which neither the wintry rain-storm, coming as an invading foe, the ruthless host (army) of the deep-roaring cloud, nor the wind carries to the hollows of the sea, battered by the all-sweeping débris."

As I write this out, I see it is not really literal. ἐπακτός ἐλθών means simply *coming from somewhere else,* not *as an invading army.* Liddell & Scott's dictionary makes it "driving in on one."

Here is another prose version (*The Extant Odes of Pindar, Translated into English,* by Ernest Myers):

"That treasure of his shall neither wind nor wintry rain-storm coming from strange lands, as a fierce host born of the thunderous cloud, carry into the hiding places of the sea, to be beaten by the all-sweeping drift."

Sir Somebody's *shingle* may be all right for χερά̨ς, though Fennell believes "it is rather wood and floating wreckage generally." It might be argued that Sir Somebody is trying to reproduce Pindar's knotty style.

By the way did you know that Russian я was originally Greek α̨, which is called alpha with iota subscript:

I never knew why they wrote this parasitic iota, and now it has occurred to me that this combination may have been pronounced like я.[1]

More miseries: most of the teeth in my upper jaw have suddenly fallen out, and Helen has just had to have one pulled. Elena has been going to the dentist for weeks so that she won't lose all of hers.

EW

1. Contrary to Wilson's evolutionary scheme, the Russian letter я had no direct Greek antecedents. Its shape and design were selected by Peter the Great during his reform of the printed alphabet in 1708–1710 and were based on an earlier Cyrillic digraph not connected in any way in either shape or sound with the ancient Greek diphthong represented by the alpha with iota subscript.

291

Dear Bunny,

Your delightful telegram enhanced my desire to drink and smoke with you and Billy. I shall have to visit Houghton Library some time in the early summer. Véra and I shall be heading for Vermont in May or early June for a reunion with three species of butterflies we especially like. We shall get in touch with you and Elena when we get to Cambridge.

I want to thank you very much for your helpful letter about Pindar. It seems that translators from the Greek have more trouble than Babette and the inimitable Elton have from the Russian.[1]

Best love,
V.

1. Babette Deutsch and Oliver Elton, Nabokov's predecessors in translating *Eugene Onegin* into English.

292

Dear Volodya: I don't know whether you know that Alice James just died.

Won't you be in Ithaca in late May or June? We have to leave here in the middle of May. I was planning to spend a little while at Wellfleet, then go to Talcottville.

EW

293

April 22, 1957

Dear Bunny,

It is beautiful here—all kinds of birds around our house in the tender woods—flickers, and waxwings, and blue jays, and the thrushes misnamed "robins."

In the first fortnight of May, depending on the season, we may travel to Vermont (and Cambridge, perhaps) for a butterfly (and a scholium), but otherwise we shall spend the summer (or most of it) in Ithaca. As long as Dmitri is away, we can offer you his room (with two beds and a bathroom), later we can put you up at the little hotel you know. We would be delighted if you and Elena could come for a visit.

We are dreadfully sorry for poor Billy James. Do you have a good dentist? We have just been for a day in NYC and had lunch with Ken McCormick and Jason. It was all very pleasant. Have to rush to a lecture. . . .

Love from both to both

I shall be 48 to-morrow.[1]

V

1. Plus one decade more.

294

Edmund Wilson
Wellfleet, Cape Cod
Massachusetts

June 12, 1957

To Volodya:

1) *Nihilist* is pronounced the way I pronounce it—not *neehilist:* see any dictionary.[1]

2) I have just been examining *Rukoyu Pushkina*.[2] There is an account, in the foreword to Part I, of Pushkin's efforts to do something with some sixteen languages which is confirmed by the notebooks that follow. On pp. 28, 90, 99, 102, 506 and 597, you find translations or quotations from English authors—including people like Barry Cornwall and Wordsworth, whom he could hardly have read in French; and on pp. 90, 98–99, you find him translating English word for word and sometimes writing the English words in. In the middle of 99, he obviously doesn't know how to deal with *wins* in the fourth stanza of *To Ianthe*.[3] He could hardly have picked up, in *Evgeni Onegin*, something of Byron's rhythms, as he did, without ever having read him in anything but French. As for Latin and Greek, there is plenty of evidence here that he knew a certain amount of Latin—in one case (p. 103), he makes a version of a passage from Juvenal. The French words he sometimes writes in, in these passages, come evidently not from cribs but from dictionaries. It seems to me that Pushkin's verse shows clearly an acquaintance with Latin poetry—tricks of style that he could not have learned from French. He had made enough headway with Greek to transcribe an ode of Sappho's and to attempt—again, word for word—a translation of the opening of the *Odyssey*. The facsimile on p. 61 of his transcription of the Hebrew alphabet shows—in his equating *aleph* to Greek *alpha*—that he had learned to write Greek characters quite fluently.

(I have conceived, by the way, a theory to account for your strange desire—in the face of incon[tro]vertible evidence—to believe that Pushkin knew no English and Turgenev little English—a theory which I expect to develop in the étude un peu approfondie which I hope to *consacrer à votre oeuvre*.)[4]

3) You are really off the track in wanting to have the coachmen or whoever they are *knock* their hands in *Evgeni Onegin*. The natural English is *slap*. You say that *knock* in this sense occurs in Cooper and Thompson, but I never remember to have seen it, and this and *beat goose* will seem outlandish to the reader. Such obsolete expressions need as much explanation as the obsolete expressions and meanings in Pushkin which you have set yourself the task of illuminating.

4) On the other hand, you are certainly right about the absence of urination in that seashore passage of *Ulysses*. I was bemused by those little Smith students.

Other matters may be left to our next encounter.

To Vera: My visit to Ithaca[5] was a godsend to me—though I'm afraid a nuisance to you—on account of my gouty condition. I finally went to New York on Tuesday to get out of my cold house and only recovered at the end of the week —though in time for Henry's wedding, which was a very festive affair, with champagne flowing, young people dancing for hours, and everybody pleased with the bride and groom.

I am back in Wellfleet till at least the 20th; after that, Talcottville again. Elena sends love, and we hope you will come to see us.

I hope that *Lolita*, as a study of amorous paternity and delinquent girlhood, will touch the American public to the point of making your fortune. If you can get her married to Pnin in Alaska and bring them home to life tenure and the American way of life in some comfortable Middle Western university, you may be able to compete in popularity with *Marjorie Morningstar* and be lecturing on young people's problems from Bangor to San Diego.

George Munn,[6] by the way, told his mother that he was fascinated by our conversation—especially by our argument over metrics. I was afraid he was being bored. Thank you for your old Russian hospitality to both of us.

As ever,
Edmund W[7]

[In Nabokov's hand at top: barely legible sketches of points 1, 2, and 3 of his reply to this letter]

1. "He tried to tell me right now that *nihilist* in English was pronounced *neehilist.*" *Upstate* (see note 5 below).
2. *In Pushkin's Own Hand*, a compilation of his sketches and jottings, edited by Lev Modzalevsky, Tatiana Zenger and Mstislav Tsiavlovsky, Moscow, 1935.
3. By Byron.
4. As sketched out in *Upstate*, this theory reads:

> "... he asserts, on no evidence whatever and contrary to the well-known facts, that Mérimée knew no Russian and Turgenev knew only enough English to enable him to read a newspaper. He denies that Russians deserve their reputation of being remarkably good linguists and says of every Russian who speaks good English that he or she had had the advantage of a governess or a tutor—though

I met in the Soviet Union a number of young Russians who had learned to speak excellent English without ever having been out of Russia. These false ideas, of course, are prompted by his compulsion to think of himself as the only writer in history who has been equally proficient in Russian, English and French ..."
(p. 160)

5. The visit of May 25–28, 1957, which was recorded by Wilson in his diary that was subsequently published in his book *Upstate* in 1971. The publication led to Nabokov's angry rebuttal in his letter to the editor of *The New York Times*, November 7, 1971, reprinted in *Strong Opinions*, pp. 218–219. For a more detailed account of this visit, see the Section "Visit to Nabokov" of Wilson's diaries in *The Fifties*, Leon Edel, editor, 1986.

6. The son of Wilson's cousin Otis Munn, who accompanied him on his visit to the Nabokovs.

7. In the available two-page copy of this letter, the figures of the numbered points read 1, 2, 3, and 5 (changed to 4 by the present editor), which suggests that a page in the middle of point 3 of the letter might be missing. Elena Wilson felt, however, that the letter is complete as it stands and that the discrepancy in the numbers was an error. This view is supported by Nabokov's numbered answers (Letter 295), where the reply to Wilson's point 3 fits the two-page text in every particular.

295

June 17, 1957

Dear Bunny,

It was good and invigorating to have you here. I hope the gout has gone for good.

1. I don't understand your observation about "nihilist." In Russian it is pronounced nee-gee (hard "g")-leest, with accent on the last syllable.

2. I have been studying the question of Pushkin's knowledge of foreign languages for about ten years now and really you should not send me to *Rukoyu Pushkina*. You will find a complete analysis of the matter in my commentary to *E.O.* Pushkin got what you call "Byron's rhythms" from Zhukovsky's versions of English poems.

3. By a singular coincidence I have just dipped into Matthew Arnold and found "the Gypsy knocks his hands." By the way, the translator's duty, as I understand it, is not to simplify or modernize an obscure or antiquated term in the original, but to render its obscurity and oddity.

Yes, I shall certainly enjoy another rencontre with you, and explain to you again and again that Pushkin knew English, Latin, etc., just about as well as Salisbury[1] knows Russian, or Auden French.

It is a delight to have Dmitri here. He is diligently working on an index for my *Onegin,* and some of his suggestions and criticisms are most intelligent and stimulating.

Love from both of us to both of you.

V

1. Harrison E. Salisbury (1908–1993), a journalist who published several books on the Soviet Union, in which he liked to quote Russian words and phrases, almost invariably getting them wrong or misspelling them.

296

Edmund Wilson
Wellfleet, Cape Cod
Massachusetts

June 20, 1957

Dear V:

1) My observation on *Nihilist* was prompted by your having corrected my pronunciation, apparently under the impression that the first syllable in English was pronounced *Nee.*

2) I learn from Troyat and Mirsky that Pushkin worked on Byron in English with the Raevskys in 1820. Opening the *Путешествие в Арзрум,*[1] I find two quotations in English from English poems, one of them from *Lalla Rookh,* as well as two quotations from Latin poems. Looking into his letters of this period, I find quite a sprinkling of Latin, including, in a letter to Gnedich of April 29, 1822, a Latin elegiac couplet, followed by a Latin hexameter, which he must have written himself and which would indicate a certain proficiency.[2] At the time I read *Onegin* in 1936, I couldn't have known much more Russian than Pushkin did English in his early stages of reading Byron, and I now realize that I sometimes misunderstood the text and undoubtedly got accents wrong, but I was able to enjoy the poem and to make English versions of passages which you were good enough to say were not so bad as the worst. It seems to me that— since you yourself learned to speak foreign languages early and didn't, I gather, study the ancient ones, of which we only know the literature without even having very much idea of how the words were pronounced—you fail to appreciate how far the literary knowledge of a language, even if imperfect, may take one. If Pushkin knew as much English as Auden knows French, he would not be at all badly off, for although Auden may not be aware that you cannot say "Le

monde est ronde,"³ I know that he has read a good deal of French. If anyone set out to discredit yourself by such methods as you use on Auden and Steegmuller, he would have no difficulty in demonstrating—by citing some of your slips in English and your notorious misapprehension of the meaning of *fastidieux*—that you knew neither English nor French—and were perhaps even shaky in Russian, since I remember your once telling me that *самодур* had nothing to do with *дурак*.⁴ (By the way, Zhukovsky didn't translate *Don Juan*, did he?—the rhythm of which, though the stanza form is different, certainly influenced *Онегин*.⁵

3) As for rendering obscure and antiquated terms in the language from which one is translating by obscure and antiquated equivalents, I am wondering how you will render *стогны*.⁶

The Joyce letters are wonderful, and at the end very tragic. They have had nothing but stupid reviews—the worst in the *London Times Literary Supplement*.⁷ How the English—including Spender—seem to want to pretend that Joyce was not important! It appears that he was immensely enthusiastic about a story of Tolstoy's called *Много ли человеку земли нужно*.⁸ I have just looked it up and read it, and though it is a good enough little story, I don't quite understand Joyce's interest in it.

As ever,

Edmund W

I'll be back in Talcottville in a few days now, if you want to prolong this polemic.

June 21, 1957

—I forgot about "Et in Arcadia ego"—Turgenev in *Переписка*⁹ has: «И мы бывали в Аркадии, и мы скитались по светлым ее полям!»¹⁰ This evidently derives from Virgil's Seventh Eclogue: "Ambo florentes aetatibus, Arcades ambo," followed later by "Huc ipsi potum venient *per prata* (through the meadows) juvenci."¹¹ Or Turgenev may have confused the two quotations. But the Soviet edition says it refers to a poem of Schiller's, which begins, "Auch war in Arkadien geboren."¹² Now Schiller is obviously thinking of "Et in Arcadia," etc., and for this Larousse refers you to Poussin's picture *Les Bergers d'Arcadie*,¹³ in which there is a tomb with the words "Et in Arcadia ego"¹⁴—But where did Poussin get this? I seem distinctly to remember that the phrase originally ended with a *vixi*¹⁵—though I sometimes imagine such things. But it must have ended with something. (Larousse explains it, J'ai vécu.) Where did you get the idea that it comes from the Middle Ages? In the picture, the *ego* does not refer to Death, as I understood you to say it originally had, but to the dead man in the tomb. The live shepherds are reading the inscription. Says Death: Even in Arcadia am I.

1. *Journey to Arzrum.*

2. The Latin verses in this letter of Pushkin's are actually a three-line quotation from Ovid's *Tristia,* cited in sequence.

3. "The world is round," with a feminine adjective modifying a masculine noun.

4. See Letter 278 and notes 2 and 3 to that letter.

5. *Onegin.*

6. An archaic and poetic word for "city square."

7. "Letters Penyeach," in the *Times Literary Supplement,* May 24, 1957. The anonymous reviewer sneers at Joyce's personality and achievement, concluding that his letters and writings belong only in academic curricula.

8. "How Much Land Does a Person Need?" translated into English as "How Much Land Does a Man Need?"

9. "A Correspondence" (a short story by Ivan Turgenev).

10. "We too have been to Arcadia, we too have roamed over her fair fields."

11. "Both in the bloom of life, both Arcadians" [...] "Hither your steers will of themselves come over to drink." Lines 4 and 11 of Virgil's Seventh Eclogue.

12. The opening line of Friedrich Schiller's poem "Resignation," which actually reads: "Auch ich war in Arkadien geboren" ("I too was born in Arcadia"). While the commentators to the recent Soviet editions of Turgenev cite the opening line of Schiller's "Resignation" as the source of the passage Wilson quotes (see note 10 above for translation), there is a much closer Russian source, both in content and in wording. This is Konstantin Batyushkov's poem "Inscription on the Grave on a Shepherdess" (1810), also familiar from its setting to music as Pauline's aria in Tchaikovsky's *The Queen of Spades.* The annotators to the academic editions of Batyushkov connect this poem and its imagery with Poussin's *Les Bergers d'Arcadie,* mentioned in this letter.

13. "The Arcadian Shepherds."

14. "Even in Arcadia am I ..."

15. "Lived."

297

Goldwin Smith Hall
Cornell, Ithaca, NY.

August 7, 1957

Dear Bunny,

This is a business proposition:

The English faculty wonders if you would consider coming to Cornell at any time during the academic year 1957–58, for four or five days, in the course of which you would be expected to give two or three talks and hobnob with the faculty. They offer you five hundred dollars. If you agree to come, the head of the faculty will write you an official invitation with all particulars. I do hope you can come, and if you do, that it might be during the fall semester, since there is a chance I might go away during the second semester.

My source for understanding *et in Arcadia ego,* meaning "I (Death) (exist) even in Arcady," is an excellent essay in Erwin Panofsky's THE MEANING OF THE VISUAL ARTS, Anchor Books, New York, 1955.

I expect to finish my commentaries to ONEGIN in the course of this month. I feel sometimes utterly exhausted and dejected, but when I read in Southey's CORRESPONDENCE what labors *he* performed every day, I feel that I am basking in indolence, as Pushkin would say.

Véra joins me in sending Elena and you our best love.

Yours,

V

298

Edmund Wilson
Talcottville
Lewis County
New York

August 9, 1957

Dear Volodya: I can't do these academic visits nowadays. Please thank them for me. Don't you want to come over here for a day or two after you have finished *Onegin?* By the way, I have lately acquired the two volumes of Mérimée's Russian studies, which include an essay on Pushkin. Also, the first half dozen volumes of the complete Goncourt journals—they have resorted to printing them in Monaco. I had supposed that the difficulty about publishing them was due to the threat of libel suits, but I find that they are terrifically indecent. The Goncourts put in everything their friends ever told them about their sexual adventures—such as how Flaubert lost his virginity—and every dirty story that was going around Paris. Have you ever read Dujardin's *Les Lauriers Sont Coupés,*[1] which gave Joyce the idea for the interior monologue? I think it is remarkably good.

Love to Vera,

EW

1. *The Laurels Have Been Cut* by Édouard Dujardin. The English translation bears the title *We'll to the Woods No More.* In his letter to Philippe (Phito) and Eva Thoby-Marcelin of August 10, 1957, Wilson wrote: "This year I read Dujardin's *Les Lauriers Sont Coupés* that Phito gave me a couple of years ago. I thought it was awfully good, a masterpiece in a small way." (*Letters on Literature and Politics, 1912–1972,* p. 470)

1958

299

Goldwin Smith Hall
Cornell Univ[ersity]
Ithaca, N.Y.

In bed, with facial neuralgia.

February 15, 1958

Dear Bunny,

I have not heard from you since the beginning of the pre-snow era. How are you? Всё хорошо?[1]

We have moved to another house much larger—but also much colder than our charming picture-window place among the cardinals, junkos, and waxwings (where you were once enthroned with your gout).

I have just *completely completed* my *Eugene Onegin: 2500* pages of commentaries, and a literal translation of the text. Dmitri is making the index. Did Doubleday send you the Lermontov book? How are your Russian studies progressing? Whatever you do, steer clear of the Goncharov-Aksakov-Saltïkov-Leskov porridgy mass.[2] Vera and I send our love to Elena. Write me *un mot.*[3]

Yours,

V.

1. "Is everything all right?"
2. "Saltïkov" is Nabokov's transcription for Mikhail Saltykov-Shchedrin (1826–1889). Nabokov's conflicting attitude toward the lesser masters of Russian nineteenth-century literature is reflected in Fyodor's first imaginary dialogue with the poet Koncheyev at the end of Chapter One of *The Gift.* On Aksakov and Nabokov, see Letter 112, note 7.
3. "A word."

Edmund Wilson
Wellfleet, Cape Cod
Massachusetts

February 23, 1958

Dear Volodya: Your letter has reminded me to send you my new book.[1] I doubt whether you will want to read much of it—though you might try "What to Do Till the Doctor Comes," my favorite chapter—but I like to keep up our exchange in the hope of getting a complete collection of your publications. I haven't been able to read these yet, because I am trying to finish up the Civil War and have to get through quantities of military memoirs and boring Southern novels.[2] I'm glad to hear you've finished the *Onegin* and look forward especially to seeing you do justice to Pushkin's knowledge of foreign languages. Who is going to bring it out? Sorry to hear you've been ill. We have been having another rather miserable winter, but not so bad as the last, and now we are cleaning up. I made a week's trip, at the end of January, to the Indian reservation in southwestern New York to assist at their New Year's ceremonies—very extraordinary but too long to write about.[3] Going into that part of the world seems always to bring on my gout—I have had it as badly as last spring. Doubleday did send me the Lermontov,[4] which I thought was very well done: you have pretty well caught the vein of the English narrative prose of that period. (On p. 161 *twinkle* ought to be *twinkling,* and it would be better to say at the end of that ¶: Since his horse invariably stopped,[5] etc.) About the chameleonlike changes of color, they are no doubt overdone, but I believe that people used to change color more often than they do now.[6] I know one old-fashioned woman who does blush like the women in books (Peggy Bacon, the artist).

Elena sends love to you both.

As ever,

EW

1. *The American Earthquake: A Documentary of the Twenties and Thirties.*
2. As part of the research for *Patriotic Gore: Studies in the Literature of the American Civil War,* on which Wilson was working.
3. As part of the research on the essays that were later to comprise *Apologies to the Iroquois.*
4. Nabokov's edition of *A Hero of Our Time.*
5. The passage to which these corrections refer reads:

In a twinkle we had galloped past the fort by way of the suburb, and entered the gorge along which the road wound, half-choked with tall grasses, and constantly crossed and recrossed by a loud brook, which had to be forded, to the great dismay of the doctor, for every time his horse stopped in the water.

6. In the "Translator's Foreword" Nabokov wrote:

The nineteenth century Russian writer's indifference to exact shades of visual color leads to an acceptance of rather droll epithets condoned by literary usage (a surprising thing in the case of Lermontov, who was not only a painter in the literal sense, but saw colors and was able to name them); thus in the course of *A Hero* the faces of various people turn purple, red, rosy, orange, green and blue.

This is followed by a paragraph that lists the various shades of pallor encountered in the novel; an appended footnote cites some rather gaudy changes of facial color that Nabokov found in the novels of Balzac.

301

Goldwin Smith Hall
Ithaca, N.Y.

March 30, 1958

Dear Bunny,

Véra and I thank you very much for your *American Earthquake*. We enjoyed many of the plums in it. What happened to the poor man whom the artist saw, but the political moralist misunderstood?[1] He keeps haunting us. The Upton Sinclair-Eisenstadt adventures are hilarious.[2]

My agents report that you will be staying at Lowell House. Do give our best regards to Perkins and his wife.[3] Dmitri had a wonderful time in that house.

We still hope to see Elena and you before we go to our native West and you to alien Europe.

Did *The Reporter* send you a copy of the issue with my story about the twins?[4]

Yours,

V.

1. Apparently a reference to the article "The Stieglitz Exhibition" and its afterword written in 1957, where Wilson recalled that Alfred Stieglitz played down the painter Charles Demuth after having earlier championed his reputation because he felt that Demuth "was either not at all the real thing or had been ruined by a craving for worldly success." (*The American Earthquake*, p. 102)

2. The article "Eisenstein in Hollywood," which is an account of Upton Sinclair's ill-starred financing of Eisenstein's film *Que Viva Mexico!* As in Letter 172, Nabokov again refers to Sergei Eisenstein as "Eisenstadt."

3. Elliot Perkins, professor of history, was Master of Lowell House at Harvard from 1941 to 1962. When Dmitri Nabokov lived there as an undergraduate he got to know him and his English-born wife Mary.

4. "Scenes from the Life of a Double Monster," which appeared in *The Reporter* on March 20, 1958.

302

Edmund Wilson
Wellfleet, Cape Cod
Massachusetts

April 7, 1958

Глубокоуважаемый Вова![1]

We are not going abroad, so I may possibly see you before you leave Cornell. My work on the Iroquois Indians may carry me over there (have I told you about it?).[2] The Siamese Twins is the beginning of a novel, isn't it?[3] I look forward to reading the rest. Nina Chavchavadze has been commissioned by Yale to translate parts of the Сказание Авраама Палицына[4] and is having an awful time. Do you happen to know if a translation into modern Russian exists or a text with linguistic notes? I can't find anything in the Widener Library but the same Soviet text she is using.

С совершенным уважением,[5]

EW

1. "Highly Esteemed Vova!" In Russian, there is a humorous incongruity between the solemn adjective and the diminutive form of Vladimir, Vova, which is a nickname used for children.

2. Wilson spent most of the summer of 1958 with the Iroquois.

3. "Scenes from the Life of a Double Monster" was begun as a novel but ended up as a self-contained short story.

4. "The Chronicle of Avraam Palitsyn." Palitsyn (d. 1626; his first name was Avraamy rather than Avraam) was a learned monk who wrote an eyewitness account of the Polish invasion of Russia during the Time of Troubles (1604–1618), much admired for its language and style.

5. "With perfect esteem."

303

Goldwin Smith Hall
Ithaca, N.Y.

May 10, 1958

Dear Elena and Bunny,

We shall be leaving on June 1. Is there any chance of your coming out here before then? We would be delighted to have you.

We have been kept very busy by proofs of various translations of *Lolita* and *Pnin*. This is why I have not written you sooner to say I did not know of any modern Russian version of the *Skazanie*.[1] Passages might be found in Russian school anthologies.

It would be nice to see you both before our departure for the West.

Sincerely,
V & V

1. See the preceding letter, note 4.

304

May 13, 1958
Wellfleet

Unfortunately I'm not leaving here till June 2. Shall be in Talcottville till after Labor Day, if you should be back before then.

Съ большимъ уваженіемъ[1]

EW

1. "With great esteem" (in old orthography).

305

May 20, 1958
Wellfleet, Mass.

Thanks for your note. I am leaving for New York State next week—so my address will be BOONVILLE RFD 1, Oneida Co. I may be making an expedition in

September which could include a stop off in Ithaca, in which case I'll call up and find whether you are back.

EW

306

Ithaca, N.Y.

May 24, 1958

Dear Bunny,

Your piece on Toile,[1] T. S. is absolutely wonderful, it is one of your very best essays, lucid, acid and wise. I realize that you still think a lot of him as a poet, and I disagree with you when you say that his verses lodge in one's head (they never did in mine—I always disliked him)—but you have pricked a ripe amber pimple and from now on, Eliot's image will never be the same.

I am hideously busy, but wanted to dash off these few words of affectionate appreciation.

Yours,

V.

Could you ask Straus to send me the Magarshack Turgenev?[2]

1. Meant to be read backwards. Wilson's essay "T. S. Eliot and the Church of England" was included in his volume of essays *A Literary Chronicle: 1920–1950*, published in 1956.
2. Turgenev, *Literary Reminiscences and Autobiographical Fragments*, translated by David Magarshack (New York: Farrar, Straus & Cudahy, 1958). The volume contained Wilson's essay "Turgenev and the Life-Giving Drop" mentioned in Letter 284.

1959

307

c/o Putnam
210 Madison Avenue
New York 16, NY.

March 2, 1959

Dear Bunny,

After long delays we have left Ithaca—for one year. I would not have been able to abandon my students if I had not found a person (Herbert Gold, a young writer) to replace me in both courses, European Masterpieces and Russian Literature. We intend to stay in New York till mid-March and then drive south-westward, to Arizona. And sometime in autumn we plan to go for a couple of months to the ancient parapets of Europe.[1]

Is there any chance of seeing you anywhere in the near future? We discovered that Elena and the twins were in town, we rang her up at the Algonquin but she had already left.

I am giving you my mailing address at the head of this letter. I can also be reached through Dmitri whose phone is Lyceum 5-0516.

My Onegin (eleven folders, 3000 typed pages) went at first to the Cornell University Press. They started to groom it for print and had actually taken care of the square brackets when an impossible clause in their contract forced me to take back my poor monster. It has now gone to another place.

I am working hard on my *Discourse on Igor's Campaign*[2] which I once translated but now have completely revamped. The commentary to it has inherited a Eugene gene and is threatening to grow into another mammoth. I hope to finish it in Flagstaff. Russia will never be able to repay all her debts to me.

Do write me a word. Véra joins me in saluting you and Elena.

Cordially,

V

1. Reference to a line in Arthur Rimbaud's poem "Le Bateau Ivre" ("The Drunken Ship"): "Je regrette Europe aux anciens parapets" (I miss Europe with its ancient parapets).
2. Nabokov chose to call the published version *The Song of Igor's Campaign*. In his annotations he explains his reasons for preferring "song" over "discourse," "narration," "sermon" or "word," all of which can be conveyed in Russian by the word *slovo* used in the title of the poem.

308

Edmund Wilson
Wellfleet, Cape Cod
Massachusetts

March 11, 1959

Dear Volodya: I was just about to write you to ask whether you had seen the news of the highly comic controversies about *Lolita* that have been going on in England. I assume that you have since you have had the Cornell Library; but if you haven't, I'll send you some clippings. The affair of the Bournemouth election sounds like Compton Mackenzie or Evelyn Waugh.[1] I'm sorry that we shan't be in New York till the latter part of April. Glad to hear you're getting off for a year. I should think you could retire for life. No: I didn't send you the pot-holder as Jason tells me you imagined—nor do I see its point.

As ever,

E.

1. Nigel Nicolson, the co-founder of Weidenfeld and Nicolson, which brought out *Lolita* in England (despite the vehement objections to the book by his parents, Harold Nicolson and Victoria Sackville-West), was having trouble getting himself re-elected to Parliament from Bournemouth. His decision to publish *Lolita* was resented by many of his constituents, as was his opposition to government policy in the Suez controversy. Nigel Nicolson lost the election by 91 votes.

309

[Véra Nabokov to Edmund Wilson]

Forest Houses
Sedona, Arizona

June 30, 1959

Dear Bunny,

Volodya asks me to write you about something that has very much upset him. As you know by now, New Directions are bringing out a new edition of *The Real Life of Sebastian Knight*. You have been kind to this book in 1941, when it was first published, and for this reason New Directions have taken it upon themselves to ask your endorsement for the jacket of their new edition. Vladimir deplores the publishers' practice of pestering famous people for endorsements before publication instead of using reviews that have actually come out. He never gives such endorsements himself. He begs you to refuse. He has written New Directions that he is against such solicitations.

The reason I am writing this letter (and not V. himself) is that he wants it mailed immediately, but, after having been writing for the last four days, he feels absolutely exhausted and wretched.

We are staying in one of the loveliest canyons of Arizona, the Oak Creek Canyon, south of Flagstaff. We shall remain here till mid-July and possibly a little longer. In the fall we shall be for a short time in New York (or on Cape Cod) before sailing for Europe.

We hope you and Elena are having a pleasant summer. We are sending our love to both of you.

Véra

310

EDMUND WILSON
TALCOTTVILLE
LEWIS COUNTY
NEW YORK

July 15, 1959

Dear Véra:

I had already written New Directions not to use that old blurb of mine, since it was now out of date. When I finally get around to doing my *étude appro-fondie*[1] of Volodya, the publishers will have something to flourish. I shall then read the whole of *Lolita* without worrying about whether it can be published, though I'll bet I've read more of *Lolita* than Volodya has of *Zhivago*. The rampancy of *Lolita*—who evidently struck a deep chord in the great American breast (note the quite different attitude in England)—seems to have opened the door to a lot of other wantons. Lady Chatterley has now been liberated, and my *Hecate County* is going to be reprinted. Just now I am reading nothing but murky old mid-nineteenth-century American books, in shabby green or brown covers, that deal with the Indians and the Civil War.

I enjoyed "The Vane Sisters," but if that is the story of which you told me that you thought *The New Yorker* had rejected it on account of its picture of New England, I can assure you that you are quite mistaken. Your satire is very mild, and even if it had been more cruel, *The New Yorker* wouldn't have cared in the least. The trouble undoubtedly was that it can't expect its readers to know about the cryptogram in the last paragraph, nor would they have felt that they could invite the reader to look for it. Nobody would have seen it in *Encounter* if the editors hadn't tipped them off.[2] I had no difficulty in solving it, but I thought that the "meter" applied to the poem that came in through the ouija-board.

I expect to be here till the end of August and then back on the Cape. In the middle of August, we are going to Cambridge, where I have a job for the winter. I hope we'll be able to see you at one or another of those places. We'd be delighted to have you come to Wellfleet.

As ever,
Edmund

1. The closest Wilson would ever come to fulfilling his promise, reiterated for years, to write a "thorough study" of Nabokov's *oeuvre* was the seven-page postscript to the revised version of his 1965 review of the *Onegin* translation, included in his book *A Window on Russia*, 1972.

2. In the last paragraph of the story "The Vane Sisters," the first letters of the words form a message for the narrator from two dead sisters he once knew.

1960

311

Hotel Astoria
Avenue Carnot
Menton (A.M.)
France

January 19, 1960

Edmund Wilson, Esq.
English Department
Harvard University
Cambridge, Mass., USA

Dear Bunny,

After spending four rather hectic months in Europe we plan to return home. We shall sail on the *United States,* on February 19th, shall spend two or three days in New York, and shall travel on to Los Angeles where we intend to remain at least six months.[1]

We visited Geneva to see my sister[2] (whom I had not seen since 1937). We stayed in Paris and London where I had to be in connection with the publication of a book of mine. We also stayed in Rome and Milan. We pushed as far as Taormina, a dreary place in Sicily. We unsuccessfully looked for a place to rent at Nervi, Rapallo, Lugano and San Remo. We finally found a flat in Menton.

Dmitri is pursuing his studies in Milan. We plan to visit him in the fall. The best French writer is Robbe-Grillet whom we met in Paris. He is being incomprehensibly lumped together with all sorts of Butors and Sarrautes by many French critics. England, like Russia of the eighteen-sixties, has a strong group of critics interested mainly in the drab School-of-Social-Comment literature.

In France, this kind of thing seems to be declining. I found Cambridge University (where I delivered a lecture) in some respects curiously provincial in comparison with its American counterparts.

We hope you are enjoying your stay at Cambridge, Mass. Did you get a copy of INVITATION TO A BEHEADING which I asked to be sent you?[3] When and where shall we see Elena and you?

The address at Menton will be good till February 15th. Do let me hear from you.

Véra joins her best regards to mine.

As ever,
V.
Vladimir Nabokov

1. Nabokov went to Hollywood on Stanley Kubrick's invitation to work on the screenplay of *Lolita*.

2. Elena Sikorski, née Nabokov.

3. The English translation of *Invitation to a Beheading* (written in Russian in the mid-1930s) appeared in 1959.

312

[Jotted on the copy of Nabokov's letter of January 19]

January 25, 1960

Dear Volodya: We are at 12 Hilliard Street, Cambridge—telephone Trowbridge 6-8179. Can't you stop off here? I gather from your Hollywood destination that *Lolita* is going into the movies. Have you read Queneau's *Zazie dans le Métro?* which has been described as France's answer to *Lolita*. If not, I think you should—though it suffers somewhat from the whimsical vein that has got into French writing: Giraudoux, Aymé, Anouilh, etc. Love to Véra.

As ever,
Edmund W.

The Levins are going out to Los Angeles in February and may be there when you are there.

313

2088 Mandeville Canyon Rd.
Los Angeles 49, Calif.

April 5, 1960

Dear Bunny,

We are in Los Angeles where we found a charming house in a blooming canyon full of good butterflies. We live very quietly. My main occupation is a screenplay I am making, but I am also occupied in reading the proofs of my ONEGIN, the proofs of my SONG OF IGOR, and Dmitri's translation of my DAR.[1]

The screenplay will keep me busy till August or September when we shall sail again for Europe. I feel happy and relaxed in lovely serene Los Angeles, and we both wish Elena and you could visit us here.

Yes, I admire greatly ZAZIE DANS LE METRO, it is quite a masterpiece in its "whimsical" genre. (Isn't all art whimsical, from Shakespeare to Joyce?) I have read some pretty awful books recently. The palm of grotesque mediocrity goes, I think, to Colin Wilson's THE RITUAL IN THE DARK.

Well, that's just a few lines to keep in touch with you. In a few months it will be 20 (twenty!) years since we first met.

Yours
V

1. *The Gift.*

314

c/o Putnam
210 Madison Ave.
New York 16, NY

October 10, 1960

Dear Bunny,

You have quite forgotten me. I am told you are living in Cambridge.

We are leaving after tomorrow for New York where we shall spend a fortnight before sailing for Europe on November 2. Might it be possible that by some happy chance you are visiting New York?

Our stay here, under the jacarandas, has been most enjoyable. The screenplay I have been working on since March is now ready, and the job is nicely done. I had seclusion and freedom, and a canyon full of butterflies.

We hope to return to California next year. Our European plans are still vague: we expect to go first to Geneva where my sister lives, and unless Dmitri can come thither from Milan, we shall go on to Italy.

Do write me a word. Véra joins me in sending Elena and you a *serdechnïy privet.*[1]

Yours
V.

1. "Cordial regards."

315

[A Christmas card with a picture of a child-angel decorating a tree in the woods, and the inscription "Meilleurs Voeux et Souhaits Sincères"]

[December 16, 1960]

Милые Елена и Здмундъ,

Поздравляемъ Васъ съ Праздникомъ и желаемъ очень счастливаго Новаго Года.

Владимиръ, Вѣра и Дмитрiй Набоковы[1]

1. "Dear Elena and Edmund,
    Season's Greetings and a very happy New Year
        Vladimir, Véra and Dmitri Nabokov"

(in Véra's handwriting and using Russian old orthography).

1961

316

57, Promenade des Anglais,
Nice, A[lpes] M[aritimes]

February 27, 1961

Dear Bunny,

Many thanks for your delightful letter in fluent Russian and for the very funny and very artistic Fatal Lozenges. I should have written you sooner but I had an intense period of inspiration that I badly needed for a long poem (part of my new novel)[1] and kept imbibing it while it lasted for hours on end. I enjoy working here but feel I should soon return to America for verbal vigor and mental ease. We have a good apartment here and the sea is present in all the windows as in Marcel's hotel at Balbec.[2] I speak French with a cornbelt accent and buy daily the *New York Herald* at Gunn's bookshop. In English and French periodicals we often see pictures of the Holy family—in the Elstree Studio—but have no contact with it.[3]

Nice is wonderfully situated being not far from Milan, and Dmitri visits us often. He will make his operatic debut in *La Bohème* in April.[4]

Roman G. tells me he saw you recently. Is there any chance of your visiting Europe in the summer? We are staying here to the end of March after which we shall be moving around for a while, so let me know soon.

How is your health? Do take care of yourself, dear friend.

Véra joins me in greeting both of you.

V.

1. *Pale Fire.*

2. At the beginning of Marcel Proust's series of novels *À la recherche du temps perdu.*

3. The film version of *Lolita* was being shot at the Elstree Studios in England at the time. Dmitri Nabokov explains that "the Holy family" refers to James Mason and other actors and actresses who appeared in the film.

4. At the performance in which both Dmitri Nabokov and Luciano Pavarotti made their operatic débuts.

1963

317

[December 1963]

HOTEL DE CASTILLE
37, rue Cambon
(Vendôme—Opéra—Madeleine)
PARIS-1er

Dear Volodya: It lately occurred to me that I have not been sending you the неприличную литературу[1] with which I need to supply you and which no doubt inspired *Lolita,* so I am including this in my Christmas packet.

As ever,

EW

Elena much enjoyed seeing you, and I am sorry that I couldn't be there, but I may make connections with you yet. Was sorry to hear about Dmitri.[2]

[Appended to this letter in the Nabokov archive was a brief press clipping, under which Nabokov wrote a two-line quotation from Vladimir Mayakovsky's poem "Conversation with a Tax Inspector About Poetry" (1926)]

Special to the World-Telegram and Sun.
　　S Y R A C U S E, Nov. 14.—Edmund Wilson, author of "Memoirs of Hecate County" and other works, today pleaded guilty to a charge that he failed to report $16,949 in income in 1957. He was fined $7500.[3]

Гражданин фининспектор,

честное слово,

позту в копеечку влетают слова.[4]

1. "Indecent literature."

2. Dmitri Nabokov became ill in August 1962 with a painful swelling of the joints which continued on and off, for the next eighteen months, before it was diagnosed and cured. See Brian Boyd, *Nabokov: The American Years*, pp. 486 ff.

3. The prosecution took place in November 1960. Wilson described his conflict with the Internal Revenue Service in his book *The Cold War and the Income Tax: A Protest* (1963).

4. "Citizen tax inspector,

my word of honor,

Words cost a poet a pretty penny."

1964

318

[Véra Nabokov to Elena Wilson]

Montreux, February 5, 1964
Palace Hotel

Dear Elena,

Would you be so very kind and send me the name of the anti-gout tablets you and Edmund mentioned when you were here? Do you know if they may produce any side effects? Our doctor does not know about them.

We hope you are having a pleasant stay in Paris. It was so very nice to see you both in Montreux.[1]

Both Vladimir and Dmitri join their fondest greetings to mine. We hope to see you and Edmund again soon.

Cordially,

Véra

1. Edmund and Elena Wilson came for a reunion with the Nabokovs and stayed at the Montreux Palace Hotel for three days, January 11–13, 1964. They had dinner with the Nabokovs and Heinrich Maria and Jane Ledig-Rowohlt (he was Nabokov's German publisher) on the 11th; on the 12th, Wilson gave a gala lunch for the Nabokovs. This was the last occasion the two writers saw each other.

319

[From Wilson to Véra Nabokov]

HOTEL DE CASTILLE
37, rue Cambon
(Vendôme—Opéra—Madeleine)
PARIS-1er

February 6, 1964

Dear Véra:

Here is a letter from my doctor, which please return. You have to take at least one of each of these pills every day; but you start by taking two until the uric acid has been eliminated. If the gout begins to reappear, go back to taking two.

I have just discovered that at dinner at Montreux I made a serious gaffe. I didn't know that Ledig Rowohlt had previously been married to the present Mrs. Feltrinelli, and said some unpleasant things about her. Mondadori, the Italian publisher, told me this, and said not to worry about my gaffe—that Rowohlt would undoubtedly agree with me.[1]

We very much enjoyed seeing you.

As ever,

Edmund

With love, Elena

1. Either Mondadori or Wilson got it wrong. Inge Feltrinelli, the wife of the Italian Communist publisher Giangiacomo Feltrinelli, was never married to Ledig-Rowohlt.

(Wilson repeated this misinformation in *The Sixties*, p. 293.) In November 1957, Giangiacomo Feltrinelli brought out the first edition of Boris Pasternak's *Doctor Zhivago*, despite protests and threats from the Soviet government. He was later to lose his life in an inept attempt to sabotage a power plant as a form of protest against the capitalist system.

320

Hotel de Castille

37 rue Cambon

Paris I

February 15, 1964

Dear Volodya:

Do you remember my attempt to translate this poem in Wellfleet? It is amusing that it should have taken two of them to produce this little non-lyric.[1]

Mary is all agog to know how she missed out on *Pale Fire*.[2] Why don't you write her? Her address is 141 rue de Rennes, Paris 6ème. Her name now is Mrs. James West.

I'm afraid we shan't be in Paris when you get here. We hope to get away at the end of this month.

Hope those medicaments make some impression on your gout.

Have you seen Chukovsky's amusing book *Живой как жизнь*[3] on what has been happening to the Russian language? He sometimes sounds a little like my complaints in the *New Statesman*[4]—he is ninety[5] years old—insists that you shouldn't say Обожаю собак, because обожать involves Вог.[6]

As ever,

EW

1. "Poem: After Alexander Blok" by Charles Tomlinson and Henry Gifford, *Times Literary Supplement*, February 13, 1964. This is an extremely free adaptation of the same poem that Wilson quoted to Nabokov in Letter 58.

2. Mary McCarthy's enthusiastic appreciation of *Pale Fire*, "A Bolt from the Blue," was published in *The New Republic*, No. 146, June 1962.

3. *Alive as Life Itself*, first published in 1962, by Kornei Chukovsky (1882–1969), literary scholar and children's poet. The book celebrates the endless possibilities of the Russian language and laments its abuse by twentieth-century usages.

4. Wilson's column on current language usages, "More Notes on Current Clichés," appeared in the *New Statesman* issue of December 6, 1963.

5. Chukovsky was 82 in 1964.

6. "Shouldn't say 'I adore dogs,' because 'to adore' involves 'God'." As often before, Wilson confused the Cyrillic and Latin alphabets, placing the Latin *B* in the Russian word for God, *Bog*, making it *Vog*.

321

Dear Bunny,

Yes, I saw that translation of Blok's poem in the Literary Supplement. The difficult bit is *ledyanaya ryab'* which, of course, is not "ice-bound," but glacial, icy-looking; and *ryab'* is not *zïb'*—not an ordinary ripple but a very fine corrugation or wrinkling of the water surface.[1]

It was grand to see you after all those years and to resume so fluently our natural intercourse.

Many thanks for the *retsept*[2] which I have started using.

We are sailing home for a month on March 18th.

Our love to Elena and to you.

As ever,

V.

[In margin]
Sorry for the transliteration!

1. For a translation of the passage Nabokov is discussing, see Letter 58, note 4.
2. "Prescription."

1971

322

Dear Bunny,

A few days ago I had the occasion to reread the whole batch (Russ., *vsyu pachku*)[1] of our correspondence. It was such a pleasure to feel again the warmth of your many kindnesses, the various thrills of our friendship, that constant excitement of art and intellectual discovery.

I was sorry to hear (from Lena Levin) that you had been ill, and happy to learn that you were much better.

Please believe that I have long ceased to bear you a grudge for your incomprehensible incomprehension of Pushkin's and Nabokov's *Onegin.* [. . .]

Yours,
Vladimir Nabokov

1. "The whole batch."

323

THE NEW YORKER
No. 25 West 43rd Street

March 8, 1971

Mr. Vladimir Nabokov
Montreux-Palace Hotel
Montreux, Switzerland

Dear Volodya:

I was very glad to get your letter. I am just now getting together a volume of my Russian articles. I am correcting my errors in Russian in my piece on Nabokov-Pushkin; but citing a few more of your ineptitudes. [. . .] I think [Solzhenitsyn] is remarkable, though somewhat monotonous—not in a class with Pasternak, but after all he has nothing to tell but his story of illness and imprisonment. I am trying to write something about him for a final chapter. I find I have some difficulty in reading Soviet Russian.

I have included an account of my visit to you in Ithaca in a book[1] that will be out this spring (don't read the stripped version in *The New Yorker*), based on twenty years of Talcottville diary. I hope it will not again impair our personal relations (it shouldn't).

Elena and I have both been in rather bad shape. I had a slight stroke, which makes it rather difficult for me to use my right hand. We are eager to leave New York, which is now absolute hell. I don't know whether I can bring myself ever to come here again.

Best regards and love to Vera.

EW

P.S. According to the Soviet edition of Chekhov, you have the date slightly wrong about the letter in which he tells of your relative's encounter with him.[2]

---

1. *Upstate: Records and Recollections of Northern New York*. See Letter 294, note 5. In his letter to the editor of the *New York Times*, published on November 7, 1971 (and reprinted in *Strong Opinions*, pp. 218–219), Nabokov wrote, *inter alia:* "What surprises me, however, is not so much Wilson's aplomb as the fact that in the diary he kept while he was my guest in Ithaca he pictures himself as nursing feelings and ideas so vindictive and fatuous that if expressed they should have made me demand his immediate departure."

2. In Chapter Three of *Speak, Memory* Nabokov has this to say about his mother's aunt, Dr. Praskovia Tarnovskaya: "One evening at Aivazovsky's [the famous painter] villa near Feodosia, Aunt Praskovia met at dinner the twenty-eight-year-old Dr. Anton Chekhov whom she somehow offended in the course of a medical conversation. She was a very learned, very kind, very elegant lady, and it is hard to imagine how exactly she could have

provoked the incredibly coarse outburst Chekhov permits himself in a published letter of August 3, 1888, to his sister."

The "outburst" in question was made actually in Chekhov's letter to his sister Maria of July 22, 1888. It reads: "She [Dr. Tarnovskaya] is an obese, bloated chunk of flesh. If she were stripped naked and painted green, she'd be a swamp frog. After a chat with her, I mentally crossed her off my list of physicians." The discrepancy in dates resulted from Nabokov's correction based on the difference between the Julian and Gregorian calendars.

Index

Within entries, "EW" stands for Edmund Wilson, "VN" for Vladimir Nabokov. Where notes of the same number, but referring to different letters, appear on the same page, they are distinguished by the annotation *top* or *bottom*.

Aaron, Daniel, 4

Adams, Henry, 223n.1

Aeschylus, 92n.1, 272n.6

Afanasiev, Alexander, 178, 179n.3, 180

Aiken, Conrad, 186

Aivazovsky, Ivan, 373n.2

Akasov, Sergei, 162n.7

Akhmatova, Anna, 24, 257n.4

Aksakov, Sergei, 162n.7, 355, 355n.2

Aldanov, Mark, 12, 38, 39n.15, 64, 65n.1, 116, 132, 135, 137, 139, 149, 151n.17, 157n.2, 177, 177n.5, 179, 179nn.4, 5, 193, 218n.1, 298

Alexander I, 338

Alexander II, 151n.17, 223

Alexandra Fyodorovna, Empress, 10, 37

Alexandrov, Vladimir E., 87n.1

Alymov, Sergei, 223, 224n.9

Anderson, Sherwood, 330, 331n.1

Andreyev, Leonid, 19, 203, 240

Annensky, Innokenty, 17, 24, 80

Anouilh, Jean, 365

Apollinaire, Guillaume, 239n.4

Appel, Alfred, Jr., 196n.1, 226n.4, 242n.8, 272n.6, 295n.1, 332n.1 *top*, 334n.4

Arnold, Matthew, 350

Aswell, Mary Louise, 69

Auden, W. H., 186, 350, 351, 352

Ausonius, 170

Austen, Jane, 20–21, 178n, 265, 268, 270–271, 283n.4, 303n.2

Aveling, Eleanor Marx, 281, 281n.4

Aymé, Marcel, 365

Babel, Isaac, 132

Bacon, Peggy, 356

Balacheff, Pierre, 238, 239n.3

Balanchine, George, 67n.2, 68n.1

Balmont, Konstantin, 50, 51n.1

Balzac, Honoré de, 20, 357n.6

Banks, Nathan, 137, 138n.5

Barbour, Thomas, 137, 138n.5

Baring, Maurice, 226

Barry, Joan, 142, 143n.6

Barth, John, 28

Basso, Hamilton, 177, 177n.5, 211

Batyushkov, Konstantin, 353n.12

Baudelaire, Charles, 21, 186, 186n.3

Beard, Charles A., 179, 179n.5

Beaumarchais, Pierre-Augustin Caron de, 19

Beckett, Samuel, 28, 336n.6

Beebe, William, 301, 301n.7

Belinkov, Arkady, 225n.3

Belinsky, Vissarion, 222, 224n.3

Belloc, Hilaire, 59

Bely, Andrei, 8, 16, 17, 23, 24, 24n.5, 80, 86, 88n.19, 112, 246

Benckendorff, Count Alexander, 264, 265n.5

Bentley, Edmund C., 284n.2

Berberova, Nina, 223n.1, 233n.7

Beresford, J. D., 160

Berkeley, Anthony, 160

Berlin, Sir Isaiah, 299

Bestuzhev-Marlinsky, Alexander, 181n.1 *bottom*, 239, 242n.1

Bièvre, Marquis de, 324

Birkett, George Arthur, 158, 158n.2 *top*

Bishop, John Peale, 19, 175n.1 *bottom*, 232, 233n.1, 234, 311

Bishop, Morris, 225, 226n.4, 237, 329

Bizet, Georges, 185n.4

Blair, Mary, 207n.1
Blake, Patricia, 228, 229n.2
Blake, William, 120n.7
Bliven, Bruce, 42, 44
Blok, Alexander, 23, 24, 80, 102n.4, 103, 106,
    172n.3, 216, 239n.4, 246, 372
Bonaparte. *See* Napoleon Bonaparte
Bondi, Sergei, 263, 265n.2
Bourke-White, Margaret, 107n.5
Bowers, Fredson, 318n.4
Boyd, Brian, vii, 79n.1, 150n.1, 200n.1 *top*,
    209, 293n.5, 299n.1, 369n.2
Boyden, Polly, 167, 168n.4
Boyden, Preston ("Bud"), 168n.4
Boyle, Kay, 64, 65n.2, 135, 136n.5
Bradbury, Walter, 197, 198n.2
Braddon, Mary Elizabeth, 20
Bramah, Ernest, 159
Breit, Harvey, 331
Breton, André, 239n.4
Brik, Lili, 5n
Broadwater, Bowden, 321, 321n.2
Brontë sisters (Anne, Charlotte and Emily),
    20
Brooke, Rupert, 87
Brooks, Paul, 315
Brooks, Van Wyck, 247n.8, 269n.8
Brown, Thomas, 136n.6
Browne, Hawkins, 282, 283n.4
Browning, Robert, 70n.5, 98
Bruce, James, 324, 325n.5
Bukharin, Nikolai, 248n.11
Bunakov, Ilya. *See* Fondaminsky, Ilya
Bunin, Ivan, 11, 23, 172n.3, 246, 300n.1
Burke, Edmund, 324
Butor, Michel, 364
Byron, George Gordon, Lord, 247n.4, 348,
    349n.3, 351

Cabell, James Branch, 333, 333n.1
Caldwell, Erskine, 72, 73n.2
Calry, Count Robert Louis Magawly-Cerati
    de, 114, 115n.4, 116
Carr, John Dickinson, 128n.6
Carroll, Lewis, 117n.1
Cervantes, Miguel de, 295, 302
Chaliapin, Fyodor, 340, 341n.4
Chamot, A. E., 48n.2

Chaplin, Charles, 142, 143n.6
Charskaya, Lydia, 27
Chavchavadze, Nina, 74, 75n.1, 99, 114, 118,
    144n.1, 168, 173, 201, 207, 208, 211, 214,
    228, 231, 358
Chavchavadze, Paul, 75n.1, 144n.1, 201, 211,
    228, 231, 260, 262, 264
Cheever, John, 28
Chekhov, Anton, 6, 8, 9, 18, 19, 21–22, 27, 28,
    48n.3, 181n.2, 232, 234, 252, 256, 260,
    261nn.4, 5, 8, 264, 265nn.6–8, 269,
    272n.1, 274, 274n.5, 275n.2, 277,
    278nn.3, 4, 286, 310, 331, 332n.1 *top*,
    373, 373n.2
Chekhov, Mikhail, 48n.3
Chekhova, Maria, 373n.2
Chelishchev, Pavel. *See* Tchelitchew, Pavel
Chernyshevsky, Nikolai, 11, 13, 14, 21–22, 25,
    233n.7, 298n.2
Christie, Agatha, 159, 160n.7
Chukovsky, Kornei, 371, 371nn.3, 5
Churchill, Winston, 87, 154
Clark, George, 146, 147, 150n.4
Clark, R. D., 200n.1 *top*
Coates, Robert, 138n.2
Cocteau, Jean, 260, 270, 336
Coleridge, Samuel Taylor, 96n
Colette, 299, 300
Comstock, John Adams, Jr., 138n.5
Comstock, W. P., 137, 138n.5
Connell, Richard, 159
Conner, Louise Fort, 191, 191n.1 *bottom*
Connolly, Cyril, 226, 227n.4, 309
Conrad, Joseph, 19, 55, 282, 283n.3, 290
Constant, Benjamin, 71
Corbière, Tristan, 239n.4
Cornwall, Barry, 348
Cournos, John, 127, 128n.5, 129
Covici, Pascal (Pat), 317, 318n.6
Cowper, William ("Cooper"), 282, 348
Crabbe, George, 282
Cross, Samuel Hazzard, 209, 209n.9, 241,
    242n.7
Cummings, E. E., 5, 5n, 311
Curran, C. H., 291n.1 *bottom*

Dahl, Vladimir, 52n.2, 256, 333, 333n.2
Dallin, David J., 254n.5

Index

D'Annunzio, Gabriele, 167

Dante, 170, 272n.6

Darnell, Linda, 310n.2 *bottom*

Davet, Yvonne, 280, 280n.4

David, Father Armand, 293, 294n.9

Davies, Joseph E., 107, 107n.7, 113n.7, 162, 162n.4

Dekobra, Maurice, 204n.16

De la Mare, Walter, 87

Demorest, Jean-Jacques, 70–71n.6

Demuth, Charles, 357n.1

Denney, Reuel, 262

Dennis, Nigel, 44, 46, 48

Derzhavin, Gavriil, 19, 122, 122n.2

Deutsch, Babette, 76, 77n.5, 346, 347n.1 *top*

DeVane, William Clyde, 70, 70n.5

Diaghilev, Sergei, 22

Dickens, Charles, 20, 125, 265, 268, 271, 273, 275

Dickson, Carter (pseud.), 128n.6

Dobuzhinsky, Mstislav, 147, 148, 150n.6

Donleavy, J. P., 344n.1

Dos Passos, John, 114, 175n.1 *bottom*, 222, 223n.1, 252, 253n.2, 332

Dostoevsky, Fyodor, 19, 101, 102, 181n.2, 197, 199, 203, 204n.13, 205, 225n.3, 302, 344

Douglas, Melvyn, 286n.2

Douglas, Norman, 206n.4

Doyle, Sir Arthur Conan, 185–186, 186n.1

DuBois, W. E. B., 97, 98n.1

Dujardin, Édouard, 354, 355n.1 *top*

Dupee, F. W., 337, 338n.1

Dzerzhinsky, Felix, 222, 224nn.6, 7, 11

Eastman, Elena, 34, 34n.3

Eastman, Max, 34, 34n.3, 116, 117n.4

Edel, Leon, 350n.5

Eichenbaum, Boris, 24

Eisenstein, Sergei, 222, 224n.4, 357, 358n.2 *top*

Elder, Donald, 133, 134, 138, 141, 142, 193–194, 199, 218, 235

Eliot, George, 313

Eliot, T. S., 92n.5, 175n.1 *bottom*, 206, 206n.1, 234, 240, 263, 282, 360, 360n.1

Ellis, Havelock, 228, 229n.1

Elton, Oliver, 235n.1, 346, 347n.1 *top*

Engels, Friedrich, 14, 37, 38, 247n.10

Epstein, Jason, 320, 322, 325, 326, 334, 337, 338, 347, 362

Erskine, Albert Russell, Jr., 57, 58n.3

Ezhov (Yezhov), Nikolai, 222, 224nn.7, 11

Fadiman, Clifton, 75, 144

Farrère, Claude, 208, 209n.6

Fasola, Roberto, 326, 326n.3

Fasolt, Sophia, 174n.5

Faulkner, William, 19, 235, 236, 237, 239–240, 256, 257, 264, 282

Fearing, Kenneth, 143n.5

Fedotov, George, 72, 73n.6

Feigin, Anna, 150

Feltrinelli, Giangiacomo, 370n.1 *bottom*

Feltrinelli, Inge, 370, 370n.1 *bottom*

Fennell, C. A. M., 345, 346

Fet, Afanasy, 21, 25, 104n.1

Feuerbach, Ludwig, 14

Field, Andrew, 110n.1, 269n.10

Fielding, Henry, 311, 312, 313

Filippov, Boris, 257n.4

Fischer, Markoosha, 151n.18

Fitzgerald, F. Scott, 19, 124, 161, 175, 175n.1 *bottom*, 227n.4

Flaubert, Gustave, 21, 191n.6, 205, 246, 247n.7, 263, 270, 273, 295, 354

Fleiss, Wilhelm, 333, 334n.1

Fondaminsky, Ilya (Ilya Bunakov), 10, 222, 224n.3

Fonvizin, Denis, 19

Forbes, Prof. William (entomologist), 98

Forster, E. M., 131

Fourier, Charles, 14

Fox sisters (Margaretta, Leah and Kate), 311, 312n.3

Francis, Arlene, 286n.2

Freeman, Elizabeth, 144

Freud, Sigmund, 97, 205, 333, 334n.1

Friedman, Harold, 323

Frisch, Karl von, 288, 288n, 291n.1 *bottom*

Galsworthy, John, 202

Gannibal, Abram, 307n.1, 324, 325n.5

Gapon, Father Georgy, 37

Garnett, Constance, 343

Gauss, Christian, 18, 187n.1

Genet, Jean, 20, 21, 27, 260, 264, 268, 270, 271, 335–336
George of Russia, Grand Duke, 75n.1
Gide, André, 270, 271, 272n.6, 280, 321
Gifford, Henry, 371n.1
Giraudoux, Jean, 268, 365
Gnedich, Nikolai, 351
Godwin, William, 23
Goebbels, Joseph, 246
Goering, Hermann, 175
Goethe, Johann Wolfgang von, 167, 168n.3, 240, 247n.10, 336n.1
Gogol, Nikolai, 7, 13, 23, 52, 75, 76n.3, 95n.1, 113n.16, 118, 125, 125n.3, 128, 141n.1 *bottom*, 156–157, 167, 168, 168n.2, 176nn.1, 2 *bottom*, 178, 182, 187n.1, 188, 188n.3 *bottom*, 233n.6, 278n.3, 286, 287n.1, 302
Gold, Herbert, 136n.4, 157n.1, 360–361
Gollancz, Victor, 288, 289–290
Goncharov, Ivan, 355
Goncourt brothers (Edmond and Jules), 354
Goodman, Paul, 259n.2
Gorky, Maxim, 6, 13, 15, 16, 40, 47, 231, 232, 234, 247nn.9, 10, 248n.11
Green, Henrietta, 139
Green, Henry, 288, 289n.2
Grégoire, Henri, 108, 109n.3, 243, 244n.4
Gresset, J. B. L., 162n.7
Grey, Zane, 271, 272n.6
Griboyedov, Alexander, 23, 112, 113nn.11–13, 129n.2
Gronicka, André van, 155n.1
Grynberg, Roman, 34n.2, 51, 63, 103, 104n.5, 108, 109n.2, 128, 161, 197, 199, 215, 230, 243, 251, 252, 254, 254n.5, 258, 282, 291, 295, 296, 298, 341, 342, 368
Grynberg, Sophie (Sonya), 34n.2, 63, 108, 109n.2, 128, 161, 298
Guerney, B. G., 112, 127, 128n.5
Gumilyov, Nikolai, 257n.4

Haardt, Sara, 160, 161n.1
Haber, Edythe C., 179n.3
Halévy, Ludovic, 184
Hammett, Dashiell, 160n.7
Hartwig, Eva Brigitta. *See* Zorina, Vera
Hasenclever, Mme, 71

Haycraft, Howard, 184n.3
Heard, Gerald (Henry Fitzgerald Heard), 124n.3
Hegel, Georg Wilhelm Friedrich, 14, 36
Heggen, Thomas, 198n.1
Heiseler, Henry von, 155, 155n.1
Hellman, Geoffrey, 217, 281
Hellman, George, 281, 281n.3
Hemingway, Ernest, 47, 215
Hersey, John, 259, 260n.2
Herzen, Alexander, 39n.3
Hessen, George, 111, 111n.1, 215, 254, 254n.5
Hessen, Iosif V., 10, 107, 107n.3
Hippius, Vladimir, 112
Hitler, Adolf, 25, 53, 68, 71, 90, 174n.5
Hogarth, William, 311
Holladay, Constance, 228, 229n.2
Holland, William Jacob, 137, 138n.4, 198
Home, Daniel, 144
Horace, 162n.6, 324, 324n.3
Houseman, Laurence, 123
Howe, Irving, 19
Hughes, Robert P., 126n.1
Hughes, Thomas, 136n.6
Hugo, Victor, 239
Hutchinson, William, 75, 77n.4
Huxley, Aldous, 49
Huysmans, J. K., 264
Hyman, Stanley Edgar, 232, 233, 233nn.4, 6, 234, 251, 260n.2

Ilf, Ilya, 175
Ilyin, Nikolai Dmitrievich, 307, 307n.2
Inchbald, Elizabeth, 282, 283n.4
Isherwood, Christopher, 49
Ivanov, Georgy, 334, 334n.4
Ivanov, Vsevolod, 203
Ivan the Terrible, 6

Jack, P. M., 64, 64n.1 *bottom*
Jakobson, Roman, 109n.3, 238, 241, 242n.7, 243, 244nn.5, 6
James, Alice, 343, 347
James, Henry, 19, 59, 206, 207, 209, 211, 227n.4, 240, 282, 308
James, William, 344, 344n.2
James, William (Billy), 343, 344n.2, 346, 347

Jannings, Emil, 97
Johnson, D. Barton, 272n.8
Johnson, Samuel, 282, 283n.4
Jones, Evan, 323n.4
Jones, Lewis, 71, 72, 166
Joyce, James, 4, 5n, 20, 24n.6, 164, 165n.6,
    191n.6, 205, 227n.4, 265, 286, 352,
    353n.7, 354, 366
Juliar, Michael, 42n
Juvenal, 348

Kafka, Franz, 219, 220n.4, 263
Kalashnikov, Mikhail ("Mishka"), 207, 208,
    209n.4
Kaliaev, Ivan, 203, 204n.13
Kannegiser, Leonid, 224n.7
Kant, Immanuel, 15
Kantemir, Prince Antioch, 87, 88n.20
Karamzin, Nikolai, 125
Karlinsky, Simon, 242n.8, 332n.1 top, 334n.4
Karpovich, Michael, 33n.1, 66, 74n.1, 147,
    150, 150n.5, 288
Karpovich, Tatiana, 147–148, 150, 150n.5
Kaun, Alexander, 155, 155n.5
Kaverin, Veniamin, 132
Kay, George de ("McKay"), 322, 323n.1 top
Kazan, Elia, 324
Keats, John, 167, 245, 271
Kees, Weldon, 108–109, 319–320
Kelly, Amy, 192, 193n.3
Kerensky, Alexander, 8, 43, 112, 142
Khodasevich, Vladislav, 11, 125, 125n.4, 126,
    126n.1, 137, 154, 172n.2
Klots, Alexander B., 291, 291n.1 bottom,
    291n.3
Klyuev, Nikolai, 257n.4
Knopf, Alfred, 76
Koestler, Mamaine, 272n.7
Koriakov, Mikhail, 236n.2
Korvin-Piotrovsky, Vladimir, 164, 165n.1 top
Kotzebue, August von, 283n.4
Kriger, Mary, 255, 257n.5
Krupskaya, Nadezhda, 15, 38, 247nn.9, 10
Krylov, Ivan, 101n.3
Kubrick, Stanley, 365n.1
Küchelbecker, Wilhelm, 77n.4
Kunina, Irina, 104
Kuzminskaya, Tatyana, 231, 231n.1, 248

Laforgue, Jules, 239n.4
Landau-Aldanov, M. A. See Aldanov, Mark
Largerqvist, Pär, 296n.1
Lasky, Melvin J., 337, 338n.1
Latimer, Jonathan, 189n.9
Laughlin, James, 12, 44, 45, 52, 55, 59, 60n.2,
    61–62, 64, 75–76, 76n.2, 99, 103, 111, 112,
    115, 116, 121, 122, 123, 124, 127, 128, 129–
    131, 132, 133, 134, 136, 142, 146, 155, 160,
    164, 171, 195, 197, 199, 211, 220, 319
Lawrence, D. H., 111, 306n.1 top, 330,
    331n.1
Ledig-Rowohlt, Heinrich Maria and Jane,
    370, 370nn.1 top and bottom
Lenin, Vladimir, 2, 4, 6, 7, 8, 9, 11, 13, 14–15,
    16, 23, 25, 27, 36, 37, 38, 39n.7, 40, 41,
    47, 107n.5, 149, 205, 213n.3, 221, 222,
    223n.1, 224n.11, 234, 236n.2, 246,
    247nn.9, 10, 257, 329, 340n.1
Lenôtre, Louis Gosselin ("Georges"), 37,
    39n.6
Leonov, Leonid, 39n.15, 133
Leopardi, Giacomo, 170
Lermontov, Mikhail, 50, 73, 75, 160, 175, 181,
    181n.1 bottom, 182, 187, 188n.3 top,
    225n.2, 242n.1, 326n.1, 333, 334, 355,
    356, 356nn.4, 5, 357n.6
Leskov, Nikolai, 355
Levin, Elena (Lena), 99, 99n.2, 171, 276, 290,
    306, 306n.1 top, 315, 332, 365, 372
Levin, Harry, 99, 99n.2, 171, 276, 290, 302,
    303n.1 top, 306, 315, 332, 365
Lewis, Sinclair, 306n.1 top
Lewis, Wyndham, 154
Ley, Willy, 291n.1 bottom, 293nn.1, 8
Lidin, Vladimir, 203
Linscott, Bob, 64
Littré, Emile, 329, 329n.1 bottom
Lobrano, Gustave Stubbs ("Gus"), 296,
    297n.3
Loti, Pierre, 204n.16
Lovecraft, H. P., 179n.3

MacAfee, Helen, 66
Mackenzie, Compton, 361
MacLeish, Archibald, 100
Maeterlinck, Maurice, 28
Magashack, David, 360, 360n.2

Malebranche, Nicolas de, 324
Malraux, André, 19, 201, 202–203, 204–205,
    206nn.2, 5, 212, 240
Mandelstam, Nadezhda, 5, 22, 24
Mandelstam, Osip, 257n.4
Mann, Klaus, 12, 44, 45, 45n.2, 47, 49, 50, 51
Mann, Thomas, 144, 164, 210, 263
Marcelin, Pierre, 235n.3
Markov, Vladimir, 110n.1, 334n.4
Marlinsky. *See* Bestuzhev-Marlinsky,
    Alexander
Marquand, J. P., 139
Martial, 136n.6
Marx, Karl, 14, 36, 38, 246, 247n.7, 281
Mason, James, 368n.3
Maturin, Charles, 117n.1
Maugham, Somerset, 64n.1 *bottom*
Maupassant, Guy de, 116, 136
Maurer, David W., 271, 272n.7
Mauriac, François, 240
Maximoff, G. P., 42, 42n, 47n.1
Maxwell, William, 69, 136n.4
Mayakovsky, Vladimir, 24, 176, 176n.3, 178,
    247n.9, 369
Mazon, André, 108, 109n.3
McCalib, Dennis, 272n.8
McCarthy, Mary, 27, 29, 45, 46, 48, 55n.8,
    63, 67, 67n.1 *bottom*, 68, 69, 70, 72, 76,
    76n.3, 95, 100, 102, 104, 108, 110, 111, 115,
    117n.3, 118, 123, 127, 128n.6, 132, 134,
    139, 144n.1, 147, 154, 157, 163n.1, 173,
    174n.3, 200, 256, 259n.2, 274, 303,
    303n.1 *bottom*, 304, 319, 320, 371,
    371n.2
McCormick, Kenneth, 194, 194n.2, 196, 198,
    199, 347
McIntyre, Robert, 172n.9
McLean, Hugh, 70n.6
Mencken, H. L., 3, 160, 161n.1, 170
Meredith, Burgess, 286n.2
Mérimée, Prosper, 184, 337, 349n.4, 354
Meyerhold, Vsevolod, 5n, 183, 183n.2
Meyers, Jeffrey, 316n.1
Michelangelo, 38n
Mickiewicz, Adam, 156
Middleton, Thomas, 234
Milton, John, 75, 271, 277
Milyukov, Pavel, 340, 341n.2 *top*

Mindszenty, Joseph Cardinal, 249, 249n.1
    bottom
Mirsky, D. S., 6, 6n, 23, 54, 55n.4, 74, 79, 80,
    101, 233n.4, 351
Mitropoulous, Dimitri, 219, 219n.1
Mizener, Arthur, 16n
Modzalevsky, Lev, 349n.2
Moe, Henry Allen, 136, 138n.2, 305, 305n.1
Molière, x, 156, 157n.4
Molotov, Vyacheslav, 233
Moncrieff, C. K. Scott, 286–287, 288
Mondadori, Alberto, 370
Mozart, Wolfgang Amadeus, 38n
Muchnic, Helen, 101–102, 104, 105, 218,
    218n.1, 238, 240, 329n.2 *top*
Munn, George, 349
Munn, Otis, 350n.6
Munthe, Axel, 209n.7
Myers, Ernest, 345

Nabokov, Dmitri, 12, 63, 65, 67, 68, 69, 73,
    74n.1, 93n.3, 96, 116, 121, 142, 143, 145,
    147, 148, 151, 152, 153, 158, 163, 166, 168,
    171, 173, 178, 186, 194, 195, 215, 217, 232,
    242, 253, 273, 280, 289, 290, 291n.2,
    294–295, 298, 308, 311, 313, 317, 322,
    328, 330, 334, 340, 341, 341n.4, 342,
    347, 350–351, 355, 357, 358n.3 *top*,
    361, 364, 366, 367, 368, 368nn.3, 4,
    369, 369n.2, 370
Nabokov, Ivan (Nicolas Nabokov's son), 335
Nabokov, Kirill (VN's youngest brother), 173,
    174n.4
Nabokov, Konstantin (VN's uncle), 204n.13
Nabokov, Nicolas (Nikolai, Nika; VN's
    cousin), 33, 33n.2, 45, 45n.4, 47, 56, 65,
    106, 135, 137, 139, 141, 143, 171, 173,
    200n.1 *top*, 209, 211, 219, 228, 229n.2,
    256, 335, 336n.2
Nabokov, Sergei (VN's younger brother),
    144n.1, 173, 174n.5, 175, 175n.2
Nabokov, Véra, vii, x, 3, 12, 39n.14, 42, 49,
    58n.2, 65, 69, 75, 76, 79, 87, 100, 102,
    103, 106, 112, 116, 119, 132, 134, 135, 136,
    142, 143, 144, 145, 147, 148, 149, 150, 152,
    155, 157, 158, 161, 166, 168, 172, 173,
    189n.12, 196n.1, 201, 209, 211, 212, 216,
    217, 219, 220, 225, 232, 235, 238, 246,

Index

251, 254, 256, 260, 262, 269, 273, 278,
282, 283, 285, 286, 287, 287n.1, 290,
294, 295, 297, 298, 303, 308, 311, 313,
315, 316, 319, 321, 322, 324, 326, 329,
330, 333, 334, 336, 338, 345, 346, 349,
354, 355, 357, 361, 365, 367, 373
Nabokov, Vladimir, works of:
  Ada or Ardor, 12, 21, 29, 55n.2, 113n.13,
    186n.3, 301n.2
  "Admiralty Spire, The," 20
  Ahasuerus, 269n.10
  "Amphibrachs," 93n.1, 94
  "Anniversary Notes," 332n.1 *top*
  "Art of Translation, The," 49n.2
  "Assistant Producer, The," 10, 107
  "Aurelian, The," 54, 55n.6
  "Ballad of Longwood Glen," 314, 314n.1
    bottom
  "Belloc Essays—Mild But Pleasant,"
    60n.3
  Bend Sinister, 9, 12, 25–26, 96n, 151, 152,
    192n.2, 197, 198, 199n.4, 200, 201–202,
    205, 207, 208, 209–211, 211n.2, 212,
    212nn.1, 2, 213, 213n.3, 215, 232, 251,
    279, 289n.2, 290, 320, 322, 323n.4. See
    also *Person from Porlock*
  "Butterflies," 230, 230n.1 *bottom*
  "Cabbage Soup and Caviar," 128n.5
  Camera Obscura, 60n.5, 173. See also
    Laughter in the Dark
  "Cloud, Castle, Lake," 46n.1
  "Colette," 227, 228n.1
  Conclusive Evidence, 221n.4, 263n.2, 278,
    280, 281, 281n.2, 286, 287, 288, 290,
    292, 298, 317, 340. See also *Other
    Shores; Speak, Memory*
  "Conversation Piece," 10, 171, 172n.6,
    175n.1 *top. See also* "Double Talk"
  Covetous Knight, The, by Alexander Push-
    kin, translated by VN, 52
  Dar, 298, 308, 366. See also *Gift, The*
  Despair, 12, 25, 69, 225, 225n.3, 251
  Discourse on Igor's Campaign. See *Song of
    Igor's Campaign*
  "Double Talk," 96n.6, 175n.1 *top. See also*
    "Conversation Piece"
  "Dream," 155, 155n.2, 188n.3 *top*
  Drugie berega. See *Other Shores*

  Empyrean Path, The, 78, 79n.2, 87,
    88n.21
  Eugene Onegin by Alexander Pushkin,
    translated and annotated by VN, 1,
    12, 13, 16, 21, 26, 27, 28, 77n.4, 88n.7,
    117n.1, 134, 135, 135n.1, 136, 138–139,
    138n.1, 232, 247nn. 3, 6, 253, 297, 298,
    300, 303n.2, 304n.4, 305, 307n.1, 311,
    311n.1, 313, 317, 320, 322, 323, 324n.3,
    330, 341n.5, 344, 350, 351, 354, 355,
    356, 361, 364n.1, 366, 372
  "Evening of Russian Poetry, An," 161,
    162n.2, 166, 166n.3, 167n.1
  Event, The, 144n.1, 150n.6
  "Execution, The," 103n
  "Exile" (article), 262, 263n.2, 284, 285n.4
  "Exile" (poem), 93, 93n.1, 94, 94n.1 *top,*
    99, 99n.1
  Feast During the Plague, The, by Alex-
    ander Pushkin, translated by VN, 52
  "First Poem," 232, 233n.3, 256, 257n.6
  "Forgotten Poet, A," 149, 150n.13, 152n.3
  "Gardens and Parks," 262, 263n.2
  Gift, The, 3, 11–12, 13, 14, 19, 25, 26, 29,
    39n.3, 75, 79n.1, 105, 112, 113n.6, 116n.1,
    144n.1, 162n.7, 177n.4, 209n.6, 224n.5,
    233n.7, 292n.2, 294n.9, 298nn.1, 2, 306,
    306n.1 *bottom,* 308n.1, 355n.2. See also
    Dar
  Glory, 102n.1, 104, 105n.1, 106nn.2, 3,
    179n.3. See also *Podvig*
  Gorny Put. See *Empyrean Path, The*
  Hero of Our Time, A, by Mikhail Lermon-
    tov, translated and edited by VN,
    326n.1, 333, 334, 355, 356, 356nn.4, 5,
    357n.6
  Invitation to a Beheading, 11, 25, 35, 35n.1
    bottom, 38, 62, 365, 365n.3
  Kingdom by the Sea, The, 215, 215n.1. See
    also *Lolita*
  La Méprise, 12, 225, 225n.3. See also
    Despair
  "Lance," 293, 293n.5, 296, 297n.2, 300,
    301n.2, 302, 303, 304n.1
  Laughter in the Dark, 25, 60, 60n.5, 65,
    69, 173, 220, 320
  Lectures on Russian Literature, 318n.4
  "Lines Written in Oregon," 313, 314n.3

Nabokov, Vladimir, works of *(continued)*:
  "Lodgings in Trinity Lane," 258n.4
  Lolita, 3, 18, 26–27, 28, 186n.3, 215n.1,
    229n.1, 295n.1, 311, 313, 314, 314nn.2 *top*
    and *bottom*, 317, 318, 318n.5, 319, 320–
    322, 325, 326n.2, 330, 331, 335, 337,
    338n.1, 340, 341, 342, 343, 344n.1, 349,
    359, 361–362, 362n.1, 363, 365, 365n.1,
    368, 368n.3. See also *Kingdom by the
    Sea, The*
  Look at the Harlequins, 12, 98n.2
  "*Lysandra cormion*, a New European But-
    terfly," 55n.7
  Mary, 163–164, 164n.1, 165n.3 *top*
  Mashenka, 163, 164, 164n.1. See also *Mary*
  "Mlle O," 102, 102n.2, 106, 107
  Mozart and Salieri by Alexander Pushkin,
    translated by VN, 13, 35, 49n.2, 255
  "Muse, The." *See* "To the Muse"
  "My Russian Education," 235, 236n.1
  "Nearctic Forms of *Lycaeides Hüb[ner]*,
    The," 104n.4, 126, 126n.3, 141, 143,
    143n.2, 152, 153, 268n.3
  "Nearctic Members of the Genus
    Lycaeides Hübner, The," 104n.4,
    143n.3, 215, 215n.3, 230, 230n.1 *top*,
    237, 237n.11, 252, 252n
  "New Species of Cyclargus Nabokov
    (Lycaenidae, Lepidoptera), A,"
    193n.7
  Nikolai Gogol, 13, 24, 26, 70, 75, 76n.3, 80,
    99, 103, 106, 126, 127, 128–129, 131, 142,
    143, 146, 155, 156, 157nn.1, 4, 167, 168,
    168n.3, 213, 240, 282, 283n.3
  Nine Stories, 211, 211n.3
  "No Matter How," 143n.7
  "Notes on Prosody," 16
  "Notes on the Morphology of the Genus
    Lycaeides," 104n.4, 143n.3, 159, 160n.1
  "On a Book Entitled *Lolita*," 229n.1
  "On Discovering a Butterfly," 103, 104n.3
  "On Rulers," 176n.3, 178, 179n.2
  "On Some Asiatic Species of Carterocepha-
    lus," 55n.7
  Otchayanie. See *Despair*
  Other Shores (Drugie berega), 209n.6,
    229n.1, 263n.2, 318, 318n.7. See also
    Conclusive Evidence; Speak, Memory

  Pale Fire, 12, 29, 51n.4, 368, 368n.1, 371,
    372n.2
  "Paris Poem, The," 132, 133nn.2, 3, 136n.3
  Perepiska s sestroi, viii
  "Perfect Past," 260, 261n.3
  Person from Porlock, The, 95, 96n, 134,
    136, 137, 138, 192n.2. See also *Bend
    Sinister*
  Person in Question, The. See *Speak,
    Memory*
  Pnin, viii, 18, 27, 28, 70–71n.6, 95n.2,
    124n.2, 162n.7, 316, 316n.2, 317, 322,
    323, 324, 325, 326, 329, 334, 341,
    341n.2 *bottom*, 343–344, 344n.3, 359
  Podvig. See *Glory*
  Poems and Problems, 60n.1, 67n.1 *top*,
    103n, 110n.1, 133n.3, 140n.4, 176n.3,
    283n.1, 332n.2 *bottom*
  "Poplar, The," 313, 314n.3
  "Portrait of My Uncle," 219, 219n.2
  "Problems of Translation: *Onegin* in
    English," 319n.1
  Pushkin, Lermontov, Tyutchev, 225,
    235n.1. See also *Three Russian Poets*
  "Rain," 332, 332n.2 *bottom*
  Real Life of Sebastian Knight, The, 12, 24,
    25, 39n.16, 45, 51n.3, 55–56, 56nn.2–6,
    57, 59n.3, 64n.1 *bottom*, 65n.2, 70n.4,
    122, 167–168, 192, 196, 210, 279, 280,
    280n.4, 288, 289n.1, 362
  "Refrigerator Awakes, The," 60n.1
  Return of Chorb, The, 140, 140nn.3, 4
  River Nymph, The (Rusalka) by Alex-
    ander Pushkin, supplied with a conclud-
    ing scene by VN, 69, 69n.2
  "Room, The," 274, 275n.3
  "Sartre's First Try," 225n.3
  "Scenes from the Life of a Double Mon-
    ster," 357, 358, 358n.3 *bottom*, 358n.4
    top
  Selected Letters, 1940–1977, viii, 70–71n.6
  "Signs and Symbols," 172n.8
  "Slava," 67n.1 *top*
  "Softest of Tongues, The," 58n.4
  "Solus Rex," 51n.4, 192n.3
  Solus Rex, 192n.3, 194. See also *Person
    from Porlock, The*
  Song of Igor's Campaign, The, translated

and with commentary by VN, 109n.6,
236, 237n.2, 238, 242, 243, 243n,
244nn.1, 5, 254, 337, 338n.2, 361,
361n.2, 366
Speak, Memory, 28, 48n.1, 102n.2, 113n.1,
174n.5, 177n.4, 185n.4, 204n.13, 209n.6,
215n.1, 219n.2, 220, 221n.4, 224n.11,
228n.1, 229n.1, 230n.1 *bottom,* 233n.3,
236n.1, 242n.9, 253, 257, 257n.6,
258nn.3, 4, 261nn.3, 4, 263n.2, 281n.2,
285n.4, 292n.2, 300n.1, 318n.7, 373n.2.
See also *Conclusive Evidence; Other
Shores*
"Spring in Fialta," 63, 69, 70n.1, 72, 135
Strong Opinions, 136n.4, 157n.1, 206n.4,
225n.3, 291n.4, 332n.1 *top,* 334n.4,
350n.5, 373n.1
"Tamara," 257, 258n.3
"That in Aleppo Once . . . ," 112, 113n.2,
118, 118n.2, 154n
Three Russian Poets, 35n.1, 50n, 52nn.1, 3,
120, 120n.10, 160, 160n.8, 164, 195, 197,
225n.1, 233, 235n.1. See also *Pushkin,
Lermontov, Tyutchev*
"Time and Ebb," 157, 158n.1 *top,* 160,
160n.7, 301n.2
"To Prince S. M. Kachurin," 214, 214n.1
bottom
"To the Muse" (or "The Muse"), 140n.4
Ultima Thule, 51n.4
"Vane Sisters, The," 293, 293n.5, 295,
295n.2, 363, 364n.2
"Visit to the Museum, The," 158, 158n.1
bottom
"Voluptates Tactionum," 283, 283n.1, 284,
284n.1
Waltz Invention, The, 106, 106n.7, 210,
211n.1
Nabokov, Vladimir Dmitrievich (VN's
father), 2, 7, 8, 9, 39n.14, 107, 107n.3,
174n.5, 268, 269n.10, 273, 340, 341n.2
top, 344
Napoleon Bonaparte, 54n, 243
Nash, Ogden, 286
Nesterov, Mikhail, 117n.5
Newman, Charles, 226n.4, 332n.1 *top*
Nicholas I, 265n.5
Nicholas II, 10, 37, 340n.1

Nicolson, Harold, 134n.1, 299–300, 300n.1,
301, 301nn.5, 6, 362n.1
Nicolson, Nigel, 362n.1
Nietzsche, Friedrich, 15
Nikolaevsky, Boris, 10, 254, 254n.5
Nimitz, Admiral Chester, 144
Norris, Frank, 117n.6

Odoevtseva, Irina, 334, 334n.4
Ognyov, N. (Mikhail Rosanov), 78
Olcott, Anthony, 242n.8
Olesha, Yury, 22, 132, 175, 218, 225n.3
Ostrovsky, Alexander, 333n.2
Ovid, 353n.1

Paine, Thomas, 23
Palitsyn, Avraamy, 358n.4 *bottom*
Panina, Countess Sophie, 232
Panofsky, Erwin, 354
Parny, Evariste, 169, 170n.1, 232, 234
Pascal, Blaise, 83
Pasternak, Boris, x, 5, 5n, 24, 27, 45, 90,
92n.6, 121n.2, 175, 218n.1, 257n.4,
370n.1 *bottom,* 373
Pater, Walter, 210
Paul, Sherman, 3
Pavarotti, Luciano, 368n.4
Pearce, Charles ("Cap"), 72, 73n.7, 95, 95n.3,
100, 101n.7, 103
Perelman, S. J., 149, 151n.19
Perkins, Agnes, 70, 70n.4
Perkins, Elliot and Mary, 357, 358n.3 *top*
Perón, Eva Duarte, 252, 253n.2
Perón, Juan, 252
Perovskaya, Sophia, 113n.15
Peter the Great, 107, 346
Petrov, Yevgeny, 175
Pilniak, Boris, 203
Pindar, 345, 345n.4, 346
Plato, 15, 180
Plinius Caecilius Secundus (Pliny the
Younger), 162
Poe, Edgar Allan, 50, 51n.1, 215n.1, 277
Pomialovsky, Nikolai, 137, 138n.3
Pope, Alexander, 19, 283n.4
Poplavsky, Boris, 238, 239n.4, 241, 242nn.8, 9
Pound, Ezra, 207
Poussin, Nicolas, 352, 353n.12

Powell, Dawn, 191, 191n.1 *bottom*
Pozner, Vladimir, 108, 109n.1, 110
Praed, Winthrop Mackworth, 245, 247n.4
Praz, Mario, 168, 287, 309
Prishvin, Mikhail, 132
Proust, Marcel, 4, 24n.5, 164, 165n.6, 191n.6,
     205, 263, 268, 286, 287, 288, 368,
     368n.2
Przhevalsky, Nikolai, 162n.7, 294n.9
Pushkin, Alexander, 1, 6, 6n, 13, 16, 20, 21, 23,
     35n.1 *top*, 38n, 41n.2 *top*, 47n.2, 48, 49,
     49n.1, 51, 52, 54, 55n.3, 69n.2, 71–77
     passim, 77n.4, 78nn.1, 2, 4–6, 79, 79nn.
     3, 4, 80, 83, 85, 87, 87–88nn.1, 3–18,
     90, 94, 94n.1 *bottom*, 94n.2 *top*, 99–100,
     101n.2, 102, 102n.3, 104–105, 104n.2,
     106, 107, 107n.8, 117n.1, 118, 119,
     120nn.2–4, 11, 121, 121n.1, 125, 135n.1,
     140n.2, 151–152, 152n.2, 153, 156, 160,
     169, 170n.1, 183, 183n.5, 184, 185n.4,
     200, 205, 232, 233n.4, 242n.1, 245–246,
     247n.3, 248, 249n.1 *top*, 265nn.2, 4,
     269n.7, 299, 303n.2, 305, 307n.1, 311,
     324, 325n.5, 329, 337, 341, 348, 349n.2,
     350, 351, 353n.1, 354, 356

Queneau, Raymond, 28, 365
Quick, Dorothy B., 160n.4

Rachmaninov, Sergei, 50, 51n.1
Racine, Jean, 19, 272n.6
Radcliffe, Ann, 20
Radek, Karl, 246, 248n.11
Raguet-Bouvard, Christine, viii
Rahv, Philip, 221, 222, 223n.1, 321, 330
Ransome, John Crowe, 311
Rasputin, Gregory, 335, 336n.3
Ravel, Maurice, 170n.1
Read, Florence Matilda, 95, 95n.2
Reade, Frank, 95, 95n.2
Reed, John, 223n.1
Remizov, Alexei, 11, 23, 24, 24n.5
Ribbentrop, Joachim von, 175
Rimbaud, Arthur, 106, 239n.4, 268, 361n.1
Robbe-Grillet, Alain, 28, 364
Rolland, Romain, 246
Roosevelt, Eleanor, 98
Roosevelt, Franklin D., 129, 143

Rooten, Luis d'Antin van, 55n.2
Rosenberg, Ethel and Julius, 314n.4
Rosenfeld, Paul, 175n.1 *bottom*
Ross, Harold, 166, 171, 232, 296, 299
Rust'hveli, Shot'ha, 34, 34n.1

Sackville-West, Victoria (Vita), 362n.1
Sade, Marquis de, 270, 309, 310
Saint-Simon, Count Henri de, 14
Salieri, Antonio, 38n
Salisbury, Harrison E., 350, 351n.1
Salt, Henry, 324, 325n.5
Saltykov-Shchedrin, Mikhail, 355, 355n.2
Sandberg, Peter, 336n.7
Sanders, George, 310n.2 *bottom*
Sandys, Sir John Edwin, 345, 345n.4, 346
Sappho, 348
Sarraute, Nathalie, 364
Sarton, May, 303, 303n.4
Sartre, Jean-Paul, 12, 219, 220n.4, 225,
     225n.3, 228, 270
Savinkov, Boris, 203
Sayers, Dorothy, 159, 160n.5
Scammell, Michael, 113n.6
Schiller, Friedrich von, 352, 353n.12
Schopenhauer, Arthur, 15
Schubert, Franz, 139
Schwartz, Delmore, 63, 64n.1 *top*
Scott, R. T. M., 159
Scott, Sir Walter, 283n.4
Scott, W. B., 271, 272n.6, 273
Sergei Alexandrovich, Grand Duke, 204n.13
Shakespeare, William, 16, 79, 80, 90, 93,
     157n.4, 178, 212, 212n.2, 255, 271, 276,
     366
Shaw, G. B., 3, 5
Shawn, William, 211, 213, 243, 302
Shchegolev, Pavel, 264, 265n.2
Shelley, Percy Bysshe, 23, 168
Shepperson, Archibald B., 66
Sholokhov, Mikhail, 218n.1
Shorer, Mark and Ruth, 306, 306n.1 *top*
Shostakovich, Dmitri, 106, 183n.2
Sikorski, Elena (Nabokov), viii, 364, 365n.2,
     367
Silone, Ignazio, 205, 206n.5
Simmons, Ernest J., 182, 182n.2, 302
Simonov, Konstantin, 175, 176n.2 *top*, 218n.1

Sinclair, Upton, 246, 357, 358n.2 *top*
Sirk, Douglas (Detlef), 310n.2 *bottom*
Sologub, Fyodor, 24n.5
Solzhenitsyn, Alexander, 28, 254n.5, 373
Southey, Robert, 354
Spellman, Francis Cardinal, 273, 274n.2
Spencer, Theodore, 249, 249n.2 *bottom*
Spender, Stephen, 335, 352
Stalin, Joseph, 4, 6, 27, 53, 87, 107n.5, 109n.1,
    127, 135, 137, 164, 165n.5, 213n.3, 221,
    222, 223, 224nn.7, 11, 225n.3, 246
Steegmuller, Francis, 352
Steffens, Lincoln, 14, 223n.1
Stein, Gertrude, 4, 5n, 175n.1 *bottom*
Stendhal, 19, 167, 324, 324n.3, 329, 329n.2
    top
Stenich, Valentin, 183n.2
Sterne, Laurence, 19, 282, 311, 312
Stevenson, Robert Louis, 268, 271, 273, 281
Stieglitz, Alfred, 357n.1
Stilman, Leon, 302
Stone, Irving, 198, 199n.1
Stout, Rex, 160n.7
Straus, Roger, 318, 319, 320, 334, 360
Stravinsky, Igor, 66, 67n.2, 68n.1
Stroheim, Erich von, 117n.6
Struve, Gleb, 17, 255, 257n.4, 334, 334nn.3, 4
Struve, Peter, 13, 14, 16
Sukhovo-Kobylin, Alexander, 23
Suvorov, Prince Alexander, 324
Svyatopolk-Mirsky, Prince Dmitri. *See* Mir-
    sky, D. S.
Sweet, Henry, 78
Swift, Jonathan, 271
Swinburne, Algernon, 234
Symons, A. J. S., 64n.1 *bottom*
Szeftel, Marc, 109n.3, 241, 242n.7

Tandy, Jessica, 280, 281n.1
Tarnovskaya, Dr. Praskovia, 373n.2
Tate, Allen, 155, 194, 198, 199, 200, 207,
    209–210, 215, 233n.1, 290, 311
Tchaikovsky, Modest, 182, 183n.1
Tchaikovsky, Peter Ilyich, 182, 183nn.2, 5,
    353n.12
Tchelitchew, Pavel, 144n.1, 156
Thackeray, William Makepeace, 35
Thieme, Hermann, 174n.5

Thiers, Louis-Adolphe, 37
Thoby-Marcelin, Eva, 355n.1 *top*
Thoby-Marcelin, Philippe (Phito), 234,
    235n.3, 355n.1 *top*
Thompson, C. Bertrand, 43, 43n.1
Thompson, Lisbet, 43, 43n.1
Thomson, James, 348
Thornton, Elena Mumm. *See* Wilson, Elena
Thornton, Henry, 217, 255, 256n.1, 265,
    265n.12, 268, 271, 281, 349
Toffler, Alvin, 291n.4
Tolstoy, A. K., 73
Tolstoy, Lev (Leo), 6, 8, 15, 19, 20, 21, 22,
    23, 24–25, 35, 54, 181n.2, 197, 215,
    223n.1, 231, 232, 234, 236, 236n.2, 246,
    247nn.9, 10, 248, 262, 284n.3, 287n.2,
    289n.4, 339n.2 *bottom*, 352
Tomashevsky, Boris, 263, 265n.2
Tomlinson, Charles, 371n.1
Toumanova, Tamara, 68, 68n.1
Toynbee, Philip, 235n.1
Trager, George L., 70, 70n.6, 114
Trilling, Lionel, 131
Trotsky, Lev (Leon), 2, 8, 15, 23, 40, 192,
    193nn.5, 6, 218n.1, 222
Troxell, Gilbert, 20n
Troyat, Henri, 351
Tseretelli, Irakly, 10, 254, 254n.5
Tsiavlovsky, Mstislav, 349n.2
Tsvetaeva, Marina, 11, 24, 48n.2
Turgenev, Ivan, 7, 13, 19, 21, 23, 59, 214,
    214n.2, 312, 334, 337, 339, 339n.2 *bot-
    tom*, 348, 349n.4, 352, 353n.9, 360,
    360n.2
Twain, Mark, 289
Tyler, Parker, 144n.1
Tyutchev, Fyodor, 23, 25, 50, 51n.2, 80, 104,
    106, 119, 120n.5, 122, 123, 124–125, 126,
    135, 135n.2, 160, 170

Ulyanov, Ilya (Lenin's father), 37, 38
Updike, John, 28
Uritsky, Moses, 222, 224nn.7, 11

Valentinov, Nikolai, 14, 16
Vaudrin, Philip, 216, 217, 218, 250, 251, 253
Verlaine, Paul, 150, 151n.20

Vernadsky, George, 108, 109n.4, 241, 242n.7, 243
Vigny, Alfred de, 123
Virgil, 170, 352, 353n.11
Vladimir, Grand Prince, 41, 41n.2 *bottom*
Vogüé, Melchior de, 27, 233n.4, 339n.2
Volkonsky, Prince Sergei, 47, 48n.2
Voloshin, Maksimilian, 81, 88n.7
Voltaire, 324, 341

Wagner, Richard, 174n.5
Walpole, Hugh, 202
Waugh, Evelyn, 189n.11, 362
Weeks, Edward, 12, 47, 48n.1, 49, 50, 52, 54, 57, 98, 106, 107, 109, 110, 112, 118, 121, 122, 124, 126, 152, 154, 158, 160, 194, 237, 238
Weinbaum, Mark, 233, 233n.7
Wellek, René, 302
Werth, Alexander, 78, 87
Wescott, Glenway, 175n.1 *bottom*
West, Mrs. James. *See* McCarthy, Mary
West, Rebecca, 304n.3
Wharton, Edith, 175n.1 *bottom*
Whicher, George, 179n.5
White, Andrew D., 223n.1
White, E. B., 237, 237n.10
White, Edmund, 28
White, Katharine, 135, 136n.4, 144, 149, 151, 152, 155, 159, 160n.3, 166, 171, 172n.8, 208, 211, 219, 219n.3, 225, 237, 237n.10, 238, 243, 296, 297n.3, 300, 313, 325
Wilbur, Richard, 189n.12
Wilde, Oscar, 6–7
Wilder, Thornton, 115, 117n.3, 227n.3, 323
Williams, Frayne, 49n.2
Wilson, Angus, 336
Wilson, Colin, 366
Wilson, Edmund, works of:
  "After writing," 100n
  American Earthquake, The, 356, 356n.1, 357, 357n.1
  Apologies to the Iroquois, 356n.3
  "At Laurelwood," 3, 9, 237n.5
  Axel's Castle, 3–4, 24n.5, 239n.4
  Bit Between My Teeth, The, 191n.1 *bottom*, 336n.5

Boys in the Back Room, 53n.1
"Brief Comments on Curious Words," 16
"Bronze Horseman, The," by Alexander Pushkin, translated by EW, 13, 41n.2 *top*, 246, 265n.3
"Bulletin No. 7: The Mass in the Parking Lot," 263n.4
"Cardinal Merry Del Val," 226, 227n.1
Classics and Commercials, 26, 39n.14, 136n.5, 143n.4, 157n.2, 160n.7, 162n.4, 165n.3 *bottom*, 179n.3, 189n.11, 220n.4, 231n.1, 282, 282n, 283n.3, 290
Cold War and the Income Tax, The, 369n.3
Cyprian's Prayer, 316, 317n.2, 342
"Dawns, dawns," 100, 100n
Dead Sea Scrolls, 317n.3
"Dissenting Opinion on Kafka, A," 220n.4
"Easy Exercises in the Use of Difficult Words," 216
Europe Without Baedeker, 169n.7, 172n.9, 174n.6, 177n.2, 206n.5, 220, 221n.2
Fifties, The, 350n.5
"Five Plays," 317n.2
Forties, The, 191n.1 *bottom*
"Francis Grierson," 235, 236n.1
"Galahad," 268, 269n.8
"Greek Diary," 174n.6, 176, 177nn.2, 4
"Helen Muchnic," 218n.1
"Intelligence of Bees, Wasps, Butterflies and Bombing Planes, The," 291, 291n.1 *bottom*, 292, 292n.2, 293n.1
I Thought of Daisy, 3, 64n.1 *top*, 155, 156n.6
"James Branch Cabell Case Reopened, The," 333, 333n.1
"Jean-Paul Sartre," 220n.4
"John Mulholland and the Art of Illusion," 143n.4
"Kipling That Nobody Read, The," 46n.2
"Koussevitzky at Tanglewood," 232, 233n.2
"Lesbia in Hell," 100, 100n
Letters on Literature and Politics, 1912–1972, 16n, 141n.1 *top*, 172n.8, 175n.1 *bottom*, 191n.1 *bottom*, 193n.4, 219n.3,

235n.3, 259n.2, 269n.2, 272n.7, 329n.2 *top*, 336n.1, 355n.1 *top*

Literary Chronicle: 1920–1950, A, 360n.1

Little Blue Light, The, 251, 251n, 255, 256n.2, 268–269, 269n.10, 280–281, 280n.1, 284, 285–286, 286n.2, 290, 316, 317n.1

"Little Museum of Russian Language, A," 39n.16

"Marxism and Literature," 23

Memoirs of Hecate County, 3, 22, 26, 64n.2, 163n.2, 176n.1, 188, 188nn.1, 3 *bottom,* 189nn.4, 6–9, 12, 192, 193, 198n.1, 199, 205, 213, 237, 237n.7, 291, 311, 342, 363, 369

"Mice, Headaches, Rehearsals," 183n.5

"More Notes on Current Clichés," 371n.4

"Mr. Holmes, They Were the Footprints of a Gigantic Hound," 165, 165n.3 *bottom*

"Mr. Joseph E. Davies as a Master of Prose Style," 162n.4

"New Jersey Childhood," 237, 237n.5

Night Thoughts, 3, 100n, 216nn.1, 2, 235n.2, 237n.5, 257n.7, 263n.4

"Nikolai Gogol—Greek Paideia," 156, 157n.2

Note-Books of Night, 100n, 101n.4, 237n.5

"Notes on London at the End of the War," 172n.9

"Notes on Pushkin," 125n.6

"Notes on Russian Literature," 88n.9, 118, 118n.1, 119, 120nn.1, 2, 122, 122n.1, 135n.2

"Omelet of A. MacLeish, The," 101n.6

"On First Reading Genesis," 317, 317n.3

"On the Margin of Moscow," 223n.1

"Original of Tolstoy's Natasha, The," 231n.1, 236, 237n.4

Patriotic Gore, 356, 356n.1

Peasants and Other Stories by Anton Chekov, selected and introduced by EW, 27, 331, 332nn.1–3 *top*

Piece of My Mind, A, 7, 27, 338, 339, 339nn.1 *top,* 4

Red, Black, Blond and Olive, 5, 223n.1, 235n.3, 253n.1, 317n.3, 322, 323n.3

"Reporter in New Mexico, A," 252, 53n.1

"Reversals, or *Plus ça change,*" 234, 235n.2

Scrolls from the Dead Sea, 312, 312n.1, 317n.3, 334, 334n.2

Shock of Recognition, The, 330, 331n.1

Shores of Light, The, 255, 257n.3, 299, 299n.2, 309, 310n.1 *top*

Sixties, The, 370n.1

To the Finland Station, x, 2, 6, 13, 14, 15, 16, 21, 23, 39n.3

Travels in Two Democracies, 5, 223n.1

Triple Thinkers, The, x, 13, 14, 23, 41n.2 *top,* 238, 239n.2, 245–248, 249n.1 *top,* 265n.3, 296, 297, 299, 330

"T. S. Eliot and the Church of England," 360n.1

"Turgenev and the Life-Giving Drop," 339n.1 *bottom,* 360n.2

Upstate, 17, 28, 229n.1, 329n.1 *top,* 333n.2, 349nn.1, 4, 350n.5, 373, 373n.1

"Vogue of the Marquis de Sade, The," 309, 310n.2 *top*

"Why Do People Read Detective Stories?" 160n.7

Window on Russia, A, 13, 26, 28, 39n.16, 51n.2, 88n.9, 118n.1, 120n.9, 125n.6, 339n.1 *bottom,* 364n.1

"Word-Fetishism," 101n.4

Wound and the Bow, The, 46n.2, 54, 55n.5, 64n.1 *top,* 215, 275

Wilson, Elena, vii, 2, 27, 201, 214, 216, 220, 231, 232, 234, 237, 239, 241, 246, 252, 256, 259, 261, 269, 277, 279, 281, 282, 287, 288, 292n.2, 295, 296, 296n.1, 298, 300, 303, 304, 308, 309, 311, 312, 315, 316, 318, 319, 322, 324, 326, 327, 328, 328n.1, 330, 331, 334, 335, 338, 341, 343, 345, 346, 347, 349, 350n.7, 354, 355, 356, 357, 361, 363, 365, 366, 367, 370n.1 *top,* 372, 373

Wilson, Helen Mather Kimball (EW's mother), 285, 286n.1

Wilson, Helen Miranda (EW's daughter), 220n.1, 227, 234, 259, 327, 328n.1, 335, 338, 339, 346

Wilson, John, 54, 55n.4, 200

Index

Wilson, Reuel (EW's son), 163, 163n.1, 200, 255, 256n.1, 259, 262, 271, 274, 277, 278, 281, 307
Wilson, Rosalind (EW's daughter), 200, 207, 207n.1, 217, 277, 285, 311, 312, 312n.1 *top*
Wilson, Woodrow, 2
Windsor, Duchess of, 96–97
Wolfe, Bertram D., 16
Wolfe, Thomas, 175n.1 *bottom*, 336, 36n.7
Wolkonsky, Prince Serge. *See* Volkonsky, Prince Sergei
Woolf, Virginia, 35, 227n.4
Wordsworth, William, 348
Wreden, Nicholas, 179n.4
Wright, J. F. C., 39n.2

Xenocrates, 345

Yagoda, Heinrich, 222, 224nn.7, 11
Yanovsky, V. S., 114, 115n.1, 116, 197
Yarmolinsky, Avrahm, 44, 44n.3, 76, 77n.5
Yeats, William Butler, 49, 255, 277
Yezhov, Nikolai. *See* Ezhov, Nikolai

Zabel, Morton D., 260n.2, 336n.1
Zabolotsky, Nikolai, 22, 257n.4
Zadek, Martin, 311n.1
Zamiatin, Yevgeny, 133
Zenger, Tatiana, 349n.2
Zenzinov, Vladimir, 149, 151n.16, 233, 33n.7
Zetkin, Clara, 15, 40
Zhukovsky, Vasily, 92n.5, 350, 352
Zola, Emile, 20
Zorina, Vera (Eva Brigitta Hartwig), 68n.1
Zoshchenko, Mikhail, 22, 132

DESIGNER: *Wilsted & Taylor Publishing Services*
COMPOSITOR: *Wilsted & Taylor Publishing Services*
TEXT: *Monotype Walbaum*
DISPLAY: *Monotype Walbaum*
PRINTER AND BINDER: *Sheridan Books, Inc.*

Index